leeds metropolitan university

Thinker, Faker, Spinner, Spy

Corporate PR and the Assault on Democracy

Edited by

WILLIAM DINAN and DAVID MILLER

Pluto Press

LONDON • ANN ARBOR, MI

First published 2007 by Pluto Press
345 Archway Road, London N6 5AA
and 839 Greene Street, Ann Arbor, MI 48106

www.plutobooks.com

Copyright © William Dinan and David Miller 2007

The right of the individual contributors to be identified as the authors of
this work has been asserted by them in accordance with the Copyright,
Designs and Patents Act 1988.

British Library Cataloguing in Publication Data
A catalogue record for this book is available from the British Library

Hardback
ISBN-13   978 0 7453 2445 6
ISBN-10   0 7453 2445 2

Paperback
ISBN-13   978 0 7453 2444 9
ISBN-10   0 7453 2444 4

Library of Congress Cataloging in Publication Data applied for

This book is printed on paper suitable for recycling and made
from fully managed and sustained forest sources. Logging, pulping
and manufacturing processes are expected to conform to the
environmental regulations of the country of origin.

10 9 8 7 6 5 4 3 2 1

Designed and produced for Pluto Press by
Chase Publishing Services Ltd, Fortescue, Sidmouth, EX10 9QG, England
Typeset from disk by Stanford DTP Services, Northampton, England
Printed and bound in the European Union by
CPI Antony Rowe Ltd, Chippenham and Eastbourne

Contents

Acknowledgements

This book has been the product of a long-term collaboration between a wide variety of people and organisations. We work as academics at the University of Strathclyde. But we are also directors of Spinwatch, the website we launched (along with co-directors Eveline Lubbers and Andy Rowell) in late 2004. This book arose out of the Corporate Spin conference we hosted in November 2004 in Glasgow.

In putting this book together we have accumulated many debts to those who have helped this process along. This collection is the first book-length product from Spinwatch and it is seeing the light of day somewhat later than it should have. This is partly due to the arrival of the G8 leaders in Scotland in 2005, which put the book on the back burner amid preparations for the demonstrations against the G8, including the Alternatives Summit held on 3 July 2005, and to work on the book *Arguments Against G8*, edited by David Miller and Gill Hubbard (London: Pluto Press, 2005).

The idea to set up Spinwatch had been in our minds for some time before the launch and it was first given concrete form at the international seminar called by Corporate Europe Observatory and hosted formally by Caroline Lucas MEP in Girona, Catalonia, in 2002. There, Miller, Lubbers and others discussed how to create a new organisation that might monitor PR and spin in Europe. In discussion with John Stauber we explored different ideas on how to develop a European version of the US quarterly *PR Watch*. It was not until late 2004 that we were able to go public with the launch of the website www.spinwatch.org at the conference on Corporate Spin held at Strathclyde University.

We are indebted to all the speakers and participants at the Corporate Spin conference for their input, ideas and suggestions. We are especially grateful to all the contributors to this collection. They have all been very patient and supportive in helping this book to press. We should also mention the contributions of all those who have contributed to the Spinwatch project by sharing information, circulating news, supporting our endeavours and donating money. We are grateful to all those who have allowed us to speak and write about corporate deception and who have encouraged our efforts. Perhaps we should mention by name Mark Ballard MSP, Davids Cromwell and Edwards, Frances Curran MSP, Mark Curtis, Steve Dorril, Bob Franklin,

Michael Sean Gillard, Tim Gopsill, Ed Herman, Olivier Hoedeman, Mark Hollingsworth, Nick Jones, Robert McChesney, Tricia Marwick MSP, George Monbiot, Greg Philo, John Pilger, Danny Schechter, Tommy Sheridan MSP, Nancy Snow, Hilary Wainwright, Barry White, Granville Williams and the following organisations: the Glasgow Branch of the National Union of Journalists, G8 Alternatives, World Development Movement, Corporate Europe Observatory, ALTER EU, and the Centre for Media and Democracy.

We would also like to thank a number of other colleagues and friends who have supported this initiative, including George Yule, Lorraine Nelson and Lynne Davies at the Department of Geography and Sociology at Strathclyde for helping to organise and manage the conference. We'd also like to thank Spinwatch's many friends, supporters and contributors. There are too many to mention here but we'd like to express our gratitude to Muhammad Idrees Ahmad, Billy Clark, Rich Cookson, Josselien Janssens, Tommy Kane, Michael Greenwell, Paul de Rooij and Bill Stevens for their input to the project.

In the latter stages of the production of the book we benefited from the beady eye of Julie-Ann Davies, who took time out from other pressing tasks to help us with copy-editing. Many thanks to her for that, and for a myriad of other contributions to the Spinwatch project.

We would like to acknowledge the support of the Economic and Social Research Council (ESRC), award R000238993, which allowed us to conduct research on corporate public relations in Britain, and to convene the Glasgow conference.

We should also say thanks (again) to Pluto Press for publishing the book and for their support for our various projects over the last ten or more years. We should mention on this occasion David Castle, Robert Webb, Anthony Winder and – of course – the (almost) always sensible interventions of Anne Beech.

Lastly, thanks to Emma Miller, Caitlin and Lewis Miller, Carol Clydesdale, and Ciara and Niamh Dinan for the inevitable sacrifices to home life that goes with this kind of work, as well as for their many other contributions to the process.

We hope that this book contributes to a greater awareness of corporate spin and to the social movements which counterpose democracy to corporate power.

DM and WD,
Glasgow,
March 2007.

Introduction:
Unearthing Corporate Spin

William Dinan and David Miller

This book intends to change how you might think about spin and
public relations. We argue that corporate spin is an important means
by which corporate power is defended and extended. This idea is not
well recognised in the mainstream media, it is misunderstood among
a surprisingly large number of well-informed and well-intentioned
activists and campaigning groups, and it is virtually unnoticed by
the general public. This misrecognition is no accident. It is part of
the project of corporate spin and the public relations industry to
deny, dissemble and disguise their work. As a result the popular
image of PR and corporate spin is that it is not really important. We
often dismiss some recent happening with the phrase 'it's just PR',
as if it were somehow trivial and unimportant. Corporate spin is
often wrongly equated with celebrity endorsements and sponsorships
geared towards selling products and services: a form of advertising
barely disguised as news that is both ephemeral and disposable.

Political spin is a different matter. The manipulations, evasions and
distortions that are ubiquitous in political campaigning in advanced
liberal democracies have done much to popularise (if that's the right
term) the idea of spin. The careful crafting of political messages, the
invention and burnishing of politicians' images, and the spread of
negative campaigning all contribute to an awareness that spin is
used by the powerful to further their own interests. Perhaps this
has also given rise to an inkling among those not interested in
party politics that this is not what democracy is supposed to be like.
Viewed in this way, the declining levels of political participation in
many industrial democracies is not quite as baffling as many liberal
commentators suggest.

The propaganda related to the war in Iraq, from the invention of
a pressing threat from Weapons of Mass Destruction, to the ongoing
efforts of the US and British administrations to 'sell' the invasion and
its aftermath, are undoubtedly the most incontrovertible exemplars
of the deadly serious nature of spin.[1] The shadow of certain American
corporations across the oil fields of Iraq,[2] and policy circles in

Washington, suggest that we might need to reappraise the nature of contemporary corporate power. To do so, we need to understand corporate spin.

The predominant images of PR and spin doctors in our popular culture veer between two poles. At one extreme we have real behind the scenes Machiavellian political fixers, media bruisers loyal to their political masters – think of Peter Mandelson or Alastair Campbell in Britain, and maybe Marlin Fitzwater (who also acted as a consultant to the television series *The West Wing*) and Karl Rove in the United States. At the other end of the spectrum we have the fictional Edina Monsoon (Jennifer Saunders in *Absolutely Fabulous*), an air-kissing, celebrity obsessed caricature public relations consultant, or the sleazy and ambitious press agent Sidney Falco (Tony Curtis in *Sweet Smell of Success*). In the United Kingdom, Max Clifford has become a household name for his ability to manage the profile of his many clients in the salacious British tabloids.

There are many other examples of spin doctors in fiction that conform to these tropes.[3] Corporate mouthpieces and lobbyists have featured, often fleetingly, in other forms of popular entertainment. Michael Moore has made something of a career of exposing the hypocrisies of such characters in his films *Roger and Me*, *Bowling for Columbine*, and in his television series *The Awful Truth*. In the United Kingdom, *The Mark Thomas Comedy Product* regularly featured corporate spin doctors trying to deflect Thomas's faux innocent inquiries. Add to this the rare drama featuring lobbyists or behind the scenes sinister corporate fixers and you've more or less sketched in the ways the media reflects the role of corporate spin in our culture. Since Seattle and the backlash against corporate globalisation we have started to see more lobbyists represented on our screens, such as in *The Insider*, the film about tobacco whistle-blower Jeffrey Wigand or the pharma execs in *The Constant Gardener*. The year 2006 saw the release of *Syriana*, which also features oil lobbyists working to manage US foreign policy, and *Thank you for Smoking*, a film about a tobacco lobbyist. Aaron Eckhart plays Nick Naylor, über-lobbyist for Big Tobacco. Naylor is spin doctor, junk science purveyor and all round bad guy, a welcome sign that the ideas in this book are penetrating the mainstream.

But the lack of scrutiny of what corporate spin doctors do, and why, is a real blindspot that impairs our view of how decisions are made, and, ultimately, our self-understanding of our political culture and society. This book is a contribution towards redressing that situation.

By bringing together the research, insights and understanding of the contributors to this volume we are trying to add an important corrective to the misunderstanding of spin as an essentially harmless surface phenomenon. Instead we would suggest that spin, the management of perceptions, beliefs and ultimately behaviours, is a deeply problematic addiction of the powerful, and that we all suffer as a result.

To extend the metaphor a little, spin is not a harmless recreational kick freely available at celebrity parties, shared by consenting adults, with little or no after effects. Instead spin should be understood as a deadly serious dependency, undeserving of its 'declassified' status, and causing much wider harm than is generally recognised. Spin fuels a black economy of insider favours, kick-backs, and deals across the media and public life which demean these institutions themselves, and undermine public trust.

Spin breeds its own culture, and insiders betray the knowing traits and manners of cliquish users. Just as drug subcultures develop their own language codes and patterns of behaviour, so too spin users adopt their own argot, using a kind of doublespeak that is unnoticed by uninitiated outsiders. Yet spin addicts do display tendencies that suggest something is amiss – the preening self-regard of some spin doctors and lobbyists, and the self-satisfaction derived from fixing things for their clients.

ABOUT THIS BOOK

The first part of this book aims to put spin in context, offering an analysis of why spin matters in the era of globalisation. Each chapter here looks at how spin works at different levels of politics and society. David Miller and William Dinan begin by setting out the case for the prosecution, arguing that the PR industry is anti-democratic in intent and effect. Leslie Sklair identifies increasing inequality and looming ecological unsustainability as the twin crises of capitalism today. He also recognises the critical role that spin and lobbying on behalf of the powerful play in perpetuating these crises. Chris Grimshaw offers us a tour of the PR industry in the form of a primer in the techniques and specialisms of spin that are available 'off the shelf' for clients to purchase as and when needed to fix the media, regulators, investors or the wider public. His chapter touches upon some of the tactics used by spin doctors that will be looked at in greater detail later in the book.

The second part examines a series of cases of corporate spin.

Laura Miller looks behind the Republican takeover of American politics, using the network of companies centred on the strategic public affairs consultancy DCI Group to illustrate the deep interpenetration of spin, lobbying and electioneering in the US system. The DCI Group represents a political machine that fundraises, lobbies and spins for clients, using techniques they pioneered for the tobacco industry. The skills include constructing fake grassroots (or 'astroturf') campaigns and creating fake news and opinion websites (online spin). Such networks can be seen as the vital political support system for the White House of George Bush Jr.

David Miller offers a detailed case study of the way the fish farming industry managed to spin legitimate health concerns about farmed salmon. This story reveals the dense personal and professional networks that criss-cross business, politics and media interests in Scotland, though these lock into wider transnational networks of corporate power. It shows how spinners and lobbyists can resist the public interest using a sophisticated and co-ordinated communication campaign that neutralises the media and cheats the public.

Convincing the public that an oil company can be green and sustainable is the strategy being pushed by BP. The denial of climate change is another option. Andy Rowell's chapter examines the role of the International Policy Network (IPN) think tank promoting Exxon-friendly ideas on climate change and GM-friendly ideas on agriculture and food. The IPN is part of a wider family of think tanks supporting free-market ideology and individual or consumer freedom, which are funded by big business (often with a US accent). These groups represent an important resource for corporate PR. The issue of GM food illustrates this form of spin, which can be seen as crucial to the way TNCs seek to manage the twin ecological and class crises of globalisation. There has been much spin associated with the issue of genetic modification as the biotech industry seeks to manage concerns raised by environmental, trade, social justice and human rights campaigners.

Jonathan Matthews draws attention to the extreme lengths to which the GM lobby will go in trying to influence public perceptions of GM foods. His chapter combines a number of themes, networks and issues already touched upon by various contributors. The distorting role of spin is seen clearly in the faking of news events around GM. The manufacture of media-friendly demonstrations to counter the real campaigns challenging corporations and their apologists, and the direct attacks on the credibility of experts in opposing NGOs, remind us that dirty tricks can be used in some cases.

Where dirty tricks end and subversion begins is sometimes difficult to say. In the study by Eveline Lubbers this is certainly not the case. In the United Kingdom the Campaign Against the Arms Trade (CAAT) was spied upon by corporate spooks with long-standing connections with British security services and defence interests. How the intelligence gathered on such activist groups is subsequently fed back into the lobbying and PR activities of the corporate client neatly illustrates the connections between this underbelly of PR and the more public face of the corporation.

The role of spin in distorting and even bypassing representative democracy is a theme that unites the section on 'PR in Action'. Uli Mueller describes the rise of business-friendly citizen initiatives (closely linked to very wealthy citizens rather than the general public) and slick PR campaigns aimed at undermining Germany's social democratic settlement. The scale of this enterprise in perception management is extraordinary and suggests that the struggle for German labour and welfare rights is intensifying and possibly entering a critical phase.

Part III looks at how networks of influencers and the powerful can steer the direction of policy and society. The section on neoliberal networks looks at the critical role these groups play in shaping the climate of opinion on particular issues and in making the private interests of different industries and corporations appear aligned to the public or national interest, as witnessed in the push for a new civil nuclear programme in the United Kingdom throughout 2006.[4]

In the past few years the world has witnessed the attempt by neo-conservative America to export its version of democracy to the wider world. The justifications for the war in Iraq since the collapse of the sham search for Weapons of Mass Destruction have centred on the notion that America wants to build a beacon democracy in the Middle East. Readers may also remember the orange-clad masses in the freezing Ukrainian winter demonstrating for democracy a few years ago – a remarkable, peaceful orange revolution, quickly followed by a 'tulip' revolution in Kyrgyzstan. Gerry Sussman exposes the spin machine behind these 'spontaneous' outpourings of popular sentiment across the former soviet states, and draws the connections between the 'popular' revolutions in this region and the geopolitical interests of the United States.

The role of corporate lobbyists has long been a concern for many observers of liberal democracies. Granville Williams charts the assault on the regulation of television as a public service in Europe, driven by transnational commercial interests.

While the machinations of lobbyists sometimes attract critical publicity from the media, it is very unusual to hear anything about the behind-the-scenes activities of financial spinners. Aeron Davis examines the role of spin in the city, and observes the distortions that pushing shares, hyping stock and moving money can have, not only for shareholders and market followers, but also for the wider economy and society.

Several contributors directly examine how lobbying and spin permeate important policy networks. William Clark describes a network of neoliberal influence comprising New Labour and the Demos think tank, and linked to an important transatlantic current in British public life, helping to align UK–US security and foreign and trade policies.

Part IV examines a range of techniques and campaigns for countering corporate spin.

Trying to describe and understand these various networks of corporate influence takes time and effort to research and disseminate. The possibility of making such resources available to those concerned about the workings of corporate spin is perhaps beginning to emerge. Bob Burton describes an exciting initiative that allows the sharing of information and knowledge between diverse activists and campaigners: SourceWatch is a web-based wiki, an online encyclopaedia of corporate spin, that profiles spin doctors, lobbyists, lobbies and campaigns. It can be a research, educational or campaigning tool of real practical use to the media, activists and the general public. SourceWatch and other such developments offer us a way to begin to understand and counter corporate spin. Once we have taken this necessary step we can begin to think about how to reverse and undo the harms of the neoliberal thinkers, fakers, spinners and spies.

The United States is not simply interested in moulding the new Europe, but is actively trying to shape old Europe too. Olivier Hoedeman's examination of the mechanics of lobbying and spin in Brussels paints a worrying picture of an unaccountable European democracy that challenges the faith of Europhiles in the European project, but gives no comfort to Eurosceptics either. We are confronted with a system of political decision making that affords privileged access to business lobbies pushing a neoliberal agenda, across the European Union. At the World Trade Organisation, European trade negotiators, urged on by big business in Brussels, seek the opening up of developing economies in order to boost profit rather than to address poverty. We are given a glimpse of the neoliberal think tanks – self-styled 'anarcho-capitalists' – inspired by the neocon takeover of Washington, trying to repeat the trick in Brussels.

Focusing on the documented experiences within two separate anti-corporate campaigns, Andy Higginbottom finds a disturbing pattern of infiltration and subversion emerging. In the case of the Columbian Trade Union SINALTRAINAL, anti-Coca-Cola union leaders are murdered by right-wing death squads.

The question of how to counter corporate spin is taken up more explicitly in the final chapter by David Miller and William Dinan. It outlines a minimum agenda for the reform of corporate spin and the thoroughgoing renovation of the democratic process.

NOTES

1. See D. Miller (ed.) *Tell Me Lies: Propaganda and Media Distortion in the Attack on Iraq* (London: Pluto Press, 2004).
2. For more detail on US corporate involvement in Iraq, see P. Chatterjee, *Iraq, Inc.: A Profitable Occupation* (New York: Seven Stories Press, 2004), and Corporate Watch's *War Profiteers* website, <http://www.corpwatch.org/article.php?list=type&type=176>, last accessed 28 August 2005.
3. Examples include Rob Lowe's character Sam Seaborn in *The West Wing*, Michael J. Fox in *Spin City*, Robert De Niro in *Wag the Dog*, Stephen Fry in *Absolute Power*, Miles Anderson in *House of Cards*.
4. For more on this, see the *NuclearSpin* website run by Spinwatch, <http://www.nuclearspin.org>.

Part I

Global Corporate Power
and Corporate Spin

1
Public Relations and the Subversion of Democracy

David Miller and William Dinan

Public relations was created to thwart and subvert democratic decision making. It was a means for 'taking the risk' out of democracy. The risk was to the vested interests of those who owned and controlled society before the introduction of voting rights for all adults. Modern PR was founded for this purpose and continues to be at the cutting edge of campaigns to ensure that liberal democratic societies do not respond to the will of the people and that vested interests prevail. PR functions, in other words, as a key element of propaganda managed democracy. This is the precise opposite of PR industry spin, which boasts that PR facilitates debate and deliberation, and is the hallmark of pluralist democracy.

It is widely accepted that the PR industry arose at the same time as the great movements for democratic reform between 1880 and 1920. In the United States this involved coping with the feared elevation of the masses. 'The crowd is enthroned' according to PR pioneer Ivy Lee in 1914.[1] Lee believed in the necessity of 'courtiers' to 'flatter and caress' the crowd. The courtiers were the PR professionals, like himself. It was essential, wrote Walter Lippmann, the most important US theorist of the trend, that 'the public be put in its place' so that 'each of us may live free of the trampling and the roar of a bewildered herd'.[2] Lippmann's view was that 'manufacture of consent' was both necessary and possible: 'within the life of the generation now in control of affairs, persuasion has become a self-conscious art and a regular organ of popular government'.[3] This development also had its counterparts in the United Kingdom, but this has been largely ignored in the UK historical record. By 1911 a hugely important and now virtually forgotten activist for big business, Dudley Docker, was organising 'business leagues' under the slogan 'pro patria imperium in imperio' (For our country; a government within a government).[4] In other words, business rule. 'If our League spreads', wrote Docker in 1911, 'politics would be done for. This is my object.'[5]

Edward Bernays was another key innovator in PR and perhaps its best known pioneer in the early twentieth century. He was one of the first to use 'front groups' – organisations set up with the intent to promote the message of Bernays's clients. Bernays shared the same view as the other PR pioneers – that public opinion must be manipulated by 'the relatively small number of persons' who understand the masses. 'It is they', he wrote 'who pull the wires which control the public mind' and 'constitute an invisible government which is the true ruling power of our country.'[6] Bernays made a career out of serving the 'small number'.

We should also mention Carl Byoir. He was very fond of using third-party techniques to manipulate public debate. Front groups could be created by 'influencing the leaders of complacent groups and by forming new "fronts"'. Byoir did both. 'It is not', he explained 'what a client says about himself that scores, but what another person says about him that carries weight'.[7] When word of Byoir's activities in the 1930s and 1940s got out, he and his client were indicted for what the judge called 'devious manipulations'.[8] Byoir's firm was fined $5,000.

From that day to this, manipulation and deceit have been the defining characteristics of the PR industry.

The main charges that can be made against public relations as a discipline are:

1. It is overwhelmingly carried out for vested powerful interests, mainly corporations.
2. It is not open and transparent about its means or even about its clients and the interests it is working for.
3. It characteristically involves deception and manipulation.
4. It does not engage in democratic debate, but rather seeks to subvert it in the interests of its clients.
5. Corporate social responsibility (CSR) and other 'ethical' activities are all subordinated to corporate strategy.
6. PR has played a crucial role at the cutting edge of corporate power in the neoliberal revolution.

Look at the client list of any big PR firm or at the lists of those lobbying firms which disclose clients.[9] You will discover that their main clients are large corporations. This in itself suggests a large imbalance in resources between citizen groups and corporations. In recent years governmental bodies have increasingly hired PR and lobbying agencies. This advances the marketisation of public services, rather than simply broadening the base of PR users in the public sector.

Second, the PR industry is allergic to openness and transparency. Some PR agencies and some corporations disclose their clients or the lobbying groups that they fund, but many don't and most do not fully disclose all this activity. More importantly, wherever there is a threat of greater transparency via regulation of lobbying, the creation of disclosure laws, the requirement to publish information about their activities, the industry opposes it. This is currently visible in the fierce efforts being made by the European lobbying industry to avert binding regulation as one of the outcomes of the European Transparency Initiative launched by Commissioner Siim Kallas.[10]

Third, PR and lobbying involve deception and manipulation. It should be said straight away that this does not mean that all PR people consciously lie, though PR does often seem to require some management of cognitive dissonance. Perhaps the least pejorative way to put this is that PR necessitates the effective operation of ideology – commitment to ideas that serve interests. In this case the interests served are almost invariably corporate. Perhaps it is unfair to talk of lying. It is plain that most corporate spin doctors and PR agency staff have little or no choice. At the most basic level their job is to attempt to align the sectional interests of their principals (employers or clients) with general interests. As public and private interests are not the same, this must of necessity involve manipulation and deception. But having said this, it is perfectly plain that there is a little more than 'innocent fraud' going on in PR.[11] We are not arguing that all public relations practitioners are actively or consciously engaged in a conspiracy against democracy. Rather, we think that one of the problems with PR and lobbying is that in seeking to position private interests as being the same as public interests the aggregate result of such spin is that the public interest is undermined.

Fourth, corporations and their PR and lobbying agencies do not engage in open and transparent debate. The alignment of sectional interests with general interests involves the use of deceptive techniques, such as front groups. Rather than corporations speaking for themselves, they disguise sources of information by funding scientists, apparently independent institutes, consumer and community groups and the like. Furthermore, much corporate political activity – or corporate spin – is not devoted to convincing the public one way or another. Often it is aimed at decision makers and regulators. In fact, opinion polls in the United States and the United Kingdom repeatedly show that the public want more effective regulation of corporations. One way in which this is undermined is by the direct involvement of corporations in political decision making via lobbying and other policy targeted activities.

Fifth, corporate involvement in 'ethical' activities such as corporate social responsibility and 'sustainable development' is actually subordinated to corporate strategy. This means firstly that corporations can appear to be 'doing good' on the one hand while continuing to lobby directly for their own interests on the other (as in the case of the involvement of Shell in the International Chamber of Commerce[12]). The mantra heard from devotees about building the 'business case' for CSR is about more than making money out of 'ethical' and 'green' activities. In fact the aim of such activities is invariably to use ethical activity as a tool to ensure that binding regulation is resisted and indeed rolled back.[13]

The sixth charge against PR is the most serious, which is that it has provided the cutting edge of the neoliberal revolution which has affected all advanced industrial countries (indeed all countries to a greater or lesser extent) from about the mid 1970s onwards.

The neoliberal revolution has been brought about by determined campaigning by corporations and their allies in the media and political elites. The cutting edge of this campaign has been waged by the public relations industry and the armies of lobbyists employed by the corporations, and by the captains of industry themselves through their peak business associations, to ensure that democratic decision making is consigned to the dustbin of history. Given the devotion of neoliberal theorists to the free market and its 'invisible hand' one might have thought that they would disdain public relations and lobbying as a market-distorting mechanism.[14] But in reality they have been assiduous in their political campaign to re-establish the unchallenged rule of business.

This has been accomplished by more than half a century of campaigning by the corporations, going back at least as far as the creation of the shadowy Mont Pelerin Society in the immediate post-war period – a gathering of free-market ideologues around Friedrich von Hayek and Milton Friedman. They met to plot how to roll back the possibility of democratic decision making and put the market in the driving seat.[15]

Out of this emerged a host of pro-business organisations determined to take on and roll back the frontiers of social democracy. In Britain this meant the creation of a series of right-wing think tanks, such as the Institute of Economic Affairs, the Social Affairs Unit, and the Centre for Policy Studies (set up by Keith Joseph). These groups supplemented the more open campaigning organisations like National Propaganda (from 1919, later called the Economic League) and Aims of Industry (from 1942). In the United States similar aims were advanced by elite business associations such as the Conference Board (from 1916), and the Business Roundtable (from 1973), the latter playing a key role in the passing of the North America Free Trade Area agreement in the 1990s.[16] Internationally one of the earliest groups was the International Chamber of Commerce (set up in 1916 and still extremely active today).

It is a well-established fact that these groups were out to enact an economic counter-revolution, which was able to take power in the United Kingdom and the United States with the election of the Thatcher and Reagan regimes in 1979 and 1980. Both governments unleashed the market on their own citizens, and on the world, giving the process of corporate-led globalisation a decisive boost.

THE GLOBAL INDUSTRY

It is crucial to recognise that the neoliberal victory was not put in place by abstract forces but had to be won by argument and action and that it proceeded by means of vastly increased investment in the machinery of information management. This helps explain the emergence and global spread of the public relations industry. In the United Kingdom the PR industry expanded rapidly in the 1980s, facilitating the process of privatisation and buoyed up by its rich pickings and consequences.[17]

The reshaping of the global communications industry in the 1990s saw a wave of mergers and acquisitions between advertising, marketing and PR agencies. PR groups with offices in over 100 countries became a reality. By the turn of the century, the industry had concentrated so much that the top four global groups owned more than half the global market in advertising, marketing, PR and lobbying combined. Most people will never have heard of these corporations which were among the top 500 global corporations in the early part of the twenty-first century. The big three, WPP, Omnicom and Interpublic, are deeply obscure organisations. WPP, a company originally called Wire and Plastic Products, used to make supermarket trolleys before it became the business vehicle for a multi-million pound communications conglomerate. Today it owns hundreds of firms engaged in spin and in putting corporate wishes into action. Among the largest and most well known are Burson-Marsteller and Hill & Knowlton, both famous for their deceptive campaigns on behalf of the world's worst corporations, torturers and dictators.[18]

The view of PR as subverting democracy is challenged by apologists for PR inside the industry and their cheerleaders in academia. James Grunig is the leading academic champion for the PR industry. He, along with the other official historians of PR, like to argue that PR might have been a bit rough around the edges when it started but that it is much better now, so much so that they cannot conceive of a democracy without it. Grunig has developed a four-part model, which is simultaneously an historical and a normative model.[19] It distinguishes successively 'press agentry', which is most commonly identified with promotional media work; 'public information', which uses one-way communication to promote a given message, perhaps in the public interest; the two-way asymmetrical model, in which feedback and perhaps market research and public opinion polling are used to manipulate audiences more effectively; and a two-way symmetrical model which is alleged to help 'create mutual understanding' between an organisation and its publics. This approach 'is considered both the most ethical and most effective public relations model in current practice'.[20] The model is intended to illustrate a historical progression from bad to good.

But Grunig's problem is that there is still a lot of bad around. An outline of the misdeeds of Lee, Byoir and Bernays draws the response that this leaves out some of the ethical pioneers – such as Arthur W. Page.[21] But even using the evidence in the hagiographical biography of Arthur Page by Noel Griese, it is difficult to discern the ethical pioneer of PR. To give only one example: Griese notes the role of Page in subverting trade union demands for improved conditions in Chile in 1946. Among other things, Page advised the mine owners to demand the recall of the US ambassador as insufficiently supportive and to pressure US financial institutions to withhold investment in Chile. He followed up by contacting his friends in the international financial institutions to encourage them to deny loans to Chile. The owners' interests were bolstered by US government pressure on the Chilean government which 'outlawed the communist party and removed 30,000 voters with communist affiliations from voting roles'.[22] Once again, we find that the 'ethical' PR practitioner is adept at manipulation and, crucially, in undermining democracy.

But the problem of empirical refutation is easily solved in the Grunig schema – any evidence of bad PR is described as belonging to one of the first three categories and not to the exalted two-way symmetrical approach. This consigns the model to the never-never land of ethical PR – omnipresent as an ideal, but not a model with any purchase on the analysis of PR in the real world. Alternatively, to the extent that the model does provide a guide for practice, it is a guide to more effective manipulation. There is, in reality, no such thing as aligning private and public interests. Only by manipulation, deceit and ideology can they be presented as the same. Grunig's work is therefore only of value to those who are interested in trying to pursue their own interests by appearing to align them with wider interests. This kind of approach is at the root of many of the deceptive practices operating under the names of Corporate Social Responsibility and 'multi-stakeholder dialogue' and other partnership and engagement programmes between corporations and their critics.

THE COMMON INTEREST

Looking back on it, these corporate missionaries might have been following the advice of Marx and Engels in one of their earliest works, written in 1846. 'Each new class which puts itself in the place of one ruling before it', they wrote, 'is compelled, merely in order to carry through its aim, to represent its interest as the common interest of all the members of society.'[23]

The essence of this work is to wage the battle of ideas across the whole political structure – not just, or even mainly, in relation to managing public opinion. The focus on public opinion has – if anything – grown comparatively less in the recent past, as the ability of ordinary people to make a difference in politics has declined. As the former spin doctor for Volkswagen and the German nuclear industry, Klaus Kocks, puts it, 'When there is no election, no-one gives a damn what the electorate thinks.'[24]

Instead PR people concentrate their efforts on direct communications with shareholders, political decision makers, and other sections of the global elite. To do so, PR specialists engage in deception. At best this means attempting to align specific corporate or class interests with the general interest. At worst it means misinformation, lies and dirty tricks.

Take just one key example, the use of the spin tactic known in the industry as the 'third-party' technique. This recognises that corporate views openly stated might garner a sceptical reception. Rather than engage in open debate, the spin doctor's advice is to disguise the source of the message by inducing others to spread it. A newer twist on this is simply to invent people or organisations with no apparent corporate connection. This gives rise to the phenomenon of the fake persuader, where corporations and their PR agencies act under false identities to try to discredit their opponents and boost themselves.[25]

The examples just quoted are usually targeted at specific constituencies of opinion. They are about managing and manipulating the information environment and enacting particular ways of doing things. This is a question not of winning the battle of ideas in the abstract, but of concretely moving society in one direction or another. It is about the way in which some information and some ideas allow certain kinds of action and decision making or, more accurately, are part of the process by which certain acts are put into practice. In other words, discussing PR is a matter not only of evaluating the progress of ideas, but of understanding how the concrete form of inequality and domination is put into practice. Ideas have no independent existence from the material conditions and struggles of life. To understand the real role of the PR industry, we should 'not explain practice from the idea but explain ... the formation of ideas from material practice'.[26] The PR industry is not some free-floating pustule on the surface of a globalising world, but the cutting edge of corporate power in its campaign to stifle democracy. What is needed is the exposure of the PR industry and a series of measures to bring it and the corporations for which it acts to heel. Otherwise democratic politics are finished.

NOTES

1. Ray Eldon Hiebert, *Courtier to the Crowd: the Story of Ivy Lee and the Development of Public Relations* (Ames, Iowa: Iowa State University Press, 1966).
2. Walter Lippmann, *The Phantom Public* (New York: Harcourt Brace and Company, 1927), p. 155.
3. Ibid., p. 158.
4. R.P.T. Davenport-Hines, *Dudley Docker: The Life and Times of a Trade Warrior* (Cambridge: Cambridge University Press, 2002), p. 74.
5. Ibid., p. 70.
6. Edward Bernays, *Propaganda* (New York: Horace Liveright, 1928).
7. Richard Tedlow, *Keeping the Corporate Image: Public Relations and Business 1900–1950* (Greenwich, Conn.: JAI Press, 1979), p. 93.

8. Ibid., p. 96.
9. See the data sources at <http://www.spinprofiles.org>.
10. For more on this, see the Alter-EU campaign website, <http://www.alter-eu.org/>.
11. J.K. Galbraith, *The Economics of Innocent Fraud: Truth For Our Time* (London: Penguin, 2004).
12. Corporate Europe Observatory, 'Shell Leads International Business Campaign Against UN Human Rights Norms', *CEO Info Brief*, March 2004, <http://www.corporateeurope.org/norms.html>.
13. This was the key fault line in the European Commission's multi-stakeholder dialogue on CSR, <http://ec.europa.eu/enterprise/csr/forum.htm>; <http://forum.europa.eu.int/irc/empl/csr_eu_multi_stakeholder_forum/info/data/en/csr%20ems%20forum.htm>. For a critique of this process see <http://www.foeeurope.org/corporates/news/eu_debate.htm>.
14. To be fair, some market fundamentalists do share this view. See for example Marvin Olasky, *Corporate Public Relations: A New Historical Perspective* (Hillsdale, N.J.: Lawrence Erlbaum Associates, 1987). Olasky went on to become an adviser to George W. Bush.
15. Richard Cockett, *Thinking the Unthinkable: Think-Tanks and the Economic Counter-Revolution 1931–1983* (London: HarperCollins, 1995).
16. John MacArthur, *The Selling of 'Free Trade': NAFTA, Washington, and the Subversion of American Democracy* (Berkeley, Calif.: University of California Press, 2001).
17. D. Miller and W. Dinan, 'The Rise of the PR industry in Britain, 1979–98, *European Journal of Communication* 15 (1), March 2000, pp. 5–35.
18. See the profiles of Burson-Marsteller and Hill & Knowlton on SpinProfiles, <http://www.spinprofiles.org/index.php/Burson-Marsteller> and <http://www.spinprofiles.org/index.php/Hill_and_Knowlton>.
19. See J. Grunig, 'Communication, Public Relations, and Effective Organizations: An Overview of the Book', in J. Grunig, D. Dozier, W. Ehling, L. Grunig, F. Repper and J. White (eds) *Excellence in Public Relations and Communication Management* (Hillsdale, N.J.: Lawrence Erlbaum, 1992), pp. 1–28; J. Grunig and L. Grunig, 'Models of Public Relations and Communication', in Grunig et al., *Excellence in Public Relations*; and J. Grunig, L. Grunig, K. Sriramesh, Y. Huang and A. Lyra, 'Models of Public Relations in an International Setting', *Journal of Public Relations Research* 7 (3), 1995, pp. 163–86.
20. Larissa A. Grunig, 'Public Relations', in Michael B. Salwen and Don W. Stacks (eds) *An Integrated Approach to Communication Theory and Research* (Mahwah, N.J.: Lawrence Erlbaum Associates, 1996), pp. 464–5.
21. Comments by James Grunig, at 'A Complicated, Antagonistic and Symbiotic Affair: Journalism, Public Relations and Their Struggle for Public Attention', Swiss School of Journalism, Lucerne, Switzerland, 18 March 2006, in response to a presentation of an early draft of this chapter.
22. Noel Grise, *Arthur W. Page: Publisher, Public Relations Practitioner, Patriot* (Tucker, Ga.: Anvil Publishers, 2001), p. 304.

23. Karl Marx and Friedrich Engels, *The German Ideology* (1846), online at <http://www.marxists.org/archive/marx/works/1845/german-ideology/>.
24. Comments by Klaus Kocks, at 'A Complicated, Antagonistic and Symbiotic Affair', Swiss School of Journalism, Lucerne, Switzerland, 18 March 2006. See also David Miller, 'Nuclear view: spin doctor defends lying', *Spinwatch*, 28 March 2006, <http://www.spinwatch.org/content/view/230/8/>.
25. George Monbiot, 'The fake persuaders: Corporations are inventing people to rubbish their opponents on the internet', *Guardian*, 14 May 2002, <http://www.guardian.co.uk/Columnists/Column/0,,715158,00.html>. See also Chapter 7 of this book.
26. Marx and Engels, *German Ideology*.

2
Achilles Has Two Heels:
Crises of Capitalist Globalisation

Leslie Sklair

My thesis is that, far from benefiting the mass of humanity and holding out the only prospect of global prosperity in the long run as its proponents claim, capitalist globalisation is intensifying two pre-existing crises – class polarisation and ecological unsustainability – and that the phenomenon of corporate spin, particularly as practised by the four fractions of the transnational capitalist class, plays a central role in prolonging the myth that there is no alternative to capitalist globalisation. As the other contributions in this volume focus on corporate spin, my focus here will be on some suggestions about how we might most fruitfully theorise and research capitalist globalisation in ways that open up alternatives to it.[1]

A necessary preliminary is to establish some clarity about our unit of analysis. There are at least three common units of analysis that different (competing) groups of globalisation theorists and researchers take to define their field of inquiry. First, the inter-national (state-centrist) approach to globalisation takes as its unit of analysis the state (often confused with the much more contentious idea of the nation state). The hyphen in 'inter-national' is deliberate, emphasising the fact that globalisation is seen as something that powerful states impose on weaker states, and something that is imposed by each state on weaker groups under its domination. This line of argument is similar to old theories of imperialism and colonialism and more recent theories of dependency. The idea that globalisation is the new imperialism is common among radical critics of globalisation, by which they often mean (but do not always say) capitalist globalisation. This view can be rejected on the grounds of theoretical redundancy and empirical inadequacy. It is theoretically redundant because if globalisation is just another name for internationalisation and/or imperialism, more of the same, then the term is redundant at best and confusing at worst. State-centrist approaches to globalisation offer no qualitatively new criteria for globalisation and, paradoxically, appear to offer at least nominal support for those who argue that globalisation is a myth. The literature on globalisation is strewn with lapses into state-centrism.

The globalist approach is the antithesis to the state-centrist thesis. Globalists argue that the state has all but disappeared, that we have already entered a virtually borderless world, and that globalisation, by which is meant invariably capitalist globalisation, is irreversible and nearing completion. The central concerns of globalists are the global economy and its governance, and they are said to be driven by nameless and faceless market forces, the globalist unit of analysis. Globalism of this variety is often referred to as neoliberal globalisation. While the inter-nationalist approach exaggerates the power of the state, the globalist approach fails to theorise correctly the role of the state and the inter-state system under conditions of capitalist globalisation. Globalists (like state-centrists) are unable to analyse adequately the changing role of state actors and agencies in sustaining the hegemony of capitalist globalisation. In particular, as I shall argue below, globalists and state-centrists both fail to conceptualise the state as a site of struggle and to probe adequately the relations between the state, its agents and institutions, and the transnational capitalist class.

The transnational approach to globalisation is the synthesis of the collision of the flawed state-centrist thesis and the flawed globalist antithesis. I consider this to be the most fruitful approach, facilitating theory and research on the struggle between the dominant but as yet incomplete project of capitalist globalisation and its alternatives. My own version of this synthesis proposes transnational practices (TNPs) as the most conceptually coherent and most empirically useful unit of analysis. Within the familiar political economy categories – economy, politics, and (somewhat less familiar) culture–ideology – we can construct the categories of economic, political and culture–ideology TNPs and conduct empirical research to discover their characteristic institutional forms in the dominant global system (manifestation of globalisation). Nevertheless, despite the fundamental differences between the inter-national, globalist, and transnational approaches, they all stem from a real if seldom recognised phenomenon, generic globalisation.

GENERIC GLOBALISATION

Because the dominant form of globalisation in the world today is clearly capitalist globalisation there is much confusion in the literature due to the inability of most theorists and researchers to distinguish adequately between what I term generic globalisation and its historical forms, actual and potential.

Generic globalisation can be defined in terms of four phenomena, moments, in both the temporal sense and in terms of social forces, of increasing significance since the middle of the twentieth century:

1. The electronic revolution, notably transformations in the technological base and global scope of the electronic mass media and to most of the material infrastructure of the world today (the electronic moment);
2. Formal political decolonisation (the post-colonial moment);
3. The subsequent creation of transnational social spaces (the spatial moment); and
4. Qualitatively new forms of cosmopolitanism (the cosmopolitan moment).

While the first two of these, the electronic and the post-colonial moments, have been the subject of an enormous amount of theory and research in recent decades, the third, the idea of transnational social spaces, is of relatively recent origin and opens up some new lines of theory and research. The last, new forms of cosmopolitanism, is in a different category. The idea of cosmopolitanism is quite ancient and had its most important modernist reincarnation in the proposal of Kant at the end of the eighteenth century for the achievement of perpetual peace through the construction of a cosmopolitan order. However, this left many questions about the relations between democracy, capitalism and human rights unanswered, and these have to be urgently asked in the transformed world of the twenty-first century. Thus, any new framework for globalisation theory and research requires systematic inquiry into the prospects for new forms of cosmopolitanism for our times.

These four phenomena – the electronic revolution, the post-colonial, transnational social spaces, cosmopolitanism – are the defining characteristics of globalisation in a generic sense. In the absence of global catastrophe they are irreversible in the long run, because the vast majority of the people in the world – rich or poor, men or women, black or white, young or old, able or disabled, educated or uneducated, gay or straight, secular or religious – see that generic globalisation could serve their own best interests, even if, in a system dominated by capitalist globalisation, it is not necessarily serving their best interests at present. This is the world most people live in – big landlords as well as subsistence farmers in villages, corporate executives as well as labourers in sweatshops in major cities, well-paid professionals as well as informal workers in tourist sites, comfortable manual workers as well as desperate migrants in transit in the hope of better lives. While there is a multitude of theory and research on how capitalist globalisation works – who wins and who loses as it conquers the globe and transforms communities, cities, regions, whole countries and cultures – there is relatively little theory and research on globalisation as a generic phenomenon, thought about and even on occasion practised outside its historical container of globalising capitalism.

This is not surprising. We live in a world of generic globalisation, but this is also a world of actually existing capitalist globalisation. So the dominant global system at the start of the twenty-first century is the capitalist global system. The most fruitful way to analyse and research it is in terms of its transnational practices.

GLOBAL SYSTEM THEORY

Global system theory is based on the concept of transnational practices, practices that cross state boundaries but do not originate with state institutions, agencies or actors (although these are often involved). Analytically, transnational practices operate in three spheres, the economic, the political and the cultural–ideological. The whole is what I mean by the global system. The global system at the beginning of the twenty-first century is not synonymous with global capitalism, but the dominant forces of global capitalism are the dominant forces in the global system. To put it simply, individuals, groups, institutions and even whole communities, local, national or transnational, can exist, perhaps even thrive, as they have always done outside the orbit of the global capitalist system, but this is becoming increasingly difficult as capitalist globalisation penetrates ever more widely and deeply. The building blocks of global system theory are the transnational corporation, the characteristic institutional form of economic transnational practices, a still-evolving transnational capitalist class in the political sphere, and in the culture–ideology sphere, the culture–ideology of consumerism. Here I focus on the transnational capitalist class, the class that creates and disseminates global corporate spin.

THE TRANSNATIONAL CAPITALIST CLASS

The transnational capitalist class (TCC) is transnational in the double sense that its members have globalising rather than, or in addition to, localising perspectives; and it typically contains people from many countries who operate transnationally as a normal part of their working lives. The transnational capitalist class is composed of four fractions, the corporate, state, technical and consumerist, as follows:

1. Those who own and control major transnational corporations (TNCs) and their local affiliates (corporate fraction);
2. Globalising state and inter-state bureaucrats and politicians (state fraction);
3. Globalising professionals (technical fraction);
4. Merchants and media (consumerist fraction).

This class sees its mission as organising the conditions under which its interests (the interests of the system of capitalist globalisation) can be furthered in the global and local context. The concept of the transnational capitalist class implies that there is one central transnational capitalist class that makes system-wide decisions and that it connects with the TCC in each locality, region and country. While the four fractions are distinguishable analytic categories with different functions for the global capitalist system, the people in them often move from one category to another.

Together, these groups constitute a global power elite, ruling class or inner circle in the sense that these terms have been used to characterise the class structures of specific countries. The transnational capitalist class is opposed not only by those who reject capitalism as a way of life and as an economic system but also by small capitalists who are threatened by the monopoly power of big business under conditions of capitalist globalisation. Some localised, domestically oriented businesses can share the interests of the global corporations and prosper, but many cannot and many have perished. Influential business strategists and management theorists commonly argue that to survive, local businesses must globalise. Though most national and local state politicians (aided by their administrators) fight for the interests of their constituents, as they define these interests, government bureaucrats, politicians and professionals who entirely reject globalisation and espouse extreme nationalist ideologies are comparatively rare, despite the recent rash of civil wars in economically marginal parts of the world. And while there are anti-consumerist elements in most societies, there are few cases of a serious anti-consumerist party winning political power anywhere in the world.

In direct contrast to proponents of the state-centrist approach to globalisation, who assume that the globalisation process is driven by businesses and their supporters in government and the state on the basis of the national interest, the transnational approach to globalisation sets out to demonstrate that the dominant mode of the capitalist class is now transnational.

Members of the TCC seek to project images of themselves as citizens of the world as well as of their places of birth and are widely publicised as devoted above all else to the pursuit of profit and corporate aggrandisement wherever the opportunity arises. Leading exemplars of this phenomenon have included Jacques Maisonrouge, French born, who became in the 1960s the chief executive of IBM World Trade; the Swede Percy Barnevik who created Asea Brown Boveri, often portrayed as spending most of his life in his corporate jet; the German Helmut Maucher, former CEO of Nestlé's far-flung global empire; David Rockefeller, said to have been one of the most powerful men in the United States; the legendary Akio Morita, the founder of Sony; and Rupert Murdoch, who actually changed his nationality to pursue his global media interests. Today, major corporate philanthropists, for example, Bill Gates and George Soros, embody the public relations thrust of the new globalising TCC.

Men such as these (and a small but increasing number of women and other 'minorities' who have fought their way to the top against formidable odds) move in and out of what has been termed the inner circles of big business around the world. The inner circle of the TCC gives a unity to the diverse economic interests, political organisations and cultural and ideological formations of those who make up the class as a whole. As in any social class, fundamental long-term unity of interests and purpose does not preclude shorter-term and local conflicts of interests and purpose, both within each of the four fractions and between them. The culture–ideology of consumerism is the fundamental value system that keeps the system intact, but it permits a relatively wide variety of choices, for example, what I term emergent global nationalisms, as ways of satisfying the needs of the different actors and their constituencies within the global system. The four fractions of the TCC in any region, country, city, society or community, perform complementary functions to integrate the whole. The achievement of these goals is facilitated by the activities of local and national agents and organisations connected in a complex network of global interlocks.

This is a crucial component of this integration of the TCC as a global class. Virtually all senior members of the TCC – globally, regionally, nationally, and locally – will occupy a variety of interlocking positions, not only the interlocking directorates that have been the subject of detailed studies for some time in a variety of countries, but also connections outside the direct ambit of the corporate sector – the civil society servicing, as it were, the state-like structures of the corporations. Leading corporate executives serve on and chair the boards of think tanks, charities, scientific, sports, arts and culture bodies, universities, medical foundations and similar organisations in the localities in which they are domiciled. Those actors, known in the terminology of network theory as 'big linkers', connect disparate networks, and in the case of the leading members of the transnational capitalist class this frequently crosses borders and takes on a global dimension. But this global dimension invariably also connects with national and local organisations and their networks. In these ways the claim that 'the business of society is business' connects with the claim that 'the business of our society is global business'. Globalising business, usually but not exclusively big business, and its interests, become legitimated beyond the global capitalist system simply as an economic imperative into the global system as a whole. Business, particularly the transnational corporation sector, then begins to monopolise symbols of modernity and postmodernity, such as free enterprise, international competitiveness and the good life, and to transform most, if not all, social spheres in its own image.

FROM TINA TO TALA

The literature on globalisation is suffused with a good deal of fatalism, popularly known as the TINA ('there is no alternative') philosophy. Even some progressive academics, popular writers and political and cultural leaders seem to accept that there is no alternative to capitalist globalisation and that all we can do is to try to work for a better world within it. While I cannot fully develop the counter-argument to this fatalism here, it seems to me to be both morally indefensible and theoretically short-sighted. Capitalist globalisation is failing on two counts, fundamental to the future of most of the people in the world and, indeed, to the future of our planet itself. These are the class polarisation crisis and the crisis of ecological unsustainability. The crisis of class polarisation – the growing numbers of the very rich and the very poor and the widening gaps between them – is at the focus of radical critiques of capitalist globalisation.

What makes this a class crisis is the fact that poverty and inequality between countries and within communities in countries is largely a question of relationship to the means of production. According to the World Bank, agencies of the United Nations and most other sources, between 1970 and 2000 the distribution of income on a per capita basis between the richest and the poorest countries and between groups within most countries became more unequal. The rich in most countries certainly became richer, both relative to the poor and absolutely. Relative to the rich, the poor were becoming poorer, and while some of the previously very poor were becoming better off in absolute terms, other groups of poor people, notably landless peasants, including many women and their children, and the families of the urban unemployed, became absolutely poorer in this period too. Global capitalism, through the unceasing public pronouncements of members of the transnational capitalist class, acknowledges many of these issues, but as problems to be solved rather than crises. Corporate executives, world leaders, those who run the major international institutions, globalising professionals, the mainstream mass media, all accept that the rich are getting richer, some of the poor are getting poorer, the gaps between the rich and the poor are widening in our globalising world. This is rarely seen as a class polarisation crisis, but that is what it is. Every few years, summits and conferences are held, expert commissions are established, targets are set, action programmes are put into practice; some targets are missed and some are achieved, and the process grinds on.

Likewise, public representatives of the transnational capitalist class accept that there are environmental problems and that something has to be done about them. The facts of ecological stress at the planetary level are clear, though their significance is not universally agreed. Agricultural lands, rainforests and other wooded areas, grasslands, and sources of fresh water are all at risk. All over the world, rivers and other aquatic ecosystems are suffering severe ecological distress. While the details of the impending ecological crisis are not widely known, most people appear to be more aware of human impacts on the environment than ever before. This is due to several factors. A series of high-profile international meetings since the 1970s, notably the United Nations Conference on Environment and Development in Rio in 1992 and the Kyoto agreement on global climate change, have made it difficult for intellectual and political elites to ignore the crisis. This is clear from even a casual look at daily papers and magazines and television all over the world. There is clearly a growing disquiet about daily environmental degradation, serious incidents and the difficulty of making environmental choices. The destruction of the ozone layer, decreasing biodiversity, worsening land, air and water pollution in many places; sudden environmental catastrophes such as those at Bhopal and Chernobyl; devastating oil spills; floods, droughts and hurricanes attributed to global warming; and advice on what we have to do to save the planet; all these are regularly reported in the mass media and popular scientific publications. And, not least, the rise in the last few decades of green movements in the North and the South exerts a continuous pressure for action on the environment.

There is mounting evidence to suggest that capitalist globalisation may be intensifying both crises. Nevertheless, as I have argued above, globalisation should not be identified with capitalism, though capitalist globalisation is its dominant form in the present era. This makes it necessary to think through other forms of globalisation, forms that might retain some of the positive consequences of capitalism (insofar as they can exist outside capitalism) while transcending it as a socio-economic system in the transition to a new stage of world history. It is time to contemplate the replacement of the ideology of TINA with the vision of TALA ('There are lots of alternatives') but in order to articulate possible alternative forms we have to be prepared to think ourselves out of the box of capitalist globalisation. To do this it is necessary to reclaim generic globalisation, and in doing this we find that there are many alternatives, one of which is outlined briefly below as a suggestion for further theory and research.

One path out of capitalism that is clear to some but quite unclear to most, takes us from capitalist globalisation (where we are), through what can be termed co-operative democracy (a transitional form of society), to socialist globalisation (a convenient label for a form of globalisation that ends class polarisation and the ecological crisis). One strategy to achieve such a transformation involves the gradual elimination of the culture–ideology of consumerism and its replacement with a culture–ideology of human rights. This means, briefly, that instead of our possessions being the main focus of our cultures and the basis of our values, our lives should be lived with regard to a universally agreed system of human rights and the responsibilities to others that these rights entail. This does not imply that we should stop consuming. What it implies is that we should evaluate our consumption in terms of our rights and responsibilities and that this should become a series of interlocking and mutually supportive globalising transnational practices.

By genuinely expanding the culture–ideology of human rights from the civil and political spheres, in which capitalist globalisation has often had a relatively positive influence, to the economic and social spheres, which represents a profound challenge to capitalist globalisation, we can begin seriously to tackle the crises of class polarisation and ecological unsustainability. But political realism dictates that this change cannot be accomplished directly, it must proceed via a transitional stage. Capitalism and socialism, as can be seen in the case of market socialism in China, are not watertight categories. Capitalist practices can and do occur in socialist societies (for example, making workers redundant to increase profits or cut losses) just as socialist practices can exist in capitalist societies (for example, trying to ensure that everyone in a community enjoys a basic decent standard of living). The issue is hegemony, whose interests prevail, who defends the status quo (even by reforming it), who is pushing for fundamental change, and how this is organised into effective social movements for change globally.

The transition to socialist globalisation will eventually create new forms of transnational practices. Transnational economic units will tend to be on a smaller and more sustainable scale than the major TNCs of today; transnational political practices will be democratic coalitions of self-governing and co-operative communities, not the largely unaccountable and unelected transnational capitalist class. And cultures and ideologies will reflect the finer qualities of human life not the desperate variety of the culture–ideology of consumerism. These sentiments might appear utopian, indeed they are, and other alternatives are also possible, but in the long term, muddling through with capitalist globalisation is not a viable option if the planet and all those who live in it are to survive.

Thus, while the discourse and practice of capitalist globalisation would seem to suggest that it is a force for convergence, the inability of the transnational capitalist class, the driver of the processes of capitalist globalisation, to solve the crises of class polarisation and ecological unsustainability makes it both necessary and urgent to think through alternatives to it. This implies that capitalist globalisation contains the seeds of divergence. The globalisation of economic and social human rights leading to what can (but need not necessarily) be termed socialist globalisation is certainly one, if presently rather remote, alternative, and there are many others. Communities, cities, subnational regions, whole countries, multi-country unions and even transnational co-operative associations could all in principle make their own arrangements for checking and reversing class polarisation and ecological unsustainability. It is likely that the twenty-first century will bring many new patterns of divergence before a global convergence on full human rights for all is established. This is unlikely to occur in a world dominated by transnational corporations, run by the transnational capitalist class and inspired by the culture–ideology of consumerism.

The conclusion I draw from this analysis is that, in the medium to long term, we will have to find viable alternatives to capitalist globalisation within the conditions of generic globalisation. This attempt to flesh out the research framework of the transnational approach to globalisation has focused mainly on capitalist globalisation, because that is where we are at now. As argued above, the twin crises of class polarisation and ecological unsustainability, crises that capitalist globalisation intensifies and cannot resolve, make it essential to start thinking about alternatives. (These crises, of course, are hypotheses within global system theory and research on them proceeds apace.) This implies that a programme of theory and research on socialist globalisation is an urgent task. The focus of any new radical framework for globalisation theory and research – in contrast to a supine social science that limits its task to describing the status quo – is clearly to elaborate such alternatives within the context of genuinely democratic forms of globalisation. But we have little chance of successfully articulating such forms unless we understand what generic globalisation is and how capitalist globalisation really works. Corporate spin is a deliberate strategy to mystify and obscure the reality of capitalist globalisation and, as such, unless we can expose it for what it is theoretically, substantively and politically, we will make little progress in the struggles to resolve the crises of class polarisation and ecological unsustainability and to create radical alternative globalisations.

NOTE

1. This chapter borrows and updates material from L. Sklair, *The Transnational Capitalist Class* (Oxford: Blackwell, 2001) and *Globalization: Capitalism and Its Alternatives* (Oxford: Oxford University Press, 2002). Copious references to all the issues discussed will be found in these two sources. My approach to corporate spin is outlined with several examples in *The Transnational Capitalist Class*, chs 6 and 7 (see especially 'Global Corporate Citizenship as a Globalizing Practice: Deconstructing Shell', on pp. 184–91).

3

A Tour of the United Kingdom's Public Relations Industry

Chris Grimshaw

One of the greatest myths of the industry: that journalists are essential to producing a newspaper.

—Conrad Black, *A Life in Progress* [1]

Public relations has become a ubiquitous practice in modern Britain, with a profound impact on the media, on government and consequently on democracy. PR is used routinely in business, in the public sector, and in the not-for-profit sector of NGOs, charities and unions. By far the largest expenditure on PR is in the business sector. This chapter examines the United Kingdom's commercial PR industry.

It is worth taking a tour of the structure of the United Kingdom's PR industry and some of the agencies within it in order to familiarise the reader with its basic 'geography'. Much of the industry enjoys and cultivates virtual anonymity and its role in modern society is therefore rarely considered. PR consultancies such as Bell-Pottinger, Hill & Knowlton or Citigate are unknown to most of the public although their activities are often aimed directly at influencing the public's opinions and tastes. This influence is directed towards marketing both products and services and also towards manipulating the political process, controlling public opinion and subverting the legislative process to further corporate interests. By some estimates as much as 80 per cent of the content of the news media is sourced from, or directly influenced by, PR. [2]

It is the often covert nature of the industry and its activities that gives it a great deal of its power. Without knowing *who* is spinning *what* messages, *where* and *how*, the public is denied a full understanding of how modern political economy functions, and without transparency there can be no true democracy. It is beyond the scope of this chapter to map out fully all the players in the industry, and due to the confidential nature of PR *what specific* messages are being spun *where* cannot be comprehensively surveyed. The aim here is to provide the reader with a general understanding of the *who,* and the *how,* of the PR industry.

WHAT IS THE PR INDUSTRY?

The United Kingdom's PR industry comprises the following groups: more than 2,700 consultants and consultancies; corporate in-house PR departments; corporate front groups; trade associations; research and 'business intelligence' companies that provide data for PR and advertising; as well as the press agencies and newswires which work to disseminate PR materials. A study commissioned by the Chartered Institute of Public Relations (CIPR) found that there are at least 47,800 individuals working in PR in the United Kingdom, and that the industry turns over roughly £6.5 billion per year.[3] The industry boasts three trade associations, of which the CIPR is one. Lobbying (or government relations, or public affairs) is now highly integrated into the public relations industry. Whilst there are still independent lobbying firms, PR companies have long since muscled into the market, and now all the major firms offer their clients lobbying services integrated with public relations. Even some very small PR outfits claim to be effective in influencing Westminster. For example, Partner PR offers effective 'political communications' at a lower cost than traditional lobbying.[4] There are many one-man-band lobbyists trading on the contacts they have cultivated over many years in governmental circles.

There is no consensus on how precisely to define PR. The CIPR defines it as 'the planned and sustained effort to establish and maintain goodwill and mutual understanding between an organisation and its publics', a definition which provides little idea of what specifically is involved. Tim Bell (of Bell Pottinger) defines it thus: 'whereas advertising is the use of paid-for media space to inform and persuade, PR is the use of third-party endorsement to inform and persuade'.[5] This definition is more illuminating, but still omits a great deal. For this author, PR is a growing body of practices used to advance *and to inhibit* messages in the media and other domains, in order to manipulate the opinions of target audiences. PR is aimed at influencing many different audiences within the general public, business and government. PR activities will be examined in some detail in the second part of this chapter.

PR consultancies come in a wide variety of shapes and sizes. Some consultancies are the UK subsidiaries of big multinational firms, whilst many more are small companies with few staff, or even individual consultants, and are often not affiliated to any of the various trade bodies for PR. Also most sizeable companies now have an in-house public relations department.

Many of the big multinational agencies are themselves subsidiaries of large conglomerates, such as WPP, Omnicom and Interpublic Group. These conglomerates own advertising, PR, lobbying, market research, media buying and other agencies and describe themselves as 'integrated communications' companies. Through their subsidiaries they offer an exhaustive range of corporate communications services, which they claim to co-ordinate more effectively than independent companies.

Each part of the industry needs some examination.

In-House PR Departments

Almost every sizeable company (and public institution) now has its own in-house PR capacity. External affairs, investor relations, press departments and so on all conduct PR for different audiences. Internal communications within a company is also a PR role.

In-house departments in large corporations are often every bit as sophisticated as commercial consultancies, as they can afford to hire the best practitioners. BNFL for instance hired Philip Dewhurst, formerly CEO of Weber Shandwick UK, as their 'corporate affairs' director.[6] There is a rapidly revolving door between the in-house and commercial consultancy sectors.

In-house PR departments answer external requests for information from journalists and the public and may also handle efforts to project particular messages to outside audiences. Their efforts are often augmented by external PR agencies, which may be hired to provide advice or to perform specialist functions such as running important campaigns or crisis communications.

As well as conducting campaigns, the PR department seeks to control information. At best, it ensures that company employees are not taken advantage of by 'unscrupulous' journalists and provides accurate information about company operations. Because inquiries are generally handled by media-trained staff, the PR department can also act as a barrier to prevent sensitive information from slipping out. At worst, the in-house PR staff engage in professional obfuscation and deception. Requests for sensitive information can be simply ignored if need be and what information is given out can be carefully 'spun' to create a desired effect. This causes considerable frustration for investigative journalists and researchers, and works against transparency and public accountability.

PR Consultancies

Most large corporations retain at least one external agency to complement their in-house provision and to help with specialist communications tasks, training or consultancy. Agencies tend to do a far greater variety of tasks and are thus able to build up a wide range of valuable skills. Many companies which cannot afford to maintain a sophisticated PR department of their own may also want to hire expert help.

The PR directory, Hollis, has the most comprehensive list of UK PR consultancies available, with over 2,700 PR consultancies,[7] of which just under 1,000 are located in London, where they have better access to the national press and broadcasters.[8] In all, the consultancy sector in the United Kingdom employs over 7,000 people and in 2003, according to the Public Relations Consultants Association (PRCA), earned fees of £700 million.[9] According to a study by the Centre for Economics and Business Research, yearly turnover for the consultancies totals £1.2 billion.[10]

Much PR work is dependent on the skill and experience of individual practitioners and so many small companies are nonetheless highly effective. Often these are started by journalists, who can use their skills to make far more money in PR than they could in the media.

Fleet Street Flair is a good example. Run by Tony Gearing, formerly deputy editor of the *Daily Telegraph*, it uses his ten years of journalism experience to conduct media relations for clients and to deliver media training. Gearing's journalistic expertise allows him to present corporate stories in a way that newspapers will consider newsworthy, a notoriously difficult task for the inexperienced. Amongst other things, his website boasts of placing stories in the press, for client LondonWaste, to help gain acceptance for a waste incinerator in the face of strong local opposition.[11]

The first multinational agencies began to appear in the 1960s, when Hill & Knowlton crossed the Atlantic to London and Paris, quickly followed by rival agency Burson-Marsteller. Since then many multinational agencies have appeared. The largest of them by revenue, Weber Shandwick Worldwide, has more than 75 offices in 35 countries with an affiliate network operating in 65 countries.

Many independent consultancies are increasingly seeking to join global, or at least multinational, affiliate networks, so they can offer an international service to their larger clients.

Through their great size and financial resources, the larger agencies are able to buy some of the best of national talent wherever they operate, ensuring a competitive advantage for their lobbying and PR operations. Most of them offer a full range of services, although some work in specialist areas. Lewis Communications for instance, which has 19 offices around the world, works mostly for information technology and biotech clients.

Conglomerates

PR and related companies have been consolidating since the 1960s. The practice of combining lobbying and PR in one agency spread rapidly in the United States and around the world. The advertising industry, with plenty of cash to spare, also began to buy up PR companies in order to extend their capabilities.

The appeal was very simple. PR tactics of media manipulation influence legislators just as much as they do the general public; lobbying operations combined with public relations campaigns can be more effective than either individually.

Chime PLC is a typical group. By revenue it is the largest PR group in the United Kingdom, with yearly revenues in excess of £60 million. Founded by Margaret Thatcher's former spin doctor, Tim Bell, it is a PR and lobbying group that also comprises advertising, media buying and research companies. Its main PR companies are Bell Pottinger, Good Relations and Harvard PR. It is itself an 'associate' of (part-owned by) the huge conglomerate WPP Group.

In the last 20 years consolidation has intensified, and at the extreme are huge multinational conglomerates, such as Omnicom, Interpublic Group and WPP, which seem to be on continuous sprees of acquisition. These are multi-billion-dollar holding companies owning scores of other companies and groups of companies. Currently the 'integrated communications' industry is dominated by a handful of these multi-billion-dollar companies. Of the global top ten PR companies only one, Edelman, remains independent. All the rest are subsidiaries of the conglomerates.

Industry Bodies/Trade Associations

A great deal of lobbying and PR is handled by industry bodies or trade associations. Almost every industry sector and sub-sector has a trade group representing their interests to legislators, regulators and the wider public. The Association of the British Pharmaceutical Industry (ABPI) or the UK Offshore Operators Association (UKOOA), represent the major companies in the pharmaceutical, and oil and gas sectors respectively. They are fundamentally PR and lobbying operations. They exist to voice their industries' views. In lobbying, industry bodies wield the collective bargaining power of entire industries, often more than even the largest corporations wield individually, and they have easy access to government. Some of them (such as the ABPI) even have offices with a Whitehall address. Naturally, individual corporations also conduct their own lobbying in parallel with the trade association. They often lobby for legislative changes or government contracts to their own advantage, whilst the trade association pursues an agenda of benefit to all its members.

Within the nuclear industry, much of the proactive PR work is carried out by the Nuclear Industry Association and the British Nuclear Energy Society, umbrella groups that represent most of the companies within the sector. These groups are much more credible than some of their member companies (such as BNFL, which is thoroughly discredited by its extraordinary history of accidents, incompetence, cover-ups and dishonesty[12]). In recent years these groups have regained some credibility in the media by abandoning the nuclear industry's traditional antagonism towards renewable power and stressing a complementary role for nuclear power in combating climate change.[13]

PR Trade Associations

The PR industry in the United Kingdom has three main trade associations, the Chartered Institute of Public Relations (CIPR), the Public Relations Consultants Association (PRCA) and the Association of Professional Political Consultants (APPC).

The CIPR is the industry body for PR professionals. It provides training and development for its members, has a code of conduct, produces research into PR and issues policy recommendations. It claims also to be dedicated to 'raising standards' within the industry. It currently has over 8,000 members.

Of the three PR industry bodies in the United Kingdom, the CIPR has the highest public profile and has become increasingly concerned with improving the industry's image. On the one hand, PR practitioners are caricatured as shallow and ridiculous, an image exacerbated by the success of the BBC's *Absolutely Fabulous*. In fact the image of 'disorganised, scatterbrained, champagne-dependent luvvies' is held even within the industry[14] and may explain why some PR people do not join the CIPR. On the other hand, a potentially some damaging image of PR, as cynical and deceptive 'spin', is emerging due to a series of corporate (and governmental) PR scandals.

The Institute of Public Relations received its royal charter in February 2005, when it became the CIPR. It had been working for chartered status for many years in the belief that this would confer a more professional image and foster the perception of higher standards. Crucially this would mean greater status for PR in the business world.

The CIPR is supposed to help with the self-regulation of the industry, although it represents little more than a sixth of the United Kingdom's PR professionals.[15] It investigates complaints against its members and may discipline them if they breach the Institute's code of conduct. However the code itself is a fairly lax set of rules, rewritten in 2000 'as a document of best practice, rather than retaining a "thou shall not" approach'.[16] However, in spite of commonplace practices against the public interest, the Institute investigates only about a dozen complaints each year. No formal record is kept of these complaints which are 'usually resolved informally' by mediation between the parties.[17] The CIPR has never terminated a membership due to complaints.

Whereas the CIPR is a body for individuals, the Public Relations Consultants Association represents member companies. The PRCA has over 120 members and has recently introduced a new class of 'observer' membership for very small agencies. Like the CIPR, the PRCA lobbies government on behalf of the industry. It also 'aims' to communicate publicly for its members though it has a lower profile than the CIPR.

The Association of Professional Political Consultants represents lobbyists. Lobbying has acquired a poor image since a string of lobbying scandals during the 1990s, and the APPC, in conjunction with the PRCA, is attempting to change that.[18] However not all lobbyists sign up to self-regulation, and they can simply resign from the APPC if they choose not to abide by the voluntary code, as lobby firm Media Strategy recently did when appointing Lord O'Neill, former chair of the trade and industry select committee, to their advisory board.[19]

There is an inherent conflict of interest for the CIPR, PRCA and APPC. Effective and transparent policing and enforcement of their own codes of conduct could have a negative impact on the image of the industry whose interests they represent.

Front Groups

Front groups are a useful asset to corporate PR work. PR agencies and corporations sponsor apparently independent groups with views sympathetic to their own. Sometimes they create such groups from scratch.

Burson-Marsteller, for instance, set up the front group 'European Women for HPV Testing' on behalf of its client, Digene. Burson-Masteller were lobbying for the NHS to adopt a new test screening for cervical cancer, which would have made hundreds of millions of pounds of new business for Digene. In order to bolster the lobbying effort, the front group was set up as an apparently independent 'grassroots' campaign. By signing up women celebrities, including Liz Hurley and Caprice, 'European Women for HPV Testing' gained extra publicity and greater leverage with government. The celebrities however were not informed of the involvement of Burson-Masteller and Digene or their role in a wider commercial lobbying campaign. Indeed, as is common practice, there was no public acknowledgement of the link. Had the story not been exposed by the *Observer*, Burson-Masteller's role would have remained a secret.[20]

Press Agencies and Newswires

Most media outlets use press agencies and newswires such as Reuters and PR Newswire to provide content when their own journalists cannot fill the pages.

The largest of these is the Press Association. Formed in 1868 by a group of newspaper publishers, the PA sells content to every national and regional daily newspaper, to broadcasters, online publishers and others. Customers take stories to print or broadcast from its news and features lists.

Much of the Press Association's content is produced by its network of journalists and photographers, and the Press Association has a reputation for impartiality. However, its independence is compromised by its relationship with the PR industry as it offers services to PR agencies: 'PA's unique position at the centre of the media industry in the United Kingdom enables us to provide support for many PR and marketing campaigns'. Space on the Press Association's newswire service is sold in bulk to other more commercial newswires and PR agencies.[21] PR agencies gain extra anonymity and respectability by having their content supplied by the prestigious Press Association.

WHAT DOES THE PR INDUSTRY DO?

Media Relations

Media relations is a core practice of PR. Influence over the media is a powerful way of shaping public opinion, and therefore attracts the attention of professional spinners. The media is the central vehicle for much of the PR industry's influence, and manipulating the media, particularly the news media, forms the basis for a great deal of PR work.

Media relations aims to influence media content by placing stories, influencing journalists as they produce stories and stopping negative stories from appearing, or by limiting the damage caused by such stories. Many other aspects of PR – crisis and issues management, brand marketing, investor relations, and so on – depend on forms of media relations work.

The relationship between the news media and the PR industry is complex and increasingly symbiotic. PR practitioners want to place their stories in the media, which in turn has become more dependent on PR to supply content to fill air time or column inches. Whilst newspapers have been steadily shedding staff over recent decades, they have simultaneously managed to produce ever fatter publications, and it is the PR industry that supplies much of the extra content.

It should be understood that PR gains influence not through dominating journalists but by providing a valuable service to them. There is considerable mistrust of PR amongst many journalists and PRs aim to improve relations by being helpful.

Placing Stories

The prime method of placing stories is by the press release. A well-made press release gives the journalist material that can be easily worked into a newsworthy article. It reduces the busy journalist's workload. Whether it concerns a new product or a controversy about the client company, the well-crafted press release enables the journalist to produce 'news' content quickly without having to conduct any research. Often press releases are reproduced with only minor amendments, and much that passes for reporting nowadays is nothing more than reworded press releases.

Targeting

In order to acquire influence, to know when to send press releases and to whom, to know how to approach media sources, the PR industry devotes enormous resources to research. The pages of *PR Week* are filled with media news and analysis. New publications and programmes, new appointments, editors' attitudes to PR, and analyses of different types of publication are the staple subject matter of the industry's main trade journal.

One recent example concerned a PR consultant who toured three newsrooms, including Sky News[22] in order to gain a better understanding of how they work. He was able to improve his appreciation of how and when to pitch stories to each news outlet and how not to annoy them. Interestingly, the journalists were quite keen to help the PR practitioner understand their operations, in the hope of receiving better content and fewer irritating approaches.

There is now emerging a small industry of research companies that maintain extensive databases of journalists, civil servants, politicians and other 'opinion leaders' and sell this information to clients in PR and lobbying. One of the most prominent of these companies is De Havilland Information Services[23] which has around 100 staff gathering information on many thousands of influential people.

Killing Stories

When bad press can be foreseen, the first hope for the PR practitioner is to stop the story from getting out. Most PR people do not like to talk openly about this practice. It is very clearly against the public interest. Some sources are quite candid about it however.

New agency Partner PR claims that

using a full array of journalistic, legal, intelligence and communications techniques, we will ensure your crisis is closed down as a public story ... When a food manufacturer faced media interest in claims its products were contaminated, we killed the story.[24]

One of the key techniques used to kill stories is to trade with journalists. Top PR people have access to many secrets and can offer one story in exchange for dropping another. Mark Hollingsworth writes of Sir Tim Bell (of Bell Pottinger):

Bell ... is a dealer in information. He establishes close relationships with journalists and editors as a way of ensuring that his client's message is conveyed to his liking. He is Mephistopheles to the reporter's Faust. Favours are offered and received: if the story about the client is spiked, the journalist is handed an even better exclusive about someone else. If the article is published, future co-operation is withdrawn.[25]

'PR is all about learning things about people they'd prefer you didn't know. Gordon's a great exponent of trading stories', said one journalist about Gordon Beattie of PR firm Beattie Media.[26]

There is no measurement of how prevalent this practice of killing stories is in the industry, and specific examples are quite rare, for the obvious reason that, when successful, the story does not appear in the media. However one Chime executive said of this practice that there is 'more and more of it',[27] and Tim Blythe, Director of Corporate Affairs at W.H. Smith, said '50 per cent of the job is keeping stuff out of the press.'[28]

Crisis Management

When a controversial story cannot be killed the crisis must be 'managed'. Crisis management is the art of putting the right spin on disasters (or at least bad news). It could mean simply making sure that customers know when business as usual will resume following a disruption in operations or services, or something as sensitive as handling media coverage of an oil spill, environmental protests against a company, product recalls, or coverage of legal and regulatory matters.

Now more than ever companies' profits are tied to their reputation, and when disaster strikes the way a company handles it can make a huge difference to its image. All the major PR companies offer crisis management services. 'The days of regarding an industrial accident that kills only one person as a minor incident to be swept under the carpet are gone', according to crisis consultant Michael Bland.[29]

Faced with a PR crisis, a company may call in crisis management specialists to handle media, government and public communications. At least one commercial insurance company will offer discounts to its customers if they have a crisis management plan on paper and can also demonstrate its feasibility through at least annual evaluated crisis simulations.[30]

Issues Management

When a crisis or controversy won't go away it becomes an 'issue' in need of long-term management. Frequently mentioned in the same breath as crisis communications, issues management is often about influencing the public perception of a broad issue over a long time scale. Monsanto's 1998 'Food, Health, Hope' advertising campaign might be described as crisis management – a response to the extraordinary backlash against GM crops in the United Kingdom – while the industry's current, less overt campaign to gain acceptance for GM might be characterised as long-term issues management.

Front groups and third-party advocates are often used in issues management. The nuclear industry's long-term efforts to gain acceptance for new nuclear power is an issues-management campaign that benefited enormously from a third-party advocate, Sir James Lovelock, the ecologist famous for his 'Gaia hypothesis'. When the media debate on nuclear power began in the summer of 2004, it was Lovelock's support for nuclear power as a solution to the problem of climate change which generated the media 'hook'.

Whilst Lovelock's views are undoubtedly sincere, his links to nuclear industry PR will certainly have helped him to gain maximum media exposure. He is a patron of the industry front group Supporters of Nuclear Energy (SONE),[31] which was set up by Margaret Thatcher's former press secretary, Sir Bernard Ingham. Ingham, who has been a director of PR firm Hill & Knowlton and a paid lobbyist for BNFL, is well known for his antagonism towards the goals of environmental groups and is also vice-president of the anti-wind-farm campaign group, Country Guardian.[32]

Dr Dejan Vercic, the Slovenian PR guru, hinted at the long-term strategic nature of some issues-management campaigns at the 2004 AGM of the Institute of Public Relations. He told the IPR's members that their greatest challenge over the next five to ten years will be to reopen the public debates on nuclear power and biotechnology and win back the industries' 'licence to operate'.[33]

Concerned with long-term high-level messaging, issues management is also sometimes known as 'strategic communications'.

Branding and Marketing

Marketing involves not only advertising and promotions. The PR industry is carving out an increasing share of the marketing business for itself. Product launches and consumer surveys have become routine fillers even for serious news sources. Radio 4's *PM* news programme recently carried a six-minute piece concerning the launch by National Express Coaches of a new service allowing customers to book two adjacent seats for themselves.[34] The programme interviewed both a National Express spokesman and former conservative transport minister Steven Norris, who happens to work for PR consultants Citigate Group, who work for National Express.[35] For the company it was great marketing. It got far more air time than an advert could provide, giving them a chance to present a positive image of themselves and an apparently independent well-known third party extolling the company's virtues. In addition, the piece was presented as news. Listeners are less likely to doubt or ignore information if it is presented in this fashion rather than in a television commercial. And all this without the cost of advertising.

Most of the big PR companies have a brand-marketing practice. Brands are regarded as intangible assets and are counted on corporate balance sheets, so they are serious business. In the modern business environment, branding is regarded as crucial to effective marketing, and simple advertising is no longer enough to mark a brand out in the public mind. In addition to the ever increasing volume of advertising to which we are now exposed, the media carry more and more 'news stories' about the latest gadget or service being offered by a company. The majority of such campaigns may be fairly innocuous, such as the launch of a new brand of crisps, but they are always about promoting consumerism.

Perhaps the most insidious aspect of this practice is its 'dumbing down' effect on the media. Due to the relationship between the media and PR, 'product news' has come to fill more and more of the press and broadcast news. As media outlets proliferate, demand for content rises and PR fills the pages like a cultural pollution.

Public Affairs/Lobbying

PR and lobbying have long been used as tools to influence legislators and governments. The potential rewards to a company of being able to influence the legislative process or government decision making are obvious. It is an area that requires specialisation and expertise to get results.

Apart from the evident corporate power they represent, lobbyists aim to wield influence by providing services to politicians. Politicians, like journalists, have limited resources and so find it hard to stay current with every issue. Like others in PR, lobbyists aim to build friendly relations with those they seek to influence, for instance by providing quality information resources (obviously sympathetic to their clients' agenda). Amongst other services, they will help to write speeches.[36]

However, many lobbying scandals over the years have revealed that lobbyists have access all the way to the top, including the prime minister's office.[37] The public affairs business has always depended greatly on the political experience and contacts of key individuals and the revolving doors between the PR business and government are constantly spinning. Most of the APPC's members freely admit to employing (former) civil servants, political party workers or politicians. Political lobbying consultancy APCO's senior consultant, Simon Milton, is also the leader of Westminster City Council. A complete list of such contacts and connections would be very long. The patterns are already well established.

Sociologist Aeron Davis argues that PR and lobbying aimed at government is one of the most successful forms of public relations. It has helped to create a situation in which corporate lobbyists have privileged access and influence in Westminster. Competing concerns are often effectively excluded from the debate over economic policy.[38] David Miller and William Dinan also note that 'PR and public affairs have seeped into the very fabric of policy and decision making in Britain and in the European political arena'.[39]

Investor Relations/Financial PR

Financial PR is the most competitive, most lucrative and highest-status branch of the PR world. Because of the specialist knowledge and high revenues associated with financial PR many of the key agencies in the area, such as Financial Dynamics, Citigate Dewe Rogerson, Tulchan, Square Mile and Brunswick are able to work almost exclusively in financial communication. However, most of the big agencies and conglomerates, such as Hill & Knowlton or Chime Communications, also have major financial communications operations.

In the financial markets information is everything. It has often been observed that trading is determined by confidence. If the markets believe that a company or commodity is going to increase in value, it will; if they think it will go down, then the herd mentality will ensure that it does. More than anywhere else, in the financial markets of the City of London, perception is reality, information is power, and so a good spin doctor is essential. In the city the PR agencies' capacity to control information, perceptions and reputations is an invaluable commodity.

Financial PR took off in the 1980s when deregulation of the financial markets and privatisation led to rich new contracts. It has been growing at an extraordinary rate ever since, feeding off the boom in mergers and takeovers. In 1986, British companies spent £37 million on financial PR. In 1996 they spent £250 million, and 'far from slowing down, as we look towards the new millennium this rampant growth is set to accelerate'.[40]

Financial spin doctors can wield enormous influence over journalists, just as they can in other PR sectors. They have incentives for encouraging journalist co-operation that other PR people do not. Michie quotes an anonymous City PR insider:

Let's say a journalist hears from an insider that a company's results are going to be ahead of forecasts, and let's say he hears this a few days before the official announcement. That gives him plenty of time to buy a few grand of shares through Aunt Mabel, write an upbeat exclusive, see the share price rocket and offload his shares, turning an easy ten percent.[41]

Such practices are not uncommon in the Square Mile. Former *Sunday Telegraph* reporter, Patrick Weever, claimed to have been unfairly dismissed for, amongst other things, refusing to co-operate with this practice known as the 'Friday Night Drop'.[42]

CONCLUSIONS

We have seen briefly that the United Kingdom's public relations industry is large and diverse, encompassing many complementary businesses. With an annual turnover estimated at £6.5 billion, PR can no longer be regarded as a fringe or specialist practice. It is now big business and an integral part of corporate operations, and continues to grow. These vast revenues are spent not only on overt communications but also to use and extend covert networks of access and influence that extend into government, the markets and the media.

The mainstream media and the public relations industry have become almost symbiotic. PR is both a cause and an effect of the commercialisation of the mainstream media. As the media cut costs, so they need more free content from PR agencies; and as they use more PR content, so PR gains greater credibility and funding to produce more, allowing the media to cut costs further. The result is a decline in investigative journalism, more superficial news and the propagation of corporate agendas, as ultimately it is the corporate sector that pays for an increasing proportion of the costs of news production. PR and lobbying derives much of its power from its anonymity and its covert mode of influence. No other industry with such influence over society is so invisible. Much of the industry's activities are poorly scrutinised and effectively unregulated. There is no accountability to society at large, only to commercial clients and shareholders, and there is no right to know about its operations. Although there is no way to quantify the political and social influence that the corporations wield through PR, we have seen in this brief tour that there is good reason to fear that that influence is extensive, anti-democratic, and often counter-productive in resolving key political, social and environmental issues. Closer scrutiny of the industry and greater public awareness of its activities would therefore be very positive developments. At the very least, some meaningful transparency should be legally enforced. Such developments might produce qualitative and quantitative information which could form the basis of an effective system of regulation for commercial PR activities.

NOTES

1. Conrad Black, *A Life in Progress* (Key Porter Books, 1993).
2. Julia Hobsbawm, 'Why Journalism Needs PR', *Guardian*, 17 November 2003; Prof. Anne Gregory, president of IPR, in speech to the IPR AGM, 23 June 2004.
3. Centre for Economics and Business Research (CEBR), 'PR Today', November 2005, p. 14.
4. *Partner PR* website, 2004, <www.partnerpr.com/what_we_do/wwd_pc.htm>.
5. Quoted in Aeron Davis, *Public Relations Democracy: Public Relations, Politics and the Media in Britain* (Manchester: Manchester University Press, 2002), p. 26.
6. Gidon Freeman, 'Dewhurst quits Shandwick for senior BNFL position', *PR Week*, 16 March 2001. In December 2006, Dewhurst became the head of PR for Russian energy firm Gazprom.
7. Hollis PR, <www.hollis-pr.com>. A free trial service is available at the website giving access to the lists. Hollis lists 2,787 companies; however, there are duplicate entries and for a few larger companies separate offices around the country are included.
8. Ibid. Hollis provides the following regional breakdown – London, 985 agencies; Midlands, 210; North West, 154; Northern Ireland, 35; Isle of Man, 1; Wales and the Marches, 77; South West, 208; Channel Islands, 5; Home Counties, 289; South East, 407; East, 84; North East, 182; Scotland, 143.

9. PRCA, 'Purchasing Public Relations: A Guide to Public Relations Consultancy For Procurement Professionals', 2005, <www.prca.org.uk/sites/prca.nsf/images/2005/$file/Purchase.pdf>.

10. CEBR, 'PR Today', p. 14.

11. <http://www.fleetstreetflair.co.uk/endorsements.htm>.

12. See, for example, <http://news.bbc.co.uk/1/hi/business/647503.stm>; <http://news.bbc.co.uk/1/hi/uk/774548.stm>; and <http://www.newscientist.com/article/mg17924020.800-secrecy-shrouds-nuclear-leak.html>.

13. Chris Grimshaw, 'It's Official: No Dark Machiavellian Conspiracy for New Nuclear Power', *Corporate Watch Newsletter* 21, December 2004, p. 3. See also <http://www.nuclearspin.org>.

14. Chris Lewis of Lewis Communications describing the IPR, in 'Survey – Creative Business: Public relations', *Financial Times*, 30 October 2001.

15. According to the CIPR's website, the CIPR has 'over 8000 members', <http://www.cipr.co.uk/About/aboutframeset.htm>. The CEBR estimates that there are at least 47,800 PR professionals in the United Kingdom: CEBR, 'PR Today', p. 14.

16. CIPR website, <www.cipr.co.uk/member_area/mem_matters/index.asp>.

17. Telephone interview with Francis Ingham, head of public affairs, CIPR, 19 October 2005.

18. Rod Cartwright, 'Thought Leader: Turning around lobbying's reputation', *PR Week*, 3 September 2004.

19. 'Britain's toothless lobbying regulator', *Private Eye*, 16 August 2005; posted at <www.spinwatch.org/content/view/1582/9/>.

20. Antony Barnett, 'Revealed: how stars were hijacked to boost health company's profits', *Observer*, 25 January 2004.

21. Telephone interview with Martin Huckett, development manager responsible for PR services, Media and Information Services, Press Association, 5 September 2002.

22. Adam Hill, 'Media relations: inside the newsroom', *PR Week*, 9 January 2004.

23. Interviews with De Havilland sales representatives. Website, <www.dehavilland.co.uk>.

24. <http://www.partnerpr.com/what_we_do/wwd cc.htm>.

25. Mark Hollingsworth, *The Ultimate Spin Doctor: the Life and Fast Times of Sir Tim Bell* (London: Hodder & Stoughton, 1997), pp. 224–5.

26. Alex Bell, 'Beattie recruits from Who's Who', *Observer*, 3 October 1999.

27. Interviewed at the IPR AGM, 23 June 2004.

28. Quoted in Davis, 'Public Relations Democracy', p. 27.

29. Amanda Hall, 'Crisis Management: Prudent Investment Is Crucial when Disaster Strikes', *PR Week*, 13 August 1992.

30. Bernstein Commmunications Inc., 'Crisis Management Predictions for 2002', <www.bernsteincom.com/docs/predictionsfor2002.html>.

31. Sir Bernard Ingham, 'About SONE', <www.sone.org.uk/content/view/42/31/>.

32. Country Guardian website, <http://www.countryguardian.net/cg.htm>.

33. Dejan Vercic, in question and answer session after his annual lecture, Institute of Public Relations, Annual General Meeting, 23 June 2004.
34. *PM*, BBC Radio 4, 20 January 2005.
35. 'Rail lobby on inside track', *Socialist Worker* website, <www.socialistworker.org.uk/archive/1709/sw170903.htm>.
36. Mark Ballard MSP, speech to 'Spin and Corporate Power' conference, Strathclyde University, 19 November 2004.
37. See, for instance, Greg Palast, 'Jack Straw's Plan to Keep it Zipped', *Guardian*, 20 July 1999.
38. Aeron Davis, 'The Rise and Impact of Corporate Public Relations in Britain', paper given at Political Studies Association conference, LSE, March 2000.
39. David Miller and William Dinan, 'The Rise of the PR Industry in Britain, 1979–98', *European Journal of Communications* 15 (1), March 2000.
40. David Michie, 'The Invisible Persuaders: How Britain's Spin Doctors Manipulate the Media' (London: Bantam Press, 1998), p. 26.
41. Ibid., p. 38.
42. John Willcock, 'BT threatened to stop advertising in Sunday Telegraph', *Independent*, 22 September 1999.

Part II

How Corporations Use Spin to Undermine Democracy

4

Powers Behind the Throne: Washington's Top Political Strategists

Laura Miller

A group of heavy-hitting corporate and political campaign strategists with close ties to the White House and roots in the tobacco industry is unobtrusively stage managing US elections and law-making. At the nexus of millions of dollars of influence-buying money sit four interconnected firms:

1. The DCI Group, a Washington-based lobbying and PR shop that specialises in creating quasi-grassroots organisations and publishes 'Tech Central Station', a website 'where free markets meet technology';
2. Feather Larson Synhorst-DCI, a telemarketing and political-consulting firm with offices in Washington, St Paul and Phoenix;
3. FYI Messaging, a political direct mail company based in Phoenix; and
4. TSE Enterprises, a Phoenix-based internet PR company that creates and hosts websites and does electronic direct mail.

The companies have overlapping clients and are most visibly linked to each other by Thomas Synhorst, a founding member of each.[1] They took in $20 million for their work to help elect George W. Bush in 2004, and they count AT&T, Microsoft and the giant trade association Pharmaceutical Research and Manufacturers of America as top clients.

The DCI Group calls itself a 'strategic public affairs consulting firm' and boasts that it handles corporate issues like political campaigns. Their website claims: 'We are a political firm and all of our partners have political campaign experience. We thrive in competitive circumstances, and are used to fluid situations and tight deadlines.' DCI Group offers services that include national, state and local lobbying; coalition building; and generating 'grasstops' and constituent support for issues. The firm has been linked to several industry-funded coalitions that pose as grassroots organisations. Perhaps this should come as no surprise, as DCI advertises its ability to provide 'third-party support' to clients. 'Corporations seldom win alone', the group's website says.

Whatever the issue, whatever the target – elected officials, regulators or public opinion – you need reliable third party allies to advocate your cause. We can help you recruit credible coalition partners and engage them for maximum impact. It's what we do best. [2]

The use of third-party front groups is common in the business of swaying public opinion. Traditionally, however, strategic influencers view the news media as the channel through which their message flows from the front group to the target audience. DCI and its affiliates offer 'direct contact' that bypasses the media entirely. The client's message is directly delivered via phone banks, regular mail and/or email. Direct contact provides the campaigners with complete control over the message. Freed from the filters created by news outlets, they can be as biased and inflammatory as the message shaper deems necessary.

'We play to win', proclaims FLSphones.com, the website of Feather Larson Synhorst-DCI. In addition to phone banks, the firm offers a 'letter desk' service, explained as follows:

Personal letters from constituents are proving to be increasingly effective in swaying legislators' opinions on hot issues. FLS can economically generate hundreds or thousands of letters on your behalf – all unique, but conveying your desired message. Each letter is personalised, individually signed and often includes a handwritten postscript from the constituent.

FLS also offers 'patch-through' calling, in which people reached via phone bank are immediately patched through to their legislators, thus generating a stream of constituent phone calls that echo the client's message: 'FLS has worked to design scripting and call systems that generate high-quality patch-through calls', the website boasts. 'Constituents are connected directly to their legislators, and in some cases are giving individual talking points to help convey your message to their elected official in a personal way.' Other services offered include automated phone calling using pre-recorded messages; inbound phone services, meaning the company provides staff to answer incoming calls to toll-free numbers; and information collection services, including emails.[3]

FLS-DCI co-founder Tony Feather, who served as a political director of George W. Bush's 2000 campaign, is also responsible for the creation of Progress for America, a soft-money group that raised and spent $28.8 million to support Bush in 2004. FLS-DCI's website prominently features a quote from top Bush adviser Karl Rove, himself a direct mail expert. 'I know these guys well', Rove states. 'They become partners with the campaigns they work with. From designing the program to drafting scripts, from selecting targets to making the calls in a professional, successful way, they work as hard to win your races as you do.'[4]

SMOKING OUT DCI'S PAST

What the DCI Group 'does best' – creating 'credible coalition partners' – is a skill that the group's managing partners –Tom Synhorst, Doug Goodyear and Tim Hyde – developed during nearly a decade of work in the 1990s for R.J. Reynolds Tobacco Company.

DCI chair Thomas J. Synhorst got his start working in the 1980s as an aide for Senator Charles Grassley (R–Iowa). In 1988 Synhorst ran Bob Dole's presidential primary campaign in Iowa, winning the state's early caucus over George H.W. Bush. He later worked on Dole's 1996 presidential bid, having by then set up the political consulting and telemarketing firm Direct Connect, Inc. Simultaneously, Synhorst worked as a Midwestern field representative for R.J. Reynolds (RJR). Some of the details of his work in that capacity can be found through internet searches of RJR's internal documents that were publicly released as part of the states attorneys' general lawsuit against the tobacco industry. As early as 1990, Synhorst's name turns up in a letter from RJR field operations manager Mark Smith. The letter outlines the tobacco company's strategy for undermining a workplace smoking ban at a Boeing plant in Wichita, Kansas. Synhorst was one of the RJR field co-ordinators put forward to meet with a Boeing employee who opposed the anti-smoking policy.[5]

The work of a field co-ordinator for RJR included keeping track of state and local smoking bans and cigarette tax initiatives; monitoring workplace smoking bans; meeting with company sales representatives; developing and supporting 'smoker's rights' groups, including setting up meetings, circulating petitions and providing materials; contacting school districts concerning RJR's youth programme; placing people at public events and meetings with legislators to support the tobacco industry's position; getting letters to the editor printed in local and regional newspapers; and creating alliances with organisations with similar concerns, such as anti-tax groups.

In one internal memo, field representatives were instructed:

Xerox like crazy. When a favourable letter to the editor is printed, getting people to copy the letters and send them to their elected officials with a note saying (essentially) 'This is what I think, too,' is key. [Letters to the editor] now become a two-step process: Step One is getting them published. Step Two is circulating them as widely as possible.[6]

The DCI Group's CEO, Douglas M. Goodyear, used to work on behalf of R.J. Reynolds. Before joining the DCI Group, he was a vice-president at Walt Klein and Associates, a PR firm whose work for RJR dates back to at least the 1980s. In 1993, Goodyear was instrumental in the creation of Ramhurst Corporation, an organisation that received money from R.J. Reynolds to ensure that tobacco industry efforts in Washington were supported by and co-ordinated with RJR's nationwide fake grassroots operations. According to internal RJR documents, in 1994 Ramhurst received $2.6 million for

executing tactical programs on federal, state or local issues; developing a network of smokers' rights groups and other coalition partners within the region that will speak out on issues important to the Company; implementing training and communication programs designed to inform activists and maintain their ongoing involvement in the grassroots movement.[7]

Synhorst was one of Ramhurst's field operators.

Timothy N. Hyde, another DCI employee, was the senior director of public issues at R.J. Reynolds from 1988 to 1997. Hyde oversaw all of RJR's PR campaigns. His weekly reports, also available in the R.J. Reynolds online archive, provide a running history of the discussion of tobacco in the public sphere and the industry's efforts to shape that discussion.

With Goodyear's expertise at co-ordinating astroturf (fake grassroots) activities in all 50 states, Synhorst's on-the-ground field experience combined with his telemarketing work, and Hyde's years of corporate work, the DCI Group offers clients a vast body of experience and contacts. The tobacco industry's efforts in the 1990s to fight regulations, taxes and lawsuits created a money-soaked training ground where dozens of political operatives and strategists learned their craft. Since most of the anti-tobacco efforts were being led by Democrats, tobacco industry money began flowing primarily into Republican coffers, further strengthening ties between 'Grand Old

Party' (GOP) political advisers and the underworld of fake grassroots campaigning.

All these factors have made the DCI Group and its sibling companies a natural choice to help top US companies such as Microsoft and highly regulated sectors such as the pharmaceutical industry as they, too, have sought to fend off regulators, consumer advocates and trial lawyers.

MACRO MONEY FROM MICROSOFT

Microsoft's decision to hire DCI came as the company faced an anti-trust lawsuit from the US Justice Department in the 1990s. By 2000, Microsoft was spending millions of dollars on contributions to Republican and Democratic campaign war chests, think tanks and ostensibly independent trade associations as well as on payments to high-powered lobbyists and public relations and political operatives. Hoping to sway public opinion and the opinion of state and federal officials, the software giant built up a wide network of supporters, with its sponsorship of those groups mostly invisible to the public.

'Microsoft has contributed to established research groups with free-market orientations, including the National Taxpayers Union, Americans for Tax Reform and the Cato Institute, which have produced studies and newspaper opinion pieces supportive of the company's legal position', the *New York Times* reported in June 2000. 'But Microsoft has also created new trade groups, the Association for Competitive Technology (ACT) and Americans for Technology Leadership (ATL), to generate support for the company through web sites and a sophisticated and largely hidden grassroots lobbying campaign.'[8]

ACT and ATL remain closely affiliated today. ATL claims to be a 'broad-based coalition of technology professionals, consumers and organisations dedicated to limiting government regulation of technology and fostering competitive market solutions to public policy issues affecting the technology industry'. In reality, however, it is mostly a shill for Microsoft. Four out of ten of ATL's other 'founding members' – Association for Competitive Technology, Citizens Against Government Waste, 60Plus Association, and Small Business Survival Committee – are themselves industry-funded organisations that consistently take their sponsors' positions. Other founders include CompTIA, a computer trade association; and the big-box stores CompUSA and Staples. These natural allies served as useful window dressing for an organisation whose main objective was defending Microsoft against anti-trust action.

Joshua Micah Marshall described the ties among ACT, ATL, DCI and Microsoft in the 17 July 2000 *American Prospect*. He noted that

while Microsoft did confirm that Synhorst's DCI had been retained as a consultant, it insisted that another DCI employee, Tim Hyde, and not Synhorst, was handling the company's account. In any event, the web of connections among DCI, ATL, and Microsoft is striking. While working for Microsoft, DCI has also provided consulting services to ATL.

Josh Mathis, who was installed by ACT president Jonathan Zuck as ATL's executive director, 'is also an employee of DCI, who still works out of the same Washington, D.C. office as Synhorst and Hyde'.[9]

ATL's domain name, techleadership.org, is registered to ACT. The site itself is hosted by Synhorst and Tom Stock's LLC, TSE Enterprises. TSE and Stock's other company Network Processing Services, LLC (which owns TSE's domain name) are connected to the websites of several industry-backed grassroots groups that advocate positions favourable to DCI clients. TSE's website describes its work as 'engineering web sites and portals, interactive multi-media, and electronic direct marketing campaign for public relations, public affairs, and political groups nationwide'.[10]

In August 2001 the *Los Angeles Times* reported that ATL was behind a 'carefully orchestrated nationwide campaign to create the impression of a surging grass-roots movement' behind Microsoft. 'The campaign, orchestrated by a group partly funded by Microsoft, goes to great lengths so that the letters appear to be spontaneous expressions from ordinary citizens. Letters sent in the last month are printed on personalised stationery using different wording, colour and typefaces – details that distinguish those efforts from common lobbying tactics that go on in politics every day.' Although FLS–DCI has not publicly claimed responsibility for generating the letters, they are consistent with the company's own description of the work produced by its 'letter desk' service: 'all unique, but conveying your desired message'.

According to the *Times*, the campaign was uncovered when Utah's attorney general at the time, Mark Shurtleff, received letters 'purportedly written by at least two dead people . . . imploring him to go easy on Microsoft Corp. for its conduct as a monopoly. The pleas, along with about 400 others from Utah citizens', included at least one from the non-existent city of Tucson, Utah.

Even living residents of real cities who wrote letters supporting Microsoft later complained that they had been snookered. According to the *Los Angeles Times*, some who were called

believed the states themselves were soliciting their views, according to the attorneys general of Minnesota, Illinois and Utah. When a caller started asking Minnesotan Nancy Brown questions about Microsoft, she thought she was going to get help figuring out what was wrong with her computer.

Another Minnesota resident contacted the state's attorney general to tell him, 'I sure was misled.'

Eighteen states' attorneys general were joining with the Justice Department in its anti-trust suit against Microsoft. Iowa's attorney general, Tom Miller, reported receiving more than 50 letters in support of Microsoft during the summer of 2001. 'No two letters are identical, but the giveaway lies in the phrasing', the *Times* wrote.

Four Iowa letters included this sentence: 'Strong competition and innovation have been the twin hallmarks of the technology industry.' Three others use exactly these words: 'If the future is going to be as successful as the recent past, the technology sector must remain free from excess regulation.'

The *Times* credited a DCI affiliate, DCI/New Media, with assisting Microsoft's 'grassroots' campaign, in concert with the Dewey Square Group, a public affairs firm with close ties to the Democratic Party.[11]

JOURNO-LOBBYISTS

AT&T and Microsoft have found some of their most consistent and enthusiastic support in articles posted on Tech Central Station (TCS), a quasi-news site that features free-market opinion and analysis pieces. Founded in 2000, TCS is 'hosted' by conservative financial columnist James K. Glassman. Shortly before the collapse of the 1990s dot-com bubble, Glassman authored a remarkably non-prophetic work titled *Dow 36,000: The New Strategy for Profiting From the Coming Rise in the Stock Market*. He is also a resident fellow at the American Enterprise Institute, a think tank funded by corporations and conservative foundations such as the Lynde and Harry Bradley Foundation, the John M. Olin Foundation and the Scaife family foundations. Until recently he was a columnist for the *Washington Post*, which finally ended the relationship after concluding that Glassman's numerous other entanglements conflicted with his role as a journalist purporting to offer expert financial analysis.

Tech Central Station is a good example of a few of those conflicts of interest, some of which are better disclosed than others. The website openly credits sponsors such as AT&T, Microsoft, Exxon Mobil, General Motors, Intel, McDonald's, NASDAQ, National Semiconductor, Qualcomm and Pharmaceutical Research and Manufacturers of America, and not surprisingly the opinion pieces published by the websites are nearly universal in supporting the interests of the sponsors. But, until recently, Tech Central Station was reluctant to acknowledge the identity of its real publisher – the DCI Group.[12]

TCS did not publicly disclose its relationship to DCI until it was uncovered by *Washington Monthly* editor Nicholas Confessore, who wrote about it in December 2003. 'After I requested comment, the web site was changed', Confessore wrote. 'Where it formerly stated that "Tech Central Station is published by Tech Central Station, L.L.C.," it now reads "Tech Central Station is published by DCI Group, L.L.C."'

The two organisations, Confessore explained,

share most of the same owners, some staff, and even the same suite of offices in downtown Washington, a block off K Street. As it happens, many of DCI's clients are also 'sponsors' of the site it houses. TCS not only runs the sponsors' banner ads; its contributors aggressively defend those firms' policy positions, on TCS and elsewhere.

'James Glassman and TCS have given birth to something quite new in Washington: journo-lobbying', Confessore continued.

It's an innovation driven primarily by the influence industry. Lobbying firms that once specialised in gaining person-to-person access to key decision-makers have branched out. The new game is to dominate the entire intellectual environment in which officials make policy decisions, which means funding everything from think tanks to issue ads to phoney grassroots pressure groups. But the institution that most affects the intellectual atmosphere in Washington, the media, has also proven the hardest for K Street to influence – until now.[13]

PROGRESS FOR THE POWERFUL

As the McCain–Feingold Campaign Finance Reform bill began working its way toward its eventual passage in Congress in 2002, long-time Republican strategists were already scheming how to get around the law's ban on soft-money contributions. They found an answer in Progress for America (PFA).

PFA was registered as a 501(c)4 (non-profit) group in February 2001 by Tony Feather, a political director of the Bush–Cheney 2000 campaign and partner at DCI Group as well as at the affiliated telemarketing and fundraising firm of Feather Larson Synhorst–DCI (FLS–DCI).

Feather set up PFA as a 'grassroots organisation that mobilises the public to contact their members of Congress about pending legislation and to write local newspapers to publicise the White House's agenda', the Center for Public Integrity wrote in 2002. During the first part of the George W. Bush administration, it led campaigns to support tax cuts, conservative judicial appointments and energy legislation.[14]

Feather told the *Washington Post* in 2002 that PFA was simply a vehicle for building grassroots support for Bush administration policies. 'Many other Republicans, however, describe it as the first organisation designed to capture some of the soft money that the political parties will be barred from accepting after November 6', wrote the *Post*'s Thomas B. Edsall.[15]

In 2001, Democrats in Montana criticised PFA for running an astroturf campaign in support of energy deregulation. An Associated Press story reported how the campaign worked:

A pollster calls you and asks questions about energy issues. Then he asks if he can write a letter summarising the conversation and mail it to you. A few days later, an envelope arrives containing a letter addressed to Sen. Conrad Burns, R Mont., on personalised stationery and prepared for your signature. The letter tells Burns you want no price controls and even fewer restrictions placed on electric power companies. You might agree with that, or you might not ... No two letters are identical, so there is no immediate indication of a letter campaign orchestrated by distant political operatives. It looks like a grassroots response, but it isn't.

When asked in an interview, Tony Feather refused to say who was paying for the letter-writing campaign.[16]

Several high-level Bush supporters and advisers have been associated with Progress for America. Ken Adelman, who would go on to become the Bush–Cheney 2004 campaign director, spoke to the *Washington Post* in 2002 and identified himself as the group's chairman. However, Adelman claimed he 'knows neither the organisation's budget nor its sources of financial support'. The address that Adelman provided to the *Post* for PFA's offices turned out to be in the 'high-rent Lafayette Center complex in downtown Washington' – the same building where the offices of FLS–DCI are located.[17]

After the Federal Election Commission decided in May 2004 to postpone regulating so-called 527 groups (named after the section of the tax code under which they are organised), PFA spun off a 527 committee called the Progress for America Voter Fund (PFAVF) that ended up pouring $28.8 million into supporting Bush in 2004.[18]

In late 2003, Feather stepped away from PFA, thus complying with the letter of the law forbidding 527 organisations from co-ordinating their activities with election campaigns. His firm, FLS–DCI, went on to do campaign work for Bush, receiving $12.8 million from the Republican National Committee and $3.6 million from Bush–Cheney 2004. Management of PFA was handed over to Chris LaCivita, an employee of FLS–DCI's sibling company DCI Group.[19] LaCivita took over as PFA's executive director, while another DCI employee, Brian McCabe, became president of the Progress for America Voter Fund.[20]

Charles Lewis of the Center for Public Integrity pointed out in March 2004 that election law specialist Ben Ginsberg, then counsel for PFA and a partner at the law and lobbying firm Patton Boggs, was 'also the chief outside counsel to the Bush campaign'.[21] During the fall of 2003, reported Peter Stone of the *National Journal*, Ginsberg talked 'across the country to prominent fundraisers', asking them to serve on PFA's advisory board and to rope in large soft-money contributions.[22] In August 2004, Ginsberg chose to resign from the Bush campaign after it was revealed that he had provided counsel to another GOP-friendly 527 group – Swift Boat Veterans for Truth.

Progress for America and its Voter Fund reveal only as much as legally required about their leadership and membership. The group's directors, advisers and chairs are not listed on their websites. But the *Washington Post* has identified a few of the groups' principal figures. In addition to FLS–DCI's Tom Synhorst, who is reported to have served as a key strategic adviser to PFA,[23] other figures include James C. Cicconi, AT&T General Counsel; C. Boyden Gray, a prominent figure in many conservative groups, including Citizens for a Sound Economy (now called Freedom Works); and Marilyn Ware, chairman of American Water in Pennsylvania and a Bush Pioneer (meaning that she personally raised at least $100,000 for his campaign).[24]

DEMOCRATIC 527s

Progress for America was by no means the only group that funnelled soft money into the 2004 presidential election. Democratic 527 groups actually took off much earlier than Republican groups, due to Republican concerns about Federal Election Commission action against 527s. PFA was only the fourth largest 527 group for the 2004 election cycle, raising $37.9 million. The largest group was the Democratic Joint Victory Campaign 2004, which brought in $65.5 million from donors including George Soros, Peter Lewis of the Progressive Corporation and Stephen Bing of Shangri-La Entertainment.[25]

During the 2004 Democratic primary, in fact, Democratic political strategists used 527 groups to target Howard Dean within their own party. Americans for Jobs and Healthcare, a group that raised funds primarily from Gephart and Kerry supporters, began running commercials in November 2003 that 'ripped Dean over his positions or past record on gun rights, trade and Medicare growth. But the most inflammatory ad used the visual image of Osama bin Laden as a way to raise questions about Dean's foreign policy credibility', CPI's Charles Lewis wrote in March 2004. At the time of the ads, Dean had been the front runner for the Democratic nomination, but the attack helped erode his support. The source of the money behind Americans for Jobs and Healthcare was not revealed until after Dean's defeat in the January 2004 Iowa Caucus put an end to his presidential hopes.

'All of this underscores the profoundly disturbing state of our politics today', wrote Charles Lewis. 'Storefront political hit squads can be created overnight, as easily as internet investment scams, with candidates and the public victimised with nowhere to turn. Political operatives continue to effectively and virtually anonymously influence electoral outcomes.'[26] Lewis was writing about Americans for Jobs, but the same can be said for the way some Republican 527 groups operated after the May 2004 Federal Election Commission (FEC) ruling.

ASHLEY AND FRIENDS

In the last three weeks leading up to the 2 November election, the Progress for America Voter Fund outspent the next largest-spending Democratic 527 group three-to-one on political ads. It bought $16.8 million worth of television and radio ad time. According to FEC data, Swift Boat Vets/POWs for Truth came in second with $6.3 million in ad spending. In third place was Democrat Harold Ickes' Media Fund, which spent $5 million.[27]

Progress for America produced two 'harshly anti-Kerry ads that have become the subjects of controversy and debate, especially in the battleground states of Wisconsin and Iowa where they are running frequently', the *Washington Post*'s Thomas Edsall wrote. Both ads closely resembled Bush–Cheney campaign ads – in one case the ads showed Kerry windsurfing and alleging flip-flopping on issues. In another case, the ads showed pictures of terrorist leaders, while the announcer declared, 'These people want to kill us ... Would you trust Kerry against these fanatic killers? President Bush didn't start this war, but he will finish it.' The Bush ad concluded: 'How can John Kerry protect us, when he doesn't even know where he stands?'[28]

'The largest single ad buy of the campaign comes from conservative Progress for America,' *Time Magazine* reported.

It shows Bush comforting 16-year-old Ashley Faulkner, whose mother died on 9/11. As it happens, the spot was made by Larry McCarthy, who produced the infamous Willie Horton ad that helped the first President Bush bury Michael Dukakis under charges that he was soft on crime. If that is the iconic attack ad, this is the ultimate embrace – to remind voters of the protectiveness they cherished in the President after Sept. 11. The ad has been ready since July, but sponsors waited until the end to unveil it.[29]

PFAVF spent $14.2 million on ad time for 'Ashley's Story', which ran on cable stations and in nine key states. According to *USA Today*, the ad was supported by a website, www.ashleysstory.com, as well as 'e-mails, automated phone calls and 2.3 million brochures' mailed to voters.[30]

A breakdown of PFAVF's spending shows that the vast majority of its money went to ad buys. Mentzer Media Services, Inc. received $23.2 million from the group for ad buys. But the second and third top recipients of PFAVF money were companies affiliated with Tom Synhorst. FYI Messaging got $1.55 million for direct mail services, and TSE Enterprises (which hosts all these organisations' websites as well as ashleysstory.com), got $907,955 for web services. Another top recipient of PFAVF money was DCI Group, LLC, which got $156,725 for consulting.[31]

NOTES

1. Limited Liability Corporation registrations for the four companies were filed with the Arizona Corporation Commission and were viewed via the State of Arizona Public Access System, <http://www.cc.state.az.us/corp/index.htm>.

2. 'Our Approach', DCI Group website, visited 11 November 2004, <http://www.dcigroup.com/2021/wrapper.jsp?PID=2021-12>.
3. 'FLS Phones: Services', <http://www.flsphones.com/services.htm>, visited 11 November 2004.
4. 'FLS Phones: Quotes', <http://www.flsphones.com/team.htm>, visited 11 November 2004.
5. 'Boeing Update', R.J. Reynolds, Legacy Tobacco Document Archive, <http://legacy.library.ucsf.edu/tid/ecm10d00>.
6. 'What RJR Will Provide To Field Support', R.J. Reynolds, Legacy Tobacco Document Archive, <http://legacy.library.ucsf.edu/tid/szf33d00>.
7. 'Public Issues 1994 Plans', R.J. Reynolds, Legacy Tobacco Document Archive, <http://legacy.library.ucsf.edu/tid/wtm33d00>.
8. John M. Broder, 'Microsoft Tries Another Court: Public Opinion', *New York Times*, 12 June 2000.
9. Joshua Micah Marshall, 'Mr. Gates Goes to Washington', *American Prospect*, 17 July 2000.
10. 'TSE Enterprises LLC: Who We Are', <http://www.tseaz.com/tse/wrapper.jsp?PID=8020-10>, visited 8 November 2004.
11. Joseph Menn and Edmund Sanders, 'Lobbyists Tied to Microsoft Wrote Citizens' Letters', *Los Angeles Times*, 23 August 2001.
12. 'About Us', Tech Central Station website, visited 11 November 2004, <http://www.techcentralstation.com/about.html>.
13. Nicholas Confessore, 'Meet the Press: How James Glassman reinvented journalism – as lobbying', *Washington Monthly*, December 2003.
14. Alex Knott and Adam Mayle, 'Impending Ban Hasn't Stopped Soft Money Rush by Presidential Hopefuls', Center for Public Integrity, 17 October 2002, <http://www.publicintegrity.org/report.aspx?aid=109&sid=200>.
15. Thomas B. Edsall, 'New Ways to Harness Soft Money in Works', *Washington Post*, 25 August 2002.
16. 'Firm polling Montanans about deregulation, sending letters to sign', Associated Press, 24 June 2001.
17. Edsall, 'New Ways to Harness Soft Money'.
18. Silent Partners, Center for Public Integrity, 'Progress for America Voter Fund', Federal Elections Commission data as of 21 October 2004, <http://www.publicintegrity.org/527/search.aspx?act=com&orgid=714>.
19. Peter Stone, 'Inside Two of the Soft-Money Havens', *National Journal* 35 (51), 20 December 2003, DCI Group, LLC listing on Lobbyists.info, visited November 4, 2004.
20. Silent Partners, 'Progress for America Voter Fund'.
21. Charles Lewis, 'Political Mugging in America', Center for Public Integrity, 4 March 2004, <http://www.public-i.org/report.aspx?aid=194&sid=200>.
22. Stone, 'Inside Two of the Soft-Money Havens'.
23. Thomas B. Edsall, 'GOP Creating Own "527" Groups: Unregulated Funds Can Be Raised', *Washington Post*, 25 May 2004.
24. Thomas B. Edsall, 'Republican "Soft Money" Groups Find Business Reluctant to Give', *Washington Post*, 8 June 2004.
25. Silent Partners, Center for Public Integrity, '2003–04 527 Activity', <http://www.publicintegrity.org/527/db.aspx?act=activity2003>, visited 11 November 2004.

26. Lewis, 'Political Mugging in America'.
27. Alex Knott, Aron Pilhofer and Derek Willis , 'GOP 527s Outspend Dems in Late Ad Blitz', Center for Public Integrity, 3 November 2004, <http://www.publicintegrity.org/527/report.aspx?aid=421>.
28. Thomas B. Edsall, 'After Late Start, Republican Groups Jump Into the Lead', *Washington Post*, 17 October 2004.
29. Nancy Gibbs, 'The Morning After', *Time Magazine*, 1 November 2004.
30. Judy Keen and Mark Memmott, 'Most expensive TV campaign ad goes for emotions', *USA Today*, 18 October 2004.
31. Silent Partners, 'Progress for America Voter Fund'.

5

Spinning Farmed Salmon[1]

David Miller

Dotted up and down the coastal lochs and around the islands of Scotland are thousands of circular or rectangular pens. Each contains thousands of farmed fish, predominantly salmon. They are a visible reminder of the economic reality of the Scottish Highlands and islands, areas in which the main form of work is in tourism, fishing, farming and in some places the military or nuclear power. Yet most of the pens, shifting gently with the swell, are not owned by locals, and they do not bring great financial rewards to the area. Instead most are owned by fish farming companies such as Marine Harvest, Skretting, Norsk Hydro or AKVAsmart. The companies themselves are not local, but are almost all part of a transnational industry which is as likely to rear fish off the coast of Norway, Canada or Chile as of Scotland.

A transnational industry requires a transnational supply chain. But the rapid expansion in fish farming has taken its toll on the natural environment, and fish feed based on natural ingredients is increasingly scarce. It 'normally takes about four kilos of wild fish to grow one kilo of farmed salmon. In this way, instead of relieving pressure on the marine environment, fish farming is actually contributing to the overfishing crisis that plagues the world's fisheries.'[2] Thus the fish farming industry has been looking for alternatives. Among the alternatives tested are substitutes like palm oil, one of the least nutritionally beneficial foods in the human diet. So although much play is made of the salmon being 'Scottish' for marketing purposes, the food that the fish receive is unlikely to originate in the local ecosystem and so will not have distinctive local qualities. Or so it might have seemed until the appearance of a paper in *Science* that sparked the crisis in the Scottish industry.

On 9 January 2004, *Science*, perhaps the most prestigious scientific journal in the world, published a study reporting that farmed salmon contained amounts of toxic chemicals known as polychlorinated biphenyls (PCBs), as well as of other chemicals, that exceeded the recommended levels advised by the US Environmental Protection

Agency (EPA). According to the EPA, 'Studies in humans provide supportive evidence for potential carcinogenic and non-carcinogenic effects of PCBs.'[3]

The following analysis is not simply about industry strategy or science communication. It is not just a study of media coverage of salmon. It is an account of how scientific research which does not fit the interests of industry can be neutralised. It is a story that involves scientists, corporations, front groups, PR firms, ministers, civil servants and journalists. It shows that the public get a dangerously distorted view of science from the media. But this is relatively trivial compared with the main conclusion which is that vested interests operating together in a corporate–state two-step are able to manage science and silence critics – even where these emanate from the most prestigious scientific journals in the world. The interests of the industry prevailed in this case by means of misinformation, manipulation and subterfuge. The implication of this for theories of democracy and governance that emphasise popular consent is that consent is not always essential for the reproduction of power.[4]

For those concerned with the amplification of risk in public discourse, this story serves as a critical test case. It undermines arguments suggesting that the problem of risk is one of public irrationality or activist misdeeds. The corporations are amongst the promoters of this view because it serves their own interests, but it is also the view of a swathe of academic opinion.

Following the publication in *Science*, the industry, in a major PR effort, led journalists, policy makers and some sections of the public to believe that we were, in fact, victims of an orchestrated attack by environmentalists. This was designed, they implied, to destroy livelihoods and undermine healthy eating advice for ideological reasons. Brian Simpson, the head of the industry lobby group Scottish Quality Salmon, and the former UK minister Brian Wilson referred to the scientific study as 'junk science' and 'pseudo-science', respectively.[5] These judgements were largely accepted by the media, even though they were wrong. This chapter tells the story of how the industry turned the story round and neutralised the issue.

THE ORIGINAL STUDY

The study on which the *Science* paper was based was undertaken at the Institute for Health and the Environment at the State University of New York, Albany, funded by the Pew Charitable Trust. The study, entitled 'Global Assessment of Organic Contaminants in Farmed Salmon', tested for levels of 'organochlorine contaminants in farmed Atlantic salmon from eight major producing regions in the Northern and Southern hemispheres'. For comparison, 'samples of five wild species of Pacific salmon were obtained from different geographic regions'. The analysis examined 14 contaminants, focusing 'additional analysis' on 'PCBs, dioxins, toxaphene, and dieldrin', which 'were consistently and significantly more concentrated in the farmed salmon as a group than in the wild salmon'.[6]

Polychlorinated biphenyls are components popularly used in electrical manufacturing until 1977, when the US Congress prohibited their use due to high levels of toxicity.[7] Dioxins are produced as a waste product of the production of some chemicals and on incineration of organic waste in the presence of chlorine. Toxaphene and dieldrin are pesticides banned in the United States in 1986 and 1990 respectively. PCBs (as a result of disposal methods) and dioxins and the pesticides (for obvious reasons) have found their way into the food chain. Along with other organochlorine contaminants, they accumulate progressively in organisms over time, meaning that those at the top of the food chain, humans, are exposed to the highest levels.

The authors stated clearly that

[i]ndividual contaminant concentrations in farmed and wild salmon do not exceed U.S. Food and Drug Administration (FDA) action or tolerance levels for PCBs and dieldrin. However, FDA action and tolerance levels are not strictly health-based, do not address the health risks of concurrent exposure to more than one contaminant, and do not provide guidance for acceptable levels of toxaphene and dioxins in fish tissue.[8]

A key reason the authors used the EPA guidelines was that these were developed to understand multiple contaminant intake rather than intake of a single contaminant.

The results showed that farmed salmon contained levels of PCBs significantly higher than that of wild salmon, with Scottish farmed salmon displaying the highest levels in the sample. The authors recommended:

The combined concentrations of PCBs, toxaphene, and dieldrin trigger stringent consumption advice for farmed salmon purchased from wholesalers and for store-bought farmed fillets. This advice is much more restrictive than consumption advice triggered by contaminants in the tissues of wild salmon.

With reference to the EPA's standards, they argued that safe consumption of the most toxic salmon (purchased in Frankfurt and farmed in the Faroe Islands and Scotland) should not exceed more than one half-portion of salmon per month.

The risks of other non-cancer ill effects (such as 'adverse neurobehavioral and immune effects and endocrine disruption')[9] were not factored into the advice because there are no recognised risk levels adopted by official agencies. This is a crucial point in relation to the most important finding of the researchers. Although they examined the concentrations of 14 contaminants, they undertook additional analysis on four (including dioxins). But the researchers only provided consumption advice based on risk levels for three of the contaminants (PCBs, dieldrin, toxaphene excluding dioxins). The key reason for this was, as the researchers told us, 'because of the international disagreement around dioxin risk assessment'.[10] In particular, there is disagreement on risk assessment between the EPA and other bodies such as the FDA and WHO. This became a key point on which the study was (wrongly) attacked.

SPINNING THE STORY

Within a week of publication, the study was effectively neutralised as a threat to the industry. To illustrate this we can examine coverage in the *Scotsman*, one of the two main 'quality' papers in Scotland. On 9 January the headline was: 'Eating farm salmon "raises risk of cancer"'.[11] The following day the story was already being questioned: 'Chemicals in fish are well known'.[12] Subsequent headlines became increasingly sceptical: 'Salmon is safe says US food expert',[13] 'Green campaigners fund salmon study',[14] 'Salmon scare report was flawed and biased'[15] and finally, 'Claims of unsafe fish run contrary to the facts, say scientists'.[16]

The arguments against the study highlighted the alleged agenda of the foundation which funded the research and claimed that the authors had not used the most appropriate standards for measuring contaminants.

ATTACK THE METHODS

The first major line of attack was simply to ignore the data and attack the standards against which the data had been evaluated. But in a stunning series of errors, the responses of the UK government and the salmon industry fundamentally misinterpreted the science and criticised the paper on grounds which were scientifically irrelevant. Scottish Quality Salmon claimed that the authors 'seem to have misapplied an already suspect risk model developed by the US Environmental Protection Agency'.[17] The director of the UK government's Food Standards Agency raised the EPA model explicitly. Sir John Krebs wrote a letter to the *Guardian* arguing that the EPA

bases its risk assessment on out-of-date science from 1991. The WHO takes into account the mechanism by which dioxins cause cancer. It concluded in 2001, using independent experts, that so long as dioxins were kept below thresholds, there would be no adverse effect upon health.[18]

In a statement at the time the FSA elaborated on this, claiming that the EPA approach 'has been evolving since 1991, but has not been finalised'.[19]

There is indeed an EPA process which has been in effect and under development since April 1991, but it is not the standard used by the authors of the paper. It is, however, useful to examine the extent to which the process that began in 1991 supports the case made by the FSA. The report 'Exposure and Human Health Reassessment of 2,3,7,8-Tetrachlorodibenzo-p-Dioxin (TCDD) and Related Compounds' was revised in 1994 and on subsequent occasions, with the most recent draft being published in December 2003.[20]

According to the FSA, Krebs' view was based on a report produced by the UK government Committee on Toxicity. This 2001 report was published under the title 'COT statement on Dioxins and PCBs'.[21] This report does not, however, seem to support the view that the EPA process is based on dated or flawed science. The COT report did take a different view on the EPA approach, but not on the basis that it was outdated.

The COT report notes that '[t]he EPA provided an excellent comprehensive review of the literature on developmental and reproductive toxicity, and although some new studies had emerged since it was written these did not have a major impact'.[22] So, on two counts (first, that the process was regularly revised and, second, that the most recent version was some two years more up to date than the FSA's own science) Krebs' statement that the process was based on 'out-of-date science' is simply wrong. In fact the EPA process was more up to date (December 2003) than the FSA's own preferred report (2001).

But, more incredibly, the FSA approach was not the standard used in the paper in *Science*. Rather, the consumption advice was based on a different EPA process which assessed a different set of contaminants (PCBs as a whole, toxaphene and dieldrin).[23] The *Science* article said nothing whatever about dioxins in relation to consumption. The researchers specifically excluded dioxins from their conclusions because of the varying regulatory standards. The FSA approach was, therefore, entirely mistaken.

Most critics of the study preferred to ignore the existence of the EPA altogether and claimed that the findings were well within health and safety limits. John Webster, sometimes described by Scottish Quality Salmon (SQS) as their 'scientific adviser', 'stressed that the PCB and dioxin levels found in Scottish salmon were significantly lower than the thresholds set by international watchdogs such as the European Union, the Food Standards Agency (FSA) or even the US FDA'.[24] This is almost true, but entirely irrelevant. It is the level of dioxins and 'dioxin like PCBs' that were lower than the WHO and EU standards. This is quite different to PCBs as a whole. In fact, neither the WHO nor the EU has established standards for consumption levels of PCBs as a whole or for toxaphene and Dieldrin. So the SQS approach was entirely irrelevant too.

The erroneous response of the FSA and the salmon industry set the tone for other official agencies in the United Kingdom, which explicitly rested on the FSA as lead adviser. Thereafter all official agencies presented a united front, downplaying the risk as being within WHO, EU and FDA guidelines. This was simply false. At best this approach was irresponsible, incompetent and scientifically illiterate. At worst, it was a calculated deception.

TARGETING HIDDEN AGENDAS AND ACTIVIST 'SPIN'

The second line of attack was to criticise the Pew Charitable Trust, which had funded the research, for having a hidden agenda. An organisation 'with ... deep pockets and aggressive political advocacy, Pew is not only the most important new player, but the most controversial on the environmental scene', according to the *New York Times*.[25] This kind of coverage was encouraged by the aquaculture industry, which described Pew as 'having taken a position against salmon farming'.[26] According to the *Observer*, Pew was the 'research body with an anti-pollution agenda' – as if this was as bad as being 'pro-pollution'.[27] Later, Scottish Quality Salmon described the Pew Trust in a press release as 'the aggressively anti-industry US environmental group'.[28] The trust funded the research in the same way that other trusts fund scientific research. '"It is based on sound science and the results are undeniable", said George Lucier, former director of the US Department of Health's national toxicological programme and author of more than 200 studies on toxic chemicals.'[29] In fact the critics largely accepted the science. Instead they attempted to smear the funding agency. The role played by the Trust 'was spelled out in the study, and highlighted by *Science* magazine ... Any suggestion that Pew interfered has been denied by all involved.'[30]

'*Science*'s editor-in-chief Donald Kennedy dismissed the allegations', reported the *Sunday Herald*.

He said that the authors were all respected members of academic institutions. 'Pew funded the study but left the authors free to publish their results without review,' ... adding that *Science*'s peer-review process 'is among the most rigorous in the scientific community'.[31]

We can conclude that the science on which the paper was based was rigorous and indeed correct, as was acknowledged even by its critics. An argument about which set of standards should have been used is clearly possible; however, the standards were not dreamt up by environmental activists but by US government officials and scientists. The Pew Charitable Trust funds scientific research on environmental pollution. But it is clear that its interests in researching pollution did not shape the conduct of the science.

This analysis has concentrated on the substance of the allegations against the study, showing that the concerns reported in the media were groundless, but not precisely how they gained circulation. Was this a conspiracy of interest by the salmon-farming industry, or was it the result of news judgements which favour controversy over routine reporting? The industry and official bodies like the FSA had their own views on the study (highlighted above). But a range of academic scientists were also quoted as critics. What was their role? Were they badly briefed? Was it a case of legitimate – if mistaken – dispute in the field of science? Or was there another reason for the inaccurate and mistaken information given out by a range of scientists?

HOW IT WORKED

Almost all the scientists quoted in criticism of the study were linked to the industry in one way or another. In some cases this is easy to discover, but in others the links required further research.

The salmon-farming industries in Scotland, British Colombia (Canada) and the United States, were at the helm of the spin machine. The key organisations involved were Scottish Quality Salmon (SQS), Salmon of the Americas (SOTA) and the Society for Positive Aquaculture Awareness (SPAA) based in British Colombia. Without the knowledge of the public in the United Kingdom and throughout the world, and of many journalists, these organisations formed a nexus of interest and action which effectively minimised the story and eliminated the public issue. They operated in tandem with PR agencies, governmental and regulatory bodies (such as the Scottish Executive and the Food Standards Agency) and even the UK Queen's property management organisation, the Crown Estate.

THE BEST SCIENCE MONEY CAN BUY

As the story broke, the international media carried quotes from a variety of university-based scientists, such as Dr Charles Santerre. He commented that he 'strongly believe[s] that all the data we have today suggests that everyone should be eating more farmed salmon'. He also stated 'I would calculate 6,000 people getting cancer over their lifetime, that's an approximation, versus potentially saving the lives of 100,000 individuals every year'. These and other statements from Santerre were reported in a wide variety of media including *The Times* (London), the *Daily Telegraph* (London), *Scotland on Sunday* (Edinburgh) and the *Press and Journal* (Aberdeen).[32] Santerre was also quoted in the *Los Angeles Times* and on *ABC News*.[33]

Further scientific testimony came from Stephan Safe, Michael Gallo and Philip Guzelian. Gallo said that, 'as a professor of public health, I would never tell anyone to limit their intake of salmon'. Philip Guzelian was quoted in an SQS media release and referred to as 'Professor of Medicine and Head, Section of Medical Toxicology at the University of Colorado Health Sciences Center'. He criticised the findings of the study, saying that the levels of PCBs found in salmon were 'not known to be of a level harmful to humans'.[34]

Given their status as academic scientists these sources were likely to be treated as credible by the media, and within hours the industry was citing their comments in the press as evidence of scientific dispute.[35] But how independent were they?

Santerre was described in the press as Purdue University's 'Associate Professor of Foods and Nutrition and an expert in the detection of PCBs'. There was no reference in these reports to the fact that Santerre was being paid as a consultant by Salmon of the Americas.[36] Santerre was taken on on 1 January 2004 specifically to combat the publicity on farmed salmon. Nor did the press report that Gallo is a regular pro-corporate commentator. He was described in an SQS press release as 'a specialist in toxicology at the Department of Environmental and Community Medicine, Rutgers University' and this description was faithfully reproduced in the press the next day.[37] But in the 1990s he was listed in an 'expert' directory circulated to journalists by the Chemical Manufacturers' Association, the American Crop Protection Association and the American Plastics Council. The directory was issued following the release of *Our Stolen Future* – a publication that warned of the adverse health effects on humans of chemicals such as PCBs in the environment.[38]

Stephen Safe and Philip Guzelian also appeared in this directory. Safe believes a link between PCBs and cancer is mythical. In 1997, in an editorial for the *New England Journal of Medicine*, he dismissed environmental concerns as 'chemophobia' fed by 'paparazzi science'.[39] His comments excited controversy when the editorial was published, as he had neglected to disclose grant receipts of $150,000 from the Chemical Manufacturers' Association.[40]

Like Santerre, Safe was described in media coverage by his academic title as 'Professor and Director of the Centre for Environmental and Genetic Medicine, Institute of Bioscience and Technology, Texas'.[41] PR Watch has identified Safe as a 'usual suspect' who regularly appears as a scientific expert 'in a variety of anti-environmental, pro-industry forums'.[42]

The merry-go-round of scientists lending their voice to industry causes continues with Guzelian, previously a paid consultant to Philip Morris (worth $100,000 a year),[43] who has appeared regularly in court as a 'long term "expert-witness"' on behalf of corporations with a history of dioxin and other toxic polluting emissions'.[44] Guzelian is a member of the advisory council of the Atlantic Legal Foundation (ALF), with a 'mission' to 'advance the rule of law by advocating limited, effective government, free enterprise, individual liberty and sound science'. ALF aims to ensure that 'courts apply correct legal and scientific principles in those cases in which scientific and other expert testimony is offered'.[45] ALF has received funding from Chevron, DuPont, Exxon Mobil, Pfizer and Texaco, as well as from prominent conservative philanthropic foundations.[46]

Guzelian is also (along with Santerre and Safe) a 'scientific adviser' to the American Council on Science and Health, a corporate front group funded by corporations including Nestlé, McDonald's, Coca-Cola, Monsanto, Exxon Mobil, Pfizer and many others. ACSH exists to downplay risks associated with the products of its funders.

THE STIRLING CONNECTION

Back on the other side of the Atlantic, on 16 January 2004 the *Scotsman* ran the headline: 'Claims of unsafe fish run contrary to the facts, say scientists'. The authors of the article, Gordon Bell and Douglas Tocher from the University of Stirling's Institute of Aquaculture, stated that 'the research study claiming links between consuming farmed salmon and risks to health through dioxins and related chemicals are, in our opinion, grossly unfair and misrepresentative of a product which is both nutritious and healthy'. This was because '[i]n 2002, we at the Institute of Aquaculture at the University of Stirling undertook a wholly independent study to measure dioxins and PCBs in Scottish farmed salmon'.[47]

That statement is interesting for three reasons. First, like industry and government bodies, it misrepresents the study in *Science* by alleging it was about 'risks to health through dioxins'. It was not. Second, it implies that the Stirling study had been intended explicitly to study levels of dioxins (and dioxin-like PCBs) – which it had not. Third, the claim that the Stirling study was 'wholly independent' merits scrutiny.

To take the latter claim first, the funding for the Stirling study came from a Natural Environment Research Council (NERC)–LINK Aquaculture initiative. NERC is a public research-funding body, but 'LINK' schemes mean that 50 per cent of the funding comes straight from industry – in this case from BioMar Ltd, EWOS Innovation, Highlands and Islands Enterprise, Marine Harvest (Scotland) Ltd, Skretting, The Highland Council and Uniq Prepared Foods (Annan) Ltd.

Marine Harvest and Skretting are subsidiary companies of Nutreco, a global food and animal nutrition company (in 2006 they were swallowed up by Panfish). Nutreco are major players in the farmed salmon industry, as they point out on their website: 'A major proportion of salmon and poultry products are put on the market through the company's own marketing and distribution channels under the company's own labels.'[48] Skretting is a salmon feed company operating in Norway, Chile, the United Kingdom and Ireland. Marine Harvest was the world's largest aquaculture company as well as producer and provider of farmed salmon. EWOS is primarily an aquaculture feeds company, as are Uniq Prepared Food and BioMar.

The study was therefore not independent, in the sense that it was part funded by industry. But what is it that the industry were interested in? It transpires that the research was part of a range of studies being carried out at Stirling on the substitution of natural fish-oil-based foods by alternatives such as vegetable oils and other sources. The reason for this is that the dramatic increase in fish farming is putting pressure on natural feedstuffs – making the industry unsustainable, in other words.

It transpires that the study undertaken in 2002 was not, as Bell and Tocher wrote in their article, 'to measure dioxins and PCBs in Scottish farmed salmon',[49] but initially sought to look at the effects on farmed salmon of using vegetable oil feeds. The end result was entitled 'Dioxin and dioxin-like polychlorinated biphenyls (PCBs) in Scottish farmed salmon: effects of replacement of dietary marine fish oil with vegetable oils',[50] and the report's content is mainly concerned with dioxin levels.

So, although their research was presented as independent, as investigating organic contaminants and as examining the same contaminants as in the paper in *Science*, in reality the study was partially corporate funded, was conducted to evaluate the potential use of vegetable oil as fish feed and was focused on a different class of chemicals than those that were the subject of the original study. These scientists at best face a serious conflict of interest, and at worst might appear to be acting as spin doctors for the industry which part funds their work.

THE FORCES AT WORK

The use of scientists by industry is not new, and nor was it the only technique used to undermine the paper in *Science*. The campaign by the industry was co-ordinated across borders, oceans and time zones. The three main organisations involved were Scottish Quality Salmon, Salmon of the Americas and the Society for the Positive Awareness of Aquaculture in British Columbia. We shall examine each in turn, starting in British Columbia.

THE SOCIETY FOR THE POSITIVE AWARENESS OF AQUACULTURE

The Society for the Positive Awareness for Aquaculture (SPAA) was an important element in a complex web of pro-industry lobbyists and communications actors. The SPAA presents itself as a 'grassroots' initiative.[51] In fact it is a front group for the salmon-farming industry. The SPAA website states that its purpose is 'to challenge the myths and misinformation surrounding the salmon farming industry worldwide'.[52]

SPAA staff at the time included Laurie Jensen and Leanne Brunt, both of whom were current or former aquaculture industry employees. Jensen, president of the SPAA, is also vice-president and sales manager for AKVAsmart Canada. AKVAsmart is 'the world's leading supplier of fish farming and information technology and also competence to the aquaculture industry',[53] operating in Australia, Canada, Chile, Norway and Scotland.

Jensen reportedly claims the 'SPAA is a non-profit society receiving no funding from the industry',[54] though the SPAA website notes that membership is open to 'any individual or corporation interested in promoting the positive awareness of aquaculture'.[55] The online membership form advertises a corporate membership rate of $250 and notes that the benefits of membership include 'recognition as a corporate sponsor'.[56] Jensen's role as a sales manager for AKVAsmart tends to undermine her protestations. According to one report of an SPAA event:

Ms. Jensen also claims that she is a 'working environmentalist,' a phrase lifted years ago from the anti-environmental campaign of the forest industry ... I found the working environmentalist phrase from Ms. Jensen to be slightly hypocritical however, based on a letter printed in the *Campbell River Mirror* back in March, in which she writes: 'I once considered myself to be an environmentalist. However, I no longer consider myself an environmentalist the way I used to. The current BC-based environmental groups ... have mostly turned into eco-terrorist groups and (have) paid protestors against anything that is resource based and economic.'[57]

FIRST DOLLAR

Both Jensen and Leanne Brunt of the SPAA are active in an organisation called First Dollar. The registrant of the SPAA internet domain name (www.farmfreshsalmon.org), Rudy Vandermey, is also a member of First Dollar.[58] According to its website, First Dollar exists to challenge misinformation and counter the misinformation and boycotts directed at BC resource industries and families, to educate British Columbians about the connection between resource industries and the service industry they generate, to encourage participation of resource workers and supporters throughout resource based communities, to facilitate networking outside and within all sectors of resource industry and to provide social networking and support.[59]

First Dollar also claims to be a 'grassroots' organisation.[60] Part of its mission is to 'encourage individuals and companies in resource based communities to educate the public and the media about the importance of resource industries to the entire province',[61]

In Brunt's campaigning with First Dollar, she is portrayed as a self-sacrificing single mother supporting local industry, whose energy and drive attract media attention most 'ordinary' citizens couldn't. The *Vancouver Sun* reported a dispute in the BC area over closure of a local mill in July 2004: 'Resource towns fight back against arriviste rock stars.'[62] It noted that performers Neil Young and Randy Bachman played a fundraising concert to support emissions testing from the mill and the assessment of dangers posed to the local environment and community. According to the *Vancouver Sun*, unlike the celebrities, 'Ms. Brunt doesn't have a publicist – not many single moms working in aquaculture do'.[63] The fact is that Brunt is herself a professional publicist. In addition to being the founder of First Dollar and founder and vice-president of the SPAA, she is also employed by the PR firm Greenspirit Strategies Ltd and is internal communications manager for Panfish Canada. Panfish is a Norwegian-based multinational and the biggest fish-farming company in the world.[64] The First Dollar website is registered to Leanne Brunt and the contact email is her Panfish account, suggesting something more than a grassroots initiative.[65]

GREENSPIRIT STRATEGIES

Brunt is listed as a 'senior consultant' at Greenspirit,[66] a 'communications consulting firm that delivers strategic planning for sustainability issues'.[67] Greenspirit was set up by Patrick Moore, one of the founders of Greenpeace, who has become a full-time campaigner for industry interests. After leaving Greenpeace in the mid 1980s, Moore ventured unsuccessfully into the salmon-farming business. Now he makes a living writing, speaking and campaigning on behalf of the logging, aquaculture, nuclear and GM industries.[68]

The January 2004 crisis saw Greenspirit update an earlier report to criticise the Hites study and attack the tactics used by environmentalists against the aquaculture industry.[69] The report, which was commissioned by the SPAA, stated:

The salmon farming industry is being subjected to a host of allegations related to environmental sustainability and human health and nutrition ... it seems clear that these findings form part of the larger effort by activists to damage the reputation of the salmon aquaculture industry by using food-scare tactics that have no basis in scientific fact.[70]

Patrick Moore's own introduction claims that activists will continue to run campaigns of misinformation against the farmed-salmon industry. Moore champions trust in what he calls 'real experts and scientists'. In his opinion, inferred from the scientific references in the report, it would seem that Patrick Moore's 'real' experts are those who – like him – are paid by industry.

The input from British Columbia was a classic use of the third-party technique, the PR ruse of creating and marshalling fake 'grassroots' organisations to create the impression of widespread support for industry interests. Laurie Jensen recounted in an aquaculture industry presentation in July 2005 how her 'small group of dedicated individuals were able to initiate change and promote the positive awareness and education of Aquaculture in British Columbia'.[71]

SALMON OF THE AMERICAS FAKE WEBSITES

In January 2004 the main fish-farming lobby group in the Americas, Salmon of the Americas, launched several fake websites to direct web traffic towards their own website. Domains such as www.pcbfarmedsalmon.com, www.pcbsalmon.com, and www.pcbsinsalmon.com were used by SOTA to offer 'concerned consumers a biased interpretation of fact and fiction about farmed salmon and PCBs'.[72]

These web domain names had been registered on 26 August 2003 by Steve Bleezarde of a company called Market Action.[73] Market Action is a PR firm headed by Alex Trent, the executive director of Salmon of the Americas. Both organisations are based in offices on Nassau Street (194 and 209) in Princeton, New Jersey. Market Action was hired by Salmon of the Americas in July 2003 just after SOTA was created by amalgamating the North and South American salmon farmers associations.[74] The websites were taken down in early 2005, when they had served their purpose.[75] The fact that they were registered in August 2003 suggests that the industry was prepared for the eventuality of criticism over four months before the publication of the paper in *Science*.

For instance, www.pcbsalmon.com

instructs readers not to worry too much about the toxins in farmed salmon because 'PCBs and similar compounds are so widespread in the environment that they are in the air we breathe, the water we drink and swim in, and the foods we eat ... They are virtually impossible to avoid.'[76]

All the websites featured links to the others, as well as to the Salmon of the Americas website, but nowhere did any of the sites indicate that they were run by the industry, a classic deceptive PR technique.

SCOTTISH QUALITY SALMON'S PR AND LOBBYING

Scottish Quality Salmon played a major part in the PR campaign to undermine the Hites study. The initial response by the SQS communications department was to mobilise 'scientific adviser' Dr John Webster. SQS worked with London PR firm Chrome Consulting to develop key messages and brief Webster. A document obtained by Spinwatch gives Chrome's own account of the campaign, written for an international PR industry competition:

Our actions during the first 36 hours of the crisis were to:
- Thoroughly review the *Science* paper, analyse inaccuracies, agree stance and brief internally
- Prepare and issue initial media statement to c.600 named UK media contacts as well as MEPs, MSPs, civil servants and via newswire distribution, some 22,500 international media outlets[77]

SQS and Chrome then issued a 'second statement focusing on the international scientific condemnation of the paper and the health benefits of regular salmon consumption'. This focused on quoting the corporate-linked scientists noted above. Chrome's account reveals the following actions:

- Liaise closely with the Food Standards Agency to clarify its stance on the issue and likely actions and advise on the Scottish Quality Salmon stance
- Update the Scottish Quality Salmon website and link statements to healthy eating information

- Monitor news coverage worldwide and act swiftly to address negative comment[78]

Chrome Consulting's assessment concurs with the analysis in this chapter that the campaign was a great success:

The very first stories to appear focused on this crisis as a major food/health scare, yet within hours media were clearly and consistently reporting doubts about the veracity of the *Science* paper's conclusions. Within a day key media became actively hostile to the paper, its authors and backers, and strongly supportive of the Scottish salmon industry. In all, some 78% of all the 843 items of monitored print and broadcast media coverage included comment and views from Scottish Quality Salmon, either directly quoted or expressed through a third party.[79]

The use of 'third-party' appeals involved scientists recruited by the industry. SQS acknowledge that they co-ordinated their spin campaign with the SPAA and SOTA and that they had regular contacts with Charles Santerre, the SOTA consultant.[80] Two out of three international links on the SQS website in June 2004 were those of Salmon of the Americas and the SPAA.[81]

THE PHILOSOPHY OF SALMON SPIN

Scottish Quality Salmon, along with the rest of the industry, sought to undermine criticism of salmon farming using classic manipulative PR techniques. This requires that ordinary citizens are seen as partly irrational and thus in need of appeals and campaigns which work at the level of 'emotion' and 'perception'. This was well understood by the early PR pioneers, such as Ivy Lee, whose view was that democracy put the 'crowd in the saddle' and that this required 'courtiers' to flatter and caress the crowd much as kings and queens had been flattered and caressed in former times. This approach was described approvingly by Walter Lippmann, one of the earliest PR theorists, as the 'manufacture of consent'.[82]

We can see this approach in the internal documents circulated between SQS and governmental bodies in the United Kingdom, which were obtained under the Freedom of Information Act. In February, March and April 2004, SQS commissioned market research to find out how the public had responded to the news about salmon. They found that 'the farmed salmon industry has had its profile raised and some people do not like what they saw'. The problem was, therefore, how to change the perceptions, rather than the industry. Thus the researchers delved into the public response which is alleged to be 'impressionistic, rather than rational'.[83] A 'rational model' in which consumers 'weigh evidence' would suggest that 'SQS should keep arguing its case to persuade doubters'.[84] 'In fact', the researchers note, 'this is not a good model'. The researchers examined both tabloid and broadsheet readers and found in the latter case that 'there was nonetheless, even for them an emotional underpinning'.[85] To counter this, 'it is essential to remember the non-rational aspect of any communication. That is, even when arguing a rational case, great attention should be given to the overall impression made, whether in advertising or PR.' 'It should not', they conclude, 'be assumed that the facts will speak for themselves.'[86]

The market research found that facts might encourage people to remember what is wrong with farmed salmon. 'A rational only response e.g. "toxins within European limits" prompts poor reaction.'[87] So, instead, the manipulative approach was taken: 'health benefits very persuasive'; 'Pew Charitable Trust and bias good secondary angle'. The strategy to be developed from these findings was:

- Don't provoke the negatives.
- Deal with the impression in balance with the facts.
- Visual imagery can be positive or negative.
- Use third-party endorsement.

'Educating consumers' therefore meant countering 'negative misinformation' and 'normalising' impressions of salmon,[88] before 'moving on to more emotive, lifestyle messages'.[89]

In the post-crisis phase, SQS provided writers with facility trips to Scottish salmon farms. Documents released under the Freedom of Information Act record that '[t]wo national consumer journalists visited Scotland and met with fish farmers at an industry event, visited SQS and a fish farm. Coverage is expected soon.' According to the documents, 'both journalists were very positive following the visit, explaining how their concerns had been allayed'.

In the recovery phase, notes Chrome Consulting, highlights included:

activity to publicise the Food Standards Agency's positive recommendations on oil-rich fish consumption (specifically including Scottish farmed salmon); and close work with the BBC to maintain fairness in its major contribution to the ongoing debate, a crisis-specific episode of the 'Should I Worry About ... ?' TV series (the answer being a resounding 'No').[90]

The success of the recovery strategy depended on changes in public resistance to salmon, which could be influenced indirectly, not least via lobbying of government.

SQS LOBBYING

SQS employed the lobbying firm Grayling, which has New Labour connections, to target the parliaments in Edinburgh, London and Brussels. In January an information shot was distributed by email to MSPs, MPs and MEPs. Grayling provided a monitoring service for SQS and advised on lines to take when approaching decision makers. The communications campaign involved SQS lobbying the Food Standards Agency. Meeting with them on 5 April 2004, SQS attempted to persuade the FSA to support them more openly.

Documents released under the Freedom of Information Act show that SQS asked for access to any new data on toxicity 'prior to publication' and offered to supply data on contamination to the FSA. But, they asked if 'it would be treated as "commercial confidential"'.[91] The FSA note of the meeting describes SQS as 'very nervous' about bad publicity and about the possible findings of government expert committees on toxicity of dioxins. They also record that 'throughout the meeting SQS appeared to want the Agency to publicly endorse the eating of farmed salmon, and in particular that produced by SQS members'. The minute also records that SQS 'would like the Agency to be more supportive of salmon as a healthy food and of their strategy for improving the quality ... of their product'.

In response, the FSA officials 'emphasised that FSA advice relates to oily fish, of which salmon is one species, and that we would not endorse the eating of any individual fish species over others'. In conclusion they noted that 'our role is to put the consumer first ... and we could not be seen as endorsing specific products or companies'.[92]

Yet by 24 June the FSA had reversed this position and specifically singled out salmon as safe to eat. 'Is the advice on eating farmed salmon different to other types of oily fish?' they asked in a FAQ page on their website: 'No, the advice on farmed salmon is the same.'[93] No wonder Chrome Consulting mentioned this in their account of spinning salmon: 'Highlights ... included: activity to publicise the

Food Standards Agency's positive recommendations on oil-rich fish consumption (specifically including Scottish farmed salmon).'[94]

The reversal is not surprising. The UK Food Standards Agency was the lead agency in determining UK and Scottish government responses. It was set up to restore public confidence in government after the Ministry of Agriculture, Fisheries and Food was discredited as being too close to industry. The FSA was compromised from the beginning by drawing on the same civil service personnel who had previously worked in MAFF. Its first head, Sir John Krebs, was a devotee of corporate science, being both an outspoken advocate of GM food and a critic of organic food.[95] Krebs was also an adviser to the Science Media Centre, the corporate-funded spin organisation which promotes GM. He had links to the Social Issues Research Centre (another corporate-funded organisation which campaigns to influence the reporting of science). He was a member of the SIRC 'Forum' on Guidelines on Science and Health Communication, along with other advocates of corporate science, such as Dick Taverne of the corporate-funded front group Sense about Science.[96]

Board members of the FSA included an adviser to Social Issues Research Centre (Jeya Henry);[97] an adviser to Sense about Science (Richard Ayre); a former vice-chair of Quality Meat Scotland (a meat industry promotional group); an owner of shares in Unilever and Cadbury Schweppes (Graham Millar); a former Mars executive and an active member of the International Life Sciences Institute (the leading food industry front group) (Maureen Edmondson); and a vice-president of the Farmers' Union of Wales (Alan Gardner).[98] The new (in 2005) chair of the FSA, Deirdre Hutton, has shares in Glaxo-SmithKline, Tesco and Unilever.[99] This is the body which consumers are supposed to believe is 'independent' of the food industry.

'NATURAL IS NOT IN IT': ADVERTISING FARMED SALMON

Chrome Consulting was responsible for the advertising campaign run by SQS in summer 2004 in order to restore confidence in farmed salmon. The campaign was designed specifically to correct 'the messages communicated by those that have tried to discredit salmon farming'.[100] In addition to general media advertising, the campaign involved distributing educational leaflets, postcards and posters to journalists and retailers. SQS reported good results for the campaign, estimating that 25,322,000 adults saw the television commercials 2.4 times, leading to 52 per cent of all adults in the

United Kingdom being exposed to their messages.[101] With the slogan 'naturally they're the best', the advertisements presented a misleading account of the industry.

The industry campaign benefited from direct state support. The Scottish Executive helped finance the propaganda campaign to the tune of £1.5 million. The industry received a further £80,000 from the Crown Estate. The Crown Estate is a property company that has 'extensive marine assets throughout the United Kingdom, including 55% of the foreshore and all the seabed out to the 12 nautical miles limit'.[102]

THE SCOTTISH EXECUTIVE CONNECTION

The public money the Scottish Executive, the devolved administration in Scotland, ploughed into the ad campaign is unsurprising since the Executive has an open commitment to the fish farming industry. On the day of publication of the *Science* study, it joined the industry chorus. Official documents show that by 4.15 p.m. on 9 January 2004, Executive spin doctor Stephen Orr had already issued a statement in the name of the minister. 'Below are lines in Allan Wilson's name given to the media', he wrote in an email to colleagues.[103] The Executive statement simply emphasised the faulty judgements of the FSA: 'The FSA have confirmed that PCB and dioxin levels in Scottish salmon are significantly lower than the thresholds set by the FSA, EU, WHO and indeed the US FDA.'

Their statement bears an uncanny resemblance to that issued by the industry: 'PCB and dioxin levels found in Scottish salmon were significantly lower than the thresholds set by international watchdogs such as the European Union, the Food Standards Agency (FSA) or even the US FDA.'[104]

The rationale for the Executive position is expressed forcefully in the 'background info' to the statement, which notes that Scotland has the third largest aquaculture/salmon industry in the world.

The industry supports more than 6500 jobs in some of the most economically fragile, fishery dependent, areas ... accounting for around 50% by value of all Scottish food exports. The salmon industry is the single most vital development in the economy of the Highlands and Islands in the last 30 years producing more income than beef and lamb combined.

Devotion to the industry is maintained despite Marine Harvest, the biggest operator, being named by the Scottish Environment

Protection Agency (Sepa) as one of the 16 worst polluters in Scotland. A fish-processing factory run by Marine Harvest in Fort William was accused by Sepa of 'unlicensed releases to the environment resulting in a report to the procurator fiscal'.[105] Marine Harvest and the rest of the industry were no doubt glad of the steadfast political and financial support they received from the Executive. On 19 April 2004 Scottish first minister Jack McConnell opened a Marine Harvest fish farm in Mallaig and was presented with a pair of gold salmon cufflinks.[106] Jack McConnell's brother Iain was at that point a fish-farm manager with Marine Harvest.[107]

CONCLUSION

The campaign to destroy the credibility, and crucially the news value, of the study in *Science* was a stunning success. Within a week it was off the news agenda. The campaign also meant that future work by the scientists involved got markedly less coverage. The industry in Scotland was able to call on government to fund its propaganda campaign on the health and safety of farmed salmon and it was able to rely on the Food Standards Agency to support their line on the science. This was so even though the FSA's analysis was at worst entirely mistaken and at best scientifically illiterate, since the paper in *Science* was widely agreed to be correct. This unedifying tale suggests that the civil service and the government, in consort with the industry, are willing to put the needs of industrial-scale aquaculture ahead of public health and sustainability.

In such circumstances, it is instructive that the International Public Relations Association awarded an international PR prize to Chrome Consulting who ran the campaign of misinformation for Scottish Quality Salmon.

The conclusion we can draw is that the public received from the mainstream media a distorted view of the potential risks and as a result they are not in a position to be able to make sensible judgements on risk. At a wider level this story also shows how decisions taken in corporate boardrooms, PR headquarters and government offices have direct effects on what information is available and on what decisions are taken, often with no input from popular opinion and with no regard for the truth. It is only by exposing this kind of deception and campaigning for democratic controls over political processes and corporations that science communication can perform a democratic function.

NOTES

1. This chapter draws upon documents uncovered via the Freedom of Information requests to the Scottish Executive, Food Standards Agency and Crown Estate as well as other unpublished documentation. Copies of all the documents referred to here can be found at the Spinprofiles website, <http://www.spinprofiles.org>. The chapter was written with the aid of research carried out by three students on my course on globalisation and anti-globalisation at Stirling University. Thanks very much to them for all their insights. I have been asked not to name them for fear of blighting their careers.
2. J. Benn, 'Norway: the rising tide of fish farming', *People and the Planet* website, posted 19 November 2003, <http://www.peopleandplanet. net/doc.php?id=2085>.
3. US Environmental Protection Agency, 'Health Effects of PCBs', 8 September 2004, <http://www.epa.gov/opptintr/pcb/effects.html>.
4. In other words, the use of the concept of hegemony (in the sense of persuasion and consent, as opposed to its original sense of leadership and force) to explain the reproduction of power relations is less than adequate. See D. Miller, 'Media Power and Class Power', in L. Panitch and C. Leys (eds) *Socialist Register* 2002 (Merlin, 2001), for a discussion.
5. Cited in D. Perry, 'Call for cash offer to Scots fish farms', *Press and Journal*, 7 September 2004, p. 10; Simpson cited in G. Harris, 'Scots farmed salmon leaps back on menu', *The Times*, 29 October 2004, <http://www.timesonline.co.uk/article/0,,2-1334836,00.html>.
6. Ronald A. Hites, Jeffery A. Foran, David O. Carpenter, M. Coreen Hamilton, Barbara A. Knuth and Steven J. Schwager, 'Global Assessment of Organic Contaminants in Farmed Salmon', *Science* 303 (5655), 9 January 2004, p. 227.
7. US Environmental Protection Agency, 'Polychlorinated Biphenyls', 8 September 2004, <http://www.epa.gov/opptintr/pcb/>.
8. Hites et al., 'Global Assessment', p. 228.
9. Ibid.
10. Jeffery Foran, personal correspondence by email, 30 March 2006.
11. J. Reynolds, 'Eating farm salmon raises risk of cancer', *Scotsman*, 9 January 2004, <http://news.scotsman.com/topics.cfm?tid=1080&id =27102004>.
12. J. Reynolds, 'Chemicals in fish are well known', *Scotsman*, 10 January 2004, <http://business.scotsman.com/agriculture.cfm?id=31392004>.
13. M. MacLeod, 'Salmon is safe says US food expert', *Scotland on Sunday*, 11 January 2004, <http://scotlandonsunday.scotsman.com/index. cfm?id=34952004>.
14. B. McConville and J. Reynolds, 'Green campaigners fund salmon study', *Scotsman*, 16 January 2004, <http://thescotsman.scotsman. com/scotland.cfm?id=55262004>.
15. J. Reynolds, 'Salmon scare report was flawed and biased', *Scotsman*, 16 January 2004, <http://news.scotsman.com/print.cfm?id=55252004>.

16. G. Bell and D. Tocher, 'Claims of unsafe fish run contrary to the facts, say scientists', *Scotsman*, 16 January 2004, <http://thescotsman.scotsman.com/scotland.cfm?id=54782004&20040927201412>.

17. Scottish Quality Salmon, 'Contaminants in the Environment', <http://www.scottishsalmon.co.uk/environment/contaminants.asp>.

18. J. Krebs, 'Health balance over farmed salmon', *Guardian*, 12 January 2004, <http://www.guardian.co.uk/fish/story/0,,1121021,00.html>.

19. Statement released under the Freedom of Information Act and described by the FSA as 'temporarily placed on our website' in January 2004.

20. Latest versions available from <http://www.epa.gov/ncea/pdfs/dioxin/nas-review/>.

21. 'Fish consumption: benefits and risks, part 8, annexe 5', COT statement on dioxins and PCBs, <http://www.food.gov.uk/multimedia/pdfs/fishreport200408.pdf>.

22. Ibid., p. 19.

23. Given in note 25 of the paper, this process is US EPA, *Guidance for Assessing Chemical Contaminant Data for Use in Fish Advisories. Volume 2: Risk Assessment and Fish Consumption Limits* (3rd edn., Washington, DC: US EPA, 2000), <http://www.epa.gov/ost/fishadvice/volume2/index.html>.

24. <http://www.scottishsalmon.co.uk/mediacentre/releases/2004/080101.asp>. Yet Webster is hardly independent of SQS, as he is billed as working for 'Scottish Quality Salmon' on the SQS website and is listed as being contactable through the SQS switchboard. See, for example, <http://www.scottishsalmon.co.uk/media/releases/170904.html>.

25. McConville and Reynolds, 'Green campaigners fund salmon study'.

26. <http://www.farmfreshsalmon.org/images/PDFS/Farmed%20Salmon,%20PCBs,%20Activist,%20and%20the%20Media.pdf>.

27. 'Handle with care', *Observer*, Observer Food Monthly, 15 February 2004, <http://observer.guardian.co.uk/foodmonthly/story/0,,1145624,00.html>.

28. Scottish Quality Salmon statement re publication of American PBDE research, <http://www.scottishsalmon.co.uk/media/releases/100804.html>.

29. R. Edwards, 'Scientists back toxic salmon study', *Sunday Herald*, 18 January 2004, <http://www.sundayherald.com/39358>.

30. Ibid.

31. Ibid.

32. LexisNexis search on 'Farmed salmon and Santerre' from 8 January 2004 to 20 January 2004.

33. Salmon of the Americas, 'Medical, health and food safety experts advise reading past the headlines in the new news about farmed salmon', 10 January 2004, <http://www.salmonoftheamericas.com/topic_01_04_press.html>.

34. 'Don't jeopardise health by cutting out salmon: respected US scientists direct vehement criticism at flawed salmon study', SQS news release, 9 January 2004, <http://www.scottishsalmon.co.uk/mediacentre/releases/2004/090104.asp>.

35. Ibid.

36. Edwards, 'Scientists back toxic salmon study'.
37. PR Newswire, 'Scottish Quality Salmon: Don't Jeopardise Health by Cutting out Salmon. Respected US Scientists Direct Vehement Criticism at Flawed Salmon Study', news release, Perth, Scotland, 9 January 2004, <http://www.prnewswire.co.uk/cgi/news/release?id=114926>; Reynolds, 'Chemicals in fish are well known'.
38. M. Dowie, 'Gina Kolata: What's Wrong With the New York Times's Science Reporting?' Nation, 6 July 1998, <http://www.mindfully.org/Reform/Gina-Kolata-Dowie6jul98.htm>.
39. From an editorial written by Stephen Safe for the New England Journal of Medicine 337, pp. 1303–4 (1997). Cited in Frank van Kolfschooten, 'Conflicts of Interest (Financial) and Bias', Annie Appleseed Project, 28 March 2002, <http://www.annieappleseedproject.org/conofinfinbi.html>.
40. Ibid.
41. J. Reynolds, 'Salmon still on the menu for top chefs', Scotsman , 10 January 2004, <http://news.scotsman.com/topics.cfm?tid=1080&id=31592004>.
42. J. Stauber and S. Rampton, 'The Junkyard Dogs of Science', PR Watch 5 (4), 1998, <http://www.prwatch.org/prwissues/1998Q4/dogs.html>.
43. Tobacco documents online, <http://tobaccodocuments.org/profiles/guzelian_philip.html>.
44. Chemical weapons working group, 'Public Health Expert Testifies to Unacceptable Health Risks from Utah Incinerator', 31 July 1996, <http://www.cwwg.org/PR_07.31.96TOCDF.html>.
45. The Atlantic Legal Foundation, <http://www.atlanticlegal.org>.
46. Sources for the preceding paragraph: ALF Annual Report, 1994; ALF, 'Our Philosophy', 2004, cited in 'Exxon Secrets Fact sheet on the ALF', <http://www.exxonsecrets.org/html/orgfactsheet.php?id=16>.
47. Bell and Tocher, 'Claims of unsafe fish'.
48. Nutreco website, <http://www.nutreco.com>.
49. Bell and Tocher, 'Claims of unsafe fish'.
50. G. Bell et al., 'Dioxin and dioxin-like polychlorinated biphenyls (PCBs) in Scottish farmed salmon: effects of replacement of dietary marine fish oil with vegetable oils', 2004, pre-publication copy of paper supplied by Bell.
51. Positive Aquaculture Awareness, 'NDP leader's call for BC farmed salmon boycott flies in the face of new evidence that shows eating salmon can help prevent Alzheimer's', news release, 7 September 2004, <http://www.farmfreshsalmon.org/images/PDFS/090704Salmonboycott.pdf>.
52. Society for the Positive Awareness of Aquaculture, <http://www.farmfreshsalmon.org>.
53. AKVAsmart, <http://www.akvasmart.com>.
54. C. Asper, 'The Stamp on the Back of my Hand', Watershed Watch, August 2003, <http://web.archive.org/web/20031207151507/http://watershedwatch.org/ww/cottus_asper.html>.
55. <http://www.farmfreshsalmon.org/D136.cfm?open27=27>.
56. <http://www.farmfreshsalmon.org/images/PDFS/MembershipFormsversion3.pdf>.

57. Asper, 'The Stamp on the Back of my Hand'.
58. <http://www.samspade.org/t/whois?a=http%3A%2F%2Fwww.farm-freshsalmon.org%2F&server=magic>; <http://www.firstdollar.ca/view.cfm?page=16>.
59. First Dollar, <http://www.firstdollar.ca/about.cfm>.
60. Ibid.
61. Ibid.
62. 'Resource towns fight back against arriviste rock stars', Vancouver Sun, 24 July 2004, <http://willcocks.blogspot.com/2004/07/resource-towns-fight-back-against.html>.
63. Ibid.
64. <http://www.greenspiritstrategies.com/D80.cfm>; <http://www.panfish.no/newsread/news.asp?docid=10115&wce=regions>.
65. <http://www.samspade.org/t/ipwhois?a=www.firstdollar.ca>.
66. <http://www.greenspiritstrategies.com/D80.cfm>
67. <http://www.greenspiritstrategies.com/D81.cfm>.
68. For more details, see <http://www.spinprofiles.org/index.php/Patrick_Moore>.
69. 'Issues in Aquaculture, Farmed Salmon, PCB's, Activists and the Media. Framed [sic] Salmon: Updated to provide commentary on the well-publicized January 9, 2004 Science (Vol. 303) study of PCB levels in farmed and wild salmon', 15 January 2004, <http://www.farmfreshsalmon.org/reports.cfm>.
70. Ibid.
71. L. Jensen, 'Mobilizing the grassroots: the ripple effect', presentation to Aquaculture Canada 2005, St John's, Newfoundland, 4 July 2005, <http://www.aquacultureassociation.ca/ac05/abstracts/awareness.htm>.
72. G. Johnson, 'Don't be Fooled: The Ten Worst Greenwashers of 2003', The Green Life, Boston, <http://web.archive.org/web/20050204001827/>; <http://www.thegreenlife.org/dontbefooled.html#Salmon>.
73. With the exception of www.salmoncolor.com, registered on 2 September 2003. Market Action's one page website is <http://www.mktact.com/>.
74. As reported by the industry information service Fishlink 8 (1), 7 July 2003, <http://www.imhooked.com/fishlink/070703.html>.
75. To view the content of the sites as they were, see the Internet Archive, <http://web.archive.org/web/*/http://www.pcbfarmedsalmon.com>; <http://web.archive.org/web/*/http://www.pcbsalmon.com>; <http://web.archive.org/web/*/http://www.pcbsinsalmon.com>; <http://web.archive.org/web/*/http://www.farmedsalmonpcb.com>; <http://web.archive.org/web/*/http://www.salmoncolor.com>.
76. Johnson, 'Don't be Fooled'.
77. Chrome Consulting, 'Scottish Quality Salmon: The Facts', Entry 204, IPRA Golden World Awards for Excellence 2005; Category 7: Recover from crisis; Entrant: Chrome Consulting Ltd.; Client: Scottish Quality Salmon, <www.nuclearspin.org/images/4/45/ChromeEntry204.pdf>.
78. Ibid.
79. Ibid.

80. Interview with Julie Edgar, Scottish Quality Salmon media manager.
81. <http://web.archive.org/web/20040619163932/http://scottishsalmon. co.uk/links/index.htm>.
82. See R.E. Hiebert, *Courtier to the Crowd: the Story of Ivy Lee and the development of Public Relations* (Ames, Iowa: Iowa State University Press, 1966); W. Lippmann, *Public Opinion* (London: Allen and Unwin, 1921), p. 158.
83. Ockwell Associates, *Qualitative research into how differing press treatments affect attitudes to salmon* (Bath: Ockwell Associates, April 2004), p. 14.
84. Ibid., p. 17.
85. Ibid., p. 20.
86. Ibid., p. 33.
87. Ibid. We should remember that the 'facts' as given by the industry were wholly misleading.
88. Ibid., p. 34.
89. Printout of SQS Powerpoint presentation to the Crown Estate on the salmon marketing campaign, undated, probably presented at meeting held on 9 June 2004.
90. Chrome Consulting, 'Scottish Quality Salmon: The Facts'.
91. FSA, minute of 'FSA Scotland Meeting with Scottish Quality Salmon (SQS)', 5 April 2004.
92. Ibid.
93. Food Standards Agency, 'Oily fish advice: your questions answered', 24 June 2004, <http://www.food.gov.uk/news/newsarchive/2004/jun/ oilyfishfaq#h_5>.
94. Chrome Consulting, 'Scottish Quality Salmon: The Facts'.
95. A. Rowell, *Don't Worry, It's Safe to Eat* (London: Earthscan, 2003), pp. 190–8.
96. <http://www.sirc.org/publik/cop_guidelines_m.html>.
97. Sankey was a board member from 2000 to 2003, <http://www.sirc. org/about/jeya.shtml>.
98. <http://www.foodstandards.gov.uk/aboutus/ourboard/boardmem/ richardayre>; <http://www.foodstandards.gov.uk/aboutus/ourboard/ boardmem/graememillar>; <http://www.foodstandards.gov.uk/ aboutus/ourboard/boardmem/maureenedmondson>; <http://www. foodstandards.gov.uk/aboutus/ourboard/boardmem/alangardner_ bm>.
99. <http://www.foodstandards.gov.uk/aboutus/ourboard/boardmem/ dierdrehutton/>.
100. Brian Simpson, chief executive of SQS, SQS media release (4 October 2004), <http://www.scottishsalmon.co.uk/media/releases/041004. html>.
101. SQS media release (4 October 2004).
102. The Crown Estate, <http://www.thecrownestate.co.uk/02_about_us_ 04_02_17.htm>.
103. Annette Stuart, email to Marianne Cook, 'FW: Quote in Allan Wilson's name on Salmon', 9 January 2004, 17.55. Released under the Freedom of Information Act.
104. <http://www.scottishsalmon.co.uk/media/releases/080104.htm>.

105. R. Edwards, 'Exposed: Scotland's filthiest companies: Polluters in "roll of shame"', *Sunday Herald*, 24 July 2005, <http://www.sundayherald.com/50953>.

106. 'Scotland's first minister visits Mallaig', *West Word*, May 2004, <http://www.road-to-the-isles.org.uk/westword/may2004.html>; registered as a gift with the Scottish Executive on 20 April 2004, <http://www.scotland.gov.uk/Resource/Doc/1066/0008094.pdf>.

107. Simon Pia's Diary, 'Brown returns for pasta and prosciutto', *Scotsman*, 11 October 2004, <http://news.scotsman.com/topics.cfm?tid=1005&id=1180992004>.

6

Exxon's Foot Soldiers: The Case of the International Policy Network

Andy Rowell

Just days after the re-election of George W. Bush in November 2004, a team of scientists and indigenous groups assembled in Reykjavik, Iceland, to hold a symposium on climate change. The scientists were worried by Bush's re-election, since he is known for his hostile position on climate change.

At the same time they knew they were about to issue an explosive report that would make news headlines across the globe, once again raising the political profile of global warming. In fact the report was so damning that its release had been delayed by the US State Department until after the American election, because the Bush administration feared that its findings would hurt its chances of re-election. 'If the report had come out it would have been a very strong piece in the presidential election in the US', said Robert Corell, the chair of the Arctic Climate Impact Assessment, the study which produced the report.[1]

Corell and his teams of scientists were releasing the findings of their unprecedented four-year study into the effects of climate change on the Arctic.[2] Undertaken by 300 of the world's leading scientists, it was no lightweight study – the main report was 15 megabytes and 146 pages long. It also had governmental backing, as it had been commissioned by the Arctic Council, a ministerial intergovernmental forum comprising the eight countries that surround the Arctic (including the United States), along with six indigenous peoples' organisations. Also involved was the International Arctic Science Committee, an international organisation appointed by 18 national academies of science.

What the scientists had found was alarming. The press release said it all: 'New Scientific Consensus: Arctic Is Warming Rapidly: Much larger changes are projected, affecting global climate.'[3] The scientists had discovered that the Arctic 'is warming much more rapidly than previously known, at nearly twice the rate as the rest of the globe, and increasing greenhouse gases from human activities are projected to make it warmer still'.[4]

The detailed findings would be enough to send a chill down the spines of the thousands of people dependent on the Arctic for their survival, but also of everyone concerned about the future of the planet:

- In Alaska, western Canada and eastern Russia average winter temperatures had increased by 4–7° Fahrenheit over the last 50 years. Temperatures were projected to increase by 7–13° F in the next 100 years.
- Arctic sea ice during the summer is predicted to decline by at least 50 per cent by the end of this century. Some models predict a total disappearance.
- Warming over Greenland is projected to lead to substantial melting of the Greenland Ice Sheet, contributing to global sea-level rise. Over the long term, Greenland contains enough melt water to raise sea level by about 7 metres (about 23 feet).
- If the Arctic Ocean becomes ice free in summer, polar bears and some seal species would be driven toward extinction.
- Arctic climate change presents serious challenges to the health and food security of some indigenous peoples, challenging the survival of some cultures.

Nor were the report's findings meant to be alarmist, as the projections on climate change were based only on 'moderate' estimates of future emissions of carbon dioxide and other greenhouse gases, not excessive levels. But there was a massive cause for concern. 'The impacts of global warming are affecting people *now* in the Arctic', said Robert Corell. 'The Arctic is experiencing some of the most rapid and severe climate change on earth. The impacts of climate change on the region and the globe are projected to increase substantially in the years to come.'[5]

Chief Gary Harrison of the Arctic Athabaskan Council, one of the indigenous organisations involved in the study, said bluntly: 'Everything is under threat. Our homes are threatened by storms and melting permafrost, our livelihoods are threatened by changes to the plants and animals we harvest. Even our lives are threatened, as traditional travel routes become dangerous.'[6]

You would expect such alarming news to make headlines around the globe, and that is what happened. The *Anchorage Daily News*, one of Alaska's most respected papers, noted: 'Climate change devours Arctic ice: Rapid melting is threatening Earth's "air conditioning", experts say.'[7] But the news also made headlines elsewhere in the United States: The *Los Angeles Times*: 'Climate Change Accelerating, Report Warns: Arctic heating is melting ocean ice and affecting species and indigenous cultures, researchers say.'[8] *Seattle Times*: 'Report says Arctic rapidly warming.'[9]

The report made headlines in the British press too. The tabloid *Daily Mail* reported it as 'The Arctic apocalypse'.[10] The liberal *Guardian* newspaper, however, normally known for its progressive stance on climate change, this time took an alternative view. 'Climate change claims flawed, says study.'[11] The *Guardian's* piece, written by Tim Radford, the paper's science editor, and a supposed specialist on the science of climate change, noted that

[a] team of scientists has condemned claims of climate catastrophe as 'fatally flawed' in a report released today ... Martin Ågerup, president of the Danish Academy for Future Studies and colleagues from Stockholm, Canada, Iceland and Britain say in their report that predictions of 'extreme impacts' based on greenhouse emissions employed 'faulty science, faulty logic and faulty economics'.

So what was the study that Radford based his report on? It was called 'The Impacts of Climate Change: An Appraisal for the Future',[12] and it was published by the International Policy Network, which describes itself as a 'non-governmental, educational and non-partisan organization'.[13]

Radford's article contained several serious omissions. Nowhere did it mention that the dissenting report was largely written by renowned climate sceptics who are at odds with the majority of the world's leading scientists. Nowhere did it say that it was published by the International Policy Network, whose key individuals have a history of right-wing pro-corporate activism.

But, most importantly, nowhere did it include that the IPN is funded by Exxon. In 2003, IPN's North America office received $50,000 for 'Climate Change Outreach' programmes from Exxon.[14] In 2004, the amount increased to $115,000 for 'Climate Change' work.[15] In 2005, the amount increased again to $130,000.[16]

This means that over the last few years Exxon has increased its funding for the IPN. But why? Because the IPN's work on climate fits perfectly into the strategy that Exxon has adopted on climate, which is to try to delay action on the issue for as long as possible, as it sees climate change as a fundamental threat to its core business, which is drilling for oil and gas. The company has responded to the issue by using the classic '3D' public relations technique: deny there is a problem; delay action; and dominate any international response.

One of the ways that Exxon has been trying to delay action on climate change is to muddy the science of climate change. The company, directly and indirectly, continues to fund a network of scientists and think tanks that try to undermine the science of climate change, just as the tobacco industry continues to try to dismiss the link between smoking and cancer, some 50 years after its own scientists conceded that there was a link. For example, one PR tobacco document from the late 1960s says: 'The most important type of story is that which casts doubt on the cause and effect theory of disease and smoking. Eye-grabbing headlines were needed and should strongly call out the point – Controversy! Contradiction! Other Factors! Unknowns!'[17]

The IPN is one of these Exxon-funded think tanks that is trying to keep the controversy about climate change open and to cast doubt on the cause-and-effect theory of global warming. These think tanks adopt varying sceptical positions in relation to climate change: they deny either that it is happening, or that it is caused by the burning of fossil fuels. Other positions adopted are that it is now too expensive to try to mitigate carbon dioxide emissions, or it is too late to try.

In 2005, the American magazine *Mother Jones* included the IPN in an article about 40 groups funded by Exxon, many of which attacked the Arctic Climate Impact Assessment report. The article noted that '[a]s the world burns think tanks and journalists funded by Exxon Mobil are out to convince you global warming is a hoax'.[18]

Seen within the context of Exxon's trying to undermine international climate science, you might argue that the IPN report deliberately tried to scupper the findings of 300 leading scientists, eight governments and numerous indigenous groups. It tried to leave the controversy open, when it should have been closed. It left the public as confused as ever about climate change. This fitted perfectly into Exxon's PR strategy.

THE HISTORY OF THE IPN

To understand the IPN as an organisation, it is necessary to study the deep-rooted personal and political connections it has to a small group of influential free-market ideologues in the United Kingdom and around the world. This close network of people continues to push a pro-business and often anti-environmental agenda, which is intellectually similar to that of many controversial industries, such as energy, chemicals and tobacco.

Until 2001, the International Policy Network was called the Atlas Economic Research Foundation UK (AERF). The precursor to AERF UK was called the International Institute of Economic Research and had been set up in 1971 with Arthur Shenfield and Anthony Fisher as original trustees. Both men were radical right-wing free marketeers.

Shenfield was an economist who at one stage was the economic director of the Confederation of British Industry, vice-president of the right-wing Adam Smith Club, and president of the equally right-wing Mont Pelerin Society.[19] Fisher, in turn, had made a fortune from broiler chickens and had started the right-wing Institute of Economic Affairs in the mid 1950s, having being inspired by F.A. Hayek's book *The Road to Serfdom*.[20]

The name of the charity was changed in 1984 to AERF UK, and for nearly 20 years it funded small projects in the United Kingdom that were linked to the Institute of Economic Affairs and the Adam Smith Institute, as well as funding small grants to like-minded think tanks in the developing world. By the late 1990s, the trustees were John Blundell, Robert Boyd, Michael Fisher and Lord Harris of High Cross, with Linda Whetstone as chairman and honorary director.

It is interesting to look briefly at some of these individuals. John Blundell has been the general director of the Institute of Economic Affairs (IEA) since 1993.[21] Lord Harris of High Cross was one of the most influential right-wing activists of his generation. He was the first director general of the Institute of Economic Affairs and is considered to have been Margaret Thatcher's mentor.[22] Michael Fisher and Linda Whetstone are the son and daughter of Sir Anthony Fisher, the founder of the IEA. Linda Whetsone is also on the board of the sister organisation in the United States, the Atlas Economic Research Foundation.[23] The mission of the US-Atlas Economic Research Foundation, according to John Blundell, who was president of the US affiliate from 1987 to 1990, 'is to litter the world with free-market think-tanks'.[24] Robert Boyd is the treasurer.

AERF UK's income throughout the 1990s was variable, but always less than £100,000 a year. However all this changed in 2001, when the name changed from AERF UK to the International Policy Network. So why the name change? Was it to hide the affiliation with the sister organisation of the same name in the United States? More importantly though, 'International Policy Network' makes it sound like an innocuous 'progressive' think tank working on policy and development issues, rather than a right-wing one. It neatly hides the political origins of the organisation. The unsuspecting public does not see a right-wing think tank funded by Exxon, all they see is an international NGO.

The Charity Commission agreed the name change. The accounts for 2001 noted that

[i]n April 2001, with the consent of the Charity Commission, it adopted the working name of the International Policy Network, IPN, by which it is now known ... In April 2001, the Trustees adopted a new plan to expand activities substantially, in line with the original conception of the Institute. Roger Bate and Julian Morris were named as International Directors ... During 2001, IPN was successful in raising funds to enable the launch of new programmes. Some of the resulting expenditure occurred within the period under review.[25]

In contrast with its previous levels of income, the IPN started receiving large amounts of money. Donations in the 12 months to 30 June 2000 were £2,987 – whereas donations in the 18 months to 2001 were £607,272. The breakdown for funds included some £152,186 from foundations and £450,269 from companies.[26]

The expanded operations were causing some logistical and financial problems that were discussed at a trustees' meeting held in London on 3 December 2001. Present at the meeting were Roger Bate and Julian Morris (the two new directors), along with three trustees – Linda Whetstone (the chair), John Blundell and Robert Boyd. The minutes of this meeting, obtained from the Charity Commission under the Freedom of Information Act, note, in part, that:

- It was noted that, in view of the increased financial cope [sic] of the Institute's operations, the accounts for the eighteen-month period to December 31st, 2001 would require audit.
- Julian Morris will produce a brief business plan for the proposed office in India.
- Julian Morris will produce a note summarising all the websites on which Kendra is working.
- Roger Bate will determine the cost of taking office space within an institute in Washington.
- The disaggregation of office costs at 2 North Lord Street was discussed, and Julian Morris agreed to establish a separate

outgoing mail bin. Phone and fax costs were separately identified and a code number would be used on the photocopier. It was proposed, and agreed with John Blundell on behalf of the IEA, that £250 per quarter should be paid by IPN to IEA to cover heat, light, power and cleaning.

- The trustees reviewed the fees paid to the two directors, approved fees of £22,500 each for the period to December 21, 2001 and resolved that from January 1st 2002, these should be at the rate of £35,000 per annum each.
- It was agreed that the address given on the website should be changed to a Post Office box number.[27]

KEY PLAYERS

The minutes raise some questions. Firstly who are Julian Morris and Roger Bate, the IPN's directors, and who is 'Kendra'? Roger Bate and Julian Morris are long-standing right-wing activists who have a history of undermining topical environmental issues. Bate and Morris are also closely connected to the IEA. Back in 1993, when John Blundell was appointed general director of the IEA, he discussed the concept of an Environment Unit with Bate.[28] The following year the IEA marked the launch of their new Unit with the publication of *Global Warming: Apocalypse or Hot Air?* by Bate and Morris.

In my book *Green Backlash*, I argued that

the bias was evident in their argument. In the chapter entitled 'An Outline of the Science of Global Warming', over half of the references of cited studies were of known climate sceptics. The recommended reading list was a wish list of right-wing counter-science. 'Hard to take seriously', was how Sir Crispin Tickell, the Prime Minister's chief environmental advisor described it. Sir John Houghton, Co-Chairman of the Scientific Working Group of the Intergovernmental Panel on Climate Change called it 'uninformed'.[29]

The following year, 1994, Bate co-founded a corporate front organisation called the European Science and Environment Forum. The website was registered to Julian Morris. John Stauber and Sheldon Rampton from *PR Watch* have outlined how by 1994 Philip Morris had budgeted $880,000 to fund a front organisation on science in the United States. In consultation with Burson-Marsteller, the company also planned a second European organisation, tentatively named Scientists for Sound Public Policy. Burson-Marsteller's documents showed that 'a countervailing voice must be created in Europe' with support from tobacco, agri-chemical, pharmaceutical, and biotech companies amongst others.

Although Scientists for Sound Public Policy never materialised, Dr Stan Glantz, an expert on the PR tactics of the tobacco industry, argues that 'it appears that the outcome was the European Science and Environment Forum (ESEF)' whose 'executive director sought funding from the tobacco companies'.[30]

As Glantz explained, Bate actively solicited tobacco money for ESEF. In 1996 Bate approached tobacco company R.J. Reynolds for a grant of £50,000 for an ESEF/IEA book on environmental risk, and the following year ESEF published *What Risk? Science, Politics and Public Health*, edited by Bate. It was not just the risks associated with smoking that ESEF wanted to debunk, it was also the issue of climate change. Many of the world's leading climate sceptics and anti-environmental academics were members of ESEF, although the most up-to-date list seems to be dated 1998. These included Bruce Ames, Sallie Baliunas, Robert Balling, John Emsley, Sherwood Idso, Zbigniew Jaworowski, Patrick Michaels, Fred Singer, Willie Soon and Gerd-Rainer Weber.[31]

Bate was an international director of the IPN from 2001 until 2003. He has now become a resident fellow at the American Enterprise Institute, the right-wing neocon think tank, whose fellows led the charge for war in Iraq. According to his biography on the AEI's website, he remains a fellow of the Institute of Economic Affairs and a director of another organisation, Africa Fighting Malaria. This latter group also received $30,000 from Exxon for 'Climate Change Outreach' in 2004.[32]

Although Bate maintains he stopped being a director of ESEF in 2001,[33] according to documents lodged by ESEF at Companies House in the United Kingdom, Bate remained a director and trustee of ESEF until at least 2004.[34] During this time ESEF funded the IPN in 2002 to the tune of £85,471 and £36,500 in 2003.[35] In November 2004, Bate, in his capacity as a director, applied for ESEF to be struck off the register at Companies House.[36] ESEF was finally struck off the Companies House register in May 2005, but it still remains a UK-listed charity, although its accounts for 2004 onwards are overdue.[37] As of early 2006 its website has disappeared too. With Bate in the United States, Julian Morris has since become the executive director of the IPN. He remains a member of the Academic Advisory Council of the Institute of Economic Affairs.[38]

In their pro-corporate and anti-environmental fight, Bate and Morris have also networked with ex-*Living Marxism* and pro-libertarian activists centred around the organisation Spiked and the Institute of Ideas. Their collaboration began in the late 1990s with two key *LM* activists, Frank Furedi and Bill Durodie, writing for ESEF and Bate writing for *Living Marxism*.

Bate wrote for Spiked Online on such topics as DDT, genetically modified organisms[39] and depleted uranium. The latter article is co-written with Professor Zbigniew Jaworowski,[40] who writes for *21st Century Science and Technology*, the magazine of conspiracy theorist Lyndon Larouche, a scientist who believes that 'The Ice Age is Coming'.[41]

Julian Morris first spoke at a Spiked conference in May 2002.[42] In January 2003, Morris debated the benefits of recycling on Spiked.[43] Two months later, in March 2003, Spiked held a conference on 'GM food labelling', co-hosted with the global PR company Hill & Knowlton and the IPN. Pro-GM speakers included Gregory Conko, the director of food safety policy at the Competitive Enterprise Institute and co-founder of the avidly pro-biotech Agbioview, and Tony Gilland, formerly of *Living Marxism* and now the science and society director at the Institute of Ideas.[44]

In May 2003 Spiked, Tech Central Station and the Royal Institution held a conference on risk, called 'Panic Attack'. It was co-sponsored by the IPN, the Social Issues Research Centre and Mobile Operators Association, amongst others. The conference fitted into the strategy of the IPN to undermine the 'precautionary principle' and show that society is becoming too risk averse. The afternoon session, titled 'The Heated Debate', included Bjørn Lomborg, the author of *The Skeptical Environmentalist* and darling of the anti-environmental movement, as well as Sallie Baliunas, the enviro-sci host at Tech Central Station, who is one of the world's leading climate sceptic scientists. On the following session on tobacco was Todd Seavey from the Wise Use group in the United States, the American Council on Science and Health, and Roger Bate, at that stage still at the IPN.[45]

That same month, May 2003, saw the Stockholm Network – a network of right-wing think tanks in Europe – hosting a conference in Geneva called 'European Barriers to Free Trade'. Julian Morris, Martin Livermore (Scientific Alliance Advisory Board and IPN fellow) and Bill Durodie (ex-*LM* and Scientific Alliance Advisory Board) all spoke, along with Prasanna Srinivasan, a fellow of the Liberty Institute, and

Stephen Pollard, senior fellow at the Centre for the New Europe in Brussels.[46]

A new strand in the assault on progressive environmental policies was seen in 2004, when the IPN participated in a debate on 'Rise and Influence of NGOs on European Economic/Regulation Policy', sponsored by the European Enterprise Institute (EEI) in Brussels.[47] Julian Morris spoke on 'NGO Accountability'. Interestingly, the director of research at the EEI is Christopher C. Horner, the counsel of the Cooler Heads Coalition at the Competitive Enterprise Institute (CEI). Cooler Heads is a coalition of right-wing and Wise Use groups determined to scupper any action on climate change.[48] The CEI has received over $2 million from Exxon since 1998.[49]

Another person with a connection to the CEI is Kendra Okonski, who is also mentioned in the 2001 trustees' minutes and is the IPN's Sustainable Development Programme director. Prior to 2001 she worked as a research assistant at the CEI in Washington.[50] Okonski has a history of counter-websites and counter-protests against progressive and environmental organisations (see Chapter 7). Okonski still remains the contact for the 'Sustainable Development Network', another guise of the IPN.[51]

The websites that are mentioned in the December 2001 trustees meeting are those of organisations that are 'partners' of the IPN. The IPN recently acknowledged that it 'supports like-minded individuals and groups around the world with websites, small grants and advice'.[52] Websites registered to Okonski include the Institute of Public Policy Analysis in Nigeria, the Inter Region Economic Network in Kenya,[53] the Liberty Institute in India[54] and the Alternate Solutions Institute in Pakistan.[55] The fact that a London NGO is assisting them might be seen as slightly ironic, since some of these groups pride themselves as Third World organisations fighting environmental groups which they consider to be modern-day imperialists too.

A QUICK OVERVIEW OF IPN CAMPAIGNS

Taking a lead from Okonski's strategy for counter-protesting, the IPN has organised counter-demonstrations and counter-websites for a number of major recent international conferences or events. Part of its strategy for these key conferences has also been to launch books on related issues; these books try to undermine the work of UN institutions or government bodies working on environmental problems, exactly as the IPN would do on climate change in

2004. As with the *Guardian* story undermining the Arctic Climate Impact Assessment, many of the links to a First World right-wing organisation are concealed or well hidden. What follows is a brief overview of some of the campaigns and connections of the IPN and other sympathetic organisations.

Africa Fighting Malaria and Campaign for Fighting Diseases

When Roger Bate was still working at the IPN, he promoted the interests of the chemical industry by advocating the continuing use of the controversial chemical DDT, a pesticide developed to counter malaria. A highly toxic chemical, designated a persistent organic pollutant (POP), DDT was the subject of Rachel Carson's seminal book, *Silent Spring*, published in the 1960s, which warned that it caused cancer and was decimating bird populations. The book is credited with giving birth to the environmental movement. It also led to the banning of the chemical in the United States and other countries in the early 1970s.[56]

Since then the chemical industry has led a rearguard action to have the chemical reinstated and once again adopted for widespread use. Bate has been part of this campaign, mainly through the organisation Africa Fighting Malaria (AFM). This was formed specifically to act as a lobbying group and website against the United Nations Programme on Persistent Organic Pollutants (POPs), held in South Africa from 4 to 9 December 2000. The Fighting Malaria website was registered on 29 October 2000, just six weeks before the UNEP conference.[57]

AFM argues that it receives no funding from the 'insecticides industry'. However, for a while much of the money for AFM came from Bate's organisation ESEF as well as from the IPN, both of which do receive corporate funding. Other funding sources that AFM admits on its website are the mining company Billiton PLC; the right-wing Earhart and Gelman Foundations; and the Marit and Hans Rausing Charitable Foundation.[58] What it does not disclose on its website is that in 2004, AFM received $30,000 from Exxon.[59]

You can also see the intertwined nature of the funding and the individuals. In 2001, both Roger Bate and Kendra Okonski were working for the Exxon-funded CEI. They co-authored a paper called *When Politics Kills: Malaria and the DDT Story*,[60] which was put on the AFM website and reworked as an article for the CEI website. Both Bate and Okonski then left the CEI, Okonski to go to the IPN and Bate to be a director of the IPN, as well as being a visiting research fellow at the AEI and a director of AFM. Bate funded the organisation through ESEF in 2002 and 2003 to the tune of £376,000 in 2002 and £352,930 in 2003.[61] The IPN also funded AFM in 2001.[62]

The organisation is fronted by Richard Tren in South Africa and Jennifer Zambone in Washington. Bate writes and speaks as a director.[63] In the run-up to the UN Meeting in 2000, AFM launched its 'Save Children From Malaria' campaign. At one stage the contact for the campaign was Kendra Okonski.[64] One of the press releases for the malaria campaign went out on 29 November 2000, the week before the UNEP meeting. The headline read: 'Sign On, Save Children's Lives from Malaria! Urges New Global Health Coalition'. One of the contacts on the press release was Christopher Klose.[65]

At the time, Klose was at John Adams and Associates, a leading PR company, whose clients include leading chemical manufacturers, the American Crop Protection Association (ACPA) and other trade associations.[66] Until earlier that year, he had spent a decade working for the ACPA, the association of pesticide manufacturers in the United States, mainly as vice-president for communications.[67] In this post, Klose developed strategic planning and crisis management strategies, directed grassroots advocacy, and developed an internet communications programme, just the kind of campaign that AFM was now running. He first dealt with ACPA as an outside adviser over the 'Alar' controversy in the late 1980s.[68]

Klose's involvement in AFM is crucial to understanding what the organisation is about. They call it a 'health advocacy group', whereas it might be argued that it is a convenient front group for the pesticide industry and right-wing activists to attack the environmental movement over their stance on DDT.

In April 2002, Kendra Okonski registered yet another domain name, www.fightingdiseases.org. The Campaign for Fighting Diseases (CFD) says it is the IPN's health campaign, but on the homepage of the CFD website the link to the IPN is not overtly apparent. The campaign was formally launched two years later, in June 2004, with remarks from the 'advisory council'. Once again the close networking is in evidence. The advisory council includes:

- Dr Amir Attaran, a scientist who works closely with Roger Bate on DDT and who is a board member of AFM;
- Professor Sir Colin Berry, from the Royal London Hospital, who is on the advisory councils of the Scientific Alliance and Sense About Science, groups that are anti-environmental and pro-GM;

- Professor William Keatinge, Queen Mary School of Medicine and Dentistry, who contributed to the IPN's spoiler report on climate published in November 2004;
- Professor Deepak Lal, Department of Economics, UCLA and co-director of the Trade and Development Unit of the IEA. He is also on the board of advisers of Liberty Institute, one of IPN's partners;
- Barun Mitra, from the Liberty Institute.[69]

A central part of CFD's work concerns malaria and the benefits of DDT. 'Central to any malaria control plan should be spraying the inside walls of residential buildings with the insecticide DDT', argues Philip Stevens, the director of Health Projects at the CFD and IPN.[70] The chemical industry could hardly have put it better.

Sustainable Development – Johannesburg, 2002

In May 2001 Okonski registered another domain name, this one called sdnetwork.net, for the Sustainable Development Network.[71] The first versions of the website appeared in July 2002, just weeks before the Johannesburg summit, with no clear mention that the SDN was linked to the IPN, apart from the fact that press releases list Kendra Okonski as press spokesperson. During the summit, the SDN and the Liberty Institute organised a 'farmer's march', which is discussed in Chapter 7, 'Biotech's Fake Persuaders'.

The Freedom to Trade Initiative – Cancun, September 2003

The IPN also set up the Freedom to Trade website seven months before the WTO meeting in Cancun in Mexico – freedomtotrade.org – although the header for this website does at least say 'IPN Freedom to Trade'. According to the website: 'The Global Freedom to Trade campaign is a coalition of NGOs who believe that freedom to trade is fundamental both for personal empowerment and development for all people in all countries.' Many of its members are in the IPN.[72]

Climate – December 2003

Between 1 and 12 December 2003, the United Nations Framework Convention on Climate Change (UN FCCC) held its ninth Conference of Parties in Milan, Italy. The main IPN counter-weapon was Kendra Okonski's book, *Adapt or Die* – which was published, with its own website,[73] in time for the conference – as well as research that supposedly showed that the majority of British consumers were against Kyoto. Once again the IPN's networking is evident in the list of contributing authors.

The foreword was by Philip Stott, a well-known British contrarian, who has worked with IPN and ESEF. Other contributors included:

- Martin Ågerup – president of the Danish Academy for Futures Studies and a fellow of the IPN;
- Indur Goklany – a visiting fellow at the American Enterprise Institute, where Roger Bate is now located;
- Martin Livermore – ex-DuPont – on the advisory board of the anti-environmental Scientific Alliance in the United Kingdom and fellow of the IPN;
- Barun S. Mitra – executive director of Liberty Institute in New Delhi, India, funded by the IPN;
- Julian Morris;
- Benny Peiser – adviser to the Scientific Alliance;
- Dr Paul Reiter – Pasteur Institute in Paris and a right-wing favourite. Reiter is also on the advisory council of the Campaign for Fighting Diseases, the IPN's health campaign;[74]
- Dominic Standish – a regular contributor to Spiked Online;[75]
- Carlo Stagnaro – a freelance journalist and IPN fellow;
- Bruce Yandle – senior associate with the right-wing PERC, Bozeman, in Montana.

What is immediately apparent about the book is the absence of climate scientists or experts on climate change. Nevertheless the IPN promoted their experts as available 'for commentary on Kyoto Protocol, COP-9 and global warming'; these included Okonski, Morris, Martin Ågerup and Margo Thorning.[76] Dr Margo Thorning is from the Exxon-funded American Council for Capital Formation as well as being managing director of its sister organisation in Brussels, the International Council for Capital Formation.[77]

In the run-up to COP-9, both Thorning and Okonski were speakers at a conference organised by the Istituto Bruno Leoni (IBL), a free-market organisation based in Turin (Italy). Other known climate-sceptic speakers included S. Fred Singer (University of Virginia), Julian Morris, and Fred Smith from the CEI, Washington.[78]

Dr Thorning's anti-climate activity goes back to the late 1990s. In 1997, Thorning attended the anti-environmental 'Wise Use' Fly-In for Freedom conference, along with another climate sceptic Dr Robert Balling. The Wise Use movement is a coalition of 'pro-use' groups in the United States, such as loggers, miners, property rights activists, off-road vehicle enthusiasts and industry associations. The 'guru' of the Wise Use movement is Ron Arnold, from the Centre for Defence of Free Enterprise (CDFE), a long-term anti-environmental advocate. Arnold's CDFE is also funded by Exxon to work on 'Global Climate Change Issues'. The Alliance for America is a Wise Use coalition that holds an annual 'fly-in' at which Wise Use groups and their sympathisers come together.[79]

At the fly-in, Thorning 'alarmed the crowd by touting statistics supporting her view that the [Kyoto] treaty would be a disaster for the economy, hurting the very people attending the Fly-In'.[80] In 1999, when three climate-sceptic senators – Sen. Frank Murkowski (R–Alaska), the energy committee chairman, Sen. Chuck Hagel (R– Nebr.), and Sen. Robert C. Byrd (D–W.Va.) – introduced an anti-Kyoto bill, Dr Thorning testified that the Kyoto agreement would hurt the US economy.[81] Two years later, Thorning defended Bush's decision to pull out of the Kyoto agreement and attacked 'Europe's hypocrisy' over the climate issue.[82]

Since then she has formed alliances with one of the leading anti-Kyoto organisations in Australia, the Institute of Public Affairs,[83] and with Dr Andrei Illarionov, President Vladimir Putin's economic adviser, who was also hostile to Kyoto before Russia ratified it;[84] and she has spoken at a conference organised by the American Enterprise Institute, along with climate sceptics Sallie Baliunas, Art Green (Exxon Mobil), James K. Glassman (Tech Central Station and AEI) and Roger Bate.[85] Both the American Enterprise Institute and Tech Central Station are also funded by Exxon.[86]

Climate – November 2004

So just as the IPN had already issued spoiler reports and books, so they issued another spoiler report that coincided with the publication of the Arctic Climate Impact Assessment. Three of the authors of Okonski's book *Adapt or Die* also wrote chapters in the IPN spoiler report: Martin Ågerup, Indur Goklany and Dr Paul Reiter.

Both Reiter and another two contributors, Prof. Nils-Axel Morner (Stockholm University) and Dr Madhav Khandekar, appeared at a briefing held by the Cooler Heads Coalition in May 2004, along with another leading climate sceptic, Patrick Michaels. The title of the talk was 'Why the alarmist view is wrong'.[87] For 'alarmist' read 'mainstream'.

These scientists are known climate sceptics, yet when the *Guardian's* science editor wrote the article, he gave more weight to their views than to the consensus of 300 scientists. He did not mention the publisher of the report, the IPN, nor the fact that they had been funded by Exxon. When challenged either to make a clarification on their website or to retract the article the *Guardian* refused. In a private email exchange, Tim Radford acknowledged that he 'did not know they were funded by Exxon when I wrote the story'.[88]

The Guardian's sister paper, the *Observer*, did report that the IPN had received funding from Exxon.[89] The article started by saying 'Climate change is "a myth", sea levels are not rising and Britain's chief scientist is "an embarrassment" for believing catastrophe is inevitable. These are the controversial views of a new London-based think-tank.'

In the *Observer* article, Julian Morris from the IPN attacked Britain's highly respected chief scientist, Sir David King, who has been outspoken about the dangers of climate change, 'David King is an embarrassment to himself and an embarrassment to his country', said Morris.[90]

The article so angered the IPN that it issued a clarification on its website: 'IPN has no affiliation with and receives no funding from any government or political party. IPN is funded by a broad range of private individuals, foundations and businesses – but is beholden to none.'[91] These were careful words: The IPN may not be affiliated to a political party but it is intertwinned with the Institute of Economic Affairs. It works closely with a whole host of other right-wing think tanks. It may be beholden to no one, but it accepts funding from Exxon and promotes a stance on climate change that Exxon would agree with.

That same month, Myron Ebell, a lobbyist from the CEI and a leading American climate sceptic, said on BBC Radio 4 that David King was an 'alarmist' with 'ridiculous views' who 'has no expertise in climate science'.[92] There is real irony in a true scientist being attacked by corporate lobbyists for knowing nothing about climate change. All it does is confuse the public and confuse the debate. But that is exactly what Exxon wants.

Denials and Delays

In January 2005, Sir David King said 'he was being followed around the world by people in the pay of vested-interest groups that want to cast doubt on the science of climate change'.[93]

Although King was talking about 'American lobbyists', the IPN's activities on climate have increasingly been criticised both in the press and by environmental groups. For example, in March 2005 the IPN was singled out by Greenpeace, Friends of the Earth, environmental columnist George Monbiot and others for being one of two lobby groups that had arisen to offer 'climate sceptics to the media'. The result of this, argued the environmentalists in a letter to the journal *Nature*, was that 'the science of climate change is under attack – an attack that is co-ordinated, well-funded and given constant play in the media. The stronger the scientific consensus on climate change becomes, the more the media suggest that the science is uncertain.'[94]

In response, the IPN argued that

[t]his is simply not true ... To the extent that we have engaged in the debate on climate change, it is because of a concern that scientifically dubious and economically illiterate claims are being used to justify policies that would undermine those institutions and thereby hinder economic development, perpetuating poverty. We believe that policies must be based on sound science and good economics.[95]

The implication that climate change is 'scientifically dubious' is one that Exxon would have been proud of.

Later that year, in December 2005, the IPN attacked an article written in the Thunderer column of *The Times* by the journalist Paul Staines which repeated the climate change 'myth' accusation. 'We have never claimed that global warming is a myth', responded Julian Morris. 'We have pointed out that many myths are perpetrated about global warming; it seems that one of these myths is that IPN thinks global warming is a myth.'

Morris continued:

Staines claims that in return for calling global warming 'a myth', IPN received $250,000 from Exxon for 'climate change outreach'. Again, this is not true. IPN has a programme on environment and sustainable development issues to which the ExxonMobil Foundation has contributed over a number of years – as it has contributed to hundreds of other causes. ExxonMobil chose to account for their funding of our programme as 'climate change outreach' but imposed no restrictions whatsoever on the way we used the funds. ExxonMobil has had no oversight of any of our projects. We would never have accepted any contribution that came with such strings.

Morris finished by categorically denying that the IPN was receiving 'ethically suspect cash' in return for promoting policies that favoured Exxon.[96]

So climate change may not be a myth, but it is certainly not something worth worrying about, according to Morris and the IPN. In September 2004, Morris had been a co-signatory to a letter published in the same newspaper, *The Times*, that said: 'There are no solid grounds for assuming ... that global warming demands immediate and far-reaching action.'[97]

If there is no need for action, there is every reason for delay. And that is exactly what Exxon wants.

Ironically, it was the *Guardian* that reported in September 2006 that, in an unprecedented step, the Royal Society had written to Exxon to demand that the company withdraw support for dozens of groups that have 'misrepresented the science of climate change by outright denial of the evidence'.[98] Those groups listed in the *Guardian* included the IPN.

NOTES

1. 'Climate Chaos: Bush's Climate of Fear', BBC *Panorama*, 1 June 2006.
2. Arctic Climate Impact Assessment website, <http://www.acia.uaf.edu/>.
3. <http://amap.no/workdocs/index.cfm?action=getfile&dirsub=%2FACIA%2Fmediakits&filename=ACIAinternationalPR%2Edoc>.
4. Arctic Climate Impact Assessment, 'New Scientific Consensus: Arctic Is Warming Rapidly, Much Larger Changes are Projected, Affecting Global Climate', press release, 8 November 2004.
5. Ibid.
6. Indigenous Peoples' Secretariat of the Arctic Council, 'Arctic Climate Assessment Proves Threat to Indigenous Peoples', press release, 8 November 2004.
7. 'Climate Change Devours Arctic Ice', *Anchorage Daily News*, 9 November 2004, <http://www.adn.com/front/story/5761865p-5695798c.html>.
8. 'Arctic Heating is Melting Ocean Ice and Affecting Species and Indigenous Cultures, Researchers', *Los Angeles Times*, 9 November 2004, p. A3, <http://www.latimes.com/news/nationworld/world/la-sci-arctic9nov09,1,4210748.story>.
9. 'Report Says Arctic Rapidly Warming', *Seattle Times*, 9 November 2004, <http://seattletimes.nwsource.com/html/nationworld/2002085775_arctic09.html>.
10. 'The Arctic Apocalypse', *Daily Mail*, 9 November 2004, p. 35.
11. Tim Radford, 'Climate Change Claims Flawed, Says Study', *Guardian*, 9 November 2004, <http://www.guardian.co.uk/uk_news/story/0,,1346489,00.html>.

12. International Policy Network, *The Impacts of Climate Change: An Appraisal for the Future* (London: International Policy Press, November 2004).
13. International Policy Network website, <http://www.policynetwork.net/main/content.php?content_id=1>.
14. Exxon Mobil, '2003 Contributions', 2004, <http://exxonmobil.com/Corporate/files/corporate/giving_report.pdf>.
15. Exxon Mobil, '2004 World Wide Contributions and Community Investments, Public Information and Policy Research', 2005, <http://www.exxonmobil.com/corporate/files/corporate/giving04_publicpolicy.pdf>.
16. Exxon Mobil, 'Public Information and Policy Research: 2005 Worldwide Giving Report', 2006, <http://www.exxonmobil.com/Corporate/Files/Corporate/giving05_policy.pdf>.
17. R. Kluger, *Ashes to Ashes: America's Hundred-Year Cigarette War, the Public Health, and the Unabashed Triumph of Philip Morris* (New York: Alfred A. Knopf, 1996), p. 324, quoting C. Thompson, memo to Kloepfer, 18 October 1968.
18. 'As the World Burns', *Mother Jones*, May/June 2005, <http://www.motherjones.com/news/featurex/2005/05/world_burns.html>.
19. Arthur Shenfield, 'Liberalism and Colonialism', Libertarian Alliance, 1986, <http://www.libertarian.co.uk/lapubs/forep/forep004.pdf>.
20. Institute of Economic Affairs website, <http://www.iea.org.uk/record.jsp?type=page&ID=24>.
21. Ibid.
22. Ibid.
23. Atlas Economic Research Foundation website, Board of Directors, <http://www.atlasusa.org/aboutatlas/board_staff.php?refer=aboutatlas>; Institute of Economic Affairs website, <http://www.iea.org.uk/record.jsp?type=page&ID=25>.
24. SourceWatch website, entry on Atlas Economic Research Foundation, <http://www.sourcewatch.org/index.php?title=Atlas_Economic_Research_Foundation>.
25. International Policy Network (IPN), 'Report and Financial Statements: Period Ended 31st December 2001', 2002.
26. Ibid.
27. International Policy Network, 'Minutes of a Meeting of the Trustees at 2 North Lord Street, London, SW1P 3LB', 3 December 2001.
28. Institute of Economic Affairs website, <http://www.iea.org.uk/record.jsp?type=page&ID=24>.
29. A. Rowell, *Green Backlash: Global Subversion of the Environment Movement* (London and New York: Routledge, 1996), p. 328.
30. A. Rowell, *Don't Worry It is Safe to Eat: The True Story of GM Food, BSE and Foot and Mouth* (London: Earthscan, 2003), p. 196.
31. Robert Matthews, *Facts Versus Factions: The Use and Abuse of Subjectivity in Scientific Research* (Cambridge: European Science and Environment Forum, 1998).
32. <http://www.exxonmobil.com/corporate/files/corporate/giving04_publicpolicy.pdf>.
33. <http://www.aei.org/scholars/scholarID.76,filter.all/scholar.asp>.

34. Companies House documents examined by the author. On the American Enterprise Institute website, Bate maintains that he was a director of the European Science and Environment Forum from 1995 to 2001.
35. ESEF, 'Notes to the Accounts for the Year Ended 31st March 2002', 2002; ESEF, 'Notes to the Accounts for the Year Ended 31st March 2003', 2003.
36. ESEF, *Register for Striking Off*, signed at Companies House, 30 November 2004.
37. Charity Commission website, listing for ESEF, accessed July 2006.
38. Julian Morris website, redirected to the IPN website, <http://www.julianmorris.com/>.
39. Roger Bate and Richard Tren, 'Let Us Spray', Spiked Online, 9 January 2003, <http://www.spiked-online.com/Articles/00000006DBCB.htm>; Roger Bate, 'Packaging Precaution', Spiked Online, 10 December 2002, <http://www.spiked-online.com/Articles/00000006DB7D.htm>; Roger Bate, 'Without DDT, Malaria Bites Back', Spiked Online, 24 April 2001, <http://www.spiked-online.com/Articles/000000005591.htm>.
40. Zbigniew Jaworowski and Roger Bate, 'Depleted Uranium: What is the Health Risk?', Spiked Online, 12 January 2001, <http://www.spiked-online.com/Articles/00000000542D.htm>.
41. Zbigniew Jaworowski 'The Ice Age is Coming! Solar Cycles, Not CO_2, Determine Climate', *21st Century Science and Technology*, Winter 2003/4, <http://www.21stcenturysciencetech.com/Articles%202004/Winter2003-4/global_warming.pdf>.
42. Spiked, 'Putting Digital Rights Management to Rights', Spiked Online website, 27 May 2002, <http://www.spiked-online.co.uk/event/2002-01.htm>.
43. Spiked Online website, <http://www.spiked-online.com/Sections/Science/Debates/Waste/>.
44. Spiked, 'GM Food Labelling: Should it Be Mandatory, and if so, What Should be Labelled?', 3 March 2003, <http://www.spiked-online.com/event/2003-01.htm>.
45. Helene Guldberg, 'Conference Report', Spiked, 9 May 2003, <http://www.spiked-online.com/panicattack/>; GM Watch website, entry on Living Marxism network, <http://www.gmwatch.org/profile1.asp?PrId=78>.
46. Stockholm Network, 'European Barriers to Free Trade', May 2003, cached at <http://web.archive.org/web/20040214224220/>, <http://www.stockholm-network.org/confs.cfm>.
47. European Enterprise Institute, 'Rise and Influence of NGOs on European Economic/Regulation Policy', 17 March 2004; cached version at <http://web.archive.org/web/20050208131517/www.policynetwork.net/events.php?StartRow2=11>.
48. European Enterprise Institute website, executive, <http://www.european-enterprise.org/items/executive/>.
49. Exxon Secrets website, <http://www.exxonsecrets.org/html/orgfactsheet.php?id=2>.
50. GM Watch website, profile of Kendra Okonski, <http://www.gmwatch.org/profile1.asp?PrId=169>.
51. Sustainable Development Network website, <http://sdnetwork.net>.

52. International Policy Network website, 'About the International Policy Network', <http://www.policynetwork.net/main/content.php?content_id=1>.
53. Network Solutions website, <http://www.networksolutions.com/en_US/whois/results.jhtml;jsessionid=D2WGTX5YMGLJQCWMEAPSFFA?whoi stoken=14&_requestid=710443>.
54. Network Solutions website, <http://www.networksolutions.com/en_US/whois/results.jhtml;jsessionid=D2WGTX5YMGLJQCWMEAPSFFA?whoi stoken=15&_requestid=710496>.
55. Network Solutions website, <http://www.networksolutions.com/en_US/whois/results.jhtml;jsessionid=D2WGTX5YMGLJQCWMEAPSFFA?whoi stoken=16&_requestid=710538>.
56. US Environmental Protection Agency, 'DDT Ban Takes Effect', 31 December 1972, <http://www.epa.gov/history/topics/ddt/01.htm>; WWF UK, 'Glossary of Chemicals', <http://www.wwf.org.uk/chemicals/glossary.asp#pops>.
57. Network Solutions website, <http://www.networksolutions.com/en_US/whois/results.jhtml;jsessionid=WP1ESI2CIJFP2CWLEALSFEY?_requestid=2421030>.
58. Africa Fighting Malaria website, <http://www.fightingmalaria.org/about.php>.
59. Exxon Mobil, '2004 World Wide Contributions and Community Investments, Public Information and Policy Research', 2005, <http://www.exxonmobil.com/corporate/files/corporate/giving04_publicpolicy.pdf>.
60. Roger Bate and Kendra Okonski, 'When Politics Kills: Malaria and the DDT Story', 5 March 2001, <http://www.cei.org/gencon/005,01986.cfm>.
61. ESEF, 'Accounts 2002'; ESEF, 'Accounts 2003'.
62. IPN, 'Financial Statements 2001'.
63. Africa Fighting Malaria website, <http://www.fightingmalaria.org/article.php>.
64. Kabissa.org website, cahed version at <http://web.archive.org/web/20030718175814/>, <http://www.kabissa.org/websites/index.php?action=view&id=94>.
65. Save Children from Malaria Campaign, '"Sign On, Save Children's Lives from Malaria!" Urges New Global Health Coalition', 29 November 2000, <http://earthhopenetwork.net/alerts_11-00_4.htm>.
66. Ibid.; John Adams Assocs, 'O'Dwyer's PR Services Report', February 2001, p. 29; P. Fogg, 'People', National Journal, 27 May 2000.
67. See article 'Endocrine Disruptors', Why Files website, <http://whyfiles.org/045env_hormone/main7.html>; David J. Hanson, 'Pesticide Law off to Rough Start; Food Quality and Protection Act Was Passed Two Years Ago, but so far EPA Has Little to Show for its Efforts', Chemical and Engineering News 76 (39), 1998, <http://www.uark.edu/depts/napiap/newsletter/news21.html>.
68. Fogg, 'People'.
69. Campaign for Fighting Diseases, 'Campaign for Fighting Diseases Launch', 18 June 2004, <http://www.fightingdiseases.org/main/event.

php?type=1&event_id=4>; Scientific Alliance Advisory Board, <http://www.scientific-alliance.org/about_us_advisory_forum.htm>; Sense About Science Advisory Council, <http://www.senseaboutscience.org.uk/index.php/site/about/27>; Liberty Guide website, <http://www.theihs.org/libertyguide/people.php/75915.html>; Campaign for Fighting Diseases website, <http://www.fightingdiseases.org/main/content.php?content_id=8>.

70. Philip Stevens, 'WHO is Failing Africa on Malaria', *Times of Zambia*, 25 April 2004, <http://www.fightingdiseases.org/main/articles.php?articles_id=407>.

71. Network Solutions website, <http://www.networksolutions.com/en_US/whois/results.jhtml;jsessionid=DIS43UKYAILLCCWLEAKSFFA?_requestid=2162895>.

72. Freedom To Trade website, <http://freedomtotrade.org/>.

73. *Adapt or Die* website, <http://adaptordie.info/home.php>.

74. Campaign for Fighting Diseases website, <http://www.fightingdiseases.org/main/about.php?content_id=1>.

75. Institute of Ideas website, <http://www.instituteofideas.com/events/attention.html>; Tech Central Station website, biography of Standish, <http://www.techcentralstation.com/102803F.html>.

76. International Policy Network, 'Experts Available for Commentary on Kyoto Protocol, COP-9 and Global Warming', 2004, <http://www.policynetwork.net/main/press_release.php?pr_id=16>.

77. American Council for Capital Formation website, <http://www.accf.org/about/margo-thorning-bio.html>; Exxon Secrets website, <http://www.exxonsecrets.org/html/orgfactsheet.php?id=77>.

78. Istituto Bruno Leoni, 'From Greenhouse Effect to Climate Control: Scientific, Economic, and Political Aspects of Global Warming', 29 November 2003, <http://www.cei.org/pdf/3758.pdf>.

79. <http://www.exxonmobil.com/corporate/files/corporate/giving04_publicpolicy.pdf>; Rowell, *Green Backlash*, pp. 14–41.

80. <http://www.ewg.org/pub/home/clear/view/CV_Vol4_No9.html>.

81. 'Global Warming Bill Introduced in US Senate', *Oil and Gas Journal*, 3 May 1999.

82. M. Thorning, 'Kyoto: Europe's Hypocrisy', *Washington Post*, editorial, 6 April 2001.

83. The Institute of Public Affairs website lists Thorning as an 'associate', <http://www.ipa.org.au/people/bio.asp?peopleid=171>.

84. M. Thorning, 'Flawed Environmental Policy; Lieberman–McCain bill Is Wrong Approach', *Washington Times*, 29 October 2003, <http://www.stopesso.com/press/00000047.php>.

85. American Enterprise Institute, 'Return to Rio, Reexamining Climate Change Science, Economics, and Policy', 19 November 2003, <http://www.aei.org/events/filter.,eventID.669/event_detail.asp>.

86. Exxon Secrets website, <http://www.exxonsecrets.org/html/orgfactsheet.php?id=9> and <http://www.exxonsecrets.org/html/orgfactsheet.php?id=112>.

87. Cooler Heads Coalition, 'Impacts of Global Warming: Why the Alarmist View is Wrong', 3 May 2004, <http://www.globalwarming.org/article. php?uid=632>.
88. M. Armstrong, email to the author, 20 January 2005.
89. Antony Barnett and Mark Townsend, 'Greenhouse Effect "May Benefit Man"', *Observer*, 28 November 2004, <http://observer.guardian.co.uk/ international/story/0,6903,1361276,00.html>; Conal Walsh, 'Denial Lobby Turns Up the Heat', *Observer*, 6 March 2005, <http://observer. guardian.co.uk/business/story/0,6903,1431306,00.html>.
90. Barnett and Townsend, 'Greenhouse Effect "May Benefit Man"'.
91. International Policy Network, 'IPN Responds to Errors Published in The Observer on 28 November', 9 January 2005, <http://www.policynetwork. net/main/article.php?article_id=646>.
92. Steve Connor, 'Lobbyists Target Government Scientific Adviser Over Climate Change', *Independent*, 17 January 2005.
93. Steve Connor, 'Americans Are Trying to Discredit Me', *Independent*, 17 January 2005.
94. George Monbiot, Mark Lynas, George Marshall, Tony Juniper and Stephen Tindale, 'Time to Speak Up For Climate-Change Science', *Nature* 434, 31 March 2005.
95. International Policy Network, 'Time to Speak up for Climate-Change Science, 31 March 2005, <http://www.policynetwork.net/main/article. php?article_id=652>.
96. <http://www.policynetwork.net/main/article.php?article_id=719>.
97. Lord Lawson of Blaby, W. Beckerman, I. Byatt, D. Henderson, J. Morris, A. Peacock and C. Robinson, 'Political Action on Climate Change', letter to *The Times*, 22 September 2004.
98. David Adam, 'Royal Society Tells Exxon: Stop Funding Climate Change Denial', *Guardian*, 20 September 2006.

7
Biotech's Fake Persuaders

Jonathan Matthews

THE FAKE PARADE

'Carrying his placard the man in front of me was clearly one of the poorest of the poor. His shoes were not only threadbare, they were tattered, merely rags barely being held together.'[1]

So begins a graphic description of a demonstration that took place at the Earth Summit in Johannesburg in August 2002. The protesters were 'mainly poor, virtually all black, and mostly women' and they had an unpalatable message for the environmental movement: 'Surely this must have been the environmentalists' worst nightmare. Real poor people marching in the streets and ... opposing the eco-agenda of the Green Left.'[2]

And seldom can the views of the poor, in this case a few hundred demonstrators, have been paid so much attention. Articles highlighting the Johannesburg march popped up the world over, in Africa, North America, India, Australia and Israel. In Britain even *The Times* ran a commentary, under the heading, 'I do not need white NGOs to speak for me.'[3]

With the summit's passing, the Johannesburg march, far from fading from view, took on a still deeper significance. In the November issue of the journal *Nature Biotechnology*, Val Giddings, a vice-president of the Biotechnology Industry Organisation (BIO), argued in a letter to the editor that the event marked 'something new, something very big' that would make us 'look back on Johannesburg as something of a watershed event – a turning point'. For the very first time, Giddings said, 'real, live, developing-world farmers' were 'speaking for themselves' and challenging the 'empty arguments of the self-appointed individuals who have professed to speak on their behalf'. To help give them a voice, Giddings singled out the statement of one of the marchers, Chengal Reddy, leader of the Indian Farmers Federation, who said 'Indian farmers need access to new technologies and especially to biotechnologies'. Giddings also noted how a 'Bullshit Award' made from two varnished piles of cow dung was given to the

Indian environmentalist Vandana Shiva, for her role in 'advancing policies that perpetuate poverty and hunger'.[4]

But if anyone deserved the cow dung, it was the man from BIO, for almost every element of the spectacle he described had been contrived. Take, for instance, Chengal Reddy. Reddy is not a poor farmer, nor even the representative of poor farmers. Indeed, there is precious little to suggest he is even well-disposed towards the poor. The 'Indian Farmers Federation' that he leads is a lobby for big commercial farmers in Andhra Pradesh. On occasion Reddy has admitted to never having farmed in his life, but his family are a prominent right-wing political force in Andhra Pradesh – his father having coined the saying, 'There is only one thing Dalits [members of the untouchable caste] are good for, and that is being kicked.'[5]

If it seems doubtful that Reddy was in Johannesburg to help the poor speak for themselves, the identity of the protest organisers also fails to inspire confidence. Although *The Times'* headline said, 'I do not need white NGOs to speak for me', the media contact on the organisers' press release was Kendra Okonski, the daughter of a US lumber industrialist who has worked for various right-wing anti-regulatory NGOs – all funded and directed, needless to say, by 'whites'. These include the Competitive Enterprise Institute, a Washington-based 'think tank' whose multi-million dollar budget comes from major US corporations, among them BIO members Monsanto and Dow. Okonski also at one time ran the website Counterprotest.net[6] which specialised in helping right-wing lobbyists take to the streets in mimicry of popular protesters.[7]

Given this, it hardly needs saying that Giddings' 'Bullshit Award' was far from being, as he suggested, the imaginative riposte of impoverished farmers to India's most celebrated environmentalist. Rather, it was the creation of another right-wing pressure group – the Liberty Institute – based in New Delhi and well known for its fervent support of deregulation, GM crops and Big Tobacco.[8]

The Liberty Institute is part of the same network that organised the rally: the deceptively named 'Sustainable Development Network'. In London, the SDN shares offices, along with many of its key personnel – including Okonski – with the International Policy Network, a group whose Washington address just happens to be that of the Competitive Enterprise Institute (CEI).[9] The SDN is run by Julian Morris, who also claims the title of environment and technology programme director for the Institute of Economic Affairs, a think tank that has advocated, amongst other interesting ideas, that African countries be sold off to multinational corporations in the interests of 'good government'.

The involvement of the likes of Morris, Okonski and Reddy doesn't mean, of course, that no 'real poor people' were involved in the Johannesburg march. There were indeed poor people there. James MacKinnon, who reported on the summit for the Canadian magazine *Adbusters*, witnessed the march first hand and told of seeing many impoverished street traders, who seemed genuinely aggrieved with the authorities for denying them their usual trading places in the streets around the summit.[10] The flier distributed by the march organisers to recruit these people played on this grievance, and presented the march as a chance to demand, 'Freedom to trade'. The flier made no mention of 'biotechnology' or of any other issue on the 'eco-agenda of the Green Left'.[11]

For all that, there were some real farmers present. MacKinnon says he spotted some wearing anti-environmentalist T-shirts, with slogans like 'Stop Global Whining'. This aroused his curiosity, since small-scale African farmers are not normally to be found among those jeering the 'bogus science' of climate change. Yet here they were, with slogans on placards and T-shirts: 'Save the Planet from Sustainable Development', 'Say No to Eco-Imperialism', 'Greens: Stop Hurting the Poor' and 'Biotechnology for Africa'. On approaching the protesters, however, MacKinnon discovered that all of the props had been made available to the marchers by the organisers. When he tried to converse with some of the farmers about their pro-GM T-shirts, '[t]hey smiled shyly; none of them could speak or read English'.[12]

Another irresistible question is how impoverished farmers – according to Giddings,[13] there were farmers on the march from five different countries – were able to afford the journey to Johannesburg from lands as far away as the Philippines and India. Here, too, there is reason for suspicion. In late 1999 the *New York Times* reported that a street protest against genetic engineering outside an FDA public hearing in Washington was disrupted by a group of African-Americans carrying placards such as 'Biotech saves children's lives'. The *Times* learned that Monsanto's PR company, Burson-Marsteller, had paid a Baptist church from a poor neighbourhood to bus in the 'demonstrators'.[14]

The industry's fingerprints are all over Johannesburg as well. Chengal Reddy, the 'farmer' that the man from BIO singled out, has for at least a decade featured prominently in Monsanto's promotional work in India.[15] Other groups represented on the march have also been closely aligned with Monsanto's lobbying and some, like AfricaBio, have enjoyed the company's financial backing.[16] It was AfricaBio who brought Reddy to Johannesburg.[17] The reason Reddy is wheeled out at events like the World Summit on Sustainable Development is that the impression of a 'representative' voice from the developing world is a powerful propaganda tool that can be used to counter environmental justice campaigners like Shiva[18] and others who oppose the corporate takeover of agriculture.

The counter-attack takes place via a contrarian lens, one that projects the attackers' vices onto their target. Thus the problem becomes not Monsanto using questionable tactics to push its products onto a wary South, but malevolent agents of the rich world obstructing Monsanto's acceptance in a welcoming Third World. For this reason the press release for the 'Bullshit Award' accuses Shiva of being 'a mouthpiece of western eco-imperialism'. The media contact for this symbolic rejection of neocolonialism? The American, Kendra Okonski.[19] The mouthpiece denouncing an Indian environmentalist as an agent of the West is ... a Western mouthpiece.

PAINT IT BLACK

The careful framing of the messages and the actors in the rally in Johannesburg provides but one particularly gaudy spectacle in a continuing fake parade. In fact, the effort to position Monsanto's soapbox behind a black man's face has, if anything, gained momentum since the Earth Summit, as from US administration platforms to UN headquarters, from Capitol Hill to the European Parliament, we've been treated to a veritable minstrelsy of lobbying.

We can pick up the trail again amidst the Martin Luther King Day observances in New York City in January 2005. That was when the Congress of Racial Equality (CORE) invited some 700 diplomats, scientists, journalists and Gotham high-school students to come and consider the 'implications and reality' of biotechnology at UN headquarters.[20] CORE's 'World Conference' included the premiere of the film *Voices from Africa*, showcasing the results of 'CORE's fact-finding trip' to the dark continent.[21]

The film opened and closed with comments by CORE's National Chairman, Roy Innis, who explained that it was his concern about hunger in Africa that led him to go there. The film concluded with Innis saying, 'We have to do everything possible to ensure that the

African farmer has access to this new technology which potentially can do so much to improve his quality of life.' In a talk on biotechnology at the Natural History Museum in London in May 2003, the world-renowned American botanist, Dr Peter Raven, noted CORE's strong concern about the obstruction of technological advancement.

Last month, the Congress of Racial Equality (CORE), one of America's most venerable and respected civil rights groups, confronted Greenpeace at a public event and accused it of 'eco-manslaughter' through its support of international policies limiting development and the expansion of technology to the developing world's poor.[22]

CORE's national spokesman, Niger Innis, described that counter-protest as 'just the first step in bringing justice to the Third World'.[23] And so it proved. In September 2003, a year after the Johannesburg fake parade, Innis presided over a mock awards ceremony at the World Trade Organisation meeting in the Mexican resort of Cancun. The ceremony included participants carrying 'Save the Children' placards while the awards went to those Innis termed advocates of 'lethal eco-imperialism'. 'Their opposition to genetically engineered foods, pesticides and energy development', Innis explained, 'devastates families and communities and kills millions every year'. Cyril Boynes Jr., the director of international affairs for CORE, said the ceremony was important 'to draw attention to the destructive and murderous policies of these eco-terrorists, as we like to call them'.[24]

Four months later CORE organised a 'teach-in' in New York entitled, 'Eco-Imperialism: The global green movement's war on the developing world's poor'. In a press release Niger Innis said that after the teach-in 'eco-imperialism' would be a household word, adding, 'We intend to stop this callous eco-manslaughter'.[25]

CORE'S rhetoric has been shaped by PR man Paul Driessen, CORE's white senior policy adviser, who moderated two of the panels at its 'UN World Conference'. Driessen is the author of *Eco-Imperialism: Green Power – Black Death*.[26] The book, which has a foreword by Niger Innis, lays at the door of the environmental movement 'the hunger and suffering of millions of the world's poor who are denied the benefits of genetically engineered food'.[27] Driessen's book is published by the Free Enterprise Press, the publishing arm of the Center for the Defense of Free Enterprise, where Driessen is a senior fellow and which has had Dick Cheney amongst its advisers. According to a review on CDFE's website, Driessen's book helps the reader 'understand why the environmental movement is engaged in the most appalling example of genocide the world has ever known!'[28]

CDFE is led by Alan Merril Gottlieb, who describes himself as 'the premiere [sic] anti-communist, free-enterprise, laissez-faire capitalist'[29] and who has spent time in jail for tax evasion,[30] and Ron Arnold, who was once a consultant for Dow Chemical, as well as head of the Washington State chapter of the American Freedom Coalition, the political arm of the Rev. Sun Myung Moon's Unification Church (which has also shared offices with CDFE). In 1991 Arnold told the *New York Times*, 'We [CDFE] created a sector of public opinion that didn't used to exist. No one was aware that environmentalism was a problem until we came along.'[31] CDFE's previous main focus had been opposing gun controls. According to the *Times*, Gottlieb shifted the organisation's focus when he realised the fundraising potential of opposing environmentalism: 'For us, the environmental movement has become the perfect bogeyman.'

The night before CORE's UN biotech conference, an annual Martin Luther King Day event, the organisation hosted a reception at the New York Hilton to honour, amongst others, Karl Rove – the Bush election strategist widely credited with having overseen black voter disenfranchisment in Florida and Ohio. This might seem a curious way of marking the MLK holiday, particularly for an organisation that features on its website images of murdered freedom riders killed during the drive for black voter registration in the Civil Rights Summer of 1964. Recently, however, those images were joined by Monsanto's logo. The organisation styled Monsanto, which also sponsored 'Voices from Africa', 'CORE's corporate partner'.[32]

CORE took its 'first step in bringing justice to the Third World' on 8 May 2003.[33] Just under a fortnight later, George W. Bush accused Europe of undercutting efforts to feed starving Africans by blocking genetically modified crops because of 'unfounded, unscientific fears'. Bush also called on European governments to 'join – not hinder – the great cause of ending hunger in Africa'.[34] The following day, the Bush administration announced plans to sue the European Union at the World Trade Organisation unless it opened up its markets to American GM products.

The WTO case was filed by the United States in the name of Africa, although Egypt – the only African country which could be persuaded to sign up in support – promptly disassociated itself. Egypt's defection prompted American retaliation: the United States withdrew from planned bilateral trade talks. But at the press conference at which the WTO case was announced, the US Trade Representative, Robert B. Zoellick, introduced a number of people of colour to express their support. One was a South African farmer, T.J. Buthelezi, who is exceptionally well travelled. In the last couple of years Buthelezi has been brought not just to Washington, but to Brussels, Pretoria, St Louis, Philadelphia, Bonn and London for GM promotionals. He was also at the Earth Summit in Johannesburg, where he took part in the fake parade.

Unlike Chengal Reddy, Buthelezi is a real farmer – just not the kind of farmer he is made out to be. Buthelezi is exhibited as a 'small farmer' leading a 'hand-to-mouth existence', or a 'small farmer struggling just at the subsistence level', as Andrew Natsios, the head of USAID, put it when introducing him to US congressmen.[35] But with two wives and more than 66 acres, Buthelezi is one of the largest farmers in his area. Aaron deGrassi of the Institute of Development Studies also suggests that Buthelezi's accounts of his experiences with GM (Bt[36]) cotton are suspiciously similar to Monsanto press releases. Farmers like Buthelezi, deGrassi says, 'are plucked from South Africa, wined and dined, and given scripted statements about the benefits of GM'.[37]

The 'principal orator' at Zoellick's press conference was C.S. Prakash, a biotech professor of Indian origin at Tuskegee University in Alabama. Prakash travels the world promoting GM crops on behalf of the US State Department. He also serves as the principal investigator of a USAID project 'to promote biotechnology awareness in Africa'.[38] But he is best known for his AgBioWorld campaign, under whose banner he has sent a stream of petitions and press releases in support of GM crops to international bodies and meetings, as well as to science journals and the media. AgBioWorld presents itself as a mainstream science campaign 'that has emerged from academic roots and values', but its co-founder and 'deputy president' is Greg Conko of the Competitive Enterprise Institute.[39] The CEI was among the organisers of the Cancun counter-protests. Conko was also an invited guest at Zoellick's press conference.

Conspicuous by its absence from Zoellick's guest list was the corporation that stood to gain most from the WTO action. But when it came to honouring Bush's election strategist at the New York Hilton, Monsanto was certainly no ghost at the feast. Presiding as chairman at CORE's celebratory dinner was Hugh Grant – not the actor but the CEO of Monsanto. A little black-washing at an MLK event was clearly a PR opportunity too good to pass up, particularly in light of other recent events. Only days before Grant's appearance, Monsanto had hit the headlines over a five-year bribery spree in Indonesia. The Monsanto executive in charge of Indonesia at the time this got underway had been Hugh Grant.[40]

Grant and Rove are not the only controversial invitees to CORE's annual King Day celebrations. Others have included the Austrian politician and 'yuppie fascist' Jörg Haider, and the right-wing radio host Bob Grant, who once called Martin Luther King a 'scumbag'. But CORE has itself become increasingly controversial since Roy Innis took the helm. Innis once branded opponents of racial segregation in the United States 'house niggers'[41] and he dismissed the struggle against apartheid as 'a vicarious, romantic adventure' with 'no honest base'. When asked in 1973 why CORE supported Idi Amin despite the Ugandan dictator's hatred of Jewish people and praise of Hitler, he is reported to have said, 'we have no records to prove if Hitler was a friend or an enemy of black people'.[42]

Innis has had no corresponding difficulty working out the enemy of black people in the case of biotech. At Cancun his son Niger handed out 'lethal eco-imperialism' awards to the European Union and Greenpeace. But there was another award – an 'Uncle Tom' award, presented to the Malaysia-based Pesticide Action Network Asia and the Pacific. PANAP is an organisation that works with small-scale farmers, landless labourers and indigenous people in countries throughout the region. Innis denounced PANAP for 'selling out its own people'. Their crime? Opposing pesticides and biotechnology in exchange, Innis claimed, for funding from wealthy foundations.

CORE, by contrast, supports pesticides and biotechnology in exchange for funding from its wealthy 'corporate partner'. In CORE's *Voices from Africa*, GM crops are presented as the only hope of salvation for resource-poor farmers. CORE's Paul Driessen pushed a similar line in his syndicated op-ed pieces timed to coincide with the 'UN World Conference'. Driessen informed his readers that 'these safe, delicious foods' were vital for Africa because they could 'replace staples devastated by disease – including Kenyan sweet potatoes'.[43]

Driessen didn't single out Kenyan sweet potatoes by accident. This flagship GM project has, with the help of the Monsanto-trained Kenyan scientist, Dr Florence Wambugu, garnered literally thousands of column inches of positive press. Wambugu has admitted that the project 'has no commercial value to Monsanto except as PR'.[44] And over the years Wambugu has more than repaid the company's PR investment. She has toured the globe, often in colourful traditional dress, talking up the GM sweet potato and preaching the gospel of transgenics. The BIO vice-president, Val Giddings, has said, 'I wish we could clone her.'

Wambugu doesn't underplay her PR claims. She told one newspaper that GM crops were 'the key to eradicating poverty and hunger in the Third World'.[45] In the journal *Nature* she claimed GM could take care of 'poverty', 'famine' and 'environmental degradation',[46] while in a Canadian paper she was quoted as saying GM could pull the whole 'African continent out of decades of economic and social despair'.[47]

Such claims often go largely unchallenged. Following a visit to Australia, one newspaper commentator asked,

Is it too cynical to suggest that having a black African as the face of a multinational chemical company is a spin doctor's dream? This seems to have lobotomised some journalists who have treated her views like the tablets from the Mount. Even the normally rigorous Jon Faine interviewed her in a way that was almost fawning [48]

The US magazine *Forbes* went so far as to name Wambugu one of 15 people around the globe who will 'reinvent the future', telling its readers, 'While the West debates the ethics of GM food, Florence Wambugu is using it to feed her country.' The article was headlined, 'Millions served: Florence Wambugu feeds her country with food others have the luxury to avoid'.[49]

What has given Wambugu her PR platform and her credibility has been the apparent success of sub-Saharan Africa's first GM crop – the virus-resistant sweet potato. According to the article in *Forbes* magazine, the results of trials in Kenya had proved 'astonishing'. Yields were 'double that of the regular plant' and the potatoes were more nutritious. For hungry Africa, we were told, 'Wambugu's modified sweet potato offers tangible hope'.[50]

But only a week or so before Paul Driessen jumped onto the sweet-potato bandwagon, the Kenyan journalist Gatonye Gathura had received a Kalam award for journalistic excellence for his article on the real results of the three year trials. Gathura's piece, 'GM Technology fails local potatoes', blew the whistle on the project's failure.[51] Far from dramatically outyielding the non-GM sweet potato, the exact opposite had occurred: 'during the trials non-transgenic crops used as a control yielded much more tuber compared to the transgenic'. The GM crop was also found to be susceptible to viral attack – the very thing it had been created to resist.

Far from 'serving millions' or 'reshaping the future', the industry's showcase project in Africa was just another part of the fake parade.

FAKE TERROR

The biotech industry in Britain in the late 1990s found itself faced with both public opposition and an often sceptical media. Even the support of Tony Blair proved powerless to stop UK supermarket chains from removing GM ingredients from their products, and many food manufacturers and fast-food outlets quickly followed suit. Public opposition also meant GM crops could not easily be approved for commercial cultivation, leading the government to embark on a series of lengthy crop trials as a way of deferring the decision.

'What inflicted the greatest damage on GM science', according to two prominent government supporters, 'was that the case for the defence was fronted by the biotech groups Monsanto and AstraZeneca'.[52] A series of initiatives was launched in order to create more sympathetic PR fronts for biotech. This led to the establishment of the Science Media Centre and other apparently independent organisations, such as CropGen and the Agricultural Biotechnology Council, both of which are run out of the office of the same central London PR agency.[53]

Things still looked bleak for biotech at the end of October 2003 after the publication of the government's crop trial results showed that GM crops were generally harmful to wildlife. The government's 'GM Nation?' public debate had also just ended with a majority saying they did not ever want GM crops grown in Britain. Media reports were generally downbeat – among the headlines: '5 to 1 against GM crops in biggest ever public survey',[54] 'Public still have no appetite for GM food',[55] 'British Government Seen Postponing GM Decision'[56] and 'Government prepares to back down over GM crops'.[57]

But then something happened to change the tone. A letter from 114 scientists was sent to Tony Blair, complaining about the lack of government support for GM during the public debate. Initial media reports said the letter was the work of Professor Derek Burke, but in later reports, it emerged that one of the new pro-GM lobby groups, Sense About Science, was behind it.

The letter attracted considerable media coverage. *The Times* reported, 'More than 100 leading scientists have made a once-in-a-generation appeal to Tony Blair to save British science.'[58] Questions demanding Blair's reply followed in both Houses of Parliament. In response, Blair was at pains to emphasise that he had not ruled out GM crop commercialisation in Britain.

Even before Blair's reassuring reply, one of the letter's signatories, Prof. Chris Leaver, noted the success of the strategy. He told the *Times Higher Education Supplement* that the letter had helped create 'some unease about the state of the debate and whether we have the full picture'. According to Leaver, 'The letter seems to have succeeded in shaking the creeping view – especially in government – that "we probably have to let the campaigners have this one".'[59]

The episode marked a victory for the biotech industry – and for Sense About Science. It had distracted the media and the government from arguments the industry cannot win – that GM is unpopular and risky – and it had successfully equated support for GM with support for British science.

This was all part of a carefully crafted PR campaign that was also intent on equating opposition to GM with violent extremism. That part of the campaign had kicked off a fortnight earlier. On the eve of the publication of the crop-trial results, an article appeared in *The Times* under the headline 'GM vandals force science firms to reduce research'.[60] The article, based on a Sense About Science press release, quoted the lobby group's director as saying, 'The burden of trying to organise the research community to pre-empt and protect from vandalism is potentially disastrous.'

Articles in the *Times Higher Education Supplement* and elsewhere went further, suggesting that the GM public debate had been 'hijacked' by 'activists' – an idea repeated in the coverage of the letter to Blair. They also claimed that scientists who supported GM were being subjected to a campaign of physical and mental abuse, leading some to leave the country for jobs abroad. One *Times Higher* article, headlined 'Scientists quit UK amid GM attacks',[61] named two scientists said to have suffered such intimidation. One was – again – Chris Leaver, a former consultant to GM giant Syngenta and a trustee of Sense About Science. The other was Mike Wilson, a Sense About Science advisory panelist.

Another *Times Higher* article – 'GM debate cut down by threats and abuse' – sounded a still more sinister note. It spoke of 'the increasingly violent anti-GM lobby', 'growing levels of physical and mental intimidation', 'hardcore tactics of protesters', 'intimidation by anti-GM lobbyists ... mirroring animal-rights activism', 'increasingly vicious protests', 'a baying mob of anti-GM activists' and 'a string of personal threats'.[62] It even contained a call for 'the government to intervene to protect researchers'. However, this article, like the others, failed to cite a single instance of a researcher being assaulted, or even of anything similar having occurred. The only specific threat cited of any seriousness was an alleged bomb hoax reported by Mike Wilson some five years earlier.

A month later the same tactic was used again in an article in *The Times*, by the chairman of Sense About Science, Lord Taverne. This was headlined, 'When crops burn, the truth goes up in smoke'.[63] Taverne claimed farmers and researchers were being 'terrorised' and spoke of 'anti-GM campaigners' adopting 'the tactics of animal welfare terrorists'. Again, no examples were given, other than the alleged bomb hoax in 1998.

The attempt to portray campaigners concerned about GM as violent fundamentalists is unlikely to have been a spur-of-the-moment inspiration on the part of Taverne and his team. It falls into a well-established strategy that has its origins on the other side of the Atlantic.

Ron Arnold, the executive vice-president of the Center for the Defense of Free Enterprise, has done more than anyone to promote the terrorist label as a means of marginalising and discrediting environmental campaigners. Even before he joined CDFE, Arnold had written a report entitled 'EcoTerrorism'. CDFE went on to publish his book *Ecoterror: The Violent Agenda to Save Nature*.[64] The terrorist terminology and Arnold's tactic of painting environmentalists as violent and dangerous were further promoted by the Wise Use movement, founded by Arnold and launched at a 1988 conference backed by, amongst others, DuPont, Exxon and the National Rifle Association. Arnold is clear about his Wise Use agenda: 'This is a war zone', he has said; and, 'Our goal is to destroy, to eradicate the environmental movement.'[65]

In order to encourage the British government to stand up to those opposing GM crop commercialisation, Sense About Science appear to have systematically employed Arnold's strategy by painting their opponents as violent extremists. Though such Wise Use tactics have never before gained a foothold in the United Kingdom, Wise Users did appear as environmental experts in the 1997 Channel 4 TV series *Against Nature*, which represented environmentalists as Nazis responsible for deprivation and death in the Third World.

Subsequent investigations revealed that the assistant producer of *Against Nature* and several of the key contributors had been closely involved with a magazine called *LM* (formerly *Living Marxism*). Just a few months after the series aired, *LM* ran an article by Ron Arnold in which he argued, 'the anti-technology Unabomber who terrorised the USA' took his cue from environmentalism. *LM*'s picture caption for Arnold's article said that for the Unabomber, 'environmentalism was the theory and assassination the practice'.[66]

LM's star columnist, the sociologist Frank Furedi, was a key contributor to *Against Nature*. Once a fervent Trotskyist, in more recent years Furedi and his followers have shifted to promoting an extreme libertarian agenda. They champion 'progress' by opposing all restrictions on science, technology (especially biotechnology) and business. To that end, Furedi has defended Monsanto in the pages of the *Wall Street Journal* and has responded to concerns over issues like GM by contacting the big supermarket chains and offering, for a suitable fee, to educate their customers 'about complex scientific issues'.[67]

The phone number for Sense About Science is the same as that for the 'publishing house' Global Futures. The only publication featured on the Global Futures website was by Frank Furedi.[68] Both the director of Sense About Science, Tracey Brown, and its programme manager, Ellen Raphael, studied under Furedi. Brown and Raphael also both contributed to *LM* and, following its demise, to its successors: the Institute of Ideas and Spiked Online.

Where Brown and Raphael led, others followed. When Sense About Science set up a working party to report on the problems of peer review, two of its members were also *LM* contributors. One was Tony Gilland, the science and society director at the Institute of Ideas and co-author of Furedi's letter to the supermarkets. The other was Fiona Fox, director of the Science Media Centre and sister of the director of the Institute of Ideas. Neither Fox nor Gilland has any background in science.

As well as writing for *LM*, Fox once headed an *LM*-connected front group – the Irish Freedom Movement (IFM), which won notoriety by its refusal to condemn any IRA atrocity, even where civilians were the target. An *LM* piece by Fox (writing under the name Fiona Foster) denying the Rwandan genocide[69] won her the condemnation of the Nazi-hunting Simon Wiesenthal Center. This was not the only *LM* article that sought to deny crimes against humanity. The magazine was sued out of existence after an article falsely accusing journalists working for the news broadcaster ITN of fabricating evidence of war crimes in Bosnia.[70]

There is an extraordinary irony in Lord Taverne, the chair of Sense About Science, fulminating against anti-GM campaigners for supposedly adopting the tactics of 'terrorists', when his own staff, and co-members of a working party he himself sat on, were contributors to a magazine notorious for having sought to excuse or deny acts of horrific violence.

FAKE BLOOD ON THEIR HANDS

The fake parade in the streets outside the Earth Summit in Johannesburg in 2002 was born in part out of a desperate need for a visible expression of support from people in southern Africa. The reason for this was made plain inside the conference centre when the US secretary of state, Colin Powell, publicly criticised Zambia for its rejection of the United States's GM maize.[71]

The backdrop was severe drought and crop failure across southern Africa. Unlike most other major donors who offered relief in the form of cash for the purchase of suitable grain, the United States had offered its surplus GM maize. Levy Mwanawasa, Zambia's president, rejected it, although only making his final decision on the matter after a team of Zambian scientists and economists, under Dr Wilson Mwenya of the National Science and Technology Council, had completed a fact-finding tour of laboratories and regulatory offices in South Africa, Europe and the United States. Their report concluded that studies on the safety of GM foods were inconclusive, and that the US maize should be rejected as a precautionary measure.[72]

From the start, the United States had responded forcefully. A Reuters headline put the US position starkly, 'Eat GM or starve, America tells Africa'.[73] Elsewhere an unnamed state department official was quoted as saying, 'Beggars can't be choosers.'[74] But despite warnings from the Americans that Zambia's policy risked a 'human catastrophe', alternative food supplies were found and no evidence emerged of anyone in Zambia having died as a consequence of the government's decision to seek alternatives to GM maize.

But that was not the impression given by the biotech lobby. In December 2002 Tony Hall, the US ambassador to the UN Food and Agriculture Agencies, called for African leaders who were reluctant to accept GM food aid from the United States to be tried 'for the highest crimes against humanity in the highest courts of the world'.[75]

It wasn't just resistance in Africa that the GM lobby were gunning for. In Europe Berndt Halling of the biotech industry lobby group

EuropaBio told the press that the food aid crisis provided a critical issue that could 'destroy' the credibility of the industry's critics: 'I want to know if they are going to accept responsibility for the people that will die as a result of the refusal of GM aid.'[76]

The tone had been set at the Earth Summit by Andrew Natsios, the head of USAID, who explained, 'The Bush administration is not going to sit there and let these groups kill millions of poor people in southern Africa through their ideological campaign.'[77] CORE's Paul Driessen was able to elaborate. 'Radical Greens', he claimed, 'spread rumors that the corn was poisonous, and might cause cancer, or even AIDS. So it got locked up in warehouses, while children starved.'[78]

It wasn't just environmentalists who were being lined up in the dock. Driessen wrote in the *Sun Herald* that as well as the 'environmental radicals', the European Union had been 'threatening to withdraw aid and ban agricultural exports from any countries that plant or distribute the [GM] grains'.[79] This claim was also made by US trade representative Robert Zoellick, who said the European Union had threatened Zambia with sanctions if it accepted the GM grain. The EU's trade commissioner described the claim as 'immoral'[80] while the EU's development commissioner called it a 'very negative lie', adding he'd like to offer the Americans a deal: 'The deal would be this: if the Americans would stop lying about us, we would stop telling the truth about them.'[81]

When no evidence emerged of anyone – let alone 'millions of poor people' – dying for want of GM food, there was a problem. To vilify the critics and destroy their credibility, deaths were essential. In 2004 Roger Bate, a fellow at the CEI, helpfully put a number on the supposed death toll. Bate told his readers how in Zambia aid workers had had to take 'food away from the mouths of starving children' and that 'perhaps as many as 20,000 Zambians died as a result'.[82] Bate offered no explanation as to how he had arrived at this figure.

The viral marketing of the crime has continued unabated. As recently as February 2005 former Syngenta lobbyist Willie DeGreef spoke at a US Grains Council meeting of his need to see the culprits identified: 'How did we get that far; who was responsible for whispering (those) messages to those policy makers ... That is something that I would rather sooner or later want to find out, because you're talking about literally crimes against humanity.'[83]

DeGreef's comments provided a springboard for Alex Avery of the Hudson Institute to name those that he said had the 'blood of the starvation victims' on their hands. At the top of Avery's list was

Dr Charles Benbrook, a former Executive Director of the Board on Agriculture for the US National Academy of Sciences. Benbrook's crime had been to tell the Zambian fact finding mission that there was no shortage of non-GM foods which could be offered to Zambia and that, '[t]o a large extent, this "crisis" has been manufactured (might I say, "engineered") by those looking for a new source of traction in the evolving global debate over agricultural biotechnology'. He added, 'To use the needs of Zambians to score "political points" on behalf of biotechnology strikes many as unethical and indeed shameless.'[84]

Not long after Benbrook made those remarks I was forwarded an email that had been sent to a leading environmental campaigner, demanding to know his position on Zambia. It had been sent by one 'Max Russell-Bennett', ostensibly a private citizen. Attached to the email was a press release from C.S. Prakash's AgBioWorld that implied that thousands had died in the Indian state of Orissa as a result of resistance to GM food aid. Prakash urged 'activists' not to repeat the same mistake in southern Africa. In reality, however, the deaths referred to had been due to a cyclone. No one had died for want of GM food aid. A check on the email's IP address revealed that it originated with Monsanto Belgium. An email from a fake person was seeking to push its recipient onto the horns of a fabricated dilemma.

Near the end of CORE's film *Voices from Africa*, there's a telling moment. Over the image of an African woman beating a club in the palm of her hand, someone says, 'We cannot just harshly or violently oppose this technology.' The film presents no evidence of violent opposition to genetically modified organisms in Africa, and, in truth, there has been none. But as Paul Driessen's boss at the CDFE reminds us, 'Facts don't really matter. In politics, perception is reality.'[85]

NOTES

1. J. Peron, 'Countermarch of the very poor', *Daily Dispatch*, 2 September 2002, <http://www.dispatch.co.za/2002/09/02/editoria/LP1.HTM>.
2. Ibid.
3. J. Shikwati, 'I Do Not Need White NGOs to Speak for Me', *The Times*, 3 September 2002, <http://www.africabiotech.com/news2/article.php?uid=16>.
4. V. Giddings, 'A turning point in Johannesburg?', *Nature Biotechnology* 20, 2002, p. 1081, <http://www.nature.com/nbt/journal/v20/n11/full/nbt1102-1081a.html>.
5. Profile of P. Chengal Reddy on GM Watch website, <http://www.gmwatch.org/profile1.asp?PrId=108>; and 'Mr Chengal Reddy, The Fake

Persuader?', *Praja Teerpu*, 1 September 2002, <http://members.tripod. com/~ngin/010902a.htm>.

6. <http://www.counterprotest.net/>. This link opens to a website headlined 'Bureaucrash' which 'is dedicated to fighting the increase of government control over our lives. Our international network of pro-freedom activists works to change the political ideology of our generation through creative activism. While most youth politics supports the growth of the already bloated government bureaucracy, we fight for personal freedom, free trade and limited government.' <http://bureaucrash.com/taxonomy_ menu/18/53/58>.

7. Profile of Kendra Okonski on GM Watch, <http://www.gmwatch.org/ profile1.asp?PrId=169>. See also the entry for Okonski on <http://www. spinprofiles.org>.

8. Profile of the Liberty Institute on GM Watch, <http://www.gmwatch. org/profile1.asp?PrId=156>. See also the entry for the Liberty Institute on <http://www.spinprofiles.org>.

9. Profile of the Sustainable Development Network on GM Watch, <http:// www.gmwatch.org/profile1.asp?PrId=154>; profile of the International Policy Network on <http://www.spinprofiles.org>; and Andy Rowell's chapter (Chapter 6) in the present volume.

10. J. MacKinnon, 'Astroturf uncovered in grassroots protest', *Adbusters*, 28 August 2002, <http://www.adbusters.org/breaking_news/joburg/03. html>.

11. 'Mass March to Summit: Street Hawkers Demand Freedom to Trade' at <http://web.archive.org/web/20030811071621/www.sdnetwork.net/ informals/march.htm>. See also the accompanying press release for the demonstration at <http://web.archive.org/web/20021207131153/www. sdnetwork.net/media/farmers_march.htm>.

12. MacKinnon, 'Astroturf uncovered'.

13. Giddings, 'A turning point in Johannesburg?'.

14. M. Peterson, 'Monsanto Campaign Tries to Gain Support for Gene-Altered Food', *New York Times*, 8 December 1999.

15. 'Mr Chengal Reddy, The Fake Persuader?'.

16. 'AfricaBio's funders', GM Watch, <http://www.gmwatch.org/p1temp. asp?pid=41&page=1>.

17. 'Crop Biotech Update', September 2002, <http://www.biotechknowledge. com/biotech/knowcenter.nsf/264530E7E8126249862S6C2C00497E5B/ $file/Crop+Biotech+Update+6+September+2002.htm>.

18. M. Ganguly, 'Green Century: Green heroes – Vandana Shiva', *Time Magazine*, August 2002, <http://www.time.com/time/2002/greencentury/ encontents.html>.

19. '"Bullshit award for sustaining poverty" awarded today to Vandana Shiva', Liberty Institute, 28 August 2002, <http://www.libertyindia.org/events/ bullshit_award_28august2002.htm>.

20. <http://www.spinwatch.org/content/view/122/>.

21. <http://www.core-online.org/Events/world_conference/voices_video. htm>

22. P.H. Raven, 'The Environmental Challenge', 2003, <http://www. agbioworld.org/biotech-info/articles/biotech-art/envirochallenge. html>.

23. M. Morano, 'Protest Planned Against Greenpeace's "Eco-Manslaughter"', Cybercast News Service, 9 May 2003, <http://www.cnsnews.com/ ViewNation.asp?Page=%5CNation%5Carchive%5C200305%5CNAT20 030509d.html>.

24. M. Morano, 'Free Market Advocates Fight Back at WTO', Cybercast News Service, 12 September 2003, <http://www.cnsnews.com/ViewForeign-Bureaus.asp?Page=/ForeignBureaus/archive/200309/FOR20030912c. html>.

25. 'Greenpeace Co-Founder Denounces Anti-Biotech Former Colleagues', American Society of Plant Biologists, press release, 15 January 2004, <http://www.aspb.org/publicaffairs/agricultural/gpbiotech.cfm>.

26. P.K. Driessen, Eco-Imperialism: Green Power – Black Death (Kenmore, N.Y.: Merrill Press, 2003), <http://www.eco-imperialism.com/content/book_ review.php3>.

27. Excerpts from Innis's foreword can be viewed at <http://www.eco-imperialism.com/content/conts_excer.php3>.

28. A. Caruba, 'Killing Millions to "Save" the Earth', 2003, <http://www. eco-imperialism.com/content/book_reviews_caruba.php3>. This review appeared on over 25 different websites in November 2003.

29. J. Halpin and de P. Armond, 'Alan Gottlieb: The Merchant of Fear', 1994, <http://www.sweetliberty.org/mof.htm>.

30. <http://www.fair.org/index.php?page=1254>; <http://www.vpc.org/ studies/reliefone.htm>.

31. T. Eagan, 'Fund Raisers Tap Anti-Environmentalism', New York Times, 19 December 1991. See also profile of the Center for the Defense of Free Enterprise on GM Watch, <http://www.gmwatch.org/profile1. asp?PrId=248&page=C>.

32. See profile of CORE on GM Watch, <http://www.gmwatch.org/profile1. asp?PrId=174>. See also K.S. Schafer, 'DDT and Malaria: Setting the Record Straight', Magazine of Pesticide Action Network North America, Summer 2006, <http://www.panna.org/magazine/summer2006/inDepthDDT. html#_sbn3>.

33. 'CORE to Protest Greenpeace race in New Jersey', press release, 8 May 2003, <http://web.archive.org/web/20030603160526/core-online.org/ news/news.htm>.

34. BBC News, 'Bush: Africa hostage to GM fears', 22 May 2003, <http://news. bbc.co.uk/1/hi/world/americas/3050855.stm>.

35. E. Masood, 'GM crops: A continent divided', Nature 426 (6964), 2003, p. 224, <www.nature.com/nature/journal/v426/n6964/full/426224a. html>.

36. Bacillus thuringiensis (a naturally occurring soil bacterium that produces a toxin which is engineered into plants as an inbuilt pesticide).

37. J. Matthews, 'GM Crops Irrelevant for Africa', Institute of Science in Society, 2003, <http://www.i-sis.org.uk/GMCIFA.php>. See also A. deGrassi, 'Genetically Modified Crops and Sustainable Poverty Alleviation

in Sub-Saharan Africa: An Assessment of Current Evidence', Third World Network, <http://allafrica.com/sustainable/resources/00010161.html>.

38. Profile of C.S. Prakash on AgBioWorld website, <http://www.agbioworld. org/about/prakash-bio.html>.

39. <http://www.agbioworld.org/about/index.html>.

40. R. Edwards, 'Monsanto boss urged to quit Scots quango over GM bribery case', *Sunday Herald*, 9 January 2005, <http://www.sundayherald. com/47036>.

41. D.Z. Jackson, 'Now a Black Separatist in GOP's Tent?' *Boston Globe*, 27 December 2002, <http://www.commondreams.org/views02/1227-03.htm>.

42. M. Tomasky, 'The Core Issue', *New York Magazine*, 14 February 2000. The article mentions the source of this remark as A. Foster and R. Epstein, 'The New Anti-Semitism' (New York: McGraw–Hill, 1974), in which the remark is quoted on p. 186 from an interview Innis gave to Africa Report in 1973, <http://nymag.com/nymetro/news/politics/columns/ citypolitic/1918/>.

43. P. Driessen, 'Skewed Ethics on Biotechnology: Anti-biotech campaigns perpetuate poverty, malnutrition and premature death', 13 January 2005, <http://www.opinionet.com/article.php?id=2696>

44. G. Thompson, 'Genetically modified food and the WTO ruling: All that glitters ... ', *Ethical Corporation*, 4 April 2006, <http://www.ethicalcorp. com/content.asp?ContentID=4199>. See also 'Monsanto's showcase project in Africa fails', *New Scientist* 181 (2433), 7 February 2004.

45. C. Lackner, 'GM crops touted to fight poverty', *National Post*, 28 June 2003, <http://www.nationalpost.com/national/story.html?id=761D55DB-D781-4939-AA17-CF12C666A066>.

46. Profile of Florence Wambugu on GM Watch, <http://www.gmwatch. org/profile1.asp?PrId=131>.

47. Lackner, 'GM crops touted'.

48. R. McKay, 'GM science can be blinding', *Herald Sun* (Melbourne, Australia), 30 July 2003.

49. L.J. Cook, 'Millions Served', *Forbes*, 23 December 2002, <http://www. forbes.com/free_forbes/2002/1223/302.html>.

50. Ibid.

51. G. Gathura, 'GM technology fails local potatoes', *Daily Nation* (Kenya), 29 January 2004.

52. T. Hunt and S. Greenfield, 'The Appliance of Science', *Independent*, 20 November 2001, <http://ngin.tripod.com/091201a.htm>.

53. Lexington Communications. For more detail see <http://www.spinwatch. org/content/view/469/9/>.

54. J. Vidal and I. Sample, '5 to 1 against GM crops in biggest ever public survey', *Guardian*, 25 September 2003, <http://www.guardian.co.uk/ gmdebate/Story/0,2763,1049103,00.html>.

55. Five Year Freeze, 'GM Food? No Thanks?', *FYF Newsletter* 18, October 2003, p. 2, <http://www.gmfreeze.org/page.asp?id=241&iType=1087>. See also <http://www.gmwatch.org/archive2.asp?arcid=1519>.

56. J. Lovell, 'British Government Seen Postponing GM Decision', 20 October 2003, <http://www.reuters.co.uk/newsArticle.jhtml?type=scienceNews& storyID=3646507§ion=news>.

57. S. Carrell, 'Government prepares to back down over GM crops', *Independent on Sunday*, 5 October 2003.

58. D. Charter, 'Scientists test Blair and find him wanting', *The Times*, 31 October 2003, <http://www.scientific-alliance.com/news_archives/biotechnology/scientiststestblair.htm>.

59. 'Scientists await PM answer on GM', *THES*, 7 November 2003, p. 52, <http://www.gmwatch.org/profile1.asp?PrId=151>.

60. *The Times*, 16 October 2003. See <http://www.senseaboutscience.org.uk/index.php/site/project/53>.

61. S. Farrar and A. Fazackerley, 'Scientists quit UK amid GM attacks', *THES*, 17 October 2003, <http://www.thes.co.uk/search/story.aspx?story_id=2004941>.

62. A. Fazackerley, 'GM debate cut down by threats and abuse', *THES*, 24 October 2003.

63. D. Taverne, 'When crops burn, the truth goes up in smoke', *The Times*, 18 November 2003, <http://www.timesonline.co.uk/article/0,,8122-899081,00.html>. Also archived at <http://www.gmwatch.org/archive2.asp?arcid=1708>.

64. R. Arnold, *EcoTerror: The Violent Agenda to Save Nature – The World of the Unabomber* (Bellevue, Wash.: Free Enterprise Press, 1997).

65. Cited in R.M. Stapleton, 'Greed vs. green', *National Parks*, 66 (11–12), 1992, pp. 32–7.

66. *LM* Archive, stored at <http://web.archive.org/web/20000611192738/www.informinc.co.uk/LM/LM108/LM108_Unabomber.html>.

67. F. Furedi, 'Succumbing to Green Scare Tactics', *Wall Street Journal Europe* (WSJE), 23 November 1998, <http://www.organicconsumers.org/ge/monsantowall.htm>.

68. The website for Global Futures <http://www.futureproof.org> appears to have been taken down (as at November 2006). The last version of the site archived is dated 11 March 2005. This can be accessed at <http://web.archive.org/web/20050311220042/http://www.futureproof.org/>.

69. F. Foster, 'Massacring the truth in Rwanda', *Living Marxism* 85, December 1995, <http://web.archive.org/web/20000308064904/www.informinc.co.uk/LM/LM85/LM85_Rwanda.html>.

70. See G. Monbiot, 'Far Left or far Right?', *Prospect*, 1 November 1998, <http://www.monbiot.com/archives/1998/11/01/far-left-or-far-right/>.

71. See Z. Toufe, 'Let them eat cake', *Extra!* November/December 2002, at Fairness and Accuracy in Reporting website, <http://www.fair.org/index.php?page=1125>.

72. <http://www.gmwatch.org/archive2.asp?arcid=283>.

73. M. Esipisu, 'Eat GM or starve, America tells Africa', Reuters, 26 July 2002, <http://www.hartford-hwp.com/archives/45/235.html>.

74. R. Weiss, 'Starved for Food, Zimbabwe Rejects U.S. Biotech Corn', *Washington Post*, 31 July 2002, p. A12, <http://www.washingtonpost.com/ac2/wp-dyn/A23728-2002Jul30?language=printer>.

75. Reuters, 5 December 2002, archived at <http://www.mindfully.org/GE/
    GE4/Zambia-Food-Refusal-Crime5dec02.htm>. See also A. Rowell and
    B. Burton, 'Rising Rhetoric on Genetically Modified Crops', *PR Watch*
    10 (1), 1st quarter 2003, <http://www.prwatch.org/prwissues/2003Q1/
    gm.html>.
76. AgBiotech Buzz, 'Of Famine and Food Aid', *Spotlight* 2 (9), The Pew Initiative
    on Food and Biotechnology, 2 October 2002, <http://pewagbiotech.org/
    buzz/display.php3?StoryID=77>.
77. P. Martin and N. Itano, 'Greens accused of helping Africans starve',
    Washington Times, 30 August 2002, <http://washingtontimes.com/
    world/20020830-2441442.htm>.
78. Driessen, 'Skewed Ethics on Biotechnology'.
79. P. Driessen, 'Affluent Activists harm the Poor', *Sun Herald*, 14 January
    2003.
80. P. Lamy, F. Fischler, D. Byrne, C. Patten, M. Wallerstron and P. Nielson,
    'EU Doesn't Tell Africa GM Foods Are Unsafe', *Wall Street Journal*, letter
    to editor, 21 January 2003, <http://www.globalegener.dk/senestenyt/
    usaeustrid.asp>.
81. Reuters, 'EU's Nielson blasts US "lies" in GM food row', 20 January 2003,
    archived at the Institute for Trade and Agriculture Policy, <http://www
    iatp.org/tradeobservatory/headlines.ctm?refID=17943>.
82. R. Bate, 'Political Food Folly: Putting food on the negotiating table',
    National Review Online, 6 August 2004, <http://www.nationalreview.com/
    comment/bate200408060856.asp>.
83. Brownfield Network, 'Biotech Rejection a "Tragedy" Among Developing
    Countries', 7 February 2005, <http://www.monsanto.co.uk/news/
    ukshowlib.phtml?uid=8572>.
84. An exchange of email correspondence between Avery and Benbrook can
    be viewed at <http://www.gmwatch.org/archive2.asp?arcid=5030>.
85. Halpin and de Armond, 'Alan Gottlieb'.

8
Fighting Dirty Wars: Spying for the Arms Trade

Eveline Lubbers

The Campaign Against the Arms Trade (CAAT) is a well-respected Quaker- and Christian-based pacifist group, which believes in non-violent protest. In the mid 1990s the group was stepping up a campaign against the £500 million sale of British Aerospace jets to Indonesia. The campaigners protested that the aircraft would be used to crush resistance in East Timor, which was seeking independence. In September 2003, the *Sunday Times* revealed that since that time BAe had been using a private intelligence company to spy on CAAT. Evelyn Le Chêne, a woman with considerable intelligence connections, sent daily reports on activists' whereabouts to Britain's largest arms dealer. The intelligence company was called Threat Response International.

This chapter is based on a detailed analysis of these secret reports. The files show how the Campaign Against the Arms Trade was subverted by infiltrators who passed on information and manipulated the activists.

Evelyn Le Chêne was identified by the *Sunday Times* as a key player in a vast private network that gathered intelligence on the identities and confidential details of nearly 150,000 activists. This information was collated and marketed to British industrial companies. BAe was only one of her clients. It paid her for at least four years – from 1996 to 1999 – to spy on opponents of the arms trade. CAAT appears to have been her main target. Six to eight agents infiltrated the group over a period of time; there is reason to believe the spying went on until the date of the exposure in the *Sunday Times* in September 2003.[1]

Previous research into the intelligence company had been conducted by Dutch grassroots organisation Buro Jansen & Janssen.[2] I was involved in an investigation in 1998 that resulted in the exposure of an infiltrator. Adrian Franks had attracted attention when he tried to extend his connections with Dutch activist groups, such as the anti-military research collective AMOK and the environmental network Aseed. The then 39-year-old Frenchman from Equihen Plage in Normandy used several surnames, and our investigation discovered he was the owner of a private intelligence company that collected information on activists. The name of this company was Risk and Crisis Analysis, and its parent company was registered in Rochester, England.[3]

This left us with a story, but also quite a few loose ends. It was established that Franks crossed the Channel regularly, so Buro Jansen & Janssen tried to interest British activist groups in the investigation. Although CAAT and Corporate Watch, as well as other organisations (like Enaat) that Franks claimed to be affiliated with, had received warnings about him from their Dutch counterparts, none of them followed up the leads. Our resources were tight. For the Dutch activists, exposing Franks was enough. The internet was in its infancy and there was no online data relating to Risk and Crisis Analysis. Nor would it have been cheap to cross the Channel and carry on the investigation abroad – not without the help, or the stimulus, of worried grassroots groups. If only we had known how close we were ...

Five years later, in September 2003, David Connett of the *Sunday Times* found an account of the Jansen & Janssen investigation on the internet. He urgently needed confirmation that Adrian Franks, who also used the name Le Chêne, was related to Evelyn Le Chêne. Connett was investigating Threat Response International, a company which advised corporations on security threats. Evelyn Le Chêne was on the board. When she was first approached by British Aerospace to carry out surveillance work in the mid 1990s, she had been running a company named R&CA Publications from an office in an industrial estate in Rochester. This was the same company that had closed down and disappeared in 1998, shortly after the Dutch exposure of one of its directors as a spy. Franks turned out to be Evelyn's son, and was still working for her company, now called Threat Response International.

THE THREAT RESPONSE SPY FILES

Because of my earlier involvement in the case, the *Sunday Times* granted me access to the spy files. The files we examined – about 500 pages – basically consisted of printed reports to BAe, made by Evelyn Le Chêne, calling herself 'Source P'.[4]

This was a rare opportunity to investigate corporate spying and anti-activist infiltration from the inside. What follows is an analysis of the spy files, an assessment of the history and practices of both Adrian Franks and Evelyn Le Chêne and some observations on what can be learned from this episode.

Daily Reports

In late 1995, when John Major's Conservative government was deciding whether to grant licences for the Hawk contract, the intelligence reports on CAAT's activities were flowing into BAe's offices at Farnborough, Hampshire on an almost daily basis.

The accounts of meetings are pretty detailed. They describe people, their habits and their willingness to participate in CAAT. They report people not having much time to engage themselves in campaign activities and cite familiar reasons such as illness, study, family and work commitments:

A. is recovering from influenza and is not participating at all for the moment. She is still interested in doing CAAT 'things' ... However, this year she has been crying off sick or as being too tired or that she has something else to do when she is asked to participate in meetings and liaisons.
B. is increasingly tied up with writing a research dissertation for a degree and since her hernia operation has not been very active. She has seldom been at home when contact has been attempted. (9 June 1997)

Le Chêne initially sent her briefings on an encrypted fax to BAe security offices on the ground floor of Lancaster House at Farnborough airfield. Later BAe set up software on her office computer so the company could access reports directly from her database. A *Sunday Times* source claimed the firm paid her £120,000 a year.[5]

Le Chêne recruited at least half a dozen agents to infiltrate CAAT's headquarters at Finsbury Park, north London, and a number of regional offices. During the four-year infiltration covered by these records, Le Chêne submitted thousands of pages of reports to BAe, which kept the company fully briefed on CAAT's meetings, demonstrations and political contacts.

Some of the information was gathered by spies attending CAAT meetings posing as activists. However, the files also show that Le Chêne's agents gained access to CAAT's IT system and databases. Le Chêne reported to BAe that diskettes of information from within CAAT had been acquired. One agent downloaded the entire contents of a CAAT headquarters computer, including a membership list, personal folders and details of private donations. Another striking aspect of the files is the repeated offer by one of the infiltrators to install a new computer system at CAAT's offices and members' homes.

Bank accounts were accessed, and Evelyn Le Chêne traced back anonymous donations to the bank where they were made.

A legacy has come through for Treat [Trust for Research and Education on Arms] for £4,000. The legacy money was anonymously donated through Draper, Crellings, Solicitors, Weybridge. This has gone into the Treat account which now stands at £4,000. (22 August 1997)

Desks were rifled, diaries were read and address books photocopied so information could be passed to BAe. CAAT members were often followed. One such target was Anna B., described in one report as a 'good-looking' 25-year-old, who was a key activist and networker for CAAT and student groups. The *Sunday Times* heard a tape recording of a phone conversation between Le Chêne and a senior officer in BAe group security which reveals that they discussed having Anna B. followed. Reports on Anna B. give details of her addresses, housemates, hairstyles, the contents of her diary and her alleged habit of smoking marijuana.

Lessons to Be Learned

Given the level of infiltration and surveillance of CAAT on behalf of BAe, what are the likely consequences for the activities of the organisation? Below I will try to explain how the information was used to counter and undermine CAAT's campaigning work.

Lobbying

The *Sunday Times* wrote that Le Chêne's agents were instructed to take a particular interest in connections between anti-arms trade pressure groups and the House of Commons. Meetings and correspondence with MPs of all three parties were closely monitored and advance warnings of any parliamentary events were forwarded to BAe.

According to a *Sunday Times* source, the agents collected a series of letters, many private, which were supplied to BAe. They included correspondence discussing British policy on the sale of arms to Indonesia with a number of leading Labour politicians such as David Clark, then shadow defence secretary, Jeremy Hanley, then Foreign Office minister, and Jack Straw, then home secretary.

When CAAT and two other pressure groups hired solicitors Bindman and Partners to seek a judicial review of the granting of export licences for arms companies, BAe was alerted to the contents of a letter sent by the firm to the then trade minister, Ian Lang.

BAe's security department filtered the information and passed it on to their in-house government relations teams so they could be one step ahead of the campaigners when lobbying in parliament.

Direct Action

Information on demonstrations and actions planned by CAAT was also highly prized by BAe. Often the reports detailed plans for upcoming demonstrations by activists at BAe's sites. At one point the files give precise information on how a small group planed an 'incursion' of a BAe plant. They intended to walk through the site, leaving behind some signs or traces of their action (varying from symbols of protest to the destruction of a Hawk fighter aircraft). In one case, the files outline where the group was to assemble, the route of their walk, who would be taking part and what they would bring. A map showing the planned route was attached to the report.[6]

In other cases Evelyn Le Chêne provided BAe with elaborate advice on how to deal with certain situations. In March 1996 CAAT set up a rapid response network to organise a 'die-in' outside the Houses of Parliament on the first Thursday after BAe announced the delivery of Hawk fighters to Indonesia. Le Chêne's advice was to plan the timing of the announcement carefully, counselling that the longer BAe delayed the announcement the more effective the CAAT protest would be. Le Chêne suggested that BAe announced the delivery to coincide with the parliamentary recess. That way, the effect of the 'die-in' – lying as if dead in front of the Houses of Parliament – would be minimised.[7]

By infiltrating CAAT so thoroughly, BAe was well placed to 'respond' to activists' protest tactics.

Every occasion required a different tactic. Where the activists' strategy was to have themselves arrested in order to use the resulting court case to draw more attention to their cause, Le Chêne suggested that BAe pressure the police to make as few arrests as possible.[8]

A similar pattern is evident in BAe's response to CAAT's 'snowball' strategy, whereby each direct action that resulted in arrests would lead to further and larger actions. In the ensuing court cases, the activists would argue that they were committing a crime (criminal damage) in order to prevent a greater crime (genocide) and that they were therefore not guilty. This defence had proved successful for Chris Cole in his 1993 'BAe Ploughshares' protest, and Evelyn Le Chêne was afraid that it would work for the four women activists awaiting trial for 'disarming' a Hawk fighter with hammers on 29 January 1996.[9] Le Chêne advised that the corporate response to these actions ought to be framed with reference to its effects on the longer-term protest. When two protesters went to a BAe site seeking to be arrested, the police merely confiscated their wire-cutters. They were reported to be annoyed, not least because they failed to generate publicity.

It is therefore difficult not to conclude that arresting activists does play into their hands and leads ultimately to larger protests in the future. On the other hand one does accept that to offer no counter would be unsustainable from a company point of view. Alternatives need to be discussed. (8 March 1996)

BAe also used Le Chêne's insider knowledge to manage larger protests. Demonstrations outside more than 60 UK BAe sites were thwarted by tip-offs from infiltrators, a key tactic being the ambush of trespassers who were then served injunctions preventing them from returning.

Counter-Work

CAAT's work was opposed and stymied by BAe on other levels. When Evelyn Le Chêne heard that BAe always sent CAAT its press releases immediately after sending them to the BBC, her advice was for that procedure to be stopped:

Don't send them or leave them to the last when it no longer matters. (11 June 1997)

When CAAT campaigners requested a copy of the Defence Manufacturers Association (DMA) members list, Evelyn Le Chêne was consulted by the director general of DMA. She advised him not to co-operate. In her report to BAe she comments:

My reply was that having such a comprehensive and up-to-date listing of all the defence support industries would cut down their own research time by 100% and likewise their expenditure for it by 200%. We are of the opinion that the recommendation was not heeded. (14 May 1997)

According to the *Sunday Times*, the sophistication of BAe's management of the activist threat was such that the names and addresses of activists were routinely run through the BAe computers to check if any were shareholders. In addition, the BAe switchboard was configured to flag up any calls from telephone numbers associated with the activists.

Disinformation

On several occasions Evelyn Le Chêne proposed feeding CAAT disinformation in order to cast them in a bad light. In February 1996 she referred to Greenpeace's climbdown over the Brent Spar incident (when they mistakenly overstated the damage to the environment of dumping the oil platform into the ocean):

On the question of sighting Hawks in the sky above Indonesia, we discussed an idea or two I had some weeks ago. You will recall that Greenpeace had an embarrassing climb-down recently because they cried wolf too often. It might be time now to have another think on the idea I had about discounting the Hawks in Indonesia story. (20 February 1996)

By the end of January 1997, CAAT had joined the Clean Investment Campaign, which targeted organisations owning shares in military hardware production companies. CAAT prepared a public document with the help of – amongst others – Corporate Watch. Le Chêne commented:

Interestingly, they still appear not to have all their facts correct which could be a point worth encouraging. (27 January 1997)

The strategy appears to have been to encourage CAAT to make claims (in good faith) which could later be used to discredit the campaign. It would be interesting to know what became of these suggestions, and what other disinformation operations have been put into effect. A fuller analysis of the Threat Response files may be able to shed more light on this matter.

Agent Provocateurism

Adrian Franks/Le Chêne made a habit of proposing more radical actions than other campaign members. He repeatedly tried to incite people towards using more violence than they intended (given the pacifist origins of the group, they tended to eschew violence). This was one of the reasons why he was not trusted by various people in a number of activist groups back in 1998.

The account in the files of one occasion when Franks irritated other activists with his proposals for a more radical approach showed his disappointment about the fact that there was 'no sign of any interest' in his suggestions. This 'assessment' (marked 'Addressee – eyes only') revealed he was sent there with a purpose.

As at time of writing this report there would appear to be NO sign of any action taking place at the Paris Air show against any company including your own ... The issue of doing something was raised three times. To have pressed harder would have been impolitic from a security point of view. (19 May 1997)

He knew he risked his cover by pushing the Issue, but he kept trying. One can only guess the strategy behind this. It could have been a tactic to provoke police action at a picket line and thus disturb the peaceful character of the protest. However, Franks's proposals had a disturbing influence on the 'spadework' of CAAT: people got irritated and vital coalition building, with organisations like Amnesty International, was thwarted due to an alleged lack of agreement on basic issues such as the character of direct action. In that sense, Franks was more than an infiltrator; we could call this the work of an agent provocateur.

True Spy

The most important informer working for Evelyn Le Chêne was Martin Hogbin, referred to as her 'excellent source'. Hogbin had been an active volunteer with CAAT from spring 1997 before joining the staff in November 2001. He resigned and left in October 2003, as soon as the initial internal investigation implicated him as a suspected spy.

Neither Hogbin nor Le Chêne co-operated with the investigations carried out by the CAAT Steering Committee and the information commissioner.[10]

The information commissioner confirmed that Martin Hogbin was forwarding information by email to a company with links to Le Chêne. Ironically, the Data Protection Act 1998 prevented the information commissioner from giving CAAT details of the company concerned.[11]

Research by the CAAT Steering Committee, comparing the spy files with events that Hogbin had taken part in, confirmed that he had started his surveillance work soon after he became actively involved with CAAT as a volunteer in spring 1997. A report on a trip to Farnborough, attributed to Hogbin, was dated 19 June that year. It was dated one day after the event, and it was a long and detailed report. Administering professional reports so soon in his activist career within CAAT might suggest that Hogbin was brought in as an infiltrator, as opposed to someone who was 'turned' or persuaded to pass on information secretly.

The Threat Response files cover the period between June 1995 and December 1997; no spy reports are available that document the period after that. But since it was proved that he continued to forward emails until the exposure in the *Sunday Times* in September 2003, it can be assumed that he also filed his reports detailing CAAT activities until that date.

The fact that he was one of the few paid staff campaigners meant that Hogbin had access to almost anything that passed through the office. This included not only reports, plans, correspondence and other paperwork, but also address books, contact files, computers, diskettes and banking details.

As national campaigns and events co-ordinator, Martin Hogbin was involved in much if not all campaigning against the arms trade. He was the main organiser of protests at BAe annual meetings. CAAT supporters bought token shares in BAe so that they could attend the annual meeting and publicly challenge directors on arms sales to repressive regimes. Hogbin was involved in organising protests against BAe plants and arms fairs, his work varying from mobilising to the practical preparations, such as taking part in 'recces' to explore the terrain of action or organising the transport of fellow activists to demonstrations.

Hogbin was also a key networker in the movement, in the United Kingdom and in Europe. He usually represented CAAT at the meetings of the European Network Against Arms Trade and co-ordinated the mobilising against EuroSatory in the United Kingdom. (Many ENAAT meetings in 1997 and 1998 were attended by Franks and Hogbin, both working for Evelyn Le Chêne.) Hogbin also played an important role in mobilising against the DSEi Arms Fair, considered the biggest military sales event in the United Kingdom.

At the CAAT office, Hogbin was a well-respected colleague and a popular member of the small staff. People thought they knew him well, and also knew his family and children. Hogbin, in his fifties, seemed like an open and honest person, devoted to the cause. He made no secret of his past career with the South African arms manufacturer Denel; his apparent change of views only added to his credibility.[12]

The fact that he was trusted did more than just complicate the investigations against him. Hogbin continued to come to anti-arms trade events even after he had left CAAT. The fact that the information commissioner had confirmed his links with Evelyn Le Chêne didn't stop people from other campaigns, both anti-arms trade and environmental, from working with him. In July 2005 he was reportedly still working for the Disarm DSEi campaign.[13]

REMAINING QUESTIONS

It is important that there is some understanding of the difficult and painful choices faced by the CAAT Steering Committee. Hopefully there will be a time for further research. The opportunity to investigate a case from both sides does not arise very often. There is much left to be learned and many questions remain unanswered. CAAT has started proceedings against one of the alleged spies, but what happened to the five (perhaps seven) others? Who else was identified? Did they play only minor roles within the organisation? Or have they subsequently left CAAT? If so, does that make it less important to find out where they have gone? Or is it too difficult to trace them after all these years?

It would surely be worth making a formal damage assessment and issuing a report that other groups could benefit from. How did CAAT deal with the internal frictions the exposure caused? How much damage was done, or rather, how did they find the resilience to continue their work? These questions relate to security issues that many activist groups need to deal with. How can openness be balanced against sensible caution? Do activist groups facing powerful and well-resourced opponents need to screen every volunteer and newcomer, and if so, how? How can activists avoid paralysis and live with the fact that they may be under surveillance?

It is alarming to realise how much time, effort and resources British Aerospace invested in undermining CAAT. That so many people infiltrated this relatively small network suggests that BAe was very concerned by the potential consequences of CAAT's activism.

CAAT's campaigning work posed a threat to BAe's reputation. A successful campaign could mean the loss of large orders. Dick Evans, BAe's then chief executive, received regular verbal briefings on the contents of Le Chêne's reports from Mike McGinty, an ex-Royal Air Force officer who headed security, the *Sunday Times* was told. This tells us something about the importance of the intelligence material for BAe.

Le Chêne also claimed to target other groups, such as Earth First! and Reclaim the Streets. The close connections and mixed membership of such groups meant that she acquired information on Friends of the Earth, the Green Party, the Campaign for Nuclear Disarmament, the World Development Movement and animal rights charities, to name just a few. So, how close was the surveillance of these groups? Le Chêne herself, as far back as 1996, boasted a database of 148,900 'known names' of CND members, trade unionists, activists and environmentalists. The most relevant to BAe was a 'hardcore' group of about 200 of whom she developed full biographies and profiles, including national insurance numbers and criminal records where possible. Which other organisations were offered this information? And which accepted?

Road Protests

CAAT was not the only group Threat Response spied upon. The protests against the Newbury bypass, for instance, receive more than average attention in the surveillance reports. Such events are reported in great detail, apparently to warn BAe against the danger of an involvement of the anti-defence groups with the environmental movement.

In the late 1990s the Newbury bypass became the focus of anti-roads groups, when thousands of protestors occupied woodland earmarked for destruction. The eight-and-a-half-mile bypass finally opened in 1998, after years of protests had delayed completion. The total cost of the project was £74 million, of which nearly a third, £24 million, was spent on security. Group 4 carried out work on behalf of the Highways Agency, as did construction companies such as Costain and Tarmac. Private security arrangements of this sort helped police many of Britain's most controversial road-building projects.

The *Sunday Times* heard tape-recorded conversations involving Le Chêne reveal that she regularly passed information from her network of agents to Group 4. She said she had agents posted permanently at Newbury who passed on to the company highly confidential personal information about protesters. This included accommodation addresses, vehicle registration details, National Insurance numbers, unemployment benefit details and income support information.[14]

The spy files reflect this work for Group 4. The detailed reports show that advanced warnings about the road protesters' plans had been forwarded to the police and the private security forces involved. Much to her frustration, Le Chêne's information was not used in the most adequate way – or rather, the way she thought was best:

The policing level was low for the amount of people present and the security guard reaction was insufficient. In fairness to the latter, it has to be said that there were not enough of them to reasonably expect control of the situation with even half the protesters present. In addition the company concerned lacks a background of control to such groups and it showed. For protesters, this is an ideal double situation. On the police side it was evident that they tried to make up for the lack of numbers by the use of horses – environmentalists being animal lovers. But this showed as well and when the police, on the second occasion, charged the oncoming handslinked protesters, the horses naturally bumped them and this let to an increase in tension and the rest is history. (13 January 1997)

The eviction of the protesters camp ended in an extremely violent confrontation with the police, now remembered as the third Battle of Newbury (the first two took place in the seventeenth century). Had the authorities listened to Le Chêne's advice, things might not have gone so far:

The numbers expected and what they would be doing and how they would do it, was known well in time and notified. It was apparently a decision on the part of the Highways Authority on how to deal with the situation that led to the low manning of police and security guards, although we are of opinion that where security guards were concerned, it was more a case of penny scrimping by cash strapped Costain. (13 January 1997)

Le Chêne claimed she had at least two people infiltrated in the Newbury bypass camp:

According to two sources at Newbury on Saturday – neither of whom knows the other – the incident that led to the arsons was the police rush with horses. This would not explain, however, the police discovery of petrol-can-type Molotovs although this latter can be made up fast anyway. (13 January 1997)

This last quote also reveals how Le Chêne assumed that the discovered Molotov cocktails might have been planted evidence.

Why a report to BAe would include such a detailed coverage of police handling of anti-road protests is not entirely clear. With anti-defence groups increasingly involved in the anti-road protest movement, Evelyn Le Chêne tried to promote herself and her knowledge of both movements.

Group 4

An unnamed Group 4 spokesman admitted buying information about protesters. He told the *Sunday Times*:

We've certainly been obtaining information about protests at our customers' sites. It is the sort of information that would be obtained in the pub about activities that may affect our customers; people or property ... We were getting information about where protesters would be and what times in advance. We would have paid for that information.[15]

On the board of Threat Response from the very beginning was Barrie Gane,[16] who also worked for Group 4, Britain's largest security firm, whose clients range from the prison service to the royal family and the government, and which advertises its ability to guard its customers against espionage, sabotage and subversion.[17] Barrie Gane is a former deputy head of MI6, tipped to succeed Sir Colin McColl. However, he decided to take early retirement from the service during a rationalisation in 1993, and to open up his knowledge and network for private intelligence companies. Corporate Watch described Barrie Gane as one of the most important former intelligence men now working for the private branch of the business. At the time *The Times* concluded that the appointment of Mr Gane signalled an upgrading of its international operation. 'Mr Gane can bring the company knowledge of international terrorism, commercial espionage and risk assessment.'[18]

Was Group 4 the only party involved in the Newbury bypass buying information from Threat Response International? In her reports, Evelyn Le Chêne claimed that the police were well informed about the numbers of activists and their plans, and that she had agents posted permanently in Newbury.

Many environmental campaigners had long suspected that they were the subjects of spying operations.

The Highways Agency explained in the *Sunday Times* that the government had funded security operations around road-building sites, but that this was the responsibility of the contractors involved. 'Clearly we worked closely with the police and the contractors to ensure that this was carried out in a lawful way', a spokesman told the paper in 2003.[19]

The Transport Department, working on orders from Treasury solicitors, spent more than £700,000 in the early 1990s employing the Southampton-based detective agency Bray's to help them identify protesters. Private detectives were seen filming people and noting down public conversations. 'Despite this, campaigners believed this type of surveillance alone could not account for some of the information contained in the dossiers issued by the department to support legal injunctions against them.'[20]

In 2002, reporter Peter Taylor made a series of documentaries called *True Spies*. In one of these he revealed how a hired spy stopped the Newbury protest. On television, Sir Charles Pollard, then chief constable of Thames Valley Police, explained why Newbury was a line in the sand. The protesters could not be allowed to win once the government had approved the building of the bypass the previous year. 'The ones who were planning and tried to carry out seriously illegal acts are very subversive in a sense of subversive to democracy', he says.[21] On the BBC website summarising the documentary, Peter Taylor also wrote: 'Special Branch resorted to their usual methods of gaining information on the opposition's plans. They recruited informers and paid them anything from £25 to larger sums of money – even up to £1,000 a week.'

Such sums may seem excessive, but they're a drop in the ocean compared to the cost of policing such a protest. A piece of vital intelligence might, for example, save tens of thousands of pounds. Despite this, with stalemate prevailing and costs still rising, Thames Valley took the unprecedented step of recruiting an agent outside normal procedures.

They'd heard of a particular individual who worked for a private security company and who had unique skills and a perfect pedigree for infiltrating the protesters. The police normally keep such companies at arm's length, since they're in the business of making money from the intelligence they gain.

Despite these reservations, Thames Valley decided to bite the bullet and hire the agent. The chief constable gave the go-ahead for a contract to be drawn up with the individual and the security company for which he worked, calculating that the value of his intelligence would far outweigh the cost of hiring him.

With the contract agreed, the agent's main task was to get as close as possible to the leaders and in particular to let his handlers know of the best time to take the main tunnel that was holding up the contractors' operations.[22]

Whether the company involved in this particular infiltration operation was indeed Threat Response International proved impossible to verify.

Peter Taylor went through his old notebooks and came up with three other companies involved in the road protests: 'Reliance

Security plus Brays and Pinkertons both of whom apparently ran their own agents.'[23]

A Freedom of Information request about the possible involvement of Evelyn Le Chêne with Thames Valley Police drew a negative response. Nor was it possible to 'trace or locate any specific records or documents to answer the question whether or not Thames Valley Police hired an agent to infiltrate the protest groups during the building of the Newbury bypass'.[24]

The chief constable who confirmed contracting the private agent on BBC television in 2002, Charles Pollard, now claims he can't remember any details. He is however not surprised no paper trail can be found: 'Of course at the time it was a very closely-guarded secret ... so secret in fact that the company was only referred to amongst the few people who knew about it under a codeword!'[25]

Whatever happened to the Newbury agent? 'His cover was so good and his information so accurate, that Special Branch then directed him to infiltrate the animal rights movement', Peter Taylor wrote.[26] This correlates with the interests Franks voiced at the time; but Franks was interested in everything that involved radical activism, so we cannot be sure.

CONCLUSION

The case of the Threat Response spy files reveals the need for a new cartography to map the shifting grounds of so-called corporate intelligence, as the boundaries between government surveillance and corporate intelligence have become blurred. Once a group is seen to pose a serious threat to powerful commercial or political interests, it is at risk of special operations orchestrated by its opponents, whether or not such assessments are factually based.

In the past, state intelligence programmes have tried to undermine successful campaigns or destabilise activist groups. Now private or privatised spy shops can access the same tools, sometimes with the support of state intelligence agencies. Though their goals may differ, depending on their clients' needs, corporate and state intelligence agencies often use the same methods of surveillance. Wider exposure, discussion and awareness of such tactics are necessary if public interest groups and campaigners are to protect themselves and the causes to which they are committed. The Threat Response files offer us a rare and important opportunity to open up this debate.

NOTES

1. *Sunday Times* insight team, 'How the woman at No. 27 ran spy network for an arms firm', *Sunday Times*, 28 September 2003; *Sunday Times* insight team, 'Security firm spied on road protesters', *Sunday Times*, 5 October 2003.
2. Buro Jansen & Janssen specialises in monitoring police and secret services in the Netherlands. Eveline Lubbers was one of the founders of this grassroots group, but left the bureau in 2003. She is now an editor of *Spinwatch*, <http://www.burojansen.nl> and <http://www.evel.nl>.
3. For an account of the 1998 research, see 'Part One of the Threat Response Files: Adrian Franks Le Chêne', at <http://www.spinwatch.org>.
4. We spent a day going through a mess of paperwork, seemingly not ordered in any way, but cleared of those files that could identify either the *Sunday Times*' sources or the spies within CAAT. Connet explained how he had obtained the files, and because the reports looked authentic, we agreed that this had to be a genuine case of infiltration.

   I was allowed to make copies from what seemed the most important files and this chapter and the Spinwatch dossier come from that selection. The quotes are to the letter, but obvious typos and references that would invade the privacy of CAAT activists have been omitted; names have been replaced with unrelated initials.
5. *Sunday Times*, 28 September 2003. See also <http://www.spinwatch.org/modules.php?name=Content&pa=showpage&pid=325>.
6. Report dated 11 June 1997.
7. Report dated 8 March 1996.
8. Ibid.
9. Report dated 8 March 1996. A few months later, the worst scenario possible for BAe unfolded. The Seeds of Hope Ploughshares activists were acquitted in Liverpool in July 1996, on the moral grounds mentioned. To keep the momentum going, the Liverpool Catholic Worker came into being. Activists founded a live-in community with East Timorese exiles and an extended live-out community with locals. When this initiative was at its height, 'Fossey' from Hull was brought in by Evelyn Le Chêne, to infiltrate and ultimately sabotage the project. See 'The Threat Response Spy Files' at <http://www.spinwatch.org/content/view/115/8/>.
10. The information commissioner enforces the Data Protection Act, as well as the Freedom of Information Act, and reports directly to parliament. He is entitled to ask for the help of the authorities to verify the claims made in the complaint. He can request data from telephone companies and intelligence agencies, and ask internet providers for the identities behind email accounts. See <http://www.informationcommissioner.gov.uk/>.
11. The commissioner also decided not to take any action against Hogbin for, though confidential, the information forwarded in the emails did not meet the narrow definition of 'personal data' as set out in a recent Court of Appeal decision and so was not covered under the 1998 Act. 'CAAT Steering Committee statement on spying', July 2005, <http://www.

caat.org.uk/about/spying.php>; see also <http://www.caat.org.uk/about/spying/spy-investigation-report.pdf>.

12. Conversations with activists who worked with Martin Hogbin.
13. 'Mike' (Mike Lewis, media co-ordinator for CAAT), 'Don't tar Disarm with this', in discussion with 'Terry' at Indymedia UK, 'The Enemy Within', 29 July 2005, <www4.indymedia.org.uk/en/2005/07/319686.html?c=on>, accessed 20 February 2007.
14. Sunday Times, 28 September 2003.
15. Sunday Times, 5 October 2003.
16. Information from Companies House, 2003 and 2006.
17. Barrie Gane worked for the Group 4 Securitas Head Office until the merger between Group 4 and Falck in 2000, at which point he transferred to Global Solutions Ltd, the custodial services division of Group 4 Falck. GSL was divested from the Group in 2004 and Gane continued to work for them as a consultant. Email correspondence with Paula Bateman, head of communications, Group 4 Securicor PLC, between 18 May and 7 June 2006.
18. Christopher Elliott, Richard Ford and James Lanale, 'Senior appointment boosts Group 4's international work', The Times, 26 May 1993.
19. The Department for Transport, incorporating the Highways Agency responsible for roadworks and their security in the 1990s, was not able to provide any information relating to the period before the department had been formed in May 2002. Before 2002 the Department for Transport was merged with up to two other government departments and therefore records were difficult to access, the Department explained in a first assessment of a Freedom of Information (FOI) request. Correspondence with Sheila Devine, Department for Transport, about FOI request, 29 March 2006.
20. Sunday Times, 5 October 2003.
21. Peter Taylor, True Spies reporter, 'Hired spy stopped Newbury protest', BBC Two , 6 November 2002, <http://news.bbc.co.uk/1/hi/programmes/true_spies/2405325.stm>.
22. Ibid.
23. Email exchange with Peter Taylor, 9 April 2006.
24. Letter by email from Chris Picking, police constable 2497, freedom of information officer for the Thames Valley Police, 15 May 2006, in answer to FOI request.
25. Email correspondence with Charles Pollard, 19–22 June 2006.
26. Taylor, 'Hired spy stopped Newbury protest'.

9
Manufacturing a Neoliberal Climate: Recent Reform Initiatives in Germany

Ulrich Mueller

Berlin, summer 2004: along the banks of the river Spree, close to the government district, there are deckchairs in the sand – an artificial 'beach club', a favourite among politicians and journalists. Close to the waterline a poster has been put up: 'High time for reforms', it reads. Below that in bold letters: 'Germany' – but half of the country's name is already covered by water. A message that is easy to understand: Germany is in deep water, reforms are necessary. In the context of the political debate in Germany in 2004 it is clear what kind of reforms this poster advocates: cutting back the welfare state, deregulating labour markets, and so on.

This image (see Figure 9.1) has been widely used in the German media to illustrate articles about the ongoing political debate. It has been a remarkable publicity coup for the organisation that staged the action: the Initiative Neue Soziale Marktwirtschaft (initiative for a new social market economy, henceforth INSM). The organisation is a well-funded PR campaign, one of many German 'reform initiatives' founded over the last few years to support and promote neoliberal policies. These organisations include Bürgerkonvent (Citizens' Convention), Deutschland packt's an (roughly translated as 'Germany is tackling it'), Klarheit in die Politik (Clarity into Politics) and Konvent für Deutschland (Convention for Germany). Using modern communications methods these campaigns advocate a political shift away from the welfare state. They have learned from social movements and they strive to appear like citizens organisations, though on closer inspection they rarely are. This chapter looks behind the façades of these new 'extra-parliamentary opposition' groups, examines a few of them, and discusses their strategies, the role of the media and the threats to participative democracy these initiatives represent.

Figure 9.1   High time for reforms. Photo: AP/ INSM

THE INITIATIVE NEUE SOZIALE MARKTWIRTSCHAFT

The INSM, one of the earliest of the new initiatives, was launched on 12 October 2000 on behalf of the employers' associations of the German metal and electronics industry.[1] The associations provide about €10 million per annum for the campaign. They founded the PR agency berolino.pr specifically to run the INSM. Its executive director, Dieter Rath, was for many years the chief press officer of the Federation of German Industries (BDI). Later Tasso Enzweiler, a journalist at the *Financial Times* Germany, was hired as an additional executive director. The core team consist of some seven people, who are supported by external PR and communication companies. The INSM claims that this external support amounts to about 20 people.

The campaign aims to change the political climate in Germany by promoting an 'entrepreneurial spirit'. Employer associations want to convince the German public of the benefits of neoliberal reforms. In particular, they want to deregulate labour markets, introduce student fees, cut taxes and welfare programmes and privatise social security. They coined the phrase 'new social market economy' for these policies. 'Social market economy' is a term which has very positive connotations in German politics and the concept is perceived as being one of the foundations of the federal republic. However, people have different perceptions about what this means. So the 'social market economy' sometimes appears more like a myth than a specific economic and social concept or project.

The term was coined in the 1950s by proponents of a market-based economic order for post-war Germany. Interestingly, those groups had close contact with neoliberals in other countries, including Friedrich August von Hayek and Milton Friedman. For them, a market economy was social in itself. Adding the word 'social' was mainly a discursive strategy to win over a public that at that time was sympathetic towards Keynesian or socialist ideas.[2] Only later did labour unions and social democrats really manage to put the social into the market economy by introducing better welfare programmes and more worker participation and protection. The term 'social market economy' changed its meaning over time into something like a market economy constrained and balanced by the welfare state and public regulation. The INSM refers to the original neoliberal concept and wants to reverse the later 'deformations'. However, by using this term they also manage to appear sympathetic to those who understand 'social market economy' in the sense of welfare state and social democracy.

The INSM generally tries not to be perceived as a campaign of employers' associations. For that purpose they enlisted the support of a number of Kuratoren (trustees) and Botschaftern (ambassadors), who, as credible third parties, represent the campaign to the public. A leading figure is the former head of the German federal bank, Hans Tietmeyer. The rest of the group consists mainly of economists, politicians and representatives of corporations, other business associations and think tanks.

These groups perform different functions for the organisations: the economists provide scientific backing and credibility. The politicians are door-openers to the political parties, but they also support the claim that the INSM is a non-partisan initiative. This claim is used to create the impression that the INSM is neutral and not party political. As parties are the dominant political actors in Germany, appearing politically neutral can be a simple matter of looking as if you are not aligned to one specific political party – while you are still connected to a particular interest, like the employers' associations in the case of the INSM. This image management has been undermined by the departure of politicians from the governing Social Democrat–Green coalition in 2004 after rising criticism both in public and within their parties. Now the campaign is only supported by two individuals from those parties; these individuals no longer have a political mandate and are not involved with current political decision making. And last but not least, the representatives of corporations, associations and think tanks link the organisation to important partners and target groups. For instance, the INSM has personal overlaps with the Mont Pèlerin Society (an international network of neoliberal intellectuals) and a number of neoliberal think tanks in Germany, such as the Stiftung Marktwirtschaft (Market Economy Foundation), the Friedrich-August-von-Hayek-Stiftung (Friedrich August von Hayek Foundation), the Walter Eucken-Institute in Freiburg and the Ludwig Erhard-Stiftung (Ludwig Erhard Foundation).[3]

The INSM uses the support of these organisations to call itself a 'nonpartisan reform movement of citizens, companies and associations'. This self-description – used in advertisements and publications – is clearly misleading. The campaign was founded and financed by employers' associations, and they provide the strategic objectives. The public third-party supporters have little or no function in the planning and co-ordination of the campaign. The board of trustees have apparently never actually met.[4] Overall, those trustees and ambassadors represent a pool of people that can be used for op-eds and comments in the print media as well as for talk shows and discussions on television. They are part of the media work of the campaign that will be analysed later. After rising public criticism, in 2005 the INSM founded a new supporting association (Förderverein) so that individuals could become supporters of the campaign. But they are still a campaign by and for the employers' associations. The Förderverein has no real function for the working or financing of the INSM. Its members pay a small fee – but these amounts don't compare to the several million euros the INSM gets from the employers' associations every year. The INSM also doesn't disclose how many members the new Förderverein actually has. Its main purpose is to strengthen the disputed legitimacy of the INSM.

BÜRGERKONVENT

The Bürgerkonvent (Citizens' Convention) is another new group advocating neoliberal reforms. It achieved public attention in May 2003 when it launched a massive publicity campaign, including television spots and advertisements in major newspapers. The question of financing for this publicity blitz quickly attracted media attention. The Convention refused to name the backers who had provided €6 million seed capital. After several months it published a long list of donor names, but no further details. The list didn't distinguish between the first major donors who had provided the start-up funding and those who had merely given small donations after the campaign launched.[5]

The spokesperson and public face of the Convention was Meinhard Miegel. He is the managing director of the board of the Institut für Wirtschaft und Gesellschaft (IWG, institute for economy and society) in Bonn. The IWG is a think tank, founded in 1977 by Miegel and the conservative politician Kurt Biedenkopf.[6] Its programme is mainly neoliberal. Miegel is also adviser to the Deutsches Institut für Altersvorsorge (German institute for pensions), financed by the Deutsche Bank group. The institute supports the privatisation of pension schemes – a policy which would provide major new sources of profit for private banks and insurance companies.

Executive director of the Convention was Gerd Langguth. His career is closely connected with the conservative CDU party, inter alia as member of Parliament, under-secretary of state and later as director of the Konrad Adenauer Foundation, a sort of think tank for the CDU. In 2004 he handed over the job as executive director to the publisher Thomas Grundmann. Wolf-Dieter Hasenclever was appointed as a second spokesperson. He works as an education expert for the German Liberals (FDP) parliamentary group – a party largely signed up to the neoliberal agenda.

The Convention uses an aggressive rhetoric against political parties and advocates neoliberal reforms. It believes that the state should be cut back to core functions and that private responsibility should play a bigger public role. This would mean, for example, reducing the existing public pension scheme to minimal basic payments. The Citizen's Convention is organised as a registered, non-profit association and is trying to build grassroots support. As of July 2005 there were 14 local conventions in different cities and a number of nationwide thematic working groups (www.buergerkonvent. de). Because of these local structures the Convention is the only 'reform initiative' that can truly claim to have at least some grassroots presence.

But the situation is contradictory. On the one hand, the Convention emphasises the role of (ordinary) citizens. On the other hand, many leading and founding members are closely connected to social and political elites. For them the Convention is an opportunity to extend their existing channels of influence to new forms of populist protest. With respect to target groups, the main actors (and their personal backgrounds) and the ideological orientation, the Citizen's Convention is clearly rooted in the conservative middle and upper class. Its founding can also be understood as a reaction on the part of conservative elites to the second defeat of the CDU in federal elections, in 2002.[7]

However, in 2004 the activities of the Convention and the attention it attracted cooled down. Creating local structures consumes much of its energy and time. Moreover, its finances seem to be quite limited after the initial funding was spent on the first large media campaign. The new campaign 'Beweg Dich' (Move Yourself) focuses on free ads in the media instead of paid advertising.

CAMPAIGNS AND INITIATIVES ALL OVER

Besides the INSM and the Citizen's Convention a number of other 'reform initiatives' have recently been launched. The PR campaign 'Deutschland packt's an' started in 2001. Its directors come from the German business television channel n-tv. The name refers to a famous speech of the former German president, Roman Herzog, arguing for Germany to get down to business and initiate economic and social reforms. The campaign focused on administrative deregulation and reforms in education, health and social security. Representatives of media companies, large corporations, PR agencies, some trade associations and the conservative-leaning polling organisation Institut für Demoskopie' in Allenbach supported the campaign. This consisted of advertisements and television spots offered free by publishers and broadcasters. But in the end the campaign turned out to be a flash in the pan.[8]

Another group is the Konvent für Deutschland (KfD, Convention for Germany), founded in 2003 to support constitutional reform of the German federal system. Its goal is a federal order based mainly on competition between the states (the Lander). The KfD wants to promote greater tax competition between states, and a reorganisation of federal powers so that states get more influence on some policies (like education) while federal decision making in other areas is stregthened. At present many decisions of the German parliament must be ratified by the Bundesrat, the representation of the Lander governments. This programme is not without political implications. As consultant Roland Berger, one of the supporters of the pressure group, put it: 'Given the current political system in Germany, Maggie Thatcher as German chancellor wouldn't have been able to implement any of her reforms.'[9]

Like the INSM, the KfD uses 'ambassadors', who include the former president of the Federation of German Industries and a representative of the Deutsche Bank as well as business consultants like Roland Berger and a number of senior politicians. There is some overlap with the INSM supporters. KfD originally didn't disclose its funding sources. Now you can find a list of corporations and foundations on their website, including a number of banks, and major German corporations such as RWE or TUI.[10] No amounts are given for the various funders. Some media reported that the initial financing came from the Deutsche Bank.[11] The Convention started with a publicity campaign, but later focused on lobbying the parties and members of an official commission to develop new options for the German federal system. The commission was set up by the German parliament and the Bundesrat. By the end of 2004 a first attempt to reform the federal system had failed. Most issues were already settled between the main parties, but a consensus on the issue of competencies for education policy couldn't be reached. The KfD is still pushing this agenda. Since 2005 it has tried to establish itself as a brand and moved back to a more publicity oriented strategy. In March 2005 it hired a press officer, and in October 2005 it organised a press workshop. In recent press interviews its ambassadors have declared their involvement with the KfD. This contrasts with earlier media appearances. A particularly memorable example was when two representatives from different political parties discussed federal reforms on TV without acknowledging they were both KfD supporters (see below).

Dieter Rickert, a German headhunter, attempted to launch a new foundation 'Klarheit in die Politik' (Clarity into Politics). Rickert is a management consultant and has many contacts among high-level businessmen in Germany. His aim was to collect €100 million per year from industry to finance publicity campaigns for liberalisation reforms.[12] He was on record as saying that he would consider his fledgling foundation a success if by 2006 the words 'social justice' were chosen as the worst words of the year.[13] Rickert envisaged cooperating with the INSM in running these campaigns. However, it turned out to be more difficult than expected to raise the projected money for the foundation. In August 2004, Rickert announced he was dropping Clarity into Politics, but was continuing to co-operate with the INSM and was trying to develop a new television show that mixed entertainment and free-market education for the public.[14]

All these new organisations and campaigns appear closely related, especially in terms of personnel. The same people appear as ambassadors and supporters of different initiatives. To some extent, the organisations are all singing from the same song sheet. But there is also some diversity and even tension between the organisations. Relations between the INSM and the Citizen's Convention are strained. The Convention uses a much more aggressive style and sees politicians as enemies. In contrast, the INSM's relations with politicians are much more instrumental: it supports politicians who push for neoliberal reforms. The INSM is itself part of the establishment and an instrument of influence for a strongly organised minority – a phenomenon attacked in the manifesto of the Citizen's Convention.[15] In return, Dieter Rickert is suspicious of these local conventions because they are hard to control.[16] So, even with similar goals and personnel, relations between the campaigns and organisations are not entirely harmonious. In May 2004, ten organisations founded a new umbrella organisation Aktionsgemeinschaft Deutschland (Action Group Germany). The groups involved are Aufbruch jetzt, BerlinPolis, Bürgerkonvent, Deutschland packt's an!, Für ein attraktives Deutschland (an initiative of the industry association BDI), the INSM, Klarheit in die Politik, Stiftung Liberales Netzwerk, Marke Deutschland and Projekt Neue Wege. But more than a year after the launch of the new organisation, little has happened.

STRATEGIES FOR INFLUENCING THE PUBLIC

As well as examining the different actors and their relationships and networks, a closer look at their strategies is necessary. The following analysis focuses on the strategies of the INSM as it is the most important and well funded of these new campaigns. One of the core strategies is to pretend to be citizen based rather than appearing to be an elite interest group. The ambassadors play a major role in that regard. For a long time, PR agencies have advised corporations to use credible third parties in their campaigns. This is true for industry associations, since they face a lack of credibility and trust similar to that which many corporations now experience. As well as lending credibility, these supporters act as important tools for public relations by writing comments and op-eds or participating in TV talk shows. In many cases the connections with pressure groups or industry-funded campaigns are not mentioned in the media. For example, in June 2004 the public TV channel Phoenix broadcast a discussion on the federal system in Germany. The two participants were Roland Herzog, the conservative former German president, and Klaus von Dohnanyi, a social democrat. It looked like a debate between representatives of two parties – but in reality both Herzog and Dohnanyi were members of the Convention for Germany, a significant fact not mentioned to the audience.

The INSM claims that its ambassadors also get invited by the media in their own right because of their prominence, which is probably true. Nevertheless, it is clear that the initiative actively supports their media appearances by arranging TV appearances and giving them media training before talk shows etc.[17] By strategically establishing senior politicians or business leaders as experts in certain fields, campaigns like the INSM can wield major influence on public debate and exploit the conventions of the current media system. The media look for big names and want people who already have media experience. They don't have much time to research new experts and establish the necessary contacts. So, they are happy to receive outside support in getting the right experts and quotes and tend to invite the same people over and over again once these experts have a media profile. These political celebrities and pundits are then introduced without mention of their links to the new pressure groups. By this mechanism, interest groups with enough resources can become dominant voices in the media while still maintaining the appearance of political debate.

The involvement of credible third parties also provides opportunities to contact and influence other important political and social actors. Parties are one example, the Catholic church is another. The INSM organised speeches and publications by Hans Tietmeyer targeted at a Catholic audience, in co-operation with Catholic organisations. They invited Cardinal Karl Lehmann, president of the German bishops' conference, for the first Ludwig Erhard lecture organised by the INSM in June 2002. In return Lehmann invited Tietmeyer and another INSM ambassador to participate in a group of advisers that was helping to prepare a new policy statement on the welfare state. The report 'Das Soziale neu denken' ('Rethinking the Social') was finally presented in December 2003. Its analysis rehearsed neoliberal arguments about a blockage of reforms (*Reformstau*) and the complexity of transfer payments by the welfare state. The statement was a success for neoliberals, as they could now claim support from the Catholic church for some of their policy analysis.

Unsurprisingly, these initiatives explicitly challenge political opponents such as the labour unions and those they perceive as 'traditionalists' and proponents of the status quo within political parties or amongst the public. The head of the German metalworkers' union IG Metall, Jürgen Peters, is criticised as a diehard and in November 2003 was proposed for the spoof award 'Blocker of the Year'. The 'election' of this 'Blocker of the Year' and the positive award 'Reformer of the Year' was organised by the INSM and the *Frankfurter Allgemeine Sonntagszeitung* (FAS), the Sunday edition of the conservative-leaning newspaper. Readers could vote on two pre-selected groups of nominees, the reformers and the blockers. Their votes counted for half the results. The other half was determined by the votes of a jury drawn mainly from representatives of the INSM. Readers were not made aware of these INSM connections. Jürgen Peters 'won' the blocker ballot, whereas the INSM ambassador Paul Kirchhof was chosen as reformer because of his new tax-cutting proposals. In 2004 this 'election' was held for a second time. After criticism of the previous election, FAS informed readers in 2004 that the INSM was funded by the employers' associations – but the INSM links of the jury members were again not mentioned.

This co-operation with the media is a good example of how these 'reform initiatives' try to limit public debate. The readers could vote, but only on a pre-selected set of nominees. This selection process already contained a major political statement: only proponents of market liberal policies were nominated as reformers whereas 'blockers' were people arguing for social justice or regulation by the state. This approach seeks to sideline critical voices, but allows for a limited plurality. Similar strategies can also be seen in advertising campaigns that ask celebrities for statements on a certain issue, such as what is the meaning of 'social'. These statements are then mixed with statements of INSM supporters and ambassadors. The ad campaign then looks like an open discussion even though the range of views is limited and biased towards the position of the pressure group.

THE MEDIA OFFENSIVE

The 'reform initiatives' seek to use the media in a very professional way. Their tactics include producing publications, websites and newsletters, ad campaigns and TV spots, as well as organising events and actions that target the media. In some cases they use protest forms that are more usually associated with grassroots activists. They also organise a large number of direct media partnerships. A forerunner in this regard is the INSM. It published a whole range of rankings, surveys and studies in collaboration with leading newspapers, magazines and TV channels.

In many cases the INSM's background is not explained – many media routinely reported the misleading claim that it is a 'non-partisan reform movement of citizens, companies and associations'. In some cases, the INSM is not mentioned at all, such as when the news channel n-tv ran a series about new working conditions which failed to mention the INSM's role.[18] In September 2005 it was revealed that in 2002 the INSM had also bought itself into a popular soap called *Marienhof*. The soap is aired by the public broadcasting station ARD, but its production is outsourced to an external TV production company. The INSM paid around €58,000 for the insertion of their messages directly into the storyline and dialogue of the soap.

The messages included the promotion of temporary work, the closer involvement of business in schooling and schools curricula, as well as criticisms of tax policy and public expenditure. The INSM now regrets the strategy of covertly inserting these messages and themes into the programmes,[19] but stands by its objective of trying to provide some basic economic education for viewers. However, a closer analysis demonstrates how these messages were part of a much wider public communication campaign at the time, targeting other key publications and events.[20] The INSM also admitted that in some cases it had bought advertising in exchange for editorial coverage.[21]

Another feature of their public relations is the use of stories that seem apolitical at first glance but that promote self-reliance, competition and hard work. These stories about self-employed or start-up companies are developed by two television production firms on behalf of the INSM and then offered to television channels. If interested, the channels pay for the actual production, but the research and promotion of these stories allow the INSM an opportunity to promote its views. Executive director Dieter Rath has deemed this form of messaging a success.[22]

STRATEGIC USE OF LANGUAGE

Within their media work, campaigns like the INSM strategically deploy certain terms, like '*Eigenverantwortung*' (self-reliance or responsibility) or '*Wettbewerb*' (competition), using them over and over again like a mantra. They refer to social myths when they use the terms '*soziale Marktwirtschaft*' or '*Wirtschaftswunder*'. Also terms like '*Chancengleichheit*' (equal opportunities) are important as they can be interpreted in a number of different ways and can facilitate new connections with various social groups and discourses. The INSM uses the slogan '*Chancen für alle*' (opportunitie for all), but doesn't explain what it means by equal opportunities. What conditions would be necessary for that? To what extent does the distribution of wealth or of cultural capital influence the opportunities of individuals? This is not addressed. 'Equal opportunities' is used as a substitute for (material) equality and as such is a legitimation for the uneven distribution of income and wealth.

Also, the INSM tries to redefine key terms of the left, especially the term 'social'. The aim is to reduce public support for social justice in the sense of redistribution of wealth. In advertising campaigns, cartoon competitions and publications, the INSM cultivates new interpretations of social, for example, 'those things are social that create jobs' or 'it is social not to rely on others' (meaning the welfare state).[23] Based on these notions it would be social to create good conditions for companies because this (might) create jobs. Or it would be social to reduce the welfare state. This turnaround of the term social has come a long way within some parts of the social democratic and conservative parties. It featured prominently in the conservative election platform in 2005.

INCLUDING DAILY LIVES

Media and framing terms are not the only weapons in the neoliberal communications armoury. The new initiatives also try to connect their activities with the daily lives of people and to target young people especially. The INSM runs a special website for schools that offers teaching materials on economic and social issues (appropriately framed) and another website targeting young people (www.wassollwerden.de). This website offers information and tips on career choice, qualifications, applications and job interviews. It looks like a neutral service, but it encourages its youthful users to internalise a concept of life based on competition, effort and self-reliance. That aim is also present in a joint campaign of the INSM with the music channel MTV (Germany), a private radio station and a lifestyle magazine. The campaign of summer 2004 focused on apprenticeships. The press release at the launch argued that the campaign was directed against the resignation and lack of motivation that allegedly underlie the falling number of apprenticeships, and warned that as a result German companies would have to struggle to find committed and eager apprentices.[24] The lack of apprenticeship positions was a political issue at that time in Germany. There was a huge debate over whether companies were 'free-riding', and it was suggested that companies should pay a fee to support the creation of new jobs. Industry strongly opposed this proposal. In the INSM–MTV campaign the structural problem was shifted to the young people themselves, with the suggestion that they should work harder and have greater self-discipline.

SUCCESSFUL – BUT NOT IN CHANGING GOVERNMENTS

The initiatives have been quite successful in shifting the political climate in Germany over the last few years. Their speakers and ambassadors are ever present in the media. This doesn't mean that shifts in the public and the political arena were only caused by those initiatives. Other think tanks (like the Stiftung Marktwirtschaft (Market Economy Foundation)), business organisations and experts played their role too. But these 'reform initiatives' were important in organising public support and marginalising critical voices. However, they are far from satisfied and they don't see their work as finished. Initiatives like the INSM see the labour market reforms implemented by the former red–green coalition as only a beginning.

So when it came to the general elections in 2005, their preferences for a new conservative–(neo)liberal government were clear. The employer associations of the metal and electronics industries have been among the biggest donors to the Conservative Party (CDU/CSU) in recent years – even while they publicly applauded Chancellor Schroeder for his attempts to 'reform' the labour markets. In the last weeks of the electoral battle, the INSM together with the economic journal *Wirtschaftswoche* published an analysis of the election platforms of the main parties, ranking the (neo)liberal party FDP first and the Conservatives second – way ahead of the Social Democrats and the Green Party.

The INSM also published a leaflet on seven questions about social justice. Six of the seven 'questions' defended the key policy proposals of the Conservatives. Conversely, when Conservative leader Angela Merkel presented her 'competence team' for the election, she appointed

Paul Kirchhof, one of the INSM's ambassadors and a proponent of radical tax reform, as an expert on taxes and fiscal policy.

The INSM and other organisations like the Market Economy Foundation prepared for the change in government. The day after the election, the conservative-leaning newspaper *FAZ* published a policy paper by the Market Economy Foundation on the next steps a new government should take, including deregulation of the labour market, gradual privatisation of pension schemes and the health system, and far-reaching tax reforms. In the evening, the public broadcaster ARD aired a story on welfare state reform, citing three experts who were all INSM ambassadors.

The INSM also organised an advertising campaign under the slogan 'The next steps decide'. The ad claimed that the mandate of the voters for the new government was clear: they should create more jobs and growth. 'Only subsequent market liberal reforms would lead us back to the top.' All this was obviously planned with the election in mind and was meant to influence the public debate and media reporting about the change in government, especially the adoption of market radical reforms.

However, the voters decided otherwise – there was no majority for a conservative–neoliberal coalition on 18 September, and no clear voter mandate. The election results in 2005 demonstrated that these attempts to promote neoliberal policies were not entirely successful. There remains resistance within German society against the cutting back of social safety nets. And while the regular repetition of such claims as 'The welfare state is not workable anymore', or 'There is no alternative to market liberal reforms' may have increased public acceptance of neoliberal reforms in some parts of society, for many people the acceptance was without real conviction. The value of social justice is still important to many. During the election the Social Democrats (although strongly influenced by neoliberal concepts themselves) chose to adopt an aggressive stance against more radical market-liberal reforms. Paul Kirchhof became the target of fierce attacks in the weeks before polling day. After the elections, a number of politicians argued for a stronger social policy in the light of the election results. But the reform initiatives persist and will continue to influence political debate. So there is still the need for intense discussion about the impact upon German democracy of this new group of industry- or elite-leaning initiatives, and for transparent and open public debate.

PROBLEMATIC CONSEQUENCES FOR DEMOCRACY

Campaigns and forms of protest are open to all interest groups. There is little point in blaming neoliberal and business-related groups for learning from social movements and combining their forms of protest with professional PR advice. However, there are some major problems with these campaigns and their strategies. The first is their lack of transparency and the attempt to conceal their real background, such as their funding sources or their links with private interests. Information is essential for transparency and democracy. It is therefore necessary that the interests and funding of these pressure groups are available to the public. This is even more important if such groups try to hide their interests behind claims that they pursue the general interest.

The use of manipulative methods in their public relations and the exploitation of weaknesses in the media constitute a second problem. The presentation of the 'Reformer of the Year' or 'Blocker of the Year' awards, the persistent use by media of seemingly independent commentators who are in reality ambassadors or supporters of pressure groups, and the presentation of news stories without reference to their origins are just a few examples of this worrying tendency.

The media reported virtually nothing about the background of the neoliberal initiatives. Only in late 2004 did the discussion on the INSM start to gain some momentum. A number of critical articles appeared in the media, especially after a union-based foundation published a study by a political scientist on the INSM. The INSM continues to mislead the public by claiming to be a citizen-based reform movement; they still publish studies and articles in co-operation with media and there is little awareness about the connections some senior politicians and business leaders have with these new pressure groups. The media use their material, interview INSM experts without disclosing their links, comply with their strategies – even on the public broadcasting stations.[25] Given their connections with economic and political elites, and their economic influence (on workers and unions via their management strategies) this further aggravates existing asymmetries in power between strong and weak interests. Those in need, consumers, or environmental concerns tend to be more difficult to organise since they are more general and diffuse.

These problems are exacerbated as political decisions (in Germany) are increasingly transferred to expert commissions outside the parliament, and private actors like consultancy firms or think tanks like the Bertelsmann Foundation become ever more involved in decision making. In this political context, democratic debates and processes threaten to collapse into closed-shop decision making on the one hand and public propaganda on the other hand. To revive this atrophied democracy, social movements and critical forces need to advocate a new democratisation and a strengthening of systems of social protection. A first step in opening up democratic debate would involve the disclosure of the backgrounds of neoliberal and industry-funded campaigns and a challenge to their methods and strategies.

NOTES

1. See their website at <http://www.insm.de>.
2. Cf. Ralf Ptak, *Vom Ordoliberalismus zur Sozialen Marktwirtschaft* (Opladen: Stationen des Neoliberalismus in Deutschland, 2004).
3. These links and overlaps don't mean that there is a formal co-ordination between these organisations. But they show the outline of the neoliberal network in Germany and the INSM's links to it. For more information on the neoliberal networks, their history and strategies see Dieter Plehwe, Bernhard Walpen and Gisela Neunhöffer (eds) *Neoliberal Hegemony: A global critique* (London and New York: Routledge, 2005).
4. Markus Grill, 'Revolution von oben', *Stern*, 17 December 2003, <www.stern.de/wirtschaft/unternehmen/magazin/index.html?id=517691>, last accessed 3 November 2005.
5. According to the news magazine *Stern*, Udo van Meeteren belonged to the initial backers of the Convention. Van Meeteren is a businessman from Düsseldorf and a major donor for the Conservative Party, CDU. But van Meeteren claims that he has donated only €5,000 to the Convention (ibid.).
6. Cf. Claus Leggewie, *Der Geist steht rechts: Ausflüge in die Denkfabriken der Wende* (2nd edn., Berlin: Rotbuch, 1987), pp. 10 ff.
7. Cf. Rudolf Speth, 'Der BürgerKonvent: Kampagnenprotest von oben ohne Transparenz und Bürgerbeteiligung', 2003, <http://www.boeckler.de/pdf/fo_buergerkonvent.pdf>, last accessed 3 November 2005.
8. Norbert Pötzl, 'Das Wollen der Vielen', *Der Spiegel* 22, 26 May 2003, pp. 38–9.
9. Grill, 'Revolution von oben'.
10. <http://www.konvent-fuer-deutschland.de/derVerein/Kuratorium/>, last accessed 20 February 2007.
11. Grill, 'Revolution von oben'.
12. See, for example, a paper prepared by Rickert for a conference on political and economic reforms in 2003, organised by the industry association BDI: Dieter Rickert, 'Was will die Initiative "Klarheit in die Politik"?', 22 September 2003, <http://www.rickert-online.de/presse/bdi_220903.html>, last accessed 3 November 2005.

13. *Rheinische Post*, 16 May 2003.
14. Cf. Dieter Rickert, 'Stiftung "Klarheit in die Politik": wie es weiterging!', letter of 30 August 2004, <http://www.rickert-online.de/presse/rundschr_300804.html>, last accessed 3 November 2005.
15. Bürgerkonvent, 'Manifest', 2003, Bonn, online at <www.buergerkonvent. de>.
16. Cf. Jan Rübel, 'Bürgerbewegungen fusionieren nicht', *Die Welt*, 11 July 2003.
17. Cf. Ulrich Rauhut, 'Analyse der Unternehmer-Kampagne "Initiative Neue Soziale Marktwirtschaft"', 2003, in 'Verschwiegen, Verschwunden, Verdrängt: Was nicht öffentlich wird', <www.mainzermediendisput. de>.
18. Ibid.
19. After the case became known, the INSM disclosed the scripts of these programmes to the professional journal *epd medien*, which reprinted them: 'Hautnah die Bedürfnisse einer Firma kennen lernen', *epd medien* 73, 17 September 2005, pp. 27–30.
20. Cf. an analysis by the NGO LobbyControl: 'INSM und Marienhof : Eine kritische Bewertung', <http://www.lobbycontrol.de/blog/download/insm-marienhof-bewertung.pdf>, last accessed 3 November 2005.
21. Cf. Volker Lilienthal, 'Drittmittelfernsehen: Der HR, Günter Ederer und die deutsche Wirtschaft', *epd medien* 37, 14 May 2003, <http://www. epd.de/medien/medien_index_14958.html>, last accessed 3 November 2005.
22. Dieter Rath Hillebrand in a radio transmission by DeutschlandRadio Berlin, 1 February 2004, transcript available at <http://www.dradio.de/dlr/sendungen/zeitfragen/226410/>, last accessed 3 November 2005.
23. Cf. INSM, 'Die Kampagne "Sozial ist ... "', 2003, <http://www.chancenfueralle.de/Datenpool/Sozial_ist.../Sozial_ist.html>, last accessed 3 November 2005.
24. Cf. INSM, 'MTV und Initiative Neue Soziale Marktwirtschaft machen Mut bei der Jobsuche', 2004, <http://www.chancenfueralle.de/Presse/Pressearchiv/Pressemeldungen/2004_ _Pressemeldungen/April_-_Juni_2004/MTV_Social_Campaign_9.6.2004.html>, last accessed 3 November 2005.
25. Regarding the responsibility of the media, see also Thomas Leif, 'Wer bewegt welche Ideen? Medien und Lobbyismus in Deutschland', in Ulrich Müller, Sven Giegold and Malte Arhelger, *Gesteuerte Demokratie? Wie neoliberale Eliten Politik und Öffentlichkeit beeinflussen* (Hamburg: VSA Verlag, 2004), pp. 84–9.

Part III

The Subterranean World
of the Power Brokers

10
Globalising Politics: Spinning US 'Democracy Assistance' Programmes

Gerald Sussman

We have 50 per cent of the world's wealth, but only 6.3 per cent of its population. In this situation we cannot fail to be the object of envy and resentment. Our real task in the coming period is to devise a pattern of relationships which will allow us to maintain this position of disparity.

—George F. Kennan, State Department Director
of Policy and Planning, 1948[1]

One of the remarkable shifts in contemporary world politics is the seemingly unimpeded involvement of foreign agencies, consultants, and public and private agencies in the organisation of national elections, including those of the former Soviet allied states. Not only did the communist party apparatuses in those countries collapse in an almost bloodless fashion, but their governing processes have since come under a system of foreign political management, led by the United States. The methods of controlling foreign elections have been modified since the headiest days of CIA cloak-and-dagger operations, but the objectives of imperial rule have remained unchanged. Today, the Central Intelligence Agency is less relied upon than the somewhat more open initiatives undertaken by such public and private organisations as the National Endowment for Democracy (NED), the US Agency for International Development (USAID), Freedom House, and George Soros's Open Society. Allen Weinstein, who helped establish NED, admitted that '[a] lot of what we [NED] do today was done covertly 25 years ago by the CIA'.[2]

Political globalisation, the neoliberal corollary to economic globalisation, is one of the less talked about and most active initiatives in world politics. Piece by piece, the United States expects to set up leaders in the former Soviet allied countries who open their state assets to transnational investment, help to isolate or force Russia into the fold, and make the world safe for the US-controlled Euro-Asian oil pipeline. Propaganda and spin are critical tools that guide the efforts of US 'democracy assistance' organisations and the local groups they train to win state power.

Russia, Ukraine, Georgia and Yugoslavia (Serbia) are among the countries in eastern Europe where American consultants, foreign service personnel, NED and its funded organisations, and other public and private agencies have recently intervened in national elections. They are joined by a long list of countries where US money has found its way to politicians and parties promoted by the White House, the State Department, and the CIA. Compared to the aggressive CIA covert actions between the late 1940s and the mid 1970s, many of these election interventions have been relatively transparent, although the presence of foreign political advisers is still regarded in many countries, such as Russia, Germany and Canada, as controversial and is kept out of the press. Carried out in the name of 'democracy building', electoral interventions are critically important to US global policy objectives, contributing to long-term state and corporate planning by solidifying American linkages to foreign governments and helping establish economic alliances. This chapter first briefly discusses early post-war US electoral interventions as a prologue to explaining the neoliberal objectives of the more recent types of political operatives and organisations. Second, it looks at the current context in discussing how the ideological pretext of 'democracy assistance' is rhetorically employed to justify the crushing of nationalist and socialist resistance to transnational corporate domination, with a particular focus on Russia and the states within its 'near abroad'. Although electoral intervention occurs in dozens of countries, the focus here is on four particularly important target countries of US interest, Russia, Yugoslavia, Georgia and Ukraine. Finally, the chapter considers how government and media management of the public understanding of world politics, by spinning their representations of foreign policy, confers legitimacy upon the notion of 'democracy assistance' and the overall good intentions of the state.

THE POST-WAR POWER CONTEXT

One of the key 'political realists' and architects of early post-war (liberal anti-communist) 'containment' policy, though considered a moderate in his cold war views, George Kennan, advised the US government in 1948 that

[w]e should cease to talk about the raising of the living standards, human rights, and democratisation. The day is not far off when we are going to have to deal in straight power concepts. The less we are then hampered by idealistic slogans, the better.[3]

A more aggressive 'roll-back' position by hardline conservatives held that the Roosevelt–Churchill–Stalin agreement at Yalta was a sell-out, and this group remained fixed on overthrowing communist party rule in Europe and any version of socialism elsewhere. The range of elite thinking in the United States never accepted anything short of US global domination; only the methods differed.

What Kennan did not consider was a composite strategy of preaching 'idealistic slogans' while destabilising governments that resist US hegemony. Hence, when George W. Bush lectured Vladimir Putin during a 2005 'summit' in Bratislava on the need to pay closer attention to 'the rule of law, a free press, a viable opposition and protection of minorities' as 'central and universal attributes of democracy',[4] the American president was simply spinning to try to capture the moral high ground and justify US imperial policies. Except for Bush's devoted following, practically anyone could observe that his administration was consistently involved in voter redistricting and voting improprieties to consolidate Republican political control; overturning numerous legal precedents to reduce taxation on the wealthy and corporate elite; warping long-established First Amendment protections under the 'Patriot Act'; paying off journalists to secretly work as shills for conservative legislative bills and presidential press conferences; threatening the opposition party's legal use of the legislative filibuster; and cutting back public sector and welfare programmes that serve the middle class and impoverished whites and ethnic minorities. His team of 'spin doctors', led by Karl Rove, was assigned the task of promoting wealth transfers in the lexicon of democratic virtues.

Dedicated political persuasion or propaganda is usually associated with authoritarian regimes that employ specialists in crafting and cultivating 'great leader' images, official ideologies and public submission – Nazi, Stalinist and fascist practices being only the starkest examples. But, as Herman and Chomsky argue, it is the capitalist 'democracies' that are most in need of, and most adept at, organised political persuasion.[5] Woodrow Wilson's Committee on Public Information (or Creel Commission) took up the scientific management of public opinion to remould isolationist attitudes into support for US entry in the First World War. The Commission's public relations/propaganda specialists included Ivy Lee, who spent his life working for American corporate robber barons and, just before his sudden death, on behalf of the business interests of the German Nazi party, and Edward Bernays, the 'father of public relations', who, during a long life, managed propaganda affairs for American tycoons and the CIA[6] and authored the claim that Wilson 'saved the world for democracy'. The Creel Commission was called 'the costliest propaganda campaign' of its day.[7]

In the early post-Second World War era, the management of 'public opinion' (heavily inflected by the wartime propaganda practices of the US Office of Strategic Services and the Office of War Information) was increasingly influenced both in the United States and Europe by conscripted media and spying organisations (CIA). Though couching it in the official category of 'democracy assistance', the United States relied on the myths engendered in the cold war to support, condone and sponsor brutally repressive dictatorial regimes in many countries – this was rationalised in intellectual circles as 'political realism'. In Europe, the CIA, the American press, local anti-communists, and 'rehabilitated' Nazis and fascists were mobilised to block socialist and communist parties from capturing political power.

Current US intervention in the political affairs of other countries is carried out by a number of different agencies, both governmental and non-governmental, which have helped organise the larger environment in which international political consultants and other operatives are able to function. And, yet, there is a fundamental and long-standing principle of international law that calls for 'the right of a people to settle its own affairs without the intervention of foreign powers',[8] which is enshrined, among other places, in the United Nations Charter. The Organisation of American States, for example, declares that 'No State or group has the right to intervene, directly or indirectly, for any reason whatever, in the internal or external affairs of any other state'.[9] Despite such a restriction, major (and sometimes minor) powers have frequently interfered with the political sovereignty of other countries. The United States has as a matter of right held the prerogative of manipulating the electoral outcomes in foreign countries, through financial and other means. Yet, when the Clinton administration came under attack for accepting alleged financial payments from Chinese government sources for his re-election campaign, the Democratic National Committee was reproached and forced to return $2.8 million in illegal or improper contributions raised by two Asian Americans.[10] Such payments, especially from a foreign communist party, are considered as subversive of the American political system, but for US state planners, the sabotage of communist and left-wing parties abroad is fair game. Spared by virtue of its power and presumed higher moral standing from honouring principles of self-determination in its foreign policy behaviour, the United States has helped install or defend many anti-democratic regimes.[11]

The collapse of the Soviet Union gave the United States an opportunity to expand its sphere of influence into formerly socialist eastern Europe, central Asia and Russia. In the 1990s, American political consultants followed the gold rush of free marketers to the region to participate in 'democracy building' efforts and to introduce US-style electioneering. Facilitating this global flow of 'non-partisan [political] expertise', USAID adopted in 1991 a 'democracy initiative' conditionality for extending grants and loans to various 'developing' countries (an act similarly adopted by the European Union two years earlier).[12] One organisation involved in this initiative, the Washington-based International Foundation for Election Systems (IFES), notes how the 'end of the Cold War in 1989 created opportunities . . . to respond to an overwhelming demand for technical non-partisan expertise in democracy and governance'. IFES claims to have field offices in 35 countries with a cadre of 1,500 consultants,[13] including big consulting names such as Stanley Greenberg (who helped direct Bill Clinton's 1992 presidential campaign). Some IFES consultants are able to turn democracy-assistance work into contracts with foreign political candidates.[14] Joseph Napolitan, founder of the International Association of Political Consultants, is on the IFES board, along with other well-known American campaign specialists.

'DEMOCRACY ASSISTANCE' AND NED

The National Endowment for Democracy (NED), which funds programmes in over 80 countries, is a quasi-private congressionally funded instrument, created by the Reagan administration in 1983, for channelling money, equipment, and political consultants and other expertise to certain countries in order 'to strengthen democratic electoral processes . . . through timely measures in cooperation with indigenous democratic forces'.[15] That is, NED's *raison d'être* is to encourage elections in countries undergoing a transition to popular electoral democracy and support others where elections have already been instituted. NED has been described as 'a full-service infrastructure-building clearinghouse' that 'provides money, technical support, supplies, training programmes, media know-how, public relations assistance, and state-of-the-art equipment to select political groups, civic organizations, labor unions, dissident movements, student groups, book publishers, newspapers, and other media'. Ironically referring to itself as a 'non-governmental organisation', its overriding purpose has been to 'destabilize progressive movements, particularly those with a socialist or democratic–socialist bent'.[16]

A number of critics in and out of government from both the left and the right see NED as an interventionist, anti-communist cold war relic falsely representing itself as non-partisan. The chairman of the board of NED, former Republican Congress member Vin Weber, is a senior partner in a consulting firm that, according to his NED personal biography, 'provides strategic advice to institutions interested in issues before, and governmental processes of, the legislative and executive branches of the federal government'. He is also a business partner with former Republican politicians and government officials Jack Kemp, William Bennett and, until her death in 2006, Jeane Kirkpatrick. The president of NED is Carl Gershman, a one-time Social Democrat, who went on to become senior counsellor to arch-conservative Jeane Kirkpatrick (who also sat on the board of the NED-funded International Republican Institute) when she was US ambassador to the United Nations under Ronald Reagan.[17] Over the years, there have been several initiatives in Congress to disband the organisation, including a recent one by a libertarian Congressional Representative from Texas, Ron Paul, who calls NED 'nothing more than a costly program that takes US taxpayer funds to promote favored politicians and political parties abroad'.[18] Currently, NED is in good favour with most Democratic and Republican legislators.

The four major organisations that NED funds are instruments of the Democratic (National Democratic Institute, NDI) and Republican (International Republican Institute, IRI) parties, the Chamber of Commerce (Center for Private Enterprise, CIPE) and the AFL–CIO (American Center for International Labor Solidarity). One of the congressional leaders behind the creation of NED, Dante Fascell, formerly chair of the House Foreign Affairs Committee (D–Fla.), said that this institutional design was intended to give each group 'a piece of the pie. They got paid off. Democrats and Republicans, the Chamber of Commerce, along with labor.'[19]

NED was supposed to provide an alternative (to the CIA) means of encouraging democratic institutions in formerly repressive states. Unlike the CIA, NED's extensive operations abroad create opportunities for political operatives, who need not assume underground lives and identities. By one estimate, the camouflaging of its imperial purposes while maintaining a seemingly transparent image makes NED a far more effective instrument of state policy than the CIA ever was[20] – a soft imperialism.

While most people in these post-authoritarian countries no doubt welcome the possibilities of transparent, multi-party politics, there has remained a widespread suspicion and sensitivity to foreign sponsorship of domestic political institutions. Even when NED's funding of Chile's 1988 election helped push a declining General Pinochet out of power, the opposition parties that benefited nonetheless expressed resentment against US interference.[21] And such suspicions are not unwarranted. The centre–right politics of CIPE and the AFL–CIO organisation are clear, and one look at the backgrounds and links of the members of the NDI and especially the IRI (listing 64 corporate and foundation 'benefactors') reveals a formidable intersection of bureaucrat–capitalists with representatives from the American Enterprise Institute and Fortune 500 energy, automobile, media and defence sectors.[22] Although corporations such as Chevron-Texaco, Exxon Mobil and Enron help fund both NDI and IRI, their influence, particularly in major NED target countries such as Venezuela, Iraq, and the rest of the Middle East, extends much further than their relatively small direct contributions would suggest. What makes NED a particularly useful instrument is that although its institutes are federally funded, their activities are not reported to Congress.

In its mission statement, IRI claims that its programmes are 'non-partisan and clearly adhere to fundamental American principles such as individual freedom, equal opportunity, and the entrepreneurial spirit that fosters economic development'.[23] However, following its 'American principles', the IRI organisation, headed by conservative leader John McCain, does not suffer a version of 'non-partisanship' that tolerates leftist organisations.[24] In the IRI world-view, freedom equates to 'free enterprise'; those who resist open-door economic policies are *ipso facto* deemed to be undemocratic. Considerably more so than NDI, IRI uses an ideological litmus test in its funding programmes.[25] Yet both organisations rely primarily on people with experience not in development work, 'but [rather] in the war rooms of presidential campaigns, in congressional and lobbying efforts, and through family relationships to top party officials'.[26]

'AMERICANS TO THE RESCUE': A RUSSIAN BRIDGEHEAD

With the collapse of the Soviet Union in the 1990s, the American electioneering industry began to operate in a more globalised environment, sustained by state funding and encouragement to establish in the name of 'freedom' new bridgeheads for neoliberal economic conquests. Russia was the electioneering plum. The first American consultants were invited to Moscow for the production of political television spots in 1993, and again for the Russian presidential election of 1996, to spin the world for capitalism and Boris Yeltsin against Communist Party (KPRF) challenger Gannady Zyuganov. Just prior to the election campaign, the United States helped bankroll Yeltsin with $14 billion in loans. German Chancellor Helmut Kohl committed an additional $2.7 billion, most of which was fully unconditional (thereby permitting its use for massive vote-buying), and French Prime Minister Alain Juppé added $392 million to the kitty, 'paid entirely into Russian state coffers'. The head of the International Monetary Fund, Michel Camdessus, committed his organisation, as a 'moral obligation', to supporting Yeltsin's privatisation plans. Most of the IMF funds went to the state treasury for discretionary spending – with the caveat that financial assistance would be suspended in the event of a Communist Party election victory.[27] 'In the end, though, the KPRF's door-to-door campaign was obliterated by the heavily researched, well-financed, media saturating, modern campaign waged by the Yeltsin team.'[28]

Operating undercover in the Yeltsin campaign were American consultants George Gorton, Joe Shumate and Richard Dresner, who had previously worked together on Pete Wilson's California gubernatorial campaign.[29] At a time when Yeltsin had very poor public opinion ratings, the three were asked to use their American razzmatazz to help spin Boris. They were joined in this task by Steven Moore, an American public relations specialist, and a Russian TV advertising production company, Video International. Dresner was a former business partner of Dick Morris and former gubernatorial campaign consultant to Bill Clinton. Morris, in turn, was Clinton's main political adviser (previously having worked for conservative southern senators Trent Lott and Jesse Helms), and acted as a liaison between the US president and Morris's friends on the Yeltsin team. Despite these close associations, the consultants denied any connections between the Russian campaign and the White House.[30]

Video International (VI) staff were trained for the election by the American advertising firm Ogilvy and Mather (part of the worldwide WPP advertising group). The campaign strategy, including use of archival footage of Stalin's brutality, was to attack the KPRF and Zyuganov with an assortment of anti-communist tactics. Within just a few years of the fall of the Soviet Union, this was an extraordinary turnaround in Russian (former Soviet) politics. As one scholar found in her interviews with VI, the company's producers mocked Zyuganov for failing to grasp the importance of political marketing,[31] which indicated yet another remarkable adaptation in Russian thinking.

VI was run by former KGB member Mikhail Margolev, who had previously spent five years with American advertising agencies. Margolev next joined the Putin public relations team for the 2000 election campaign. Since then he has became a 'senator' in the Federation Council, Russia's legislative upper chamber. He and other close advisers to Putin have been receiving 'first-hand insights into strategies and techniques of American campaign practice',[32] a tutelage they presumably assume will assist their leader's grand political ambitions. Another VI company executive, Mikhail Lesin, became Putin's press minister. Lesin is known in Russia for harassing media outlets that are critical of the Putin government,[33] marking the growing authoritarian style of that leadership.

The American campaign consultants worked closely with Yeltsin's daughter and campaign operations manager, Tatyana Dyachenko, passing on to their Russian counterpart the American techniques of spin doctoring.[34] According to a published news report, 'they advised the campaign on organisation, strategic and tactical use of polls and focus groups' with a 'central campaign message of anti-communism', a role they shared with Burson-Marsteller and other American public relations firms.[35] They also urged Yeltsin to assert authoritarian control and to think in terms of how to make the state-run television stations 'bend to your will'. Boasting that they had saved Yeltsin from certain defeat and Russia from a return to the cold war, the consultants admitted to employing a host of manipulative tactics in their advertising strategy to sow fear among Russians,[36] a style that has been well-rehearsed by many Republican political strategists. A *Time Magazine* report on these events came with the brazen cover lead, 'Yanks to the Rescue' – later inspiring a Showtime (cable TV) film, *Spinning Boris*, about how the heroics of American political consultants 'saved Russia from communism'.[37]

The consultants' political ads, mostly aired over state-run television and radio stations, which Yeltsin fully controlled,[38] repeatedly pitched the theme that a Zyuganov victory would bring back a command economy and a climate of terror.[39] For 'personality' styling designed to capture the youth vote, the Americans asked Yeltsin to appear at rock concerts and had him 'dance' onstage at one of them. Some of Yeltsin's Russian advisers did not approve of the stunt.[40] Ignored in the campaign slogans, and by the Clinton administration, were the out-of-control economy, Yeltsin's poor health and alcohol addiction, and his broad use of repressive policies. Despite his autocratic tendencies, disregard for constitutionally guaranteed freedoms, frequent money-laundering scandals, and brutal war in Chechnya, Yeltsin received the unreserved endorsement of the leaders of the main market economies, as if open markets were the only real measure of a democracy.[41] A *Time* correspondent rationalised the American intervention in pure Machiavellian logic: 'Democracy triumphed – and along with it came the tools of modern campaigns, including the trickery and slickery Americans know so well. If these tools are not always admirable, the result they helped achieve in Russia surely is.'[42] Russians too have learned the dark arts of Machiavellian political chicanery. Moscow hosts a Centre of Political Consulting, more popularly known as 'Niccolo M' – referring to the famed theorist of political manipulation and spin. By 2002, Niccolo M, whose organisers were trained in NED-funded seminars by the NDI and IRI,[43] was joined in Russia's new electioneering business by several other new political consulting groups, such as the Centre of Political Technologies, that help design campaign strategies and arrange contacts between businesses and Kremlin officials. Niccolo M staff used all the methods learned from their mentors, including candidate marketing, polling, focus groups, direct mail, phone banks, heavy use of the mass media, attack ads and 'spin doctoring'. Following the 1996 election defeat, the KPRF began studying Western campaign manuals and adopting the same tactics.[44] For tighter control over policy making, Russian business groups have learned to give their money directly to the consultants rather than to candidates,[45] a practice that corresponds to soft-money election financing in the United States.

An NDI assessment congratulated itself on the role it played in transforming Russian society through the introduction of American electioneering techniques. Under US influence, Russian political parties, the study confidently claimed, were now

targeting their communication to voters based on demographic and geographic information . . . conducting research on voter attitudes through focus groups and polling . . . small meetings, coalitions with civic groups, door knocking, phone banks, and public leafleting; organizing more sophisticated press operations *that attempt to create news and respond to events* . . . Much of this change can be attributed to NDI training.[46]

If the United States influenced Russian politics as much as the NDI claimed, then the ascension of Vladimir Putin suggests that American campaign practices have little to do with institutionalising democracy.

In fact, American 'democracy assistance' to Russia has been part of a larger programme to transform that country into an open-market economy and place it under the control of stable and reliable pro-capitalist, pro-US elected officials, regardless of their anti-democratic history or inclinations. In early 1990, Harvard University's Institute for International Development (HIID), which 'served as the gatekeeper for hundreds of millions of dollars in USAID and G-7 taxpayer aid, subsidised loans, and other Western funds' sent a team of economic 'shock therapists', led by Jeffrey Sachs. HIID's influence extended to the co-ordination of $300 million in USAID grants that went to the global public relations firm Burson-Marsteller and the 'big six' international accounting firms operating in Russia to help sell the privatisation programme.[47] Working closely with Anatoly Chubais, Yeltsin's first deputy prime minister, minister of finance and chief of staff, HIID support led to the conversion of major state enterprises to private ownership. The Harvard group actually 'drafted many of the Kremlin decrees' to this effect.[48]

SAVING UKRAINE AND OTHER 'TRANSITIONAL DEMOCRACIES'

Beyond Russia, NED, especially the IRI, has concentrated its funding efforts heavily in the former Soviet bloc states.[49] By 1990, American political consultants were already training future campaign counterparts in other former communist party-run states, including such 'transitional democracies' as Poland, Czechoslovakia and Hungary. In the 1980s, even before the collapse of Polish communist control, NED had already provided Lech Walesa's Solidarity union movement with $5 million,[50] even as the Reagan government was

smashing labour organisations in the United States. In Czechoslovakia (now the separate Czech and Slovak republics) that year, local
party leaders accused NED of funding two favoured political parties
associated with Vaclav Havel, while ignoring 21 others that were also
competing for public office. And although NED denied its political
interference, a US government budget document made it clear that
the organisation's funds given to one of the two Czechoslovakian
groups, Civic Forum, were explicitly intended 'to prepare for the
June 8 election and consolidate their position as Czechoslovakia's
premier democratic movement'. German, British and Canadian
political organisations were among other foreign groups assisting
the country's Christian Democratic Party.[51] The Hungarian Socialists,
led by Peter Medgyessy, brought in two Washington lobbying firms
to help with public opinion research in Medgyessy's 2004 re-election
bid. As one business publication explained, the eastern European
revolutionaries of 1989 'have been shunted aside by pushy, smooth-
talking pollsters and consultants'.[52]

In Bulgaria, with the collapse of the Soviet Union, the Bulgarian
Communist Party reformulated itself as the Bulgarian Socialist Party
and won the national elections in June 1990, capturing the offices of
president and prime minister, and taking control of the parliament.
The BSP was subsequently overthrown in a *coup d'état* that, according
to a widely cited study, was 'engineered and financed by the US
National Endowment for Democracy'.[53] In December 1994, the BSP
was returned to power, and a former Communist Party leader became
prime minister. In Albania, NED also financed destabilisation, which
led to the collapse of the government headed by former communists.
The country's Democratic Party remained in power through what
even President Clinton recognised as 'irregularities of the elections'.[54]
Although the methods of US intervention in other countries' electoral
processes have somewhat changed since the cold war, its hegemonic
goals apparently have not.

In the Romanian election of 1992, IRI provided support for the
main opposition (anti-communist) parties and co-sponsored with
NDI an observer team; at least one member of each institution was
a political consultant working with an opposition candidate. IRI's
goal was to block the re-election of the former communist Ion Iliescu,
whom they claimed had 16 American consultants working for him.[55]
A memo the IRI crafted for the political opposition, which made
it appear that the American organisation was little more than an

instrument of the Bush (senior) administration and the Republican Party, was leaked to the Romanian national press.[56]

If the semi-public, semi-private nature of NED blurs the distinction between official and unofficial conduct of foreign policy, the political intervention of individual American citizens does so even more. When President Eduard Shevardnadze (formerly foreign minister of the Soviet Union under Gorbachev) was forced to resign as head of state in Georgia after a rigged election and a national uprising that followed in late 2003, the billionaire financier and international political activist George Soros was seen as having a substantial hand in orchestrating the transfer of power. Soros, whose organisations are involved in the destabilisation of nationalist regimes, had been funding the opposition television station Rustavi 2, the newspaper *24 Hours*, and the Georgian youth movement Kmara, just as he had supported another student movement, Otpor, in Serbia three years earlier. Otpor was centrally involved in organising the overthrow of Slobodan Milosevic.

Georgian student leaders acknowledged that they had imitated the Serbian revolt step by step. 'Otpor activists ran three-day classes teaching more than 1,000 Georgian students how to stage a bloodless revolution. Both trips were funded by Soros' Open Society Institute.'[57] Soros might have been the more visible foreign hand in Shevardnadze's defeat, but USAID, NDI, IRI, Freedom House and the State Department were also involved in various ways in steering the outcome of the country's election. Richard Miles, US ambassador in Belgrade, who had been a key player in the overthrow of Milosevic, was transferred to Tbilisi, where he 'repeated the trick', by coaching Mikheil Saakashvili on methods to bring down Shevardnadze.[58] The Ukrainian president at the time, Leonid Kuchma, insisted that Shevardnadze's defeat was a 'western engineered coup'.[59] The United States touted Saakashvili's 96.24 per cent margin of victory in January 2003 as a legitimate expression of electoral democracy.[60]

As the United States has central interests in Georgia's Baku Ceyhan pipeline, and the Bush administration worried about Shevardnadze's ongoing oil deals with the Russians, it is likely that the country's opposition was lent a covert hand by the CIA.[61] Clearly, the White House's first choice to replace Shevardnadze was Saakashvili, a George Washington University and Columbia University law school graduate, and the United States supplied his campaign with pollsters, strategists and consultants.[62] Following Shevardnadze's forced departure, the United States raised $14 million to help pay Georgian government salaries, and Saakashvili was swept into office in January 2004. To help assure his victory, Saakashvili's supporters in parliament were able to force a re-registration, which reduced registration lists by one-third and thereby guaranteed an official turnout of 50 per cent (of registrants), the minimum required to make the election stand.[63]

The November 2004 presidential election in Ukraine provided another opportunity for US and western European governments to seek to influence a political reorientation of eastern Europe away from its Soviet legacy. The US and EU favourite was Viktor Yushchenko, someone whom the United States and its European allies saw as likely to bring Ukraine into NATO and to adopt the general programme of the WTO. As head of the Ukrainian central bank in the early 1990s, Yushchenko, whose American wife had worked in the Reagan administration, enthusiastically followed the IMF programme of structural reforms. Economic restructuring led to wildly inflated local commodity and service prices, severely reduced real wages, and a downturn in the overall health of the economy that put the Ukrainian people in serious jeopardy.[64]

Yushchenko's rival for the presidency was the prime minister, Viktor Yanukovych, the candidate supported by Kuchma, the outgoing president, and the Russian president, Vladimir Putin, but whom the State Department regarded as corrupt and unacceptable, threatening sanctions if he 'stole' the election. Several agencies of the US government, together with private organisations, including the NDI and IRI and Soros's International Renaissance Foundation, contributed millions to Yushchenko's campaign, while an executive of American PR firm Rock Creek Creative boasted of having created a website for the US/EU candidate that served as a 'virtual freedom plaza for the democracy movement' in Ukraine.[65] They were joined in support of Yushchenko by the Konrad Adenauer Foundation and Friedrich Ebert Foundation of Germany and the European Peoples Party (Christian Democrats). With considerable irony, the Bush administration sent to Kiev as emissaries for fair elections former president and CIA director George Bush senior and former secretary of state Henry Kissinger, well known for his destabilisation initiatives in south-east Asia and Latin America. It is also a case of 'situational ethics' that on the basis of its funded exit polls, the IRI disputed the initial election victory declaration for Yanukovych, while the same method of determining electoral outcomes was treated as irrelevant in places like Florida (2000) and Ohio (2004).

Both the United States and the European Union funded pre-election and exit polling for Yushchenko, defining beforehand a Yanukovych victory as an unfair election. Unfazed by such obvious partisanship, the American Bar Association helped the cause by training Ukrainian judges, including five of the Supreme Court judges, who overturned the results of the November poll and called for a new election.[66] And as in Yugoslavia and Georgia, the momentum behind the Western-backed opposition candidate Yushchenko was a foreign-funded student movement, Pora. Indeed, it was no secret that leaders from both Serbia's Otpor and Georgia's Kmara were brought in to provide tactical training for the Pora activists.

Three prominent politicised NGOs in Ukraine, the International Centre for Policy Studies, the Western Ukraine Regional Training Centre, and The Centre for Political and Legal Reforms have visible links to Yushchenko. According to a US House Republican from Bush's home state of Texas, Ron Paul, the first was funded by George Soros and the latter two by the US government. Millions of dollars for the Ukrainian election also poured in from USAID through the 'Poland–America–Ukraine Cooperation Initiative', which is run by the private 'democracy assistance' organisation, Freedom House. The direct links of this and a number of other nominal political 'reform' groups to Yushchenko are highly visible.[67] Although the US government and NGOs made a lot of noise about the alleged voting fraud on the Yanukovych side, vote-rigging in Yushchenko-leaning western Ukraine was no less conspicuous.

Moreover, as Jonathan Steele noted in the *Guardian*, the US government did not show any similar outrage about the massive manipulations that took place during Yeltsin's election in 1996, the Azerbaijan presidential vote in 2003, the unconstitutional ouster of Shevardnadze in Georgia, or the 2002 attempted military coup in Venezuela against the popular president, Hugo Chávez.[68] It is also widely reported that the IRI helped to instigate and choreograph large street demonstrations, as well as to design branded symbols of resistance, such as clenched fists, in advance of the recent elections in Belgrade, Tbilisi and Kiev.[69] These uprisings and icons, in turn, were dutifully reported by the mainstream American media, with little investigation, as indicators of a sweeping popular, pro-Western tide. The same media, as submissively behaved as the controlled press in dictatorships ever was, ignored the massive protests in the United States, Britain and many other countries on the eve of the US invasion of Iraq.

GLOBAL ELECTIONEERING: THE BIG SPIN

After the communists seized power in Beijing in 1949, the US State Department began a purge of its ranks over the issue of 'who lost China'. This reflected a long-held imperial assumption that less developed nations and peoples are mere vassals to dispose of at the pleasure of the superpower. US interventionist behaviour has never depended on genuine respect for democratic principles, yet its rhetoric, a tribute to the sensibilities of ordinary people, is always cast in that light. Between 1798 and 2005, the United States engaged in well over 200 separate acts of direct military intervention (103 *before* 1895), not including the genocidal wars against Native American nations on the continent itself. Whereas, until quite recently, the United States relied extensively on providing aid to dictatorial regimes throughout the world (which it has not abandoned), in a communication-intensive world environment, it is now considered more politically palatable to accomplish its neoliberal ends through the discursive framing of 'democracy assistance'.

With respect to Anglo-American designs on Russia and eastern Europe, nothing much has changed since British foreign secretary Lord Balfour declared in 1918 (the year of the British–French–US military intervention in Russia): 'The only thing which interests me in the Caucasus is the railway line which delivers oil from Baku to Batumi. The natives can cut each other to pieces for all I care.'[70] Beyond the broad geopolitical strategy of controlling the oil reserves that beckon foreign intervention in the states of the Caspian Sea and central Asia, there is the allure of new frontiers for transnational capitalist penetration. The need for political legitimacy and domination embodied in the expression 'democracy assistance' is shared by a range of transnational corporate and state interests and their local compradors, which rely on public relations propagandists and electioneering mercenaries in the hope of capturing footholds in the region. Rick Ridder, a political consultant and former president of the International Association of Political Consultants, said with reference to the consulting gold rush in Mexico in preparation for the 2000 elections in that country: 'If there's one thing Americans can teach Mexicans it is this: Democracy is a booming business.'[71]

Indeed, 'democracy assistance' is a growth industry. With the adoption of American-style elections, there's unlimited work for campaign strategists, pollsters, focus group specialists, fundraisers, speech-writers, web designers, media buyers, political advertisers, and direct mail, telemarketing, public relations, communications, voter analysis and other electioneering professionals. The election of 'free-market' politicians and parties is the gateway through which all sorts of international carpet-baggers are certain to follow. At the same time, there's no certainty that Western expertise and capital will always be welcome or successful. There remains much suspicion in the world about the motives behind NED and 'democracy assistance'. Poles have referred derisively to the presence of foreign campaign consultants and public relations professionals as the 'Marriot brigades' – referring to their favourite place of lodging.[72]

The imperial methods behind NED and US 'democracy assistance' programmes conflate democracy with neoliberal expansionism. This discussion of Russia and eastern Europe is only a snapshot of the work that the superpower and its minions have taken up in the service of transnational domination and the world war against national sovereignty and socialist alternatives to global capitalism. In pro-Western repressive client states, such as Pakistan, Egypt, Saudi Arabia, Singapore, Kazakhstan, Equatorial Guinea, Israel and Colombia, and many former military dictatorships that have opened themselves to transnational corporate enterprise, elections are used by ruling elites and endorsed by their foreign patrons in order to 'reap the fruits of electoral legitimacy without running the risks of democratic uncertainty'.[73] In the long term, the failings of faux-democracy are likely to give rise to a more authentic discourse of internationalism based on respect for peace, human and civil rights, sovereignty and co-operative participatory development – and without recourse to political spin and other forms of neocolonial hegemony.

NOTES

1. Cited in William I. Robinson, 'Low-intensity Democracy: The new face of global domination', *Covert Action Quarterly* (Fall 1994), p. 45.
2. William Blum, *Rogue State: A guide to the world's only superpower* (Monroe, Maine: Common Courage Press, 2000), p. 180.
3. Cited in William Robinson, *Promoting Polyarchy: Globalization, US intervention, and hegemony* (Cambridge: Cambridge University Press, 1996), p. 1.
4. Ian Traynor, 'US president acknowledges ties with Russia have weakened', *Guardian*, 25 February 2005 (online edition).
5. Edward Herman and Noam Chomsky, *Manufacturing Consent: The political Economy of the Mass Media* (New York: Pantheon Press, 1988).
6. By the time of his death in 1995 at the age of 103, Bernays's resumé in commercial and political persuasion listed many of the wealthiest

corporations in the country as clients, and it also had a few notable foreign policy credits. One of his charges was to help organise a propaganda campaign in the 1950s against Guatemala's reformist and democratically elected president, Jacobo Arbenz, on behalf of his client, the United Fruit Company. The company, with vast landholdings throughout Central America, detested Arbenz's efforts to tax its banana exports and institute a land reform-programme for landless peasants, which would have meant nationalising United Fruit plantations. Together, Bernays and the company instigated US intervention in Guatemala, which led to a 1954 CIA-organised military coup, whose officers engaged in a wave of violence, torture and terror against real and imagined opponents (Noam Chomsky, *Necessary Illusions: Thought Control in Democratic Societies* (Boston: South End Press, 1989), p. 29; Tom Lewis, *Empire of the Air: The Men Who Made Radio* (New York: HarperCollins, 1991), p. 183). Guatemala was one of the early post-war targets of political consultants in the service of covert foreign policy objectives.

7. WNYC, 'The father of public relations' (transcript of part of the New York-based radio series *On the Media*), 17 January 2003.

8. Lori F. Damrosch, 'Politics across borders: Nonintervention and nonforcible influence over domestic affairs', *American Journal of International Law* 83 (1), (October/November 1989), p. 7.

9. Ibid.

10. Michael Pinto-Duschinsky, 'Overview (project precis)', in International IDEA (ed.) *Handbook on Funding of Parties and Election Campaigns* (Stockholm: Institute for Democracy and Electoral Assistance, 2001), p. 7.

11. A shortlist includes Marcos, Suharto, Pinochet, Mobuto, Somoza, Trujillo, Batista, Diem, Chiang, the Shah of Iran and Saddam Hussein; the royal Saudi family; the military dictatorships in South Korea, South Vietnam, Pakistan, Nigeria, Guatemala, El Salvador and Thailand; the juntas and paramilitaries in Greece, Brazil, Haiti, Honduras, Argentina, Colombia, Mexico, Paraguay and Uruguay; and the apartheid regimes in South Africa. William Robinson, whose list of aided dictatorships is more extensive and detailed, concluded that '[d]espite all the rhetoric on "electoral democracy" and emphasis on "free and fair elections", the United States is only concerned with assuring procedurally clean elections when the circumstances or results favor US interests'. Robinson, *Promoting Polyarchy*, p. 111.

12. Ankie Hoogvelt, Globalisation and the Postcolonial World: The new political economy of development (Baltimore: Johns Hopkins University Press, 1997), p. 173.

13. International Foundation for Election Systems (IFES), 2003, <http://www.ifes.org>.

14. John Maggs, 'Not-so-innocents abroad', *National Journal* 32 (25), 17 June 2000, available online through Ebsco Host.

15. Damrosch, 'Politics across borders', p. 19.

16. Bill Berkowitz, 'NED targets Venezuela', *Z Magazine Online*, May 2004, <http://www.zmagsite.zmag.org/May2004/berkowitzpr0504.html>.

17. National Endowment for Democracy (NED), <http://www.ned.org>, accessed 2 February 2005.
18. Ron Paul, 'National Endowment for Democracy: Paying to make enemies of America', 11 October 2003, online at <http://www.antiwar.com/paul/paul79.html>.
19. David Samuels, 'At play in the fields of oppression', *Harper's*, May 1995 (online edition).
20. Robinson, *Promoting Polyarchy*, pp. 110–11.
21. Barbara Conry, 'Loose Cannon: The National Endowment for Democracy', foreign policy briefing paper no. 27 for the Cato Institute, 8 November 1993, <http://www.cato.org/pubs/fpbriefs/fpb-027.html>.
22. International Republican Institute (IRI), 2003, <http://www.iri.org/help.asp>.
23. Becky Shelley, 'Political Globalisation and the Politics of International Non-Governmental Organisations: The case of village democracy in China', *Australian Journal of Political Science* 35 (2), 2000 (online edition).
24. IRI is often partnered in its anti-leftist 'non-partisanship' with another NED-funded organisation, the AFL–CIO's Free Trade Union Institute. In the 1980s, one of the FTUI's 'democracy assistance' projects was a $1.5 million grant in support of a right-wing extremist group, the National Inter-University Union, for the purpose of blocking what the labour group saw as dangerous communist influences in François Mitterand's socialist government. Conry, *Loose Cannon*.
25. Thomas Carothers, 'The Resurgence of United States Political Development Assistance to Latin America in the 1980s', in Laurence Whitehead (ed.) *The International Dimensions of Democratization: Europe and the Americas* (New York: Oxford University Press, 1996), p. 137.
26. Samuels, 'At play in the fields of oppression'.
27. Fred Weir, 'Betting on Boris: The West antes up for the Russian election', *Covert Action Quarterly*, Summer 1996, pp. 38–41.
28. Sarah E. Mendelson, 'Democracy Assistance and Political Transition in Russia', *International Security* 25 (4), 2001, available online through Ebsco Host.
29. After saving the world for capitalism, Gorton, Shumate and Dresner went on to work on the gubernatorial campaign of Arnold Schwarzenegger to save California from the Democrats.
30. 'US Republicans reportedly helped Yeltsin engineer election win', Deutsche Presse-Agentur, 7 July 1996 (online edition).
31. Mendelson, 'Democracy Assistance', p. 76.
32. Fritz Plasser and Gunda Plasser, Global Political Campaigning: A worldwide analysis of campaign professionals and their practices (Westport, Conn.: Praeger, 2002), p. 22.
33. Michael Kramer, 'Rescuing Boris', *Time Magazine*, 15 July 1996 (online edition); Mendelson, 'Democracy Assistance', p. 73.
34. 'US political consultants take bow for Yeltsin victory', Deutsche Presse-Agentur, 9 July 1996 (online edition); Kramer, 'Rescuing Boris'.

35. Deutsche Presse-Agentur, 'US political consultants take bow'; Janine R. Wedel, *Collision and Collusion: The strange case of Western aid to Eastern Europe* (New York: Palgrave, 2001), p. 143.
36. Kramer, 'Rescuing Boris'.
37. Andrei Zolotov Jr., 'Hollywood spins Yeltsin spin doctors', *Moscow Times*, 3 June 2002 (online edition).
38. Following his American consultants' advice, Yeltsin fired the head of state-run television and radio, whom he regarded as too critical of his government (Kramer, 'Rescuing Boris'). Zyuganov, on the other hand, faced a more hostile press and much tougher questioning (Ellen Mickiewicz, *Transition and Democratization: The Role of Journalists in Eastern Europe and the Former Soviet Union*, in Doris Graber, Denis McQuail and Pippa Norris (eds) *The Politics of News: The News of Politics* (Washington, D.C.: CQ Press, 1998), pp. 35–50). The manipulative use of state media did not appear to trouble the 'free-speech'- and 'free-enterprise'-loving American advisers.
39. Daniel Hellinger, 'Democracy Builders or Information Terrorists?', *St Louis Journalism Review* (September 1996), pp. 10–11.
40. Mark Stevenson, 'America's newest export industry: Political advisers', Associated Press, 29 January 2000.
41. Mendelson, 'Democracy Assistance'.
42. Kramer, 'Rescuing Boris'.
43. NED's annual funding allocation, at the time $30 billion, was also used to assist the campaigns of 41 Duma members in the Russian parliament. Norman Solomon, *The Habits of Highly Deceptive Media: Decoding Spin and Lies in Mainstream News* (Monroe, Maine: Common Courage Press, 1999), p. 75. With offices in Moscow, the NDI and IRI have been heavily involved in party and political activist training in many regions of Russia, backed by more than $15 million during the 1990s. Mendelson, 'Democracy Assistance', pp. 75–6.
44. Julie Corwin, 'The business of elections', Radio Free Europe/RadioLiberty, 11 September 2002, available online through LexisNexis; Mendelson, 'Democracy Assistance'; Plasser and Plasser, *Global Political Campaigning*, p. 35.
45. Corwin, 'The business of elections'.
46. Cited in Thomas Carothers, *Aiding Democracy Abroad: The learning curve* (Washington, D.C.: Carnegie Endowment for International Peace, 1999), p. 152 (emphasis added).
47. The 'big six' were Deloitte and Touche, Coopers and Lybrand, KPMG Peat Marwick, Arthur Andersen, Ernst and Young and Price Waterhouse.
48. Wedel, *Collision and Collusion*, pp. 125, 142, 241.
49. Carothers, *Aiding Democracy Abroad*, p. 144.
50. Jim Abrams, 'Endowment fund promotes democracy, spawns controversy', Associated Press, 29 October1993 (available through LexisNexis).
51. Stephen Engelberg, 'US grant to 2 Czech parties is called unfair interference', *New York Times*, 10 June 1990, p. A8; Conry, 'Loose Cannon'; Robert V. Friedenberg, *Communication Consultants in Political Campaigns: Ballot box warriors* (Westport, Conn.: Praeger, 1997), p. 203.
52. 'Spinning', *The Economist*, 3 April 2004, p. 56.

53. Gerald Sussman, *Global Electioneering: Campaign Consulting, Communications, and Corporate Financing* (Lanham, Md.: Rowman & Littlefield, 2005).
54. William Blum, 'Will Humans Ever Fly?', *Peace Review* 9, 1 March 1997 (available on Academic Search Premier database).
55. Carothers, *Aiding Democracy Abroad*, p. 149.
56. Ibid., pp. 132–3, 145.
57. Daan van der Schriek, 'Georgia: "How good the revolution has been!"', *World Press Review*, 7 December 2003 (online edition).
58. Ian Traynor, 'US campaign behind the turmoil in Kiev', *Guardian*, 26 November 2004 (online edition).
59. Tom Warner, 'Saakashvili may win 80% of vote in Georgia', *Financial Times*, 4 January 2004.
60. John Laughland, 'The revolution televised', *Guardian*, 27 November 2004 (online edition).
61. Eric S. Margolis, 'Shevy's Big Mistake: Crossing Uncle Sam', *Toronto Sun*, 30 November 2003 (online edition).
62. Ian Traynor, 'Analysis: How Shevardnadze went from Glasnost hero to hated lame duck – and who will succeed him', *Guardian*, 24 November 2003 (online edition).
63. Tom Warner, 'Poll landslide for Saakashvili', *Financial Times*, 3 January 2004.
64. 'The Ukrainian crisis: More than it seems', *Catholic New Times* (Canada), 19 December 2004 (accessed through LexisNexis).
65. Annys Shin, 'Local PR firm caught in worldwide web of bad press', *Washington Post*, 7 March 2005 (online edition).
66. Max Boot, 'Exporting Ukraine', *New York Sun*, 31 December 2004 (online edition).
67. Ron Paul, 'Massive interference in Ukrainian politics', 9 December 2004, <http://www.indybay.org>.
68. Jonathan Steele, 'Ukraine's postmodern coup d'etat', *Guardian*, 26 November 2004 (online edition).
69. Ian Traynor, 'US campaign behind the turmoil in Kiev', *Guardian*, 26 November 2004 (online edition).
70. John Laughland, 'Georgia on my mind', *Guardian*, 1 April 2004 (online edition).
71. Esther Schrader, 'Mexico imports American-style campaigning', *Los Angeles Times*, 27 August 1999, p. A17.
72. Wedel, Collision and Collusion, p. 45.
73. Andreas Schedler, 'The Menu of Manipulation: Elections without democracy', *Journal of Democracy* 13 (2), 2002, pp. 36–7.

11
Behind the Screens: Corporate Lobbying and EU Audiovisual Policy

Granville Williams

Unless information is generated by sustained public debate, most of it will be irrelevant at best, misleading and manipulative at worst. Increasingly information is generated by those who wish to promote something or someone – a product, a cause, a political candidate or officeholder – without arguing a case on its merits or explicitly advertising it as self-interested material.[1]

The development of media policy in the early twenty-first century has become the focus for determined lobbying at a national, European and international level by governments, media trade associations, global media groups and conservative think tanks. One consequence is that media policy is shaped, not by a process of public debate and the presentation of alternative arguments, but rather through the partial presentation of information, filtered and selected to favour the interests of commercial media groups. This chapter analyses the reasons for this development, the consequences, and what we need to do about it.

Lobbying as part of an open process of persuasion is a perfectly legitimate way for organisations to influence public debate and shape the formation of policy, but when it becomes covert, conducted with lack of transparency, and has goals which, unless challenged and publicised, only benefit corporate interests, it is deeply damaging to the democratic process. We do have positive (albeit rare) examples of open debate and participation by a wide range of interests in the development of media policy. Two historical episodes, one from the United States and one from the United Kingdom, illustrate this point.

In the United States 'the sole instance in modern US history in which the structure and control of an established mass medium would be a legitimate issue of public debate' occurred between 1928 and 1934.[2] In what he calls a 'revisionist' analysis of this episode in US broadcasting history, American academic Robert McChesney challenges other accounts which view the public as 'passive, ignorant and mostly nonexistent before the corporate juggernaut that dominates public policy' and describes how strands of American society coalesced into a broadcasting reform movement: 'Elements of education, labor, religion, the press, civic groups, and the intelligentsia created the opposition and reflected a general social dissatisfaction with the contours of the emerging commercial system.'[3] In its various activities to influence public opinion, Congress and the White House, the broadcasting reform movement faced an uphill struggle to persuade the legislators that a significant section of US broadcasting (25 per cent) should be allocated to non-profit organisations. The National Association of Broadcasters (NAB), representing commercial broadcasters, was already honing the lobbying skills which have since given it enormous political clout. In 1933, as the Federal Radio Commission issued a questionnaire to elicit information for a report, NAB established an emergency fund to 'provide the American public with the real facts about the American broadcasting industry'. A letter to NAB members appealing for funds stated: 'The entire American Plan of broadcasting, based on private ownership and advertising support, is now definitely under fire.'[4]

The important point about the media reform movement was that it challenged a basic tenet of emerging US broadcasting policy, the notion that the airwaves were solely for private exploitation and that network-dominated, advertising-financed broadcasting was its natural structure. Although it failed in that objective it drew in a range of organisations and stimulated discussion on alternative media policies.

In 1954 the UK Conservative government passed the Television Act, leading to the creation of ITV. It was preceded by the first determined piece of corporate lobbying to reshape UK media. A coalition of Conservative MPs associated with the Broadcasting Policy Committee, radio and television set manufacturers, major British and American advertising agencies, and financial institutions dedicated their efforts towards the introduction of commercial broadcasting in Britain.

One feature of the campaign for commercial television was that it was a very public, open debate with two umbrella organisations presenting their views, the National Television Council (NTC) opposing, and the Popular Television Association (PTA) supporting the introduction of a new commercial service. There was, however, a clear difference in the effectiveness of the two organisations in the way in which they presented their cases. The PTA ran a sophisticated public relations campaign, with the vast bulk of its material distributed as 'news' so that it was not identified as PTA propaganda. A stream of articles was distributed to a mailing list of 1,400 newspapers, written under newsworthy names, including the Oxford historian A.J.P. Taylor and the Surrey and England fast bowler Alec Bedser. Negative stories about the BBC were circulated and the members of the PTA (it claimed 12,000 members although because it had a policy of secrecy neither its membership nor its financing could be verified) were urged to write letters to newspapers calling for the immediate introduction of 'Competitive Television' – the word 'commercial' was studiously avoided. The Aims of Industry was set up in 1942 as a free-enterprise corporate lobby group and established its reputation for conducting anti-nationalisation campaigns for the sugar and iron and steel industries. It provided two members to work for the PTA and also co-operated in the distribution of features, news stories and films.[5]

The US and UK media systems had developed along different paths from the 1920s, but they both had regulatory and ownership constraints placed on them by government legislation. All this began to change in the 1970s and 1980s as old systems of regulation and government intervention were abandoned, and a whole new series of terms and concepts emerged, exemplifying changed economic, political and cultural realities: deregulation, privatisation, free trade, globalisation, neoliberalism. Of course, as Bourdieu points out:

The neoliberal vulgate, an economic and political orthodoxy so universally imposed and unanimously accepted that it seems beyond the reach of discussion and contestation, is not the product of spontaneous generation. It is the result of prolonged and continual work by an immense intellectual workforce, concentrated and organized in what are effectively enterprises of production, dissemination and intervention.

He cites the example of the 'tens of thousands of professional lobbyists who, in Brussels, haunt the corridors of the European Commission, the European Council, and the European Parliament'.[6]

Corporate Europe Observatory (CEO) has done a great deal of work to alert people to the particular vulnerability of the policy-making process in Brussels to corporate lobbyists:

The number and intensity of connections with business varies within different Commission directorates, but the phenomenon appears only to be increasing.

Corporations and their lobby groups also often provide useful information for the understaffed and disconnected Commission bureaucracy. In fact, it can be said that corporate lobby groups act as a replacement for the citizen-based constituency which the Commission lacks.[7]

The reason for the burgeoning lobbying presence in Brussels was that during the late 1980s and early 1990s the European Commission was drafting the directives which would form the framework for the operation of the single European market. One such directive, 'Television Without Frontiers' (TWF), which became operative in October 1989, had within it the requirement that European television channels should carry at least 50 per cent of European-originated programming.[8] The directive has become the focus of massive lobbying efforts since then, but in 1989 it was only at a late stage in the directive's development that the US government and powerful trade groupings like the Motion Pictures Association of America (MPAA), under its well-connected president, Jack Valenti, became aware of the quota proposal which was designed, for both economic and cultural reasons, to protect European film and broadcasting and prevent a flood of US audiovisual imports. Jack Valenti alerted President Ronald Reagan, who in turn contacted Margaret Thatcher, and the two words 'where practicable' were added to the directive as a result of the intervention of the then foreign secretary, John Major.[9] The two words crucially weakened the directive and allowed satellite and cable channels, particularly children's channels, to carry a majority of US programming.

After the directive was implemented, US efforts moved to another forum, the negotiations on the General Agreement on Trade and Tariffs (GATT), in which Jack Valenti sought to mobilise opposition to the directive, whereas European Union negotiators were mandated to seek an explicit exemption for the audiovisual sector. Valenti used the close links between Hollywood and the Clinton administration to reinforce opposition to the directive. At a meeting on 15 October 1993, the president, Valenti and 16 leading Hollywood figures issued a statement which asserted that audiovisual services must be included in any GATT agreement.[10] In the end it was the EU position, strengthened by the insistence of the French government's determination to defend the European cultural exemption, which won through. In order to conclude the GATT negotiations the United States conceded, and the directive remained in force. The US government, however, realised that it had to clarify its global audiovisual lobbying strategies and intensify its efforts. A 1995 US government document outlined specifically the areas of activity to be pursued to achieve this. Its introductory paragraph describes 'a systematic approach on the part of the US Government to the growing number of audiovisual problems ... that our audiovisual industry faces in its global operations' and then identifies Europe as one of the key regions. The document outlines a detailed integrated strategy on how to roll back and liberalise trade in audiovisual products, involving the US government, trade associations like the MPAA, individual media companies, and 'experts in broadcasting and intellectual property areas'. US government and private sector representatives 'should participate in international seminars and conferences to explain the US position and develop contacts with private sector and government officials' and make efforts to 'obtain favourable reports of US activities in the press'. What is striking about the document is the total commitment to free-market assumptions, the seamless linking of shared interests and the concerted drive to win over a broad group of government ministers, officials and private sector representatives in the countries and regions targeted for lobbying.[11] A range of lobby groups began to pay much more attention to media policy debates within the EU, and in the revision process leading to the 1997 TWF directive, one UK journalist described the scenes in the European Parliament on 12 November 1996 over a determined battle on one amendment to the directive to delete the words 'where practicable', and another to include new technology-driven services:

The spectacle in the European Parliament over the last couple of days has been extraordinary. All the world's communications giants, all those with their snouts in the great European broadcasting trough, were there, leaning, lobbying, paying, threatening. Some, like Berlusconi, actually have their own staff of MEPs ...

There was the full might of the American administration, promoting the interests of its movie and television industry. Bertelsmann, Kirch, Murdoch, Turner, Reuters, British Telecom, Sony, Microsoft, Deutsche TV – the list is endless. All the big global players had their lobbyists there.[12]

The TWF directive was due for revision again in 2002, but the Commission finally managed to produce a consolidated text in March 2007. The delay has mainly been due to intense lobbying by different groupings with an interest in radically reshaping the directive. Two of these groupings are worth highlighting. The World Federation of Advertisers (WFA) through its European Action Group boasts a key role in postponing the revision of the directive and 'has been heavily involved in both preparatory research and EU Commission hearings'. The WFA promotes itself as a socially responsible organisation, concerned, for example, about the impact of advertising on the young and therefore a supporter of media literacy (through the Media Smart programme to teach primary school children in the United Kingdom to think critically about advertising). At one conference, organised by its UK affiliate, ISBA, with the EU director general for health and consumer protection, Robert Madelin, in attendance, Larry Light, executive vice-president and global marketing officer for McDonald's Corporation, demonstrated the spirit of responsible advertising by unveiling a global marketing campaign aimed at promoting a healthy diet and an active lifestyle to children.[13] The WFA has a clear agenda in terms of the revision of the TWF directive. The first is absolute defence of the 'country of origin principle', which means that what is legal in one European country must be accepted in another. In Scandinavian countries domestic restrictions on advertising aimed at children could not therefore apply to programming beamed into homes from satellite systems outside the countries. The second is an absolute insistence on self-regulation 'which holds a number of advantages over legislation in that it can quickly adapt to changing social sensitivities by revising and updating itself – and all this with no extra costs to the consumer'. The WFA has also lobbied fiercely on new advertising techniques – split-screen virtual advertising and interactive advertising. Here again, 'light touch regulation is more appropriate since it will allow these technological innovations to develop and spread'.[14]

Another organisation which has put considerable energies into lobbying the European Parliament and European Commission on the revision of the Television Without Frontiers directive is the International Communications Round Table (ICRT), representing 25 leading media, computer and communications companies, including Time Warner, Walt Disney, News International/News Corporation, Reed Elsevier, Sony Entertainment, Bertelsmann, Philips, Siemens and Microsoft. It argues that the aim of a future directive 'should be to create a liberal and clearly less restrictive regulatory framework for the audiovisual sector to replace the TV without Frontiers directive'. It too rejects regulation: 'Content, in particular broadcasting content, must be free from the straightjacket of regulation developed in a different – historically changed –media world.' Quotas on EU-originated programmes are 'no longer viable or justifiable in a global and technologically converging environment'. On advertising, the EU should 'trust more market forces and self-regulation':

the advertising rules in the TV Without Frontiers Directive are classic examples of how technological progress can render obsolete legislation that was intended for the television of the 1980s ... The time is thus ripe for a determined modernisation and deregulation of restrictions on TV advertising.[15]

When EU President José Barroso announced the new Commission members in November 2004 he made clear that the priorities would be greater liberalisation, agreed as part of the Lisbon agenda, and he appointed economics, trade and competition commissioners to ensure that pro-market, free-trade policies were pursued. These themes were picked up by Viviane Reding, the information and society commissioner with responsibility for the TWF directive, at the Bertelsmann Forum (an important forum at which deregulatory policies for the media are promoted) in Gütersloh, Germany. She voiced her opposition to new restrictions on advertising as being contrary to the Lisbon agenda and its focus on economic reforms, and indicated that existing restrictions on TV advertising might be reformed to foster the competitiveness of the European media industry.[16] In this new phase in the development of the EU, a comment made by the Corporate Europe Observatory in 1999 is more pertinent than ever: 'No analysis of the EU's current neoliberal economic strategies – which involve promoting deregulation and privatization in virtually all areas and subordinating every policy field to the objective of international competitiveness – can ignore the activities of corporate lobby groups.'[17] This is certainly the case with the revised TWF directive.

The other major target of corporate lobbying activity is public service broadcasting (PSB), and the scale of activity, at national and European levels, has increased noticeably. A grouping of European commercial media organisations, the Association of Commercial Television in Europe (ACTE), the Association Européenne des Radios (AER), and the European Publishers' Council (EPC) intervened in the debate with *Safeguarding the Future of the European Audiovisual Market*.[18] This document essentially threw down the gauntlet, charging the EU in the audiovisual sector with 'a lack of political will, unimaginable in other sectors' by allowing market distortion through massive subsidies to publicly funded broadcasters (PFBs), which the report defines as 'TV and radio broadcasters with public service remits funded either wholly through State Aid or through a combination of State Aid and commercial revenues including advertising'. The report uses data from the 15 member states before EU enlargement to argue that PFBs have a privileged position: 'PFBs received State Aid equalling a massive €15 billion (more than €82.2 billion between 1996 and 2001). The magnitude of this subsidy effectively makes PFB the third most subsidised "industry" in Europe.' The report also cites numerous examples where, they claimed, PFBs breached EU competition law, but the EU had not acted against them. PFBs have also been placed in a privileged position, compared with private radio and TV broadcasters, because they could use a 'predictable, stable and reliable income stream' to build a 'position at the expense of private radio and TV broadcasters as well as press and internet publishers'. Another charge in the report is that PFBs are weakly regulated, so they are able to build audience share through scheduling popular programming on their main channels in prime time to compete with commercial broadcasters. Serious, distinctive programming covering the arts and current affairs is scheduled elsewhere. In adopting such tactics, the report claims, they move away from their PSB remit. What is important about this document is that its policy proposals have clearly influenced the new EU Commission.

In March 2005, for example, the EU competition commissioner, Neelie Kroes, made a strong statement about the role and financing of some PSB activities in the Commission's response to complaints made by Verband Privater und Rundfunk und Telekommunkation e.V. (the umbrella organisation of commercial broadcasters in Germany) that the German PSB channels ARD and ZDF had some website services that were more to do with e-commerce than with a public service remit. The Commission

requested clarifications from Germany, Ireland and the Netherlands about the role and financing of public service broadcasters ... the Commission's preliminary view is that the current financing system is no longer in line with EC Treaty rules requiring member states not to grant subsidies liable to distort competition (Article 87).[19]

It is clear from the above analysis of media policy issues that the long-established social-market broadcasting model, which is still promoted and defended by bodies like the Council of Europe, is under threat.[20] The body of ideas associated with the defence of the European cultural and audiovisual space embodied in the original 1989 Television Without Frontiers directive is also being eroded. A simple measure of this change is to compare the policy debates in both the European Commission and the European Parliament in the 1990s with current debates. There was a Commission Green Paper on media concentration in 1992,[21] and an active group of MEPs who argued fervently for a strengthened Television Without Frontiers directive. Carole Tongue, a UK MEP and spokesperson for the Socialist Group on Media Issues, produced *Culture or Monoculture? The European Audiovisual Challenge,*[22] which expressed strong concerns about the 'Americanisation' of European culture and the potential loss of distinctive national or regional cultural identities. Today these issues are discussed differently. The culture commissioner, Viviane Reding, has eschewed a 'one size fits all' directive on media ownership and media concentration. Instead national governments or competition law should deal with this issue. Even the Television Without Frontiers directive is the subject of a study about the effectiveness of the quotas to promote European and independent works.[23]

In the United Kingdom, a good example of the application of corporate lobbying on media policy was the review instituted by the Department of Culture, Media and Sport (DCMS) into the operations of BBC Online. For a number of years the BBC has been subjected to a rolling programme of reviews: *News 24* was examined in 2002 as a result of complaints by News International about unfair competition against its own 24-hour news service, *Sky News*, and currently two separate reviews are being conducted into the BBC digital television and radio operations. In 2001, the launch of two digital channels for children, CBeebies and CBBC, was also challenged, unsuccessfully, by Disney, News Corporation and Viacom. The genesis of the *Report of the Independent Review of BBC Online*[24] was the lobbying efforts of the British Internet Publishers Alliance (BIPA), which several years ago began to argue that the dominance of BBC Online had a detrimental effect, by inhibiting commercial investment in other online initiatives.[25] Also local and regional newspapers in the United Kingdom, through their organisation, the Newspaper Society, have been unhappy with the way BBC Online has developed local content which intrudes on their business activity. The chair of the online report, Philip Graf, is former chief executive of Trinity Mirror, which owns national newspaper titles (the *Daily Mirror, Sunday Mirror* and the *People*), but is also the owner of over 200 local and regional newspapers in the United Kingdom. The report's recommendations were seen by BIPA as a victory for their lobbying efforts: in future the BBC's online activities must be carefully monitored, with a priority given to coverage of news, current affairs and education; the BBC board of governors should appoint two new governors, one with new media experience and another with competition law experience; and the BBC should source 25 per cent of its content from outside suppliers, except for news.[26] Intriguingly, the contact for further information on BIPA's response to the Graf report is Angela Mills Wade, the same person who is listed as the contact for further information on the EPC/ACT/AER report discussed above.[27] She is a ubiquitous lobbyist who worked for Rupert Murdoch's News International for several years and is now executive director of the European Publishers' Council.

CHALLENGING THE POWER OF CORPORATE LOBBYING

When policy is left to be fought over by powerful commercial interests behind closed doors with no public awareness or participation – by what self-interested commercial parties call 'experts' – one gets what one would expect: a media system that serves powerful corporate interests first and foremost. As the axiom goes, if you are not at the table you are not part of the deal.[28]

One significant recent move to highlight the issue of corporate lobbying was the open letter by a platform of NGOs, in October 2004, to the EU president, José Barroso. It made the point that '[t]housands of lobbyists, assisted by an army of public affairs consultants, today play a powerful and increasingly undemocratic role in the EU political process. As a first step in addressing these problems Europe needs far stricter ethics and transparency requirements.' It argued that '[w]ithout a radical improvement of the registration and reporting obligations for lobbyists working to influence the European institutions, there can be no effective democratic scrutiny over EU policy-making', and suggested that

Europe should learn from the lobbying disclosure legislation in place in the United States and Canada and oblige firms and organisations targeting the EU institutions (with a lobbying budget over a certain threshold) to submit regular reports giving details on the issues they are lobbying on, for which clients and with what budget.[29]

The open letter has certainly raised the level of interest, prompting good media coverage, and also an acknowledgement by the EU vice-president, Siim Kallas, of the scale of lobbying and the problem: '2,600 interest groups have a permanent office in the capital of Europe. Lobbying activities are estimated to produce 60 to 90 million euro in annual revenue. But transparency is lacking.' He criticised the weakness of 'self imposed codes of conduct [which] have few signatories and have so far lacked serious sanctions' and suggested that 'their transparency is too deficient in comparison to the impact of their activities'.[30]

There is also another deep-rooted problem that needs to be addressed in terms of corporate lobbying and the media. Concentrated media power, symbolised by global media groups such as Time Warner, Viacom and News Corporation, also confers political power. For years, American media companies have invested millions of dollars in lobbying to ensure favourable company-friendly legislation.[31] In the United Kingdom and Europe the same techniques and influence are being deployed both by global media groups and by powerful EU-based media groups, which identify common policy goals in challenging public service broadcasting and pursuing deregulatory policies for commercial media. At the opening of this chapter we cited two positive historical cases of public debate shaping media policy. We can now add two more recent examples. In 2003 there was a remarkable mobilisation of public opinion in the United States against the Federal Communication Commission's proposal to relax media ownership rules, described as 'a remarkable and unprecedented moment in U.S. media history', when during the first nine months of 2003 some 3 million Americans registered their opposition to relaxing media ownership rules.[32]

In the United Kingdom the case of the BBC is instructive. It was under attack on two fronts in 2003/4. Firstly, over the sequence of events following the death of the government scientist, Dr David Kelly, which led to the Hutton Inquiry and Report and the resignation of the director general, Greg Dyke, and the chair of the BBC governors, Gavyn Davies. Secondly, as debates began on renewal of the BBC Charter in 2006, radical new ideas on the BBC's future were proposed, including the replacement of the licence fee by subscription.

A number of UK organisations (Campaign for Press and Broadcasting Freedom, Public Voice, the National Union of Journalists, Voice of the Viewer and Listener) were active in raising public awareness about the threats to the BBC. One result of this activity was that when the DCMS began its extensive consultation process in preparation for its Green Paper, the culture secretary, Tessa Jowell, acknowledged powerful support for the BBC:

Through opinion polls, focus groups, public meetings and our website we got the views of thousands of listeners, viewers and online users. Their views – your views – were very clear. The BBC is liked and trusted by millions. Its services are valued and enjoyed. It is seen as having a vital role to play in news and in sustaining and informing our democracy.[33]

After a period of intense lobbying by sections of the press and commercial media deeply hostile to PSB, the recommendations in the Green Paper for the renewal of the Charter for ten years and the continuation of the licence fee represented a victory for its defenders.

Both examples have to be qualified. They are victories in what is a long and very unequal struggle between the vested commercial interests of the media and corporate lobbying groups, and those organisations and individuals who want diverse and accountable media. But they are victories nonetheless, and important foundations to build on.

POSTCRIPT: UPDATE ON TWF – JULY 2006

A draft directive amending the TWF Directive was published on 12 December 2005. The timetable is to have an agreed directive in place by December 2006 and an obligation on member states to incorporate its policy proposals into national law by 2010. The directive will also have a new title, an Audiovisual Media Services (AMS) Directive.[34] Attempts to include new media in the previous directive revision of 1997 were resisted, but one major change in the new draft directive is the inclusion within its scope of 'on demand' audiovisual material over the internet and mobile phones. In the words used by the Commission, the scope of the directive would be widened to include both television broadcasting ('linear') and new media ('non-linear') services. Also the draft directive proposes to end the ban on product placement ('surreptitious advertising') and liberalise advertising rules.

A UK coalition, which includes the government, the media regulator Ofcom, the Broadband Stakeholder Group (BSG), the Digital Content Forum, and Intellect, the trade association of the UK hi-tech industry, have all registered their strong disagreement with the arguments presented by the Commission for the extended scope of the directive. An energetic lobbying campaign has been taking place in the United Kingdom and Europe to win broader support for this critical position.

The intensity of the United Kingdom's disagreement with the Commission's approach was strikingly demonstrated at the joint UK Presidency/EU Commission audiovisual conference, 'Between Culture and Commerce', held in Liverpool, 20–22 September 2005 to discuss responses on six position papers drawn up by Commissioner Viviane Reding's Information Society and Media Directorate.[35] The conference, organised jointly by the European Union Information Society and Media Directorate and the DCMS, drew together industry representatives, regulators and government officials from the EU, EU candidate and EFTA countries. The structure of the conference involved working groups discussing the specific issue papers and also a series of keynote speeches.

UK viewpoints were featured prominently. On the day the Liverpool conference opened, 20 September, Intellect and the BSG issued a joint plea to the EU Commission – 'go back to the drawing board'. In uncompromising language the press statement considered 'the proposed approach to policy regulation to be totally unworkable, and an attempt by the EU to regulate the internet via the backdoor'. The proposals were 'premature', 'unjustified', 'inappropriate' and 'unworkable' and 'what the EU must do now is stop the process in its tracks and begin the consultation process again. This time we ask that the EU engage with all of the industry stakeholders who will be affected by the proposed Directive … '.[36] The chair of the media regulator Ofcom, Lord Currie, was also critical. He concluded his speech, 'So Ofcom's view, boiled down to its essential, is one of scepticism about the case made for the extension of scope in so far as it seeks to extend regulation to services currently in their infancy, and concern about the practicalities involved.'[37]

Certainly at the Liverpool conference there was the clear sense that the UK position did not appear to win significant support amongst conference participants. Commissioner Reding ended the conference by declaring, 'The listening phase is over and the time for concrete texts has come.' However the arguments presented at Liverpool by the various UK political, regulatory and industry interests opposed to the draft AMS Directive have continued to be energetically promoted and there is now a determined lobbying campaign gaining momentum at a national and European level, involving an alliance between the broadcasting, telecommunications, technology, new media and advertising sectors. They represent businesses and organisations operating in the United Kingdom, across the EU and globally.[38]

The UK position seems to be isolated, with only Slovakia supporting it, and a recent change of government there may result in that support being withdrawn. In December 2006 the European Parliament debates the final form of the draft AMS directive and only then we will be able to see to what extent the lobbying by the UK coalition has been effective.

NOTES

1. C. Lasch, The Revolt of the Elites and the Betrayal of Democracy (New York: W.W. Norton, 1995), p. 174.
2. R.W. McChesney, Telecommunications, Mass Media and Democracy: The Battle for the Control of US Broadcasting, 1928–1935 (New York: Oxford University Press, 1993), p. 37.
3. Ibid., p. 3.
4. Ibid., p. 147.
5. H.H. Wilson, Pressure Group: The Campaign for Commercial Television (London: Secker & Warburg, 1961), pp. 171–5.
6. P. Bourdieu, Firing Back: Against the Tyranny of the Market (London: Verso, 2003), pp. 11–12.
7. B. Balanyá et al., Europe Inc.: Regional and Global Restructuring and the Rise of Corporate Power (London: Pluto Press, in association with Corporate Europe Observatory, 2000), p. 4.
8. Europa, 'Regulatory Framework, the "Television Without Frontiers" directive', 2004, <http://europa.eu.int/comm/avpolicy/regul/regul_en.htm>.
9. The issue is discussed in John Cole's memoirs, As It Seemed To Me (London: Weidenfeld & Nicolson, 1995). Douglas Hurd, home secretary at the time, 'particularly admired the skill with which Major handled the Prime Minister during a heavy piece of American lobbying. President Reagan, surprisingly, telephoned her himself about a low-level problem, a European broadcasting directive, which seemed to exclude non-European material. After what Hurd thought was a marvelous Major performance at the Council of Ministers, Thatcher was able to tell the President that the directive was going to go through anyhow, but that Britain had won a clause – "where practical", or some such.' Cole's interpretation suggests this was an insignificant matter, but for the American film and television industry the threat of quotas would have a major impact on audiovisual exports to Europe.
10. B. Grantham, Some Big Bourgeois Brothel (London: John Libbey, 2000), p. 125.
11. The full text of the document, 'USG Global Audiovisual Strategy Phase 1: January–April 1995', is available at <http://www.spinwatch.org>.
12. P. Toynbee, 'The sinister sound of democracy trickling away', Independent, 13 November 1996.
13. WFA, 'European Commission gives advertisers a three-point plan for effective advertising self-regulation', 11 March 2005, <http://www.wfanet.org/news/article_detail.asp?Lib_ID=1513>.

14. WFA, 'The View from Europe', 13 July 2004, <http://www.wfanet.org/docfiles/A1366D914.pdf>.
15. ICRT, 'ICRT comments on the Commission's work programme on the evaluation of the TVWF Directive', April 2003, <http://www.icrt.org/pos_papers/2003/030402_BO.pdf>; ICRT, 'Joint EU Media Association Position Paper on Public Broadcasting', 2 May 2003, <http://www.icrt.org/pos_papers/obwg.htm>; ICRT, 'ICRT comments on the Commission's Communication on the Television Without Frontiers directive', March 2004, <http://www.icrt.org/pos_papers/2004/040224_BO_TVWF.pdf>.
16. V. Reding, 'How Competitive is the Media and Communications Industry in Europe?', 11 April 2005, <http://europa.eu.int/information_society/newsroom/cf/newsbytheme.cfm?displayType=sp>.
17. Balanyá et al., Europe Inc., p.xii.
18. ACT, AET, EPC, Safeguarding the Future of the European Audiovisual Market, (Brussels: ACT/AER/EPC, 2004), available at <http://www.epceurope.org/presscentre/archive/safeguarding_audiovisual_market_300304.pdf>.
19. Europa, 'State Aid: Commission request Germany, Ireland and the Netherlands to clarify role and financing of public service broadcasters', IP/05/250, 3 March 2005, <http://europa.eu.int/rapid/pressReleasesAction.do?reference=IP/05/250>.
20. Council of Europe, Media Diversity in Europe, Media Division, Toynbee Directorate General of Human Rights (Strasbourg: COE, 2002).
21. Council of the European Communities, Pluralism and Media Concentration in the Internal Market (Brussels: CEC, 1992).
22. R.W. McChesney, The Problem of the Media: US Communication Politics in the 21st Century (New York: Monthly Review Press, 2004), p. 252.
23. V. Reding, 'The Future of European Media Policy', 22 April 2004, Westminster Media Forum, London, <http://europa.eu/rapid/press-ReleasesAction.do?reference=SPEECH/04/192&format=HTML&aged=0&language=EN&guiLanguage=fr>.
24. DCMS, 'Report of the Independent Review of BBC Online', 2004, <www.culture.gov.uk/NR/rdonlyres/>.
25. Members of BIPA include News International, Commercial Radio Companies Association, Trinity Mirror New Media, EMAP, Guardian Unlimited, The Publishers Association, Associated New Media and the Telegraph Group.
26. For a robust response to the Graf report and its proposals, read Tony Lennon, 'The BBC's Future', Free Press 141, July–August 2004. Available at <http://www.cpbf.org.uk>.
27. BIPA, 2004, <http://www.bipa.co.uk/getArticle.php?ID=316>.
28. McChesney, The Problem of the Media.
29. CEO, 'European Commission Must Act to Curb Excessive Corporate Lobbying Power', 25 October 2004, Amsterdam, <http://www.corporateeurope.org/barroso.html>. For a detailed account of developments since the open letter, see also <http://www.alter-eu.org>.
30. S. Kallas, 'The need for a European transparency initiative', 3 March 2005, <http://europa.eu.int/rapid/pressReleasesAction.do?reference=SPEECH/05/130&format=HTML&aged=0&language=EN&guiLanguage=en>.

31. Center for Public Integrity, 'Networks of Influence: The political power of the communications industry', 28 October2004, <http://www.publicintegrity.org/telecom/report.aspx?aid=405>; C. Layton, 'Lobbying Juggernaut', *American Journalism Review*, November–December 2004, available at <http://www.ajr.org/Article.asp?id=3748>.
32. McChesney, *The Problem of the Media*.
33. DCMS, *Review of the BBC's Royal Charter: A strong BBC, independent of government* (London: DCMS, 2005), p. 2.
34. 'Proposal for a European Parliament and Council Directive', amending Council Directive 89/555 COM (2005) 646, final.
35. Issues Papers for the Liverpool Audiovisual Conference available at <http://europa.eu.int/comm/avpolicy/revision-tvwf2005/ispa_scope_en.pdf>. The papers were: 'Rules Applicable to Audiovisual Content Services'; 'Right to Information and Right to Short Reporting'; 'Cultural Diversity and the Promotion of European and Independent Audiovisual Production'; 'Commercial Communications'; 'Protection of Minors and Human Dignity: Right of Reply'; 'Media Pluralism: What Should Be the European Union's Role?'
36. Intellect, 'TV without frontiers must go back to the drawing board, says hi-tech industry', press release, 20 September 2005, <http://www.intellectuk.org/press/pr/pr_200905_tvwf_back_to_drawing_board.asp>.
37. D. Currie, 'Introductory remarks to the Liverpool Conference', 21 September 2005, <http://www.ofcom.org.uk/media/speeches/2005/09/liverpool_conf>.
38. Digital Content Forum, 'Webpage launched for industry response on the draft Audiovisual Media Services (AMS) directive', 2005, <http://www.dcf.org.uk/information/industrynews/AMSDirective>.

12

Spinning Money: Corporate Public Relations and the London Stock Exchange

Aeron Davis

This chapter looks at a form of corporate spin which has received little attention in the literature.[1] Attention is normally focused on the impact of corporate public relations on the public or of lobbying on government. Instead this chapter examines the activities and consequences of corporate spin when it is directed at other corporate and financial elites. I would argue that such corporate elite-to-elite spin has had consequences for society and the economy that are just as important. However, the mechanisms have been a little different.

This chapter focuses on the promotional activities that take place around the trading of company shares in the London Stock Exchange (LSE). In 2003 some £1.35 trillion in company shares were traded on the Exchange. For most company chief executives, it is large shareholders to whom they are answerable on a day-to-day basis. Since 85 per cent of corporate shares are managed by professional fund managers, working on behalf of large financial institutions, companies focus their communications upon these financial elites. Thus, in the corporate sector, financial public (or investor) relations is considered a vital activity, as communicators attempt to spin their companies to brokers and elite investors. On the investment side, institutional shareholders mostly consist of banks, pension funds and insurance companies. In other words, most people's pension money, insurance money and other savings, as well as government debt, is managed by an elite group of fund managers who are themselves the focus of corporate and other forms of financial PR. Corporate spinning at this level, therefore, has the potential to have two sorts of impact on wider society. On the one hand, levels of personal savings, mortgages, insurance payments and pensions rise and fall with the spin-saturated market. On the other hand, spin-influenced investment decisions have a strong impact on management behaviour, employment patterns and capital deployment.

THE RISE OF THE FINANCIAL SPIN MACHINE

Both information and promotion are central to the workings of stock markets and it is often difficult to identify where one ends and the other begins. For regulators and financial theorists the production and dissemination of 'price-sensitive' information is essential for markets to function efficiently. For those who analyse and invest in markets, this information is vital for making investment decisions. At the same time, financial markets are highly competitive places. Companies compete with each other to get investors. Stockbrokers and investment banks compete to offer financial services. Fund managers compete to manage external investors' money and outperform their rivals. Each is therefore concerned to promote their products and services to others. Promotion and information go hand in hand. Thus, for one former participant and observer, the City of London is best described as 'the great expectations machine'.[2] In the opinion of one experienced fund manager, 'I think the whole business has changed. It's now basically a huge marketing machine to get people to deal.'[3]

The information and promotion machine has expanded its capacity tremendously in recent years (see Figure 12.1). Much of this has been driven by publicly quoted companies themselves. Industry surveys (see Public Relations Consultants' Association (PRCA) annuals) reveal that, through the 1980s and 1990s, corporate public relations capacity expanded more than 11-fold.[4] Within that expansion, three

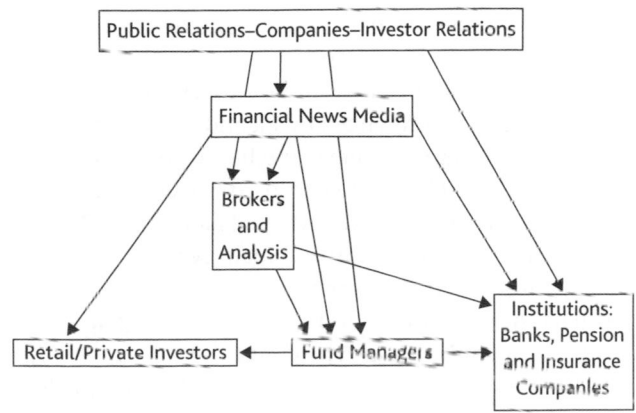

Figure 12.1   Lines of Spin in the London Stock Exchange

of the top four PR occupations were geared towards communications with other corporate and financial audiences.[5] For some years, it was financial public relations that had the biggest expansion. Financial PR professionals attracted the most kudos and the largest remuneration packages.[6] The 1990s also witnessed the further growth of investor relations and the creation of the Investor Relations Society. This was a specialist financial PR occupation, which oriented its communications towards the large institutional investors.

One function of these financial promotional operations is to communicate with financial regulators and policy makers in government. However, their main day-to-day activity involves communicating with City elites, to ensure a 'full share price', get support in takeover activity, raise further investment, and maintain good relations with major shareholders. Being so focused, both company managers and financial communicators attempt to manage the financial media, while simultaneously focusing their attentions on those City insiders who can influence the market. According to one ex-fund manager: 'There's quite a large group of people at the moment who think the main task of managing a company is managing the expectations of investors ... This is a sort of self-fulfilling prophecy. If you tell people that their job is X and nobody tells them differently then their job is X.'[7]

Communications output is on several levels. One of these is the financial news media. What studies there are of financial journalism in the 1980s and 1990s[8] all tend to confirm that financial and business news has been one of the growth areas in news production generally. Financial and business journalism has expanded and, despite little public interest, now makes up approximately a third of broadsheet news space. Equally importantly, these studies tend to confirm that financial news is more influenced by PR and advertising than is any other sector of the national news media. A poll produced by the PRCA[9] found that the *Financial Times* used considerably more public relations material than any other national paper, with 26 per cent of its output being PR-generated in the main section and 62 per cent in the companies and markets section. As a consequence, financial journalism has been reformed and shaped to fit the goals of financial promotion. In Parson's words: 'The danger is that, as in the past, the financial press may become more participants and "puffers" than observers and more extensions of PR companies than independent commentators and reporters.'[10]

However, spinning the financial media is only one part of the promotional activity that goes on in the LSE. As regulation has evolved, so the amount of public information released and spun by companies has increased. Annual and biannual reports and accounts are released, as well as quarterly updates and regular announcements on company developments that are deemed 'price sensitive'. These are released in printed and electronic forms as well as being relayed via the Regulatory News Service (RNS) of the Exchange.

In addition, private forms of information dissemination and promotion are widespread. Company chief executives and finance directors, in conjunction with investor relations specialists, spend increasing amounts of time talking to fund managers and analysts. According to an investor relations survey in the late 1990s over three-quarters of chief executives have more than eleven one-to-one meetings with fund managers per year, and 10 per cent of chief executives spent a third or more of their time on investor relations.[11] According to another study company managers averaged 52 one-to-one meetings per year with analysts and/or fund managers.[12] Investor relations specialists also devote much of their attention to brokers' analysts. Analysts are employed specifically to research, analyse and make assessments of companies, and have greater knowledge and resources than journalists. Their assessments are widely circulated to investors and also appear regularly in financial news reports. According to several accounts the investor relations function has been central to a rapid increase in controlled, private information disclosure between companies and analysts.[13] By the end of the 1990s, 77 per cent of analysts had at least weekly contact with their investor relations counterparts.[14]

One can add to this numerous informal telephone conversations, emails and meetings between managers, communicators, analysts, journalists and fund managers. The result is an intense and extensive communications network that is oriented around the promotion of shares, services, trading and other financial activities in the LSE.

SPINNING IN THE LONDON STOCK EXCHANGE

Financial spinning works on many levels. Most promotional activity, at a basic level, is about maintaining a strong share price by ensuring continuing demand for the shares amongst the investment community. Existing shareholders must be kept happy and new investors encouraged to buy the shares. As such, corporate spin operations seek to present positive financial data that suggests continuing future profits. Simple accounting measures, such as corporate earnings, profits and dividends, give some indication. However, even simple measures can be creatively presented. There are also many unknown and speculative factors. Things like expected 'growth rates' and the future 'market share' in a sector are difficult to predict. Predicting the success of new products and investments, as well as wider social and economic developments, is harder still.

All of which leaves ample scope for financial communicators to manage the presentation of accounting and other 'price-sensitive' information.[15] As one chief executive of a financial PR company explained:

The market isn't all that efficient. If it were, then there would be no reason for us to exist. In the long term you can outperform the market by looking at your audiences, seeing what they believe and giving them what they want ... There are many things you can do which amount to telling them the truth about your company in a structured and interesting way which plays to their prejudices and interests.[16]

Companies also promote their management teams as part of the presentational process. One survey of fund managers found that

[c]hief executive reputation accounts for 40 per cent of a company's reputation ... [and that] 75 per cent of respondents believe the CEO's reputation will enhance the company's ability to attract investment capital and earn the company the benefit of the doubt in times of crisis.[17]

As a result, chief executives, finance directors and other senior figures make great efforts to promote themselves, through a mixture of media coverage and meetings with powerful City figures. As one senior fund manager recounted:

Chris Gent of Vodaphone was extraordinarily charismatic. I think the company was identified with him and he had an extraordinary impact ... You find yourself being deluded by impressions. I find I have to check myself from being deluded all the time. It's people trying to hypnotise you with presentation. The world is presentation.[18]

If companies make up the first level of market spin, stockbrokers and their analysts make up the second. Brokers get commissions from investors to do the buying and selling of company shares. Until deregulation of the LSE in 1986 (the big bang) commission rates were fixed and, therefore, brokers attracted clients largely on the basis of their financial analysis and advice. Such analysts came to be regarded by journalists and many fund managers as the authoritative 'experts' on companies. However, since deregulation, broking houses, which have been bought up by investment banks, have had conflicting roles. They now draw commission from multiple activities and are more likely to encourage takeover activity, hype companies they work with, puff up investment fashions, and extol the virtues of investing in stock markets generally.

Consequently, since deregulation, analysts have been increasingly prone to promote buying and investment fashions generally. They now make far more 'buy' recommendations than 'sell' ones. By 2000, only 1 to 2 per cent of recommendations were to 'sell' companies. Even though the stock market was in clear decline for the next three years, the ratio of buy to sell recommendations was still five to one.[19] Not only do brokers over-promote individual shares; they also promote and puff up investment fashions. Bioscience, telecommunications, media, internet, oil and gas company stocks have all been fashionable market sectors in the last decade. Over-investment, as well as investment bubbles and crashes, have been the result. In the words of one investor relations specialist,

investment is a fashion business. There is no doubt. It's just like clothes, houses, universities – they are all fashion businesses ... what you don't know over a long time is whether a company is just riding the fashion or genuinely doing well because of the management.[20]

A third level of financial spinning, which involves brokers, fund managers and stock market insiders, is the promotion of the stock market itself. Brokers thrive on all sorts of trading and other financial activities. The more they are involved, the more their commissions mount up and, consequently, the more they like to promote share investment in general. As Smithers and Wright explain:

Whereas a scientist rejects a hypothesis if it is inconsistent with the data, stockbrokers habitually reject data that are inconsistent with their hypotheses ... A stockbroker's 'hypothesis' is that stocks are wonderful. Any stockbroker who discards this hypothesis will rapidly become both unemployable and unemployed ... Scientists are paid to pursue the truth; stockbrokers to sell stock.[21]

Fund managers, similarly, benefit from persuading large external institutions to put their money into the stock market, to be managed by their company. Most fund managers, regardless of their performance, are paid a fixed commission as a percentage of the amount of money they manage. Their primary aim is thus to manage more money and draw more investment generally into the stock market, as opposed to the bond, currency or property markets, or other rival stock markets. As a senior financial actuary explained:

One flawed structure undoubtedly is the financial model of fund managers, whose income is a percentage of funds under management ... It leads to behavioural activities of increasing transactions, when the market is down, to keep your revenue up. And what happens, when the market is up and there are lots transactions but you are covering your overheads, is that you get outrageous bonuses, which upset people. So it's a completely flawed way of charging for a product.[22]

This promotion of stock markets was apparent throughout the 1990s in the lead-up to the 2000 crash. Numerous books, by fund managers and market insiders, made wildly over-optimistic claims about the future growth of stock markets. Books, such as Siegal's *Stocks for the Long Run* and Glassman and Hassett's *Dow, 36,000*,[23] were bestsellers that hyped the markets. Financial media commentators also contributed to the culture of 'irrational exuberance' that engulfed insiders and external investors, both large and small.[24] Although fund managers, brokers and others all stand to gain from such promotional activity, many of them also appeared to believe the hype themselves. Research by Shiller found that, in 2000, after strong market falls, 97 per cent of professional investors still agreed that the market was the best place to invest in and 80 per cent believed that the market would go back up within two years.[25]

The fourth level of promotion is that of market ideology itself. Such an ideology means that markets are always right and market participants are not responsible for any negative repercussions that might result from market activities. On a daily level this means a belief in the stock market as a miraculous mechanism which lies at the heart of any properly functioning economy. According to this 'efficient markets' philosophy, participants in markets are rational; any irrational individuals or market movements will always be smoothed over by the long-term forces of the market itself; and stock markets are the most efficient way to invest capital in the economy. As one fund manager explained, referring to a frequently cited Warren Buffet quote,

in the short term the stock market is a voting machine. In the long term it's a weighing machine. In other words the stock market, by and large, is efficient at allocating capital, that's what 'stock market' means – market for stock coming from capital. So it allocates capital, takes it away from companies that aren't getting the right returns and allocates it to areas where, risk adjusted, they are making higher returns. So it is efficient every time.[26]

On the larger scale, market ideology is the belief that free-market thinking provides the solution to all social and political problems. As several City observers have noted, being pro-market and supporting pro-market political parties is the established norm.[27]

In effect, massive amounts of promotionally-oriented material is produced and consumed by financial elites within, and adjacent to, the stock market. Companies promote themselves and their shares. Brokers and investment banks promote their services and general market activities, from trading to takeovers. Fund managers promote their services and share investment generally. All involved within the London Stock Exchange promote the LSE itself. Many are not just involved in this promotional activity, they also buy into it.

THE SOCIAL AND ECONOMIC CONSEQUENCES OF FINANCIAL SPIN

What are the consequences? How does financial elite-to-elite spinning impact upon wider society, economics and politics? I would say on two broad levels. One is that financial elite communication and decision making, like most promotional spinning, is overly focused on internal market matters. This means that non-market factors are excluded from the discussion and evaluation process. The other is that investors, large and small, have been persuaded to place large amounts of public and private money into the unpredictable stock market machine. Once there, it is, in many cases, effectively gambled with impunity.

Starting with this first issue, management goals and financial reporting are overly influenced by the agendas of financial spin. The management of corporations becomes primarily oriented towards persuading investors that shareholder profits will improve in the short to medium term. Employee conditions, the environment, long-term research investment and development, are all secondary considerations. Any survey of City opinion reveals that companies are judged on things like the reputations of their management and their returns on capital investment. Treatment of customers, employees, social responsibility, etc. are mentioned by only a few per cent of respondents.[28] Similarly, mainstream financial and business reporting is equally unconcerned with such considerations. Nor is financial reporting particularly taken up with wider debates about economic or fiscal policy, economic theory, globalisation, or the part played by business in the environment or community. It's almost all about selling to investors – big and small.[29]

This becomes especially significant when company managers and key investors are agreeing the strategic development plans for companies. Such plans are always centred on increasing returns to shareholders. They involve such things as 'productivity drives', making 'efficiency savings' and takeover activity, which, in turn, impact directly on employees. Job cuts, flexible contracts, multitasking, longer hours, benefits and pensions cuts, and environmental pollution are some of the results. Since these things are a minor consideration next to shareholder returns, they can be ignored. This is also significant when one looks at the inherent investment biases contained in the market. Long-term research and development has been significantly lower in the United Kingdom than its major competitors. Decline of the industrial base has been significantly faster. Investment in new companies and smaller market-quoted companies is weak.[30] For many fund managers and company managers the demand for short-term returns gets louder with each decade.

The second general impact concerns the misallocation and waste of capital in society more generally. That is a concern to wider society because it usually involves using public and personal money that might be better and/or more securely invested.

Throughout the 1980s and 1990s, financial spin was centrally implicated in the large transfer of public and personal capital into the LSE, particularly into the shares market. Between 1979 and 1996 there were 59 major public sales of government-owned businesses[31] and these now make up approximately 20 per cent of the value of shares traded on the LSE. There has also been a steady succession of life assurance companies and building societies which gave up their mutual status in order to raise capital on the LSE. Each of these movements shifted large amounts of public finances that were publicly managed into the hands of powerful private investment companies. Not only did former public institutions become tradable commodities, they invested much of their surplus capital (the majority in many cases) into the stock market. Pension companies, above all, placed the majority of their funds with professional fund managers operating inside the shares market. However, so did many banks. Similarly, many people were advised to put their personal savings into a series of government sponsored investment schemes which put money directly into shares. Quite clearly, treasury officials, corporate managers, pension fund trustees, the boards of insurance companies and high street banks, all became convinced that the London equities market was the best place to invest any surplus capital.

At the same time, as already stated, fund managers are disproportionately paid according to how much money they manage, not according to their performance. They take risks with money that is not theirs. They lose nothing if those risks fail, but earn big bonuses if they succeed. In effect they gamble with other people's money and calculate risks to themselves rather than their clients. As one experienced ex-fund manager explained:

The problem is quite simple. There are these conflicts of interest between stockbrokers, fund managers and owners of capital. And it's not the fault of the stockbrokers and fund managers – it really isn't. If you've got a business risk which overrides the asset risk of the client you can't afford to take it.[32]

But, then, as several insiders acknowledged to me, why should fund managers be in a position to evaluate investment issues on any socially minded or client-oriented basis? Most fund managers and institutional investors know absolutely nothing about the industries of which they are effectively masters. Most do not have any experience of working in industry and have no industrial qualifications. They are fixated on the financial issues that are driven by spin. As one company chairman put it:

Putting the non-executives in charge of the business is a bit like taking me to the Olympics and saying 'well it's a choice between XXX, who occasionally runs for the bus, and Darren Campbell who trains seven days a week, and we'll stick XXX in the 200 metres'. How can they set the strategy? Madness. Madness. The fund managers are in charge but none of them know how to run a business.[33]

Such City spin, combined with ignorance, short-sightedness and self-interest, have resulted in heavy costs to the public. At many times in history, 'irrational exuberance' has resulted in stock market bubbles and crashes. In these cases, large amounts of outside investors' money are wasted on redundant infrastructure, research and companies that go bust. The most recent occurrence of this was in 2000. Stock market investment had reached completely irrational levels – far beyond anything reached just before the 1929 Wall Street Crash. As can be seen in Figure 12.2, which relates to the US markets, the prices paid

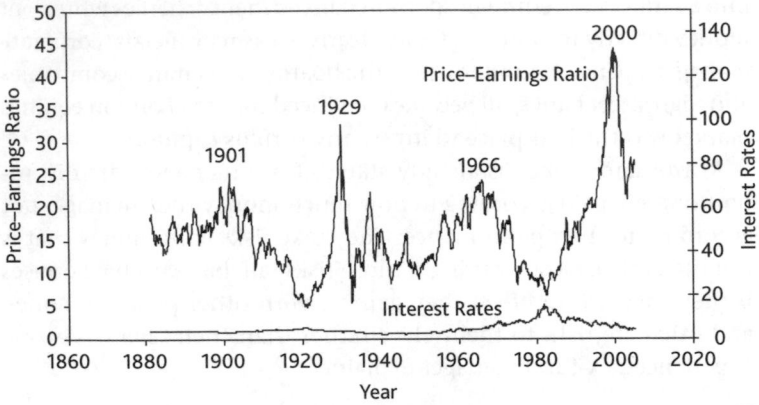

Figure 12.2   The Price–Earnings Ratio of the S&P Composite Stock Index 1881–present

for companies, relative to their earnings, meant that they could not possibly offer any sort of reasonable returns on investment.[34] The crash came, and it dragged the UK market down heavily for three years. Approximately £500 billion was wasted on useless investment in infrastructure as new hi-tech and internet companies tried to gain dominant market shares. Pension funds were left with large shortfalls. Insurance companies were in danger of not having enough assets to cover their liabilities. Endowment mortgages reaching their expiration date were no longer able to pay off mortgages. Personal savings plans lost large sums. Through the eleven-year period of boom and bust, all these investors – big, small, public, private – would have made a greater return if they had put their money in a high-interest account. Many businesses and individuals would not have gone under.

WHAT IS TO BE DONE?

The possible solutions to such problems involve challenging spin at its centre. They amount to countering spin and dominant market thinking at the place where such ideas and practices develop; for example, amongst financial elites in the City. Spin cannot simply be done away with. Rather, information and reporting need to follow agendas that are not set by spin and the promotional goals of market insiders. Financial decision makers, at all levels, need to broaden their informational inputs beyond such agendas.

One important step is to attempt to restore financial journalism. It used to be a place where economics and policy were discussed and where the reader was something more than an investor and/or consumer of financial products. Non-financial elite sources must try to get a say in financial and business news. Such news needs to be brought, more often, out of the business pages, where few people read it. Financial issues need to be made more relevant to the public, at least beyond a discussion of the budget once a year. By such means, those people at the heart of it all, from fund managers to regulators, might be made more publicly accountable for their actions. We know all about our politicians and public representatives. But we know next to nothing about the people who manage far bigger amounts of public money than most cabinet ministers.

Second, non-market thinking must make more of an impact on the workings of the market. The policy-setting and regulatory bodies, from the Treasury to the Financial Services Authority, need to have more input from non-economists and non-City insiders. At the moment, most regulation is self-regulation, and most assessments of the City are done by conventional economists and/or City insiders. Corporate managers all follow narrow market remits and are guided by classical economic assumptions. A large proportion of the 100-plus people I have interviewed inside the market, from financial PRs to brokers to fund managers, have experiences which suggest that market thinking frequently falls down in practice. For some of these insiders, 'efficient markets' are regarded as the extreme rather than the norm. As a senior fund manager said to me, 'I actually think, in fact my whole interest in my declining years, is to write about the dysfunctionality of markets – and it's a complete contradiction to how I came in. I actually think the market is potentially dangerously dysfunctional.'[35]

Third, those who invest public money and set the incentives and rewards in the financial sector need, themselves, to be more financially literate and socially aware. Too often, those who invest our money, from pension fund trustees to mortgage companies, are not aware of the risks of investment and are thus easily spun. Too often they do not appear to question the actions and remuneration of fund managers and business leaders. Consequently, they also ignorantly set the targets for fund managers to act in ways that are detrimental to their own members and fail to question the activities of financial elites.[36]

NOTES

1. This chapter draws on two lengthy periods of research conducted by the author (1998/9 and 2004). This research, which includes over 100 interviews with market participants, has looked generally at the impact of public relations and communications on the London Stock Exchange (LSE).

2. T. Golding, *The City: Inside the Great Expectations Machine* (2nd edn., London: FT/Prentice Hall, 2003).

3. Interview with Tony Dye, founder and director of Dye Asset Management, 7 April 2004.

4. See D. Miller and W. Dinan, 'The Rise of the PR Industry in Britain, 1979–98', *European Journal of Communication* 15 (1), March 2000, pp. 5–35.

5. See A. Davis, *Public Relations Democracy: Public Relations, Politics and the Mass Media in Britain* (Manchester: Manchester University Press, 2002).

6. See annual surveys in *PR Week* and PRCA handbooks.

7. Interview with Andrew Smithers, ex-fund manager, director of Smithers & Co., 20 April 2004.

8. See W. Parsons, *The Power of the Financial Press: Journalism and Economic Opinion in Britain and America* (London: Edward Elgar, 1989); H. Tumber, '"Selling Scandal": Business and the Media', *Media, Culture and Society* 15 (3), 1993, pp. 345–61; J. Tunstall, *Journalists at Work* (London: Sage, 1971); A. Davis, *Public Relations Democracy* (Manchester, Manchester University Press, 2002).

9. *PR Week*, 1 July 1994.

10. Parsons, *The Power of the Financial Press*, p. 213.

11. Investor Relations Society, *Investor Relations in the UK: Current Practices and Key Issues* (London: Business Planning and Research, 1998).

12. C. Marston, *Investor Relations Meetings: Views of Companies, Institutional Investors and Analysts* (Glasgow: Institute of Chartered Accountants of Scotland, 1999).

13. C. Marston, *Investor Relations: Meeting the Analysts* (Glasgow: Institute of Chartered Accountants of Scotland, 1996); Marston, *Investor Relations Meetings*; J. Holland, *Corporate Communications with Institutional Shareholders: Private Disclosure and Financial Reporting* (Glasgow: Institute of Chartered Accountants of Scotland, 1997).

14. Investor Relations Society, *Investor Relations in the UK*.

15. On this, see D. McCloskey, *The Rhetoric of Economics* (Brighton: Wheatsheaf, 1985); T. Smith, *Accounting for Growth: Stripping the Camouflage from Company Accounts* (2nd edn., London: Century Business, 1996).

16. Interview with Nick Miles, chief executive of Financial Dynamics, 17 August 1998.

17. See *PR Week*, 3 April 1998, p. 2.

18. Interview (anonymous) with fund manager, 2004.

19. See Financial Services Authority, 'Investment Research: Conflicts and Other Issues', discussion paper, 15, July 2002, p. 12.

20. Interview (anonymous), 1999.

21. A. Smithers and S. Wright, *Valuing Wall Street: Protecting Wealth in Turbulent Markets* (New York: McGraw Hill, 2000), p. 34.
22. Interview with Jeremy Goford, principal at Tillinghast Towers Perrin, immediate past president of the Institute of Actuaries, 29 September 2004.
23. J. Siegal, *Stocks in the Long Run* (3rd edn., New York: McGraw Hill, 2002); J. Glassman and K. Hassett, *Dow, 36,000: The New Strategy for Profiting from the Coming Rise in the Stock Market* (New York: Random House, 1999).
24. See accounts by R. Shiller, *Irrational Exuberance* (Princeton, N.J.: Princeton University Press, 2001); J. Cassidy, *Dot.Con* (London: Penguin/Allen Lane, 2002).
25. Shiller, *Irrational Exuberance*, p. xiii.
26. Interview (anonymous) with fund manager, 2004.
27. B. Hill, 'Britain: The Dominant Ideology Thesis After a Decade', in A. Abercrombie, S. Hill and B. Turner (eds) *The Dominant Ideology Thesis* (London: Unwin Hyman, 1990), pp. 1–37; W. Hutton, *The State We're In* (London: Vintage, 1996); J. Boswell and J. Peters, *Capitalism in Contention: Business Leaders and Political Economy in Modern Britain* (Cambridge: Cambridge University Press, 1997).
28. For example, see MORI, 'Captains of Industry', London, November 1998; MORI 'Attitudes of UK Institutional Investors and City Analysts', London, Summer 2000.
29. See Parsons, *The Power of the Financial Press*; A. Davis, 'Public Relations, Business News and the Reproduction of Corporate Elite Power', *Journalism: Theory, Practice and Criticism* 1 (3), 2000, pp. 282–304.
30. See Hutton, *The State We're In*; Golding, *The City*; HM Treasury, *Budget and Pre-Budget Reports*, London, HMSO, November 1998–November 2003.
31. See H. Gibbon (ed.) *Privatisation Yearbook 1997* (London: Privatisation International, 1997).
32. Interview (anonymous) with fund manager, 2004.
33. Interview (anonymous) with company chairman, 2004.
34. This diagram comes from R. Shiller, *Irrational Exuberance* (Princeton, N.J.: Princeton University Press, 2001). It is also publicly available on Shiller's own website at <http://www.irrationalexuberance.com/index.htm>. A price–earnings ratio is the price of a company divided by its annual earnings. The higher the figure the lower the returns on investment and, usually, the higher the expectations about future returns from investors.
35. Interview (anonymous) with fund manager, 2004.
36. On this matter, see P. Myners, *Institutional Investment in the United Kingdom: A Review* (London: HMSO, 2001).

13

The Atlantic Semantic:
New Labour's US Connections

William Clark

Demos is a well-known think tank in British public life. Many people probably know it as a kind of left-wing organisation that forms part of an ideas factory for the New Labour administration, along with other think tanks and policy organisations like the Institute for Public Policy Research (IPPR). However, if we begin to analyse what Demos does, and how it relates to government and other powerful interests in society, a more interesting story emerges.

Think tanks occupy a curious political space in contemporary Western society. They aim to be useful to policy makers but are often beholden to sponsors, who are usually the large corporations. Although important, their role has largely been under-theorised and under-examined. Think tanks have a long pedigree in shaping policy and the climate of opinion, beginning with influential groups like the Mont Pelerin Society[1] at the vanguard of the neoliberal revolution throughout the latter half of the twentieth century, and followed up enthusiastically by organisations like the Institute for Economic Affairs (IEA),[2] the Adam Smith Institute, the Centre for Policy Studies and many others. These groups were avowedly right wing in orientation and philosophy. This partially explains how Demos and the IPPR came to be regarded as left-leaning organisations. This chapter is an attempt to tease out the connections between Demos and the traditional neoliberal think tanks on the one hand and corporate lobby groups and state and intelligence agencies on the other. It suggests among other things that Demos played a role in the final phase of the attempt by the corporations and the political right to draw the teeth of the labour movement and turn the Labour Party into a party of big business.[3] The story starts with the response of the US and UK governments to the threat from the left posed most obviously by the Labour Party policy of unilateral disarmament and the rising strength of the Labour left in councils up and down the country.

A passage in the MI6 and CIA operative Brian Crozier's memoir *Free Agent* gives us a racy starting point for a study of the development of covert projects against the British left from the mid 1980s and the role of the United States therein. Crozier reports being summoned to Heathrow Airport for an important meeting with a prominent financier, well known in conservative political circles, on 27 February 1985. The financier was fresh from a dinner the previous evening at Chequers with Mrs Thatcher, Keith Joseph and another US-based 'tycoon'. 'The theme for the discussion', reports Crozier,

was neither the Soviet threat ... nor the state of the economy, nor a general election. It was an insidious domestic problem: the challenge to the government of the self-styled 'People's Republics' in the Greater London council and a number of municipal councils.[4]

Thatcher wanted to take out full page ads in the press warning of this. The financier had other ideas: 'What was needed was a full counter-subversion programme, using the enemies' own methods. There was only one man capable of helping such a programme with his existing organisation. And he named me', reports Crozier. Crozier was scheduled to meet the prime minister the next day in any case, and at the meeting she explained that she was 'turning to the private sector for help' because her plan to carry out counter-subversion activities from within government had been blocked. The 'great financier' proposed a 'suitably substantial budget' which would be made up of contributions by four business 'tycoons'. Crozier got to work.

The problem of what to do about the left in the United Kingdom had already been of concern in the White House. Rewind nearly two years, and we find the first known mention of the concept of a 'successor generation', at a meeting motivated by the rising anti-US feeling represented in the campaign against the siting of Cruise and Pershing missiles. Reagan, wary of the security of US military bases in Europe and of growing anti-Americanism, was reactivating cold war networks.[5] The US ambassador to Ireland was recalled and tasked with developing a strategy to defeat the opposition. The meeting, on 21 March 1983, was intended to recruit 'private sector donors' to help. Present at the meeting, according to declassified National Security Council papers, were President Reagan, James Goldsmith (US-based financier and a close acquaintance of Crozier's), Rupert Murdoch and George Gallup, as well as the US Information Agency's Charles Wick.

The meeting was 'focused ... specifically on our needs in Europe', according to a memo by the CIA director of operations.[6]

This was a natural business opportunity for Crozier and his fellow cold warriors. They intended to promote a pro-American orientation amongst key opinion formers in Britain. Reagan told the meeting that 'a special concern will be the successor generations ... who will have to work together on defense and security issues'.[7]

Two years later, in 1985, the first meeting of the 'British American Project for the Successor Generation' (BAP) took place. This brought together '24 Americans and 24 Britons aged between 28 and 40 who by virtue of their present accomplishments had given indication that, in the succeeding generation, they would be leaders in their country and perhaps internationally'.[8] BAP's Atlanticist 'Successor Generation' would engage future leaders of the left and right in a new special relationship, in order to shape their thinking and sentiment towards the world's superpower. Implicit in Tom Easton's analysis is that these moves tapped into older establishment anti-left networks: for example, those who had previously worked under the rubric of the CIA-funded Congress for Cultural Freedom (CCF).[9]

Crozier – who had been involved in the setting up of the Social Democratic Party (SDP) (which succeeded in splitting the left vote in the 1983 and 1987 UK general elections) – was commissioned by the then prime minister, Margaret Thatcher, to engage in less sophisticated subversive operations against prominent opponents of Conservative government policy, ranging from supporters of nuclear free zones to Ken Livingstone, the Greater London Council, the Communist Party of Great Britain (CPGB) and the leadership of Militant, the radical socialist group.[10] A record of this remains, in the form of a propaganda publication attacking socialism, co-authored with his friend Arthur Seldon of the Institute of Economic Affairs (IEA).[11] A few years later Seldon would join Demos and sit on the board beside the CPGB's Martin Jacques, whom Seldon and the IEA had previously regarded as a red threat.

Crozier's projects against the left seem complementary to those overseen by Conservative minister Michael Heseltine, which focused on CND, the scale of which is only now emerging.[12] Anti-left moves were also escalating within the Labour Party in the mid 1980s: openly against Militant and under the cover of 'modernisation' in the formation of the Institute for Public Policy Research, BAP, the Atlantic Council and the Labour Finance and Industry Group (LFIG). Peter Mandelson, perhaps New Labour's pre-eminent political fixer and manipulator, was a key figure in these networks and was then working with the consultancy SRU.[13]

My focus here is on the 'Atlanticist' connections within Demos and its satellite organisations that formed the company 'The Mezzanine', named after the open-plan office complex in central London which they all shared. I would argue that the key to a fuller understanding of the emergence of New Labour requires some understanding of the interplay between the various proxy forces that sought to legitimise New Labour's façade. One way of doing this is to examine the microcosm of organisations based around Demos in the Mezzanine. Rather unusually, all the groups who sublet office space (squeezed in below and above two floors used by government departments, opposite the headquarters of Shell, a major Demos funder) were members of the Mezzanine trading company. It appears that all these organisations worked in concert.

At one level the nexus of New Labour connections knotted together in the Mezzanine looks very much like a revival of the CCF network. There appears to be a certain continuity from the Marshall Plan of the 1940s, to CIA involvement with Labour politics in the 1950s and 1960s, to the Social Democratic Party breakaway in the early 1980s, through to New Labour's pro-American tendency today. The argument is that this is part of a long-term process of influencing and undermining the British left in the interests of US foreign policy, and ultimately US capital. Those surprised by the loyalty of Blair to the Bush gang after 9/11 might be interested in some of the backstory outlined here.

DEMOS

The CV of Demos's founder, Geoff Mulgan, doesn't mention his membership of BAP in 1996, nor whether he was a member of Militant;[14] nor does it clarify what his position was in organising the 'Red Wedge' showbiz publicity stunt for the Labour Party.[15] This is now seen as having been created outside the Labour Party Young Socialists, precisely because they were dominated by Militant and were openly hostile to the Labour Party leadership.[16] Peter Mandelson (who joined BAP in 1988) has confessed: 'All this stuff was born when I was communications director, when I really was chasing Militant, when I really was being thrown into battle against the Benns and the Livingstones and the Derek Hattons of this world.'[17]

Mandelson has continued this anti-left mission with his think tank the Policy Network, also based in the Mezzanine, which has links to US 'third-way' organisations. 'Mandelson said he would be using the Network's high profile platform to launch an attack on the policies of the anti-globalisation protesters.'[18] The Policy Network includes many of Blair's inner circle: Lord Adonis, Roger Liddle, Adair Turner, Philip Gould and Anthony Giddens.[19]

A kind of idle dehumanisation has marked Mulgan's output at Demos. He invented the term 'underwolves' to demonise young people 'disconnected from society' who increasingly 'threaten the social order', updating Charles Murray's work on 'the underclass', which distinguished between a 'deserving' and an 'undeserving' poor, falsely justifying the withdrawal of state provision. This was the beginning of Demos's interest in 'social exclusion'.[20]

From 1990 to 1992 Mulgan was special adviser to Gordon Brown when he was shadow Trade and Industry secretary.[21] Mulgan described himself as 'the Clinton campaign's link to Labour, which involved lots of telephone calls with the Americans'. How these contacts came into existence is unspecified.[22] Mulgan was part of a 1995 'secret committee' led by Peter Mandelson 'to examine policy changes'[23] that were central to the modernisation of the Labour Party. This group met at Westminster on alternate Fridays. Set up just before Blair flew to meet Rupert Murdoch in 1995, it was officially described as a group of outside experts 'helping to write sections of speeches and background papers' for the Labour leader. Some senior MPs noticed that this committee was actually an exclusive policy-making forum – among those notably excluded were Gordon Brown and Robin Cook. The group contained no MPs, preferring Roger Liddle (then City economist, sometime lobbyist, later special adviser to Blair as prime minister and now serving in the European Commission in Brussels, working for Trade Commissioner Peter Mandelson), Derek Scott (both former SDP members), Patricia Hewitt (then at global accounting firm Andersens) and television producer Michael Wills (later a Labour MP). It was here that Blair was urged by Mandelson and Liddle to use the SDP, which they described as 'broadly based and free from special interests',[24] as a party model. Both Scott and Mulgan would later accompany Blair on the first big government jaunt to the United States in February 1998.[25]

Mulgan's eventual government appointment to the prime minister's Policy Unit converted Demos's experiments into new shibboleths surrounding social exclusion, welfare to work, the family, the voluntary sector and other issues dealing with the poor. The appointment was attacked by the Tories as an example of 'cronyism' and the creeping politicisation of the civil service under Labour.[26] Mulgan, as director of the Performance and Innovation Unit (PIU) at the Cabinet Office and then director of Blair's Forward Strategy Unit in Number 10, was one of the first New Labour appointees to cross the line from political adviser to fully-fledged civil servant.

Mulgan is also a trustee of the *Political Quarterly* (with Richard Holme of BAP), Green Alliance (part of Rio Tinto's greenwash) and *Prospect* magazine. There is an American Demos and an American *Prospect* magazine (with the CCF's Daniel Bell on board) Mulgan's book *Connexity* cites Bell's *The Cultural Contradictions of Capitalism* as its guiding light. The former director of the CIA-funded *New Leader*, Bell, in *The End of Ideology*, held that Marxist theories of class struggle were redundant since economic affluence had made the working class indistinguishable from the middle class.[27] This was during the Vietnam War.

Mulgan's precise role is as opaque and ambiguous as his writings. As Demos's 'policy entrepreneur', he pushed various ideas into Labour to aid in the concoction of an artificial intellectual consensus around certain key issues. His use and promotion of the 'end of ideology' dictum mimics the 1950s cold war in that it is centred on manipulating existing viewpoints of the left rather than the creation of new ones.[28]

Demos imported a range of (mostly American) pro-market fads, such as the US Communitarian movement, but reached new lows of propaganda with Philip Bobbitt (LBJ's nephew) at the Institute of Contemporary Art (ICA) on 25 July 2002, who argued that war 'was inevitable'. Bobbitt is a key figure in the US planning elite. He was Reagan's legal counsel from 1980 to 1981, was on the Select Committee on secret military assistance to Iran and the Nicaraguan 'opposition' from 1987 to 1988 and was director for intelligence at the NSC from 1997 to 1998. He is a member of the Commission on the Continuity of Government, and director for intelligence, senior director for critical infrastructure and senior director for strategic planning at the National Security Council.[29]

'SINISTER POLITICAL ENDS'

A key stage in the development of Demos occurred with the involvement of Tim Pendry, who was paid by the Labour Finance and Industry Group (LFIG) to help Mulgan advance Demos along specific lines:

The solution was simple: to reposition the think-tank towards the people with the spare money and the motivation to invest as 'insurance' for the future. I might easily lay claim to the invention of 'public/private partnership' ideology to achieve this; but, in fact, it was a logical outgrowth of the 'New Times' model. I, therefore, advised the creation of an Advisory Board (as ideological cover) with 50% private and 50% public sector participants and the targets were then found to meet the revised ideological need. These targets were to be reassured by the company they kept and by modern design and management methods and then asked to support a 'non-political' ideas programme for the modernisation of the Left. [30]

Pendry adds that Demos and the other organisations it shared offices with in the Mezzanine were 'used' for 'much more sinister political ends' by what he terms the 'centralist national security state'.[31]

In 1993 the Demos advisory board included three key figures from the Institute for Economic Affairs (IEA). The late Arthur Seldon was vice-president of the Mont Pelerin Society (MPS), past presidents of which have included von Hayek and Milton Friedman. The MPS was instrumental in launching the Heritage Foundation, the conservative think tank founded by the Coors family. Seldon also advised the Independent Institute, a business lobby exposed in the *New York Times* as an over-energetic proponent of Microsoft's cause during its anti-trust trial. Leaked internal Institute documents showed that Microsoft secretly contributed $203,217 during 1999, specifically funding lobbying.[32]

Seldon was also a member of the Israel Centre for Social and Economic Progress (ICSEP), which was run by Daniel Doran, a former Israeli intelligence officer and special consultant to the US Embassy in Tel Aviv in 1957, and a Mont Pelerin member. The US ICSEP board includes Irving Kristol, while the UK ICSEP has Sir Stanley Kalms (treasurer of the Conservative Party between 2001 and 2003), Lord Harris (IEA and MPS), Lord Young (British Telecom, Cable and Wireless, and British Aerospace), Sir Sigmund Sternberg and Sir Ronald Cohen (who each donated £100,000 to the Labour Party in 2001)[33] and Gerald Ronson, the convicted fraudster.[34]

Seldon had further right-wing connections, with the Adam Smith Institute and the Centre for Policy Studies (CPS). As recently as June 2000 the IEA hosted the 'Aims of Industry Free Enterprise Awards', with Aims' Sir Nigel Mobbs. Seldon was on the Advisory Council of the Libertarian Alliance whose journal *Free Life* describes Demos as part of '[a] cavalry of Trojan horses within the citadel of leftism. The intellectual agenda is served up in a left wing manner, laced with left wing clichés and verbal gestures, but underneath all the agenda is very nearly identical to that of the Thatcherites.'[35]

As well as co-authoring *Socialism Explained* with Brian Crozier, Seldon also edited *The Radical*, founded in 1988 by Stephen Haseler and Neville Sandelson (who was initially a very right-wing Labour MP before becoming one of the founding members of the SDP, supporting Thatcher's radicalism and the anti-subversion lobby).[36] Haseler has also written for Demos (and worked for the Greater London Council (GLC)). Haseler worked for the 'left face' of the US National Strategy Information Center (NSIC) which funded Brian Crozier and was at the centre of a vast network of anti-communism and front organisations; his involvement illustrates a continuity with previous CIA relations with Labour. Haseler also worked with Roy and Joe Godson, who, in the 1970s, through the Atlantic Council, had set up the Labour Committee for Transatlantic Understanding, now called the Trade Union Committee for European and Transatlantic Understanding, which incorporates Peace Through NATO, the group that had been central to Michael Heseltine's MoD campaign against CND in the early 1980s.[37]

The second IEA figure to join Demos was Sir Douglas Hague, also involved with the CPS and a former member of the 1981 'Policy Unit', which provided the basis for Conservative Party strategy up until 1989. Hague was a member of the International Economic Association, founded in 1950, which organises events such as the Wilton Park conferences of the British Foreign Office and the Anglo-American get-togethers at Ditchley Park (just about everybody mentioned here is a member of the Ditchley Foundation). He also has connections with the Adam Smith Institute (ASI), and with Arthur Seldon spoke at their 'Open Society', alongside Patricia Hewitt and disgraced lobbyist Derek Draper (who led a 'Next Generation Group' (BAP) recruitment meeting in the House of Commons).[38]

Graham Mather is the third Demos and IEA director. Founder of the European Policy Forum, Mather had no problem with the IEA's game 'to get government out of providing schools and hospitals, cut taxes and give vouchers to the poor'.[39] His resignation from the IEA in 1992 came after several months of infighting between Mather, Lord Harris and Seldon following Thatcher's removal from power by Tory MPs. As the result of targeted leaks, the Charity Commission investigated the IEA's charitable status, claiming it was covertly acting as a political organisation. Embarrassed patrons at the time included the governor of the Bank of England and the chairman of the Stock Exchange. The IEA offshoot Civitas also occupied an office in the Mezzanine.

Mather came to prominence as head of policy at the Institute of Directors (IoD). His principle interest is 'the advance of markets into government itself'.[40] Mather sees himself as part of a 'priesthood of believers in the market', pushing a libertarian right ideology against the 'threat ... from socialism', and has found a spiritual home in Demos.[41] In 1990 it was noted that the IPPR's Patricia Hewitt felt a common cause with Mather:

There is even, between the rival think tanks, agreement on the part of the new agenda ... That has reached the point where the IEA and IPPR are planning a joint seminar ... 'It is not', Mr Mather says, 'a consensus on solutions. But there is a consensus on objectives.' Patricia Hewitt says: 'We may even be able to agree on some of the methods.'[42]

LORD SNOOTY AND HIS CHUMS

Another key figure on the early Demos board of directors was Lord Stevenson. A multimillionaire banker and management consultant and a key figure in BAP, Stevenson has been chairman of numerous companies, notably Manpower Inc, whose board member Rozanne L. Ridgway was president of the Atlantic Council of the United States (a vehicle for supporting NATO) and a director of Boeing, as well as being a member of the elite policy-planning groups the Brookings Institution and the George C. Marshall Foundation. Recruitment is a key aspect of Stevenson's work. As chairman of the media group Pearson, which owns the *Financial Times* and *The Economist*, he placed Marjorie Scardino (again of the Atlantic Council of the United States) as chief executive.

Stevenson says he first met Mulgan when he was giving a talk to the Council on Foreign Relations (CFR) in New York. Stevenson recruited Peter Mandelson for his secretive consultancy SRU in 1990, in between Mandelson's time as Labour's communications director and his election as an MP. Stevenson was an under-recognised gateway for big business access to New Labour, saying that 'Blair has involved businessmen to a huge extent ... In fact he has almost delegated power to them, I think there is a legitimate question about the extent to which that is actually right.'[43]

The *Sunday Times* also reported that Stevenson 'helped to fill the posts' and states that the 'Rebranding Britain' exercise, intended to give a New Labour makeover to British identity, was a distraction from the influx of big business into the government's 'taskforces'.[44] Stevenson moves easily between corporate power-broking and social policy think tanks that provide seemingly informal initiatives exploiting the ambiguous terrain between state and private sector. He attended the 1995 Bilderberg globalist conference meeting and remained on the Demos advisory panel until 2004.

Stevenson's involvement with Demos also brought in Martin Taylor, general secretary of the annual Bilderberg conference.[45] Among other activities, Taylor chaired the IPPR's expert commission on Public Private Partnerships (PPP). Critics noted that the IPPR's report amounted to a friendly warning to the government to start privatising health and education provision in ways that do not galvanise public opposition.[46] In an appearance before the Select Committee on Public Administration, Taylor enthusiastically stated (until interrupted by Lord Hollick, also Demos) that '[a]ny intelligent government would long to be free of the incubus of the Health Service; it is a source of constant ministerial embarrassment and it is set up to be for the next ten years'.[47] Somehow the NHS sucks blood out of the people like a vampire ...

Demos also gained Bob Tyrrell, 'Futurologist' and former chairman of the Henley Centre, a 'marketing and strategic planning consultancy' owned by WPP Group (which also owns PR firms Hill & Knowlton and Burson-Marsteller). Several Demos members have connections with the Henley Centre, and it was used (with Lord Stevenson's SRU) by Demos to sound out New Labour concepts to the City and vice versa.[48]

Formerly of the *Financial Times*, Demos's Ian Hargreaves is a member of the Centre for European Reform (CER). This is a lobby group closely associated with the American Enterprise Institute and the Atlantic Council.[49] The CER lobbies for various Atlanticist positions, often working closely with political lobbying consultancy APCO. Peter Mandelson speaks frequently at CER meetings, which are funded by WPP, *The Economist*, Pearson, the German Marshall Fund of the United States, and a group of banks and arms companies connected to the directors. Thought of as a 'New Labour think tank', the CER was set up by Nick Butler of BP (also of the World Economic Forum and

Chatham House, the leading elite British think tanks and equivalent of the Council on Foreign Relations). Butler, who is linked to the right wing of the Labour Party, was a key figure in setting up BAP, stating that their aim was to groom the future Labour leadership because '[t]he traditional British left-wing remained deeply suspicious of the United States, particularly on foreign policy and security issues. The British American Project (BAP) was made to counter this suspicion and encourage admiration for US-style "market forces".'[50]

CER director Charles Grant is former defence editor of *The Economist*. He writes on UK/US intelligence and works closely with the Foreign Office, collaborating with individuals such as Roger Liddle and Mark Leonard of the Foreign Policy Centre and the American Enterprise Institute. He was on an official list of approved Labour Party candidates leaked to the *Independent*.

The Atlantic Council of the United Kingdom was formed in 1994 when the British Atlantic Committee and Peace Through NATO (PTN) joined forces. PTN was the group used by Michael Heseltine to undermine CND. Again we see continuities in personnel with anti-left operations dating back to the days of Thatcher and Crozier. CER's office, which they shared with the Tory Reform Group, was at 29 Tufton Street, Westminster. The office was also used by the Action Centre for Europe which gathered together Lord Carrington (chair of BAP), Lord Howe, Lord Brittan, Kenneth Clarke, Stephen Dorrell, Christopher Patten and others. The Conservative Group for Europe (much the same line-up) is also tucked in there. The European Movement's offices are just down the road, at number 11.

THE OFFICE

Although invisible to the mainstream press, Demos's location and context, the Mezzanine, was a curious gathering of newly created groups with interlocking directorships. These were supplemented by fake grassroots organisations, wealthy funding bodies and other think tanks, some of which will be briefly mentioned below to conclude this chapter.

The Foreign Policy Centre has direct connections with the intelligence services through MI6's Baroness Meta Ramsay, also of the Atlantic Council, a Demos benefactor and LFIG member. Steven Dorril's history of MI6 states that Ramsay was secretary of the International Student Conference that allegedly acted as a CIA front. Its offshoot 'shared an office' with the overseas Students Trust which Dorril also states had intelligence connections and worked within the NUS. Along with the IPPR, the FPC was named as offering access for cash.[51] John Lloyd, former editor of *Time Out* and the *New Statesman*, was associated with both the FPC and Demos.

Lloyd's Demos publication *The Protest Ethic* appears to be heavily influenced by Samuel Huntingdon's *Clash of Civilisations*, asserting that Muslims are intrinsically more hostile than any other religious civilisation. Lloyd will happily argue that '[t]he anti-war movement ... is guilty of the worst kind of moral equivalence, equating Bush and Blair with Saddam and Bin Laden. It has been seduced by anti-Americanism.'[52] Lloyd develops this theme in *The Protest Ethic*, when he writes:

The only political grouping now using the tactics developed by the global movements – sporadic use of violence and opposition-ism through uncontrollable and unpredictable networks – is Bin Laden's al-Qaeda ... taking the destructive potential of such tactics and strategies to a far more lethal extreme.[53]

The Mezzanine's phoney grassroots organisation Community Action Network (CAN) is run by Ian Hargreaves's wife Adele Blakebrough, with Demos director Tom Bentley as a trustee.[54] In 1997 CAN was introduced by the late Geoffrey Tucker (a lobbyist whose clients included British Nuclear Fuels, British Gas and McDonald's) to GTech, who promptly gave them £130,000. Tucker brokered the marriage between commercial security printers De La Rue Holdings and GTech to create Camelot.[55] CAN became a neat way of placing paying executives onto lottery-distributing decision-making committees.

Someone who quietly slipped into the New Deal Task Force and DTI Competitiveness Council was CAN's Amelia Fawcett (who has dual US and UK citizenship).[56] Prior to joining Morgan Stanley, she worked for the international US CIA-connected law firm of Sullivan & Cromwell.[57] Fawcett stated that 'Morgan Stanley asked me to set up a government coverage function to monitor UK and EU governmental initiatives, support the privatisation effort and look for business opportunities with government'.[58] The picture of cosy lobbying and privileged access to Number 10 is clear:

Ten young social entrepreneurs, all sponsored by the Coca-Cola Youth Foundation, were recently taken by CAN to Number Ten Downing Street. This is part of a programme of activities which CAN is implementing to inspire and encourage them to develop their social entrepreneurial skills further. They met

Geoff Mulgan of the Policy Unit and discussed ideas and issues that concern them. Geoff has given the group and all CAN members e-mail access via CAN HQ into the Policy Unit so the dialogue with government can continue.[59]

Unsurprisingly Coca-Cola Great Britain is represented on the board of CAN, through Christopher N. Banks, managing director.

Ashoka is another American organisation located in the Mezzanine. It too is devoted to 'social entrepreneurs'. It was founded in the 1960s by Bill Drayton, who claims he 'intrapreneured' the introduction of 'emissions trading' while serving in the US Environmental Protection Agency.[60] A former consultant with McKinsey & Co. (Ashoka 'fellows' operate through partnerships with McKinsey, and Hill & Knowlton[61]) the 'Ashoka Society' was based at both Harvard and Oxford Universities and has ties to the Carnegie and Rockefeller Foundations. Part of its work involves public–private partnerships and social engagement, which is often code for controlling public forums and organising 'independent' groups as pro-corporate spokespeople to divide critics.[62]

Even organisations like the Mezzanine's Carnegie Youth Trust have dubious connections. Many post-war scholars who specialised in international studies were sponsored by the OSS/CIA, with funding by the Carnegie, Rockefeller and Ford Foundations. The first OSS Secret intelligence chief in London, Whitney Shepardson, was director of the Carnegie Corporation's British Fund and president of the CIA-funded Free Europe Committee.[63]

The Carnegie Endowment for International Peace 'incubated' the German Marshall Fund of the United States and John Foster Dulles led the board; the organisation cites CIA reports to this day.[64] Its Massachusetts Avenue address in Washington is shared by BAP, the Nitze School of Advanced International Studies, Heritage Foundation, CATO Institute, CFR, Brookings Institution and the British Embassy, so you don't have to walk far. It was Allen Dulles's idea to organise most CCF funding at arm's length, through a 'consortium' of 'philanthropic foundations, business corporations, and other institutions and individuals, who worked hand in hand with the CIA to provide the cover'.[65]

And this can be seen in our last organisation, ERA, which described the Mezzanine as 'an open plan trading floor or market place ... where new relationships are negotiated and new ideas turned into practical opportunities'.[66] Although nominally a charity, its purposes appear rather more like an expensive boutique consultancy. The board includes familiar names: Baroness Ashton, Anthony Giddens, Ian Hargreaves, Will Hutton, Lord Stevenson and Linda Tarr-Whelan, a former US ambassador to the United Kingdom who runs the US Demos – funded by the Ford Foundation, the Rockefeller Foundation and the Carnegie Corporation.[67]

This chapter has sought to describe a nexus of interests and organisations centred on one particular locale, the Mezzanine, and one notable organisation, Demos. Readers are of course free to draw their own conclusions from this coalescence. However, it is worth noting the patterned, almost structured way such policy actors and charity groups associate and interpenetrate. The case of Demos and the Mezzanine represents a network of actors with shared connections and, crucially, shared interests. They represent a little-examined and poorly understood current in British public life. But we should beware of looking to conspiracy theory for an explanation. Much of what has been discussed here is not secret, but is openly available on the public record if you know where to look. As William Domhoff, a leading expert on elites and power structure research, notes:

We study visible institutions, take most of what elites say as statements of their values and intentions, and recognize that elites sometimes have to compromise, and sometimes lose. Conspiracists study alleged behind the scenes groups, think everything elites say is a trick, and claim that elites never lose.[68]

Domhoff notes several problems with the conspiratorial world-view that don't fit with the available evidence. For instance, the notion that a tiny wealthy clique with an obsessive desire for power is really conspiring secretly to rule the world is unsustained: 'It makes more sense to assume that leaders act for their usual reasons, such as profit-seeking motives and institutionalized roles as elected officials.' Such a perspective is useful when looking again (or indeed for the first time) at groups like Demos. Such policy-orientated groups merit careful study and scrutiny. The analysis offered here draws together different pieces of evidence to offer an alternative account of the role of think tanks and para-political organisations in the conduct of politics and policy.

We can draw some conclusions. First, that the policy entrepreneurs around Demos are thoroughly entwined with the right-wing networks which promoted Thatcherism and with their US equivalents, not least through the British American Project. Second, that the intelligence and foreign policy connections are many and complex, linking this nexus with the UK and US intelligence services and with the US foreign- and defence-policy establishment. Third, that the interpenetration of the think-tankers, lobbyists and New Labour is striking. These networks, actors and organisations are all part of the life support system for the New Labour government. They contribute to the climate of opinion by shaping discourse and debate, and both encourage and enable the neoliberal policy agenda.

The analysis presented above directly challenges the mainstream histories of this period that are available. Doubtless some will try to dismiss this account as somehow fanciful or conspiracist. The focus here has been to document and describe some of the actors and their political projects as a way of unspinning the story of New Labour and reconceptualising the taken-for-granted accounts of the 'modernisation' of the Labour Party over the last 20 years.

NOTES

1. See D. Plehwe, B. Walpen and G. Neunhoffer (eds) *Neoliberal Hegemony: A Global Critique* (London: Routledge, 2005), especially ch. 2; D. Miller and W. Dinan, *The Cutting Edge* (London: Pluto Press, forthcoming).
2. For more detail, see R. Cockett, *Thinking the Unthinkable; Think-tanks and the Economic Counter-revolution 1938–83* (London: Fontana, 1995).
3. David Osler, *Labour Party PLC* (Edinburgh: Mainstream Books, 2002).
4. All quotes in this paragraph are from B. Crozier, *Free Agent: The Unseen War 1941–1991* (London: HarperCollins, 1993), p. 250–1.
5. S. Dorril, 'American Friends: the Anti-CND Groups', *Lobster* 3, February 1984.
6. Papers submitted to the report of the Congressional Committee investigating the Iran-Contra Affair (House Report No. 100–433/Senate Report No. 100–216, Washington, 1988), cited in T. Easton, 'The British American Project for the Successor Generation', *Lobster* 33, Summer 1997, <http://www.unclenicks.net/bilderberg/www.bilderberg.org/bap.htm>.
7. <http://www.unclenicks.net/bilderberg/www.bilderberg.org/bap.htm#Tom>.
8. Ibid.
9. See F. Stonor Saunders, *The Cultural Cold War: The CIA and the World of Arts and Letters* (New Press: New York, 2004).
10. Crozier, *Free Agent*, p. 250.
11. B. Crozier and A. Seldon, *Socialism Explained* (Sherwood Press: London, 1984).
12. 'Operational Selection Policy OSP11: Nuclear Weapons Policy 1967–1998', revised November 2005, National Archives, p. 7, paragraph 5.17, <http://www.nationalarchives.gov.uk/documents/osp11.pdf>; Dorril, 'American Friends'.
13. D. Macintyre, *Mandelson and the Making of New Labour* (London: HarperCollins, 2000), pp. 248, 311.
14. N. Cohen, 'Up for Grabs', *New Statesman*, 23 October 2000.

15. Red Wedge was a celebrity-led initiative to engage young voters in the political process before the 1987 election. It was linked with the Labour Party and included musicians Billy Bragg and Paul Weller, and comedians Lenny Henry and Ben Elton.

16. J. Tranmer, 'Wearing badges isn't enough in days like these', *Cercles* 3, 2001, p. 134, <http://www.cercles.com/n3/tranmer.pdf>.

17. *Guardian*, 26 September 2002.

18. K. Ahmed, 'Mandelson back as think tank head', *Observer*, 9 September 2001, <http://www.policy-network.net/php/article.php?sid=6&aid=257>.

19 Cohen, 'Up for Grabs'.

20. G. Mulgan and H. Wilkinson, *Freedom's Children* (London: Demos, 1995).

21. Hansard Debates, 5 December 1991.

22. G. Bedell, *Independent On Sunday*, 24 January 1993.

23. *Guardian*, 15 and 18 July 1995.

24. Ibid.

25. House of Commons Hansard, written answers for 19 October 1999 (pt. 20), <http://www.publications.parliament.uk/pa/cm199899/cmhansrd/vo991019/text/91019w20.htm>.

26. M. McHale, 'Geoff Mulgan: Thinker of the unthinkable', *Public Finance*, 8 December 2000, <http://www.publicfinance.co.uk/features_details.cfm?News_id=7231>.

27. D. Bell, *The End of Ideology: On the Exhaustion of Political Ideas in the Fifties* (New York: Free Press of Glencoe, 1960). In the American edition of '*The End of Ideology*', Bell states that the book is a collection of articles 'prompted' by Irving Krystol (now with the neoconservative American Enterprise Institute), Michael Josselson and Melvin Lasky ('an old comrade'), which first appeared in *Commentary* and *Encounter*, and that the longer essays were presented at CCF conferences. Bell states that he worked for the CCF (1955–57) as director of international seminars, and cites a CCF conference in 1957 'under the auspices of St Antony's College, Oxford'.

28. G. Mulgan, *After the End of Politics*, occasional paper 2 (Sheffield: University of Sheffield, February 1994).

29. Phillip C. Bobbitt, biography, School of Law, University of Texas, <http://www.utexas.edu/law/faculty/profile.php?id=pbobbitt>.

30. T. Pendry, 'Demos: Fashionable ideas and the rule of the few', *Lobster* 46, Winter 2003.

31. Ibid.

32. Uriel Wittenberg, 'The Independent Institute', 1999, <http://www.urielw.com/deception2.htm>.

33. Red Star Research. Sternberg made large donations to the Labour Party in the late 1970s. He is a fellow of the Institute of Directors and is vice-president of the Labour Finance and Industry Group (he was deputy chairman from 1972 to 1993). Cohen had donated £100,000 to Labour in 1999 and was given a knighthood in 2000, <http://www.red-star-research.org.uk/subframe3.html>.

34. Israel Centre for Social and Economic Progress website, <http://www.icsep.org.il/about/organization.shtml#uk-friends>.

35. B. Micklethwait, Review of A. Etzioni, *The Parenting Deficit* (Demos, Paper No. 4, London, 1993), *Free Life* 23, August 1995, <http://www. btinternet.com/~old.whig/freelife/fl23etzi.htm>; <http://www.seangabb. co.uk/freelife/flhtm/fl23etzi.htm>.

36. Crozier, *Free Agent*, p. 147. Haseler was a founder member of the SDP and the National Association for Freedom.

37. T. Easton, 'Who were they travelling with?', *Lobster* 31, 1996, <http:// www.lobster-magazine.co.uk/articles/l31whowh.htm>; Dave Parks and Greg Dropkin, 'Backing Barry: The NATO Publisher and the PCS Coup', 5 July 2002, <http://www.labournet.net/ukunion/0207/pcs2.html>; see also Julian Lewis's account claiming that he was 'the person who collected and supplied nearly all the material used by Michael Heseltine and Ray Whitney to expose the Left-wing affiliations of CND leaders so damagingly before the 1983 election'. Julian Lewis, 'I exposed CND links', *Tribune*, 29 July 1988.

38. <http://www.adamsmith.org/policy/bulletin/b18.htm>.

39. *Guardian*, 4 May 1999.

40. *Financial Times*, 16 March 1992.

41. *Independent*, 12 December 1990.

42. Ibid.

43. *Sunday Times*, 21 June 1998.

44. Ibid.

45. D. Estulin, 'The World in the Palm of Their Hands: Bilderberg 2005' (online journal), 24 May 2005, <http://www.mindfully.org/WTO/2005/ Bilderberg-Millennium-World24may2005.htm>.

46. J. Shaoul, 'Britain: Government think tank sets out plans for privatisation of essential services', World Socialist website, 6 July 2001, <http://www. wsws.org/articles/2001/jul2001/ippr-j06.shtml>.

47. Select Committee on Public Administration, 'Minutes of Evidence, Examination of Witnesses (Questions 160–179)', 15 November 2001, <http://www.publications.parliament.uk/pa/cm200102/cmselect/ cmpubadm/263/1111504.htm>.

48. Macintyre, *Mandelson and the Making of New Labour*, p. 248.

49. Atlantic Council board members include Lord Robertson (NATO, BAP), Lord Dahrendorf (former warden of St Antony's College, Oxford, who has close ties to MI6), Lord Hannay (former ambassador to the UN and the EU), Lord Haskins (LFIG and Demos), Catherine Kelleher (professor, US Naval War College), John Monks (general secretary of the TUC), Dame Pauline Neville-Jones (former chair of Joint Intelligence Committee, governor of the Ditchley Foundation, director of QinetiQ – set up by the MoD to work with the Carlyle Group in running the government's Defence Evaluation and Research Agency) and Baroness Smith of Gilmorehill (the widow of Labour leader John Smith and a director until 2000 of the corporate spying firm Hakluyt).

50. Red Pepper profile, 'Nick Butler, Chief Group Policy Adviser for BP', <http://www.redpepper.org.uk/natarch/butler.html>.

51. A. Barnett, 'Think-tanks face claims of "cash for access" deals', *Observer*, June 30 2002, p. 5.

52. *New Statesman*, 17 February 2003.

53. J. Lloyd, 'The Protest Ethic: How the anti-globalisation movement challenges social democracy', 1 January 2001, <http://www.demos.co.uk/publications/protestethic>.
54. Bentley was an adviser to David Blunkett when he was secretary of state for education. Bentley went on to become the executive director for policy and cabinet for the premier of Victoria, Australia, from September 2006, <http://www.demos.co.uk/people/tombentley/blog>.
55. <http://www.brisinst.org.au/resources/sanderson_wayne_can.html>.
56. Fawcett biography at <http://www.telegraph.co.uk/money/main.jhtml?xml=/money/2005/03/10/ccfifty10.xml&menuId=242&sSheet=/money/2005/03/10/ixcoms.html>.
57. On Sullivan & Cromwell and the CIA, see E. Masud, 'Millions Spent Subverting "Enemies", Stifling Dissent', 15 February 2001, <http://www.twf.org/News/Y2001/0215-CIAfunds.html>; <http://www.answers.com/topic/john-foster-dulles>; also to be found in Christopher Simpson, Bankers, Lawyers and Linkage Groups: The Splendid Blond Beast (Monroe, Maine: Common Courage Press, 1995); <http://www.thirdworldtraveler.com/Genocide/Bankers_Lawyers_SBB.html>; <http://www.britannica.com/ebi/article-9321907>; and Nancy Lisagor and Frank Lipsius, 'A Law Unto Itself: The Untold Story of the Law Firm Sullivan & Cromwell', Business History Review 63 (2), Summer 1989, pp. 432–4, <http://links.jstor.org/sici?sici=0007-6805(198922)63%3A2%3C432%3AALUITU%3E2.0.CO%3B2-%23>.
58. <http://www.justpeople.com/contentnew/People/Interviews/Financial/AmeliaFawcett.asp>.
59. Web archive of CAN site at <http://web.archive.org/web/20010108023100/http://www.can-online.org.uk/activity/1999-05.htm>.
60. <http://www.ashoka.org/about/leadership>.
61. <http://www.ashoka.org/partners>. The website testimonial reads: 'Hill & Knowlton provides pro bono marketing and communications services to Ashoka and Ashoka Fellows. This global partnership is critical to advancing the profession of social entrepreneurship by providing strategic communications counsel, media and presentation training and other consulting services – including serving as organizational board members for Ashoka Fellows. To date, 25 offices on 5 continents have contributed to this rewarding effort. Hill & Knowlton is enabling social entrepreneurs to gain greater support for their ideas and to share best practices around the world.'
62. <http://www.youthventure.org/home.asp>; Larry Lohmann 'Whose Voice Is Speaking? How Opinion Polls and Cost-Benefit Analysis Synthesize New "Publics"', first published May 1998, <http://www.thecornerhouse.org.uk/item.shtml?x=51962>.
63. R. Harris Smith, OSS (Berkeley, Calif.: University of California Press, 1972).
64. See for example the CEIP pages on WMD in Iraq, <http://www.ceip.org/programs/npp/un-iraq.htm>.
65. A. Johnson, 'The Cultural Cold War: Faust Not the Pied Piper', New Politics 8 (3), Summer 2001, <http://www.wpunj.edu/~newpol/issue31/johnso31.htm>.

66. <http://www.era-ltd.com/about_us/where.shtml>.
67. 'Miles Rapoport Named President of Demos, New Public Policy Network', 6 March 2001, <http://www.commondreams.org/news2001/0306-10.htm>; <http://www.era-ltd.com/about_us/ad_council.shtml>.
68. G.W. Domhoff, 'There are no Conspiracies', March 2005, <http://www.publiceye.org/antisemitism/nw_domhoff.html>.

Part IV

Fighting Back:
Campaigning Against Spin and
Rolling Back Corporate Power

14
Unmasking Public Relations

Bob Burton

At the January 2005 World Economic Forum held in the snowbound Swiss resort of Davos, Richard Edelman, the president and chief executive officer of the public relations company Edelman, reviewed the icy winds of public opinion buffeting the reputations of governments and global corporations.

Releasing the results of the sixth annual 'Edelman Trust Barometer', a compilation of market research results from 1,500 college-educated 'opinion leaders' who earn over US$75,000 a year across six countries, Edelman noted a substantial drop in public trust in corporations, governments and the media and a corresponding jump in support for non-governmental organisations.[1] 'The trust void in institutions – business, government, media – is being filled by NGOs, whose trust ratings have trended up in U.S., from 36% in 2001 to 55% in 2005. NGOs are now the most trusted institution in every market except China', he stated in a media release accompanying the results.[2]

Edelman invoked the results to bolster the perennial bid by PR companies for a larger slice of the corporate promotional budgets. 'Approximately nine of ten people across all markets believe information conveyed by articles or news stories more than advertising, and more than 80% of respondents overall do not believe information unless they see or hear it from multiple sources', he stated.

In a February 2001 presentation to the Conference Board on Global Corporate Citizenship, Richard Edelman reviewed the findings of that year's Trust Barometer which probed 'trust, favourability, credibility on five key issues'. For corporations and governments, the results were sobering.[3]

According to Edelman activist, non-government organisations (NGOs) 'are winning'. 'The crisis of confidence in government and corporations provides opening for NGOs', Edelman's Powerpoint presentation noted. The evidence, he suggested, was to be found in recent European controversies: 'Shell/Brent Spar and Monsanto/GM Foods show failure of old model of persuasion.'

Edelman is the world's largest private PR company, employing 1,800 staff in 39 offices worldwide and, according to *O'Dwyers PR Daily*, boasts a client list that includes Microsoft, Pfizer, Unilever, Home Depot and numerous government agencies. Within the PR industry, Edelman is a heavy hitter when it comes to pushing pharmaceuticals, hustling high technology products, reassuring investors and promoting food.

In an article outlining the 2005 survey results, Richard Edelman extolled the 'necessity of corporate social responsibility' (CSR) and noted that the high NGO rankings meant that 'partnerships between public-interest groups and business can make for a clear advantage'.[4]

A 'clear advantage', that is, for his corporate clients. In his 2001 presentation, even Edelman flagged the question, 'Will co-operation with business lead to subversion of NGO credibility?'

Edelman seeks to sell itself as a PR company that can build bridges with at least some of their clients' critics. 'Our experience to date is positive: Chiquita–Rainforest Alliance, Home Depot–Forest Stewardship Council', Richard Edelman noted in 2001.

In his presentation, Edelman sketched 'what smart companies do' to handle NGOs. 'Have affirmative program to identify NGOs interested in your issues, reach out to moderate elements to forge relationships, try to have positive agenda that leads your industry', and 'be prepared to fight in the event of extremism'.

Edelman had advice on 'how to tackle hostile NGOs' too. 'Use similar tone/tactics as NGOs – use advocacy language', he suggested, as well as using 'new media aggressively – Internet chat room monitoring, active posting of material'.

Edelman also suggested that the use of a divide-and-conquer strategy could be effective. 'Invite NGOs for discussions – amplify relationships with centrist NGOs – make sure they are part of the solution, that they have a stake in the outcome', he noted.

Of course, Edelman's presentation was a pitch to corporate and government movers and shakers that his company was there to help, for a fee. 'We understand how to mobilize credible third parties and to operate in a multiple stakeholder environment', Edelman noted.

Within the PR industry, replacing corporate executives and government officials with more credible messengers is known as the 'third-party' technique. Writing in the September 2002 edition of *Pharmaceutical Executive*, Nancy Turett, the president and global director of Edelman Health, wrote that the heart of PR is third-party credibility. Third-party messages are an essential means of communication for validating scientific credibility, for legitimizing products, for building brand and disease awareness, and for building defenses against crises. As advocates develop louder voices, pharma companies must forge alliances and win allies.[5]

In a 2004 interview, Edelman's London associate director - health, Paul Keirnan, matter-of-factly said of the technique that 'it is not putting words in the mouths of opinion leaders. It is basically using a third party to put forward what are the facts without it being seen to be spun, if you like, by the pharmaceutical company.'[6]

In a presentation to a 1995 advertising conference in Sydney, the then senior Burson-Marsteller executive, Armada Little, said, 'developing third party support and validation for the basic risk messages of the corporation is essential. This support should ideally come from medical authorities, political leaders, union officials, relevant academics, fire and police officials, environmentalists, regulators.'[7]

According to the 2005 Trust Barometer findings, '[e]xperts who are seen as having no vested interest in the welfare of a company – "doctors or healthcare specialists" (>56%), "academics" (>49%), "a person like yourself" (>49%), and "representatives of NGOs" (>47%) are the most trusted spokedspersons'.[8]

The success of the PR industry has more to do with its invisibility to the public than the sophistication of the techniques it employs. Visibility of PR companies in a debate carries the risk of the message being discounted as 'spin' and disbelieved.

Of course, not all PR is Machiavellian. Some PR campaigns would be universally accepted as serving the broad public interest, such as anti-smoking awareness or effective crisis communications in times of natural disasters. Others could, at worst, be described as mostly harmless.

But as the PR industry primarily caters for those with deep pockets, it gravitates towards serving the needs of those with wealth and power in our society.

For these reasons few PR companies openly disclose who their current clients are, or, if they do, are very wary of disclosing exactly what issue it is that they are working on. Even within the ranks of PR, there is criticism about the contradiction between PR companies advocating that clients embrace 'transparency' while they themselves remain secretive.

In a December 2003 online survey on corporate social responsibility *PR Week* noted that anonymous participants commented on 'the irony that one part of a communications business could pronounce on CSR while another division represented Third World dictators'. As one sceptical PR participant wrote, 'It's very difficult to have a robust, defensible and enforceable CSR policy in PR if your job is to make big dirty corporate cock-ups look less bad.'[9]

But if PR practitioners are so critical about their own industry, why is there so little specialist reporting on the PR industry? Is it that the activities of the industry are considered so bland that its invisibility to the media-consuming public is warranted?

PR AND JOURNALISM

The success of much of what the PR industry does relies on exploiting the weaknesses of modern journalism. While surveys indicate that much media coverage originates from some PR activity, many in the PR industry – often former journalists themselves – will disarmingly insist that there is little to report on beyond the harmless peddling of press kits.

A search for recent mainstream media coverage mentioning even just the larger companies – Hill & Knowlton, Edelman, Burson-Marsteller, Weber Shandwick, Porter Novelli, Fleishman-Hillard or those in the Ogilvy PR group – would be lucky to turn up a handful of references. Even then, a significant proportion of those stories will cite PR industry insiders as informed commentators.

The most effective PR relies on the meticulous but invisible cultivation and deployment of allies while marginalising dissenting views. The muddy footprints of PR lead to some interesting places: think tanks, regulators, non-profit groups, minister's offices, trade associations and unions.

Many of the strategies routinely used in the PR trade were pioneered by the tobacco industry, deep-pocketed companies desperate to defeat or delay tobacco control measures. As a result, the millions of pages of publicly accessible internal industry documents shed light on the strategies used in many public-policy debates.

For example, recent documents illustrate the largely hidden phenomena of corporate tobacco lobbyists courting favour with the editorial boards of major US news organisations. In 1999 the then president, Bill Clinton, announced plans to sue major tobacco companies under the Racketeer-Influenced and Corrupt Organisations

Act, on the grounds that they defrauded smokers by concealing health risks.

Philip Morris (PM) hired the PR firm BSMG (now part of Weber Shandwick, the world's largest PR firm) to craft a plan aimed at undermining public and political support for any legal action. BSMG's PR strategy was quietly to meet with the editorial boards of many major media outlets, while simultaneously mobilising conservative allies 'to help provide an "echo chamber" of opinion consistent with our messages'.[10]

Suggestions on how to hide Big Tobacco's message behind the mask of such 'third parties' included the establishment of a speakers' bureau 'to expand the stable of surrogates to carry our message', and 'placement of surrogates on local radio programs or other activities'.

The goal, explained BSMG, was 'to build a steady drumbeat of discussion' about why the government's case against Big Tobacco was without merit. Once the echo chamber was ready, PM would offer briefing materials to a number of influential conservative columnists – including Jacob Sullum, George Will, William Safire, Paul Gigot and James K. Glassman – and set up editorial board briefings in the top 25 media markets.

This, according to a later iteration of the PR plan, was not just to provide information on PM's position, but also to 'identify the key editorial writer for each paper and assign an industry spokesperson to continue the dialogue with the writers and maintain communications and rapid response'.[11]

While many in the media dismiss the suggestion that corporate sponsored trips influence coverage, a British American Tobacco internal memo revealed its confidence in the practice.[12]

In 1994 BAT's Corporate Communications division pondered whether it could sponsor a visit to BAT's London head office for South American editors and journalists. They noted in frustration that some media organisations refused corporate sponsored trips for journalists and would only cover the costs themselves if they were convinced it was 'not just a junket or a pure publicity exercise'.

'In this respect, freelancers can be a better bet as they are more open to having their trip paid for, and they are less likely to "bite the hands that feed them" as they will want to safeguard their place on any future trips', they candidly wrote.[13]

While it is not surprising that the courting of journalists and editorial boards goes unreported, aggressive campaigns targeting media outlets occasionally backfire. In April 1998 the *Los Angeles Times* revealed that Edelman had drafted a campaign plan to ensure that a dozen state attorneys general did not join anti-trust legal actions against Microsoft. Part of the plan included generating letters to the editor, opinion pieces and articles by freelance writers supporting Microsoft. [14]

According to the documents, a goal of the campaign was to counter 'negative, reactive coverage that is driven by state attorneys general', and it aimed to generate a pile of press clippings that it described as 'leveragable tools for the company's state-based lobbyists'.

While discussion of the threat posed by PR is commonplace in journalism forums, it is a concern that is not reflected in the allocation of editorial beats. While the global mainstream media sports numerous columnists and writers on everything from astrology to yachting, to the best of my knowledge there are none with the sole remit of investigating the PR industry. (Those that come closest have a focus on either a merged PR/marketing round or a very broad media round.)

The lack of mainstream media reporting on PR reflects, in part, an assumption that PR continues to play a minor role, simply explaining clients' and employers' decisions. On the contrary, the last decade has seen the most senior PR advisers move to the heart of decision making in corporations and, more recently, governments.

Yet most PR campaigns remain invisible, because they exploit the fault lines in the media industry, with editors under pressure to cut costs and journalists expected to produce more stories with fewer resources. As the most extraordinary PR campaigns are the best hidden, and leaked documents are rare, there are few fast-and-easy stories that can be cherry-picked by general reporters.

In a post-Davos entry in his weblog Richard Edelman noted that one take-home message from the 2005 conference was that 'the news hole is shrinking. TV is providing news with more feature and entertainment value to keep audiences. The key dilemma is what is interesting versus what is important.'[15]

In the absence of the time and resources to investigate PR campaigns properly, many journalists rely on the use of the word 'spin' to hint at the underlying PR strategy and tactics. However, an over-reliance on the word 'spin' may well be counter-productive by implying that PR is solely about word games, the petty gatekeeping tricks of minders or spur-of-the-moment stumbles.

Many in the PR industry argue, and with some justification, that the lack of reporting on PR is simply a recognition that most journalists are unwilling to bite the hand that feeds them. Some even describe the relationship between PR and journalism as a 'partnership'. Perhaps another factor is that most major media corporations use PR and lobbying campaigns to advance their own commercial interests with regulators and the public.

Of course individual journalists can increase the visibility of PR companies by simply taking a few words to mention the company name and who they are representing in a story. This at least enables a company's client list – something that is often treated as a trade secret within the PR industry – to be assembled over time.

If there is a paucity of mainstream reporting on the PR industry, what then of the PR trade press, such as *O'Dwyers PR Daily*, the *Holmes Report* and *PR Week*? Such publications both benefit from and are hampered by their close proximity to the PR industry.

To their credit, *O'Dwyers PR Daily* tracks disclosures on lobbying required under US government regulations, while *Holmes* regularly carries lengthy and often fascinating features in which industry insiders discuss issues with their peers. While these publications provide valuable information on specific companies' campaigns and are often critical of industry excesses, much of what is covered consists of what PR companies want to announce, such as new accounts won or staff recruited.

PR AND NGOs

Edelman is just one of the large PR companies that offers clients its services as a key to courting or curbing the public advocacy of NGOs. If NGOs have been widely identified within the PR industry as primary targets what is the response of NGOs?

Amongst many of the larger NGOs there is a seemingly widespread indifference to researching and critiquing the PR companies that target them. This is especially noticeable amongst the most senior staff. Why?

Often senior NGO staffs, like many journalists, are inclined to believe that PR campaigns and the industry generally are relatively benign and warrant little attention. On top of that, many are overwhelmed with the daily challenge of organisational maintenance and tactical campaigning.

It is also easy for low-visibility strategies and campaigns to fly under the radar of overworked and under-resourced staff. For some, discounting the potential impact of PR campaigns is a way of shunting the issue off to the 'too-hard basket' in the hope that it will go away.

It is also not uncommon for NGO activists to downplay revelations about a PR company campaign as not being directly relevant to them. Commonly the argument advanced is that it wasn't their group or movement, that it occurred elsewhere or it was some time ago. After all, if those who have regular exposure to PR companies don't report on the existence of the PR industry, who's to know what they are up to?

Commonly, however, the trigger for a personal interest in understanding PR strategies is after they have come across hard evidence that their own campaign or organisation has been targeted. The more savvy activists recognise that the better they understand and anticipate PR strategies that may be used against them, the better the chance they have of winning.

Amongst many supporters of NGO groups working on labour, women's, environmental, human rights and indigenous issues, there is a thirst for information on what the PR industry does and how it affects the issues they care about.

Others in the NGO community lay the welcome mat out for PR company representatives. Some of the larger NGOs employ PR companies or have them work on their behalf pro-bono. Even pro-bono work for an NGO is not without its benefits for the PR company, as its executives gain valuable insights into the organisation and others it works with.

While NGOs can hire PR companies with a progressive reputation – such as Fenton Communications in the United States – simply using a PR company underpins a reticence to speak out about the industry generally. And it is not without its hidden risks. In 2000 the International Fund for Animal Welfare was stunned to learn that the PR company Shandwick (now Weber Shandwick) it had used to run a campaign in the United Kingdom to ban fox hunting was also promoting an expansion of whaling on behalf of the Japanese Whaling Association. IFAW terminated the account.[16]

Nor do those NGOs who view their organisations as potential beneficiaries of PR-devised 'divide-and-conquer' strategies have any incentive to speak out about the activities of the PR industry.

One of the notable developments in the last decade or so has been the 'revolving door' between activism and the PR industry. Former Friends of the Earth UK chairman Des Wilson subsequently became the vice-chairman of public affairs for the PR behemoth Burson-Marsteller. He then went on to become director of corporate and public affairs for BAA, the company which wanted to overcome community opposition to the expansion of London's airports. (In July 2000 Wilson retired from the position, though he remains an adviser to BAA.)

Others have given the door a good spin. Former journalist Jonathan Wootliff worked with major PR companies including Fleishman-Hillard and Hill & Knowlton before going on to head the communications section at Greenpeace International in Amsterdam.

After a short stint with Greenpeace, Wootliff went on to become an account director with Edelman and is now a 'corporate responsibility consultant who specialises in helping multinational companies to build productive relationships with NGOs', including companies such as Coca-Cola, BP, and the Indonesian paper and pulp producer, APRIL.[17] In one presentation, when he was working for Edelman, Wootliff reassured his business audience that 'not all NGOs are there to beat up on industry'.[18]

Another variation on the 'revolving door' theme involves those who work for PR companies while continuing to play an active role in NGOs. Peter Melchett headed Greenpeace UK until January 2001, when he joined the CSR practice of Burson-Marsteller. While Melchett was required to resign from all positions in Greenpeace, he continues as policy director of the UK Soil Association, the peak organic food and farming organisation in the UK.

Across the Atlantic, Bennett Freeman, who in mid 2003 became a colleague of Melchett's in Burson-Marsteller's CSR practice, sits on the board of directors of the US division of the global aid group, Oxfam. He is also a member of the Business and Economic Relations Group of Amnesty International USA.[19]

Given the ambivalence about PR amongst NGO groups, it is not surprising that attempts to document and investigate PR strategies aimed at countering community campaigns has been patchy at best.

When the US anti-environmental movement relaunched itself in the early 1990s, several foundations supported Clearinghouse on Environmental Advocacy and Research (CLEAR), a project of the Environmental Working Group, which established an online database to track the activities of corporate front groups and lobbying. It aimed at assisting frontline activists wanting to get past suspiciously reassuring names of previously unknown groups.

While CLEAR's work was invaluable, its Achilles heel was its ability to attract long-term funding and track the globalisation of anti-environmentalism. At the very time that US anti-environmentalism was morphing from an oppositional extra-parliamentary movement to one involving insiders within the ascendant Republican Party, funding for CLEAR's work dried up. Other groups, such as Greenpeace, published guides documenting the growth in corporate front groups.[20]

Perhaps the tobacco control movement, bolstered by millions of pages of internal industry documents obtained from legal actions, has been the most successful movement in documenting corporate PR strategies. These documents, which are still pouring out at a rate of thousands of pages a month, have proved crucial in unmasking the industry's third-party allies and blunting its divide-and-conquer strategies.

ASSEMBLING THE PR JIGSAW

With both mainstream journalism and many NGOs becoming ever more enmeshed with PR, what hope is there of unmasking the seemingly ever-growing influence of the influence industry?

The initial efforts at investigating aspects of the PR industry in the 1980s and 1990s came from writers such as Joyce Nelson[21] and Susan Trento.[22] In 1993 veteran environmental and community activist John Stauber established the Wisconsin-based Center for Media and Democracy (CMD). At the time it was the only watchdog group tracking the PR industry.

Despite meagre resources, the work of CMD and its flagship publication *PR Watch* grew in popularity. *Toxic Sludge is Good for You* by Stauber and co-author Sheldon Rampton is regarded by activists and PR industry insiders alike as a classic.[23] More recently, CMD has been joined by the UK-based Spinwatch to track the European end of the PR industry.

While interest in umasking PR is now much greater than it was a decade ago, the reality is that the combined annual budgets of CMD and Spinwatch would represent a tiny fraction of the daily billings of the global PR industry. No one really has a good tally on the total turnover of the PR industry but it is generally thought to be growing annually by double digit figures.

In many respects, documenting the PR industry is harder than assembling one of those hair-pullingly hard 4,000 piece jigsaws. Harder because at the outset we don't really know how many pieces there are, what their shape is or where exactly to find them. The nature of the industry is that most of its participants crave invisibility and willingly disclose relatively little. Often only one or two pieces of the jigsaw come to light at a time. Despite this, the evolution of the web and new software that facilitates collaborative research and writing open up exciting possibilities.

SOURCEWATCH

In October 2003 I started editing SourceWatch (www.sourcewatch. org, which until January 2005 was named Disinfopedia) for CMD. SourceWatch is based on open-source wiki software that enables anyone at any time to add to or edit articles in an online database aiming to track the public relations industry and others shaping public debate.

My initial reaction to the project was one of scepticism. How can a high quality standard of writing and referencing be achieved if anyone can change the articles? It seems counter-intuitive, but once a critical threshold of core contributors is achieved the quality of contributions is surprisingly high. Those who are regular contributors have a substantial investment in ensuring that new contributions meet agreed standards, such as the need to reference key points.

One of the features of wiki software is that publishing an article is only marginally more technically difficult than compiling a basic word-processing document. Tracking changes and reverting vandalism is equally easy. The low technical threshold also opens the door to a much greater pool of volunteer contributors.

By recruiting a pool of volunteer contributors and editors, wiki software allows a small investment in staff time to be leveraged to produce a substantial body of work. It can also facilitate global collaboration on local topics. For example, a contributor in Japan contributed to a series of profiles on think tanks and climate-change sceptics based on tobacco industry documents accessed from the University of California's online Legacy Tobacco Documents Library.[24] A click on a link in the articles and curious readers can view the source document.

The volume of traffic – over 8 million pages served in 2004 alone – should dispel any misconception that a specialist web publication caters for only a small audience. The unique content of the articles also helps ensure that pages score high in Google searches, driving traffic to the pages.

For example, the day the Republican-linked group the Swift Boat Veterans for Truth was launched, a SourceWatch contributor started a page on them. Once the group launched their television advertisements attacking presidential aspirant John Kerry over his war record, traffic to the page – ranked number 2 on a Google search – soared.[25]

As has occurred with other articles, it was noticeable how material and leads appearing in the article were taken up in mainstream news reports, as time-pressed journalists Googled for background information on the group.

Wikis have other advantages too. Where a traditional approach to profiling a PR company or a tactic would be for an individual patiently to assemble material until an article could be compiled, a wiki facilitates an incremental approach to pooling pieces of the jigsaw. A reference to a client here or a document there quickly builds to provide a substantial information base that can underpin a more extensive article.

Wikis such as SourceWatch are not perfect. The quality of contributions can vary, making some articles editing-intensive. There is also an inevitable churn rate of contributors which can leave the articles they created stranded unless new contributors update them. There is also a tendency to rely overly on web-accessible material for references.[26]

However, SourceWatch is just one element of the new technologies that are helping to fill part of the void left by the retreating mainstream media.[27] My initial scepticism about the potential of wikis has been replaced with the realisation that assembling the PR jigsaw has become a lot easier.

The PR industry has noticed too. Trevor Cook, a director of the Australian PR firm Jackson Wells Morris and a blogger on PR, reflected on the case in which a conservative commentator, Armstrong Williams, was paid US$240,000 as a subcontractor to PR company Ketchum to help tout controversial Bush administration changes to education policy. Cook pointed to SourceWatch as 'the type of service that can help us put together the jigsaw and make our media environment more transparent'.[28]

NOTES

1. Edelman, *Sixth Annual Edelman Trust Barometer: A Global Study of opinion leaders*, January 2005, <http://www.edelman.com/image/insights/content/Edelman_Trust_Barometer-2005_final_final.pdf>. (Notably, the survey did not ask about the public standing of the PR industry.)
2. Edelman, 'Trust Shifting from Traditional Authorities to Peers, Edelman Trust Barometer Finds: U.S. Corporations Face "Trust Discount" in Europe and Canada', media release, 24 January 2005, <http://www.edelman.com/news/ShowOne.asp?ID=57>.
3. R. Edelman, 'The Relationship among NGOs, Government, Media and Corporate Sector', presentation to the Conference Board on Global Corporate Citizenship, 28 February 2001, <http://www.sourcewatch.org/upload/f/ff/EdelmanNGOPresentation_-2-28-01.pdf>.
4. R. Edelman, 'The Principles of Building Trust: Sixth Annual Edelman Trust Barometer – A global study of opinion leaders', January 2005, p. 3, <http://www.edelman.com/image/insights/content/Edelman_Trust_Barometer-2005_final_final.pdf>.
5. N. Turett, 'Thriving Amid Uncertainty: Relationships Reign', *Pharmaceutical Executive*, 1 September 2002, <www.pharmexec.com/pharmexec/article/articleDetail.jsp?id=29984>.
6. B. Burton and A. Rowell, 'Unhealthy spin', *British Medical Journal* 326, May 2003, pp. 1205–7, <http://bmj.bmjjournals.com/cgi/content/full/326/7400/1205>.
7. A. Little, 'A green corporate image: More than a logo', proceedings of Green Marketing Conference, 25 and 26 June 1990, p. 12. (Amanda Little was with Burson-Marsteller in Australia at the time. She has subsequently worked for Hill & Knowlton and now runs her own Sydney-based company, Intermedia Consulting.)
8. Edelman, 'Trust Shifting'.
9. A. Ray, 'CSR: The live debate', *PR Week*, 5 December 2003, <http://www.prweek.com/news/news_story.cfm?ID=197492&site=1>.
10. BSMG Worldwide, 'Communications Plan', 2 February 1999, Bates no. 2071722605/2611, <http://legacy.library.ucsf.edu/tid/qaq06c00>.
11. S. Williams, 'Communications Plan: Supersized', BSMG Worldwide, 25 February 1999, Bates No. 2071722733/2741, <http://legacy.library.ucsf.edu/tid/fbq06c00>.
12. D. Eberwine, S. Aguinaga Bialous and S. Shatenstein, 'The Tobacco Files', *Perspectives in Health Magazine* 8 (1), Pan American Health Organisation, 2003, <http://www.paho.org/English/DD/PIN/Number16_article3_3.htm>.
13. Ibid.
14. G. Miller and L. Helm, 'Microsoft Plans Stealth Media Blitz; Publicity: Campaign to conjure image of public support called just a proposal by firm', *Los Angeles Times*, 10 April 1998, pp. 1 and 8, <http://www.latimes.com>; <http://www.smoogespace.com/gaming/torg/mail-archive/199804/0087.html>.
15. R. Edelman, 'News from Davos', 1 February 2005, <http://www.edelman.com/speak_up/blog/>.

16. G. Freeman, 'IFAW axes Shandwick to bring PR in-house', *PR Week*, 22 September 2000, <http://www.prweek.com/news/news_story. cfm?ID=110847&site=1>.
17. Association for Sustainable and Responsible Investment in Asia, 'Conference Speakers: Jonathan Wootliff, Corporate Responsibility Consultant', July 2004, <http://www.asria.org/events/singapore/july04/ Speakers/Jonathan_Wootliff>.
18. Gareth Harding, 'NGOs trounce companies, media in trust ratings war', *TerraViva*, InterPress Service, 13 December 2001, <http://www.undp.org/ dpa/frontpagearchive/december00/13dec00/tv121300.pdf>.
19. Burson-Marsteller, 'Burson-Marsteller Names Bennett Freeman to Lead Corporate Responsibility Unit in U.S: Former Deputy Assistant Secretary of State for Democracy, Human Rights and Labor Adds Leadership and Expertise to Growing Specialty Area', media release, 15 May 2003, <http://www.bm.com/pages/news/releases/2003/press-05-15-2003>; Burson-Marsteller, 'Bennett Freeman'>; <http://www.bm.com/pages/ bios/freeman?subsecLoc=2006>.
20. See for example M. Megalli and A. Friedman, *Masks of Deception: Corporate Front Groups in America* (Washington, D.C.: Essential Information, 1991); Carl Deal, *The Greenpeace Guide to Anti-Environmental Organizations* (Berkeley, Calif.: Odonian Press, 1993).
21. Joyce Nelson, *The Sultans of Sleaze: Public Relations and the Media* (Monroe, Maine: Common Courage Press, 1989).
22. See Susan B. Trento, *The Power House: Robert Keith Gray and the Selling of Access and Influence in Washington* (New York: St Martin's Press, 1992).
23. J. Stauber and S. Rampton, *Toxic Sludge Is Good for You: Lies, Damn Lies and the Public Relations Industry* (Monroe, Maine: Common Courage Press, 1995).
24. See <http://legacy.library.ucsf.edu/> for information on how to search the 7 million pages of internal industry documents.
25. As of March 2005, the total number of visits to the Swift Boat Veterans for Truth has reached 338,000, the majority of which occurred between August and November 2004.
26. Citing web-accessible material allows for quick checking of the original source, but it has its limits too, as earlier offline material not online or in LexisNexis, such as books and newspaper articles, are ignored.
27. Dan Gilmour, *We the Media: Grassroots Journalism by the People, for the People* (Sebastopol, Calif.: O'Reilly, 2004).
28. T. Cook, 'Buying Influence', *Walkley Magazine* 31, February/March 2005 (Media Entertainment Arts Alliance), pp. 23–4.

15
Corporate Power in Europe: The Brussels 'Lobbycracy'

Olivier Hoedeman

Over the last two decades, corporations, industry lobby groups and PR firms have been magnetically drawn to Brussels. The reason, of course, is the greater powers that the European Commission, the European Parliament and other EU institutions have gained as the result of a series of new European Union treaties. Today well over 50 per cent of all laws and regulations of the 25 EU member states result from EU decision making – for environmental issues it is over 80 per cent. A conservative estimate is that over 15,000 full-time lobbyists work to influence the EU institutions, most of them from offices in the four square kilometres around the European Commission and the European Parliament, the so-called European quarter. Over 70 per cent of these lobbyists represent big business. The Brussels corporate lobbying scene numbers over 1,000 lobby groups, hundreds of public relations and public affairs firms, numerous law firms offering lobbying services, dozens of corporate-funded think tanks, as well as hundreds of EU affairs offices run by individual corporations.[1] The annual turnover of corporate lobbying in Brussels has reached levels of between €750 million and €1 billion.[2]

A German member of the European Parliament told the *International Herald Tribune* about his daily experiences with lobbyists: 'They phone me, they pick me up downstairs, they write me a hundred letters a day. It is not possible to get from here to the entrance and not see any lobbyists.'[3] Another indication of the steep growth in the number of lobbyists in Brussels is the complaint by the Society of European Affairs Professionals (SEAP) about the lack of space in the European Parliament. In an open letter in the spring of 2004, this club of professional lobbyists expressed its dissatisfaction with the fact that its members sometimes have to stand when they want to attend parliamentary committee meetings. The European Parliament buildings are enormous, but still not big enough to accommodate the ever-growing ranks of lobbyists.

It should be stressed that corporate lobby groups did not simply react to European unification. The European Roundtable of Industrialists (ERT), through strategic partnership with the European Commission, has played a very active role in shaping and accelerating the process of European integration.[4] In the second half of the 1980s and the first half of the 1990s, this powerful club of 45 CEOs of the largest European corporations was instrumental in promoting market-driven integration, paving the way for the neoliberal reforms that have swept Europe in recent years.

LOBBYISTS' PARADISE

A political culture has emerged in Brussels in which professional lobbyists play a far stronger role than in any of the individual EU member states. While there is certainly a legitimate role for lobbying, it is problematic when it becomes the dominant form of doing politics, as seems to be the trend in Brussels decision making. Democracy, after all, was meant to involve much more than one-to-one meetings between professional power brokers and decision makers who often have very little interaction with the voters. One of the reasons for the strength of this model is the absence of a genuine European public debate and the relative weakness of pan-European civil society networks and social movements which, despite some advances, remain underdeveloped on the EU level.

For corporate lobby groups and the booming Brussels PR industry, these are almost ideal conditions under which to work. When PR giant Burson-Marsteller claims that there are 55,000 lobbyists in Brussels, this is because its definition also includes European Commission officials, as well as European parliamentarians and their assistants. Everyone aiming to influence decision making, Burson-Marsteller argues, is a lobbyist, whether they are a 'hired gun' lobbying consultant, an 'EU affairs' manager for a large corporation, a civil society campaigner, a Commission or government official or a democratically elected parliamentarian. While this definition is fortunately not yet broadly accepted, it is illustrative of the status which lobbying professionals currently enjoy in Brussels decision making.

With lobbying being the name of the political game, it is no wonder that courses on how to lobby are a major growth area in Brussels. On a hot day in July 2004, for instance, over 100 people were packed into a room in the Marriot Hotel, each having paid over €300 for an afternoon crash course in 'effective lobbying in Brussels' organised by

Burson-Marsteller and the widely read weekly the *European Voice*. The afternoon was chaired by Rinus van Schendelen, an influential Dutch academic, who defends the status quo by claiming that lobbying in Brussels is simply 'a marketplace of ideas' in which different interests balance out each other, and Craig Winneker, who runs the Brussels branch of the hardline US 'free-market' think tank Tech Central Station.

'I need lobbyists, I depend on lobbyists', a UK MEP told the participants. Indeed, MEPs are often overwhelmed by the number of detailed issues they have to decide on and therefore develop a sometimes unhealthy dependency on lobbyists. The same MEP stressed that he does not want general opinions on political questions; he wants lobbyists to give him concrete text amendments that he can submit for voting in committees or plenary sessions of the European Parliament. This practice has become routine in the European Parliament, and as a result amendments drafted by industry lobbyists (and occasionally by civil society groups) often end up as EU law. Parliamentarians are in danger of becoming mere intermediaries, transferring lobby-group demands into the EU's decision-making machine. With this kind of political culture emerging it is no surprise that, after their time in the Parliament, many MEPs go through the revolving door to join the corporate lobbying world. Examples include UK Liberal Democrat MEP Nick Clegg and Labour MEP David Bowe, both of whom joined the Brussels team of lobbying firm GPlus Europe after leaving the European Parliament in 2004.

Similarly, a growing number of European Commission officials cannot resist the temptation to go through the revolving door and straight into lobbying for industry, often on issues they held responsibility for while working in the Commission. Two high-profile examples are Jim Currie, former director-general of DG Environment, and Jean-Paul Mingasson of DG Enterprise.[5] Currie left the Commission in 2001 to become paid non-executive director of British Nuclear Fuels, a company in the field which Currie was responsible for overseeing while in DG Enterprise. Mingasson went to the EU employers' federation UNICE in 2004, where he works as a top lobbyist. Although European Commissioners are obliged to take a year's cooling-off period before taking up a corporate job on an issue within their field of authority, there are no such restrictions for other Commission officials.

This political culture is also fertile ground for a large number of hybrid organisations operating around the EU institutions where the dividing line between business and politics is blurred at best. One example is the Transatlantic Policy Network, an influential network of parliamentarians and business leaders lobbying together for the creation of an EU–US free-trade zone. In April 2004, the European Parliament approved a resolution embracing the Transatlantic Policy Network's proposal for launching negotiations with exactly this goal. The resolution was pre-cooked by German Christian–Democrat parliamentarian Elmar Brok, who simply cut and pasted sentences from a Transatlantic Policy Network document into the draft Parliament resolution. Brok is a leading member of the network and on the payroll of multimedia multinational Bertelsmann AG, one of the network's corporate members.[6] A dozen or more other parliamentarians involved in the debates on this resolution, including German Social Democrat MEP Erika Mann, also belonged to the network, but never disclosed their double roles.[7]

KOFI ANNAN IN BRUSSELS

Avenue de Cortenbergh 118, a five-floor building in the centre of the Brussels European quarter, is a corporate lobbying and public relations microcosm, full of law firms, PR firms, individual corporations and trade associations. Unilever's EU lobbyists are neighbours to PR firms Hill & Knowlton and Burson-Marsteller as well as an organisation called the Bromine Science and Environment Forum (BSEF). The latter name suggests an academic body or an environmentalist organisation, but this 'forum' is a front group set up by Burson-Marsteller on behalf of the chemical companies producing toxic bromine flame-retardants, to fight a possible EU ban on these products.[8] Until recently, the corporate nature of BSEF and the key role of Burson-Marsteller in its operations were kept vague or simply hidden. In fact everyone working for BSEF from the Cortenbergh 118 offices is a Burson-Marsteller consultant. To add to the impression of a house of mirrors, Burson-Marsteller's Brussels office also runs several other bromine industry outfits, such as the Alliance for Consumer Fire Safety in Europe (ACFSE) and the European Brominated Flame Retardant Industry Panel (EBFRIP), which consists of three of the four BSEF member corporations. The mechanism whereby corporations and PR firms establish front groups and various forms of pseudo-NGOs has been part of the corporate lobbying toolbox in the United States for several decades, but Brussels is now unfortunately catching up in the area of deceptive lobbying and PR practices.

Unilever is one of the companies investing heavily in EU lobbying. Its main Brussels lobbyist, Charles Laroche, explained to the workshop participants at the Marriot Hotel that his company's lobbying starts at the earliest stage, before the European Commission begins work on drafting new legislation. Laroche describes Unilever as a political machine on all levels: 'lobbying must be in the blood of the company'. For the bulk of its lobbying, Laroche explained, Unilever therefore does not need public affairs consultants. Unilever only uses out-house consultants for specific purposes, such as the initial steps in preparing a lobbying campaign, in the phase when the company does not yet want to be noticed. In an article in the *International Herald Tribune*, Laroche claims that he represents the needs of consumers. 'Citizens are also consumers', Laroche says. 'We go into the Parliament and read through draft legislation with them and ask, "What is in this for the consumer?"' A corporate lobbyist getting away with pretending to be a consumer advocate? Welcome to Brussels!

Lobbying in the EU capital is frequently described as being softer and more consensus-seeking than the often very aggressive approaches that are common practice in Washington.[9] But the gap is narrowing fast, as EU industry increasingly shifts towards more aggressive lobbying strategies. Among the lecturers at the 'Effective Lobbying in Brussels' course at the Marriot was Chrissie Simmons, who runs one of the hundreds of 'EU Affairs' consultancy firms in Brussels. Simmons, a former GlaxoSmithKline lobbyist, outlined the main strategies that corporations can choose for their EU lobbying. She recommended first trying 'the Kofi Annan' strategy, in combination with 'the third-party' strategy. Doing a 'Kofi Annan', in Brussels lobbyist-speak, means engaging with decision makers to reach a compromise and thus avoid worst-case regulation scenarios, while 'the third party' means striking deals with NGOs and unions. These two approaches have in the last decade been the most common industry lobbying strategies in Brussels, but more aggressive approaches like 'the dentist' (first 'pull out the worst teeth' from a disliked piece of legislation and then come back for further 'treatment') and 'the gunship' (aggressive lobbying including threats of relocation if policy proposals are not dropped) are gaining ground. In an interview in May 2005, EU lobbying veteran Daniel Guéguen predicted that Brussels lobbyists are likely to become more ruthless, employing 'borderline' strategies. He said: 'I think we are moving towards tougher lobbying strategies, towards more sophisticated approaches to economic intelligence that will probably involve practices such as manipulation, destabilisation or disinformation.'[10]

RIGHT-WING WINDS

One of many examples of the ongoing shift to non-conciliatory tactics is the recent call by employers federation UNICE for a moratorium on all social initiatives until the EU has reached the so-called 'Lisbon Agenda' goal of being the most competitive economic bloc in the world. After intense lobbying by UNICE and the European Roundtable of Industrialists (ERT), EU governments in the spring of 2004 agreed to introduce so-called business impact assessments for all existing and new EU policies. The EU's Kyoto commitments for fighting climate change are first in line to be reassessed, which may further weaken efforts to combat climate change. Even before these reassessments have started, one piece of EU environment and health protection initiative after the other has been downscaled in the last few years due to industry complaints over alleged competitiveness impacts, the proposed REACH system for registration and testing of chemicals being the worst example. The original REACH proposal, presented in February 2001, aimed to secure registration and testing of over 100,000 chemicals currently used by industry in Europe. It would end the existing patchwork of regulations that allows 99 per cent of all chemicals to be used without having passed sufficient environmental and health assessment. This proposal sparked the largest ever industry lobbying campaign in Europe.[11] The chemical industry council CEFIC took the lead, with German giant BASF in a key role, and with active backing from US chemical corporations and the Bush administration. Scaremongering, flawed impact studies and delay tactics were part of the aggressive counter-campaign that seriously weakened REACH. In October 2003, the European Commission presented a seriously watered-down version of the original proposal, full of loopholes that would allow industry to continue production and sales of dangerous chemicals. As decision making enters the last phases, industry continues to lobby for further weakening, thereby obstructing the only real possibility for improving the dangerous regulatory vacuum around chemicals in Europe for many years to come.

The full corporate choir cheered when José Manuel Barroso took over as European Commission president in October 2004 and announced that the Lisbon competitiveness goals would be given absolute priority during his presidency.[12] Barroso's EC team marks a further shift towards more undiluted neoliberalism. As the *Wall Street Journal* noticed with approval, 'all important economic positions went to avowed free-marketers'. In the months after the new European Commission started work, neoliberal hardliners such as Neelie Kroes (competition) and particularly Peter Mandelson (international trade) have tightened their grip on the Commission's political course; but opposition is growing. When Barroso unveiled his economic strategy blueprint in February 2005, he was heavily criticised by centre–left MEPs, as well as by trade unions and civil society campaigners. According to the *Financial Times*, Barroso's programme 'marks a clear break with European thinking of the recent past, when environmental concerns and improving workers' rights were given the same priority as the need to generate growth'.[13]

Ironically, the European Commission's appetite for deregulation increased dramatically after the double 'No' to the proposed EU Constitution in referenda held in France and the Netherlands. The Commission has failed to acknowledge that a large part of the population in both countries rejected the constitution because they found it too neoliberal and at odds with the goal of a social Europe. Instead, Commission President Barroso and Commissioner Verheugen presented high-profile initiatives to slash 'absurd' laws and reassess regulatory initiatives that might bring additional costs to industry. Trade unions and environmental NGOs fear this will also negatively impact important social and health regulations, such as a proposal regulating the use of potent greenhouse gases in refrigerators and air-conditioning, discussed by the European Parliament throughout 2005. Verheugen explains his crusade as follows: 'When I started meeting with companies back in February it became my conviction that overregulation is the most important obstacle for investment and job creation in Europe.'[14]

Meanwhile, Trade Commissioner Mandelson has enthusiastically continued the tradition of awarding privileged political access and influence to big business lobby groups. A prime example is the European Services Forum (ESF), a lobby coalition of large European services corporations working to influence the negotiations on services liberalisation (GATS) in the World Trade Organisation (WTO). The ESF was established in 1999 at the initiative of the European Commission, which wanted an EU-level corporate lobby group that could assist the EU in the GATS negotiations. The group helped draft the EU's demands for services liberalisation in the rest of the world, which includes the liberalisation and privatisation of essential public services like water and education. European Commission documents obtained by CEO leave no doubt that the Services Forum enjoys very intimate relations with EU trade negotiators.[15] The ESF regularly participates in meetings of the Article 133 Committee (consisting of Commission and member state trade officials). On some occasions these meetings even take place at the ESF offices in central Brussels, followed by joint cocktail parties.[16]

THE THINK TANKS BOOM

Since the second half of the 1990s, a handful of centre–right think tanks have operated in Brussels, of which the European Policy Centre and the Centre for European Policy Studies are the most prominent. While competing for attention, these think tanks all cover roughly the same political territory and they are without exception deeply dependent on corporate membership fees. In the last few years they have been joined by a significant number of new think tanks promoting a more radical 'free-market' ideology, empowered by the neoliberal political climate and backed by corporate funding. The most visible of this new generation of think tanks is the Lisbon Council, which has cleverly named itself after the EU's competitiveness agenda. The Lisbon Council describes itself as a 'Brussels based citizens-action group', but these are not average citizens. Its spokespeople come straight from the World Economic Forum and the *Wall Street Journal*. With a media-savvy approach that has made the established Brussels think tanks watch with envy, the Lisbon Council launches fierce attacks on civil society groups, trade unions and anyone else it considers an obstacle to the sweeping neoliberal reforms it desires. In March 2005, when almost 100,000 people took part in a pan-European demonstration against the proposed EU Services Directive (widely known as the Bolkestein Directive), Lisbon Council director Anne Mettler lashed out in the media: 'This is ignorance at best and stupidity at worst.'[17] In fact the protests against the Bolkestein Directive are entirely rational; the directive's country-of-origin principle would seriously undermine social standards across Europe.[18]

Ideologically next of kin to the Lisbon Council, but even more radically right wing, are think tanks like the Centre for the New Europe (CNE), the European Enterprise Institute, Institut Economique Molinari, and several affiliates of US think tanks, such as the International Council for Capital Formation and Tech Central Station. Although their funding sources are a well-protected secret, there is little doubt that the work of these think tanks is overwhelmingly financed by donations from corporate giants who see their commercial interests best served by advocating free-market fundamentalism in the heart of Europe. Not only are these think tanks promoting an economic-jungle society with few limits on corporate activity, they are also more than willing to help big business fight specific environmental and health regulations. Therefore they routinely serve as de facto fronts for corporations. Exxon Mobil for instance, a virulent opponent of the Kyoto protocol, in 2004 donated respectively $80,000 and $115,000 to the 'Global Climate Change Education Efforts' of the Centre for a New Europe and the International Policy Network, a like-minded think tank based in London. The main liaison channel for European 'free-market' think tanks is the London-based Stockholm Network, which claims to have 123 member organisations. As part of its quest for winning the 'battle of ideas' the Stockholm Network regularly organises workshops in Brussels to improve the fundraising strategies and media outreach skills of neoliberal think tanks from around Europe.

DEBATE ABOUT LOBBYING DISCLOSURE HEATS UP

Despite the ever-growing volume of lobbyists and the growing political influence of big business, lobbying towards the EU institutions is virtually unregulated. In contrast, the United States and Canada developed lobbying disclosure and ethics legislation in the 1990s, obliging lobbyists to register and report which issues they work on and how much money is spent. Although this has not resulted in curbing corporate lobbying power, which in the United States has reached disastrous levels due to the dependence of politicians on corporate campaign finance donations, these laws do secure a level of transparency around lobbying that is absent in Europe. The European Parliament has a register of over 5,000 lobbyists with access passes, but this list only includes names and organisations. The European Commission has traditionally been decidedly hostile to proposals to regulate lobbying. In October 2004, an open letter signed by a large number of NGOs called upon Commission President Barroso 'to act immediately to curb the excessive influence of corporate lobby groups over EU policymaking'.[19] 'As a first step in addressing these problems', the letter argued, 'Europe needs far stricter ethics and transparency requirements.' In line with tradition, the Commission responded by referring to the voluntary codes of conduct of SEAP and other clubs of professional lobbyists.[20] These codes lack the obligation for external transparency and are far too weak to prevent deceptive and otherwise unethical lobbying practices.

It therefore came as a major surprise to most when on 3 March 2005 European Commissioner Siim Kallas announced his European Transparency Initiative (ETI).[21] In a high-profile speech, Kallas highlighted the influence of the over 15,000 lobbyists in Brussels and complained about 'the complete lack of mandatory regulation on reporting and registering of lobbying operations in the EU'.[22] Kallas was careful to stress that he sees 'nothing wrong with lobbies' as such, because 'each decision-making process needs proper information from different angles'. The problem, according to Kallas, is that 'their transparency is too deficient in comparison to the impact of their activities'. Kallas's European Transparency Initiative provides an unprecedented opportunity for the emergence of EU rules forcing lobby groups to report about their activities. To ensure meaningful transparency, these reports should be fully accessible to the European public in an online searchable database. Only this degree of transparency would enable far more democratic scrutiny and thus contribute to curbing excessive corporate lobbying power. But the opposition is going to be fierce.

Among the staunchest opponents is the Society of European Affairs Professionals (SEAP), whose *raison d'être* since its foundation in 1997 has been to prevent any form of binding regulation around lobbying. After Kallas's surprise speech, SEAP's Rogier Chorus told the media that he was 'a bit puzzled' by the move. SEAP had launched a revised lobbying ethics code only weeks before. [23] While this voluntary code remains very weak and lacks any form of external transparency obligations, SEAP argues that there is no need for regulation.[24] But even if SEAP's code were to be far stronger and mandatory, it would still not be a solution. SEAP only has 150 individual members, a tiny minority among over 15,000 Brussels-based lobbyists.

A somewhat more subtle form of opposition comes from EUlobby. net, a website run by veteran lobbyist Christian de Fouloy.[25] De Fouloy welcomed Kallas's initiative but at the same time promotes his own commercial website – a form of yellow pages for lobbyists – as an alternative to regulation. Another grouping defending the status quo of unregulated lobbying is the European Public Affairs Consultancies Association (EPACA), a new association of Brussels-based public affairs firms officially launched in January 2005. A few months earlier, in a letter to Corporate Europe Observatory, EPACA had already rejected calls for disclosing lobbying by its members on EU chemicals regulation (REACH), while stating that there is 'a legitimate discussion to be had about the appropriate levels of disclosure and registration by all interest groups'.[26] EPACA brings together 38 firms, including APCO, Burson-Marsteller, Edelman, Hill & Knowlton, Houston Consulting Europe and Weber Shandwick Adamson.[27] In May 2005, John Houston, president of EPACA, told the *Financial Times* that 'there was no evidence the present system of self-regulation was ineffective'.[28] Shortly afterwards, the *Wall Street Journal* revealed that Houston had played a central role in the lobbying efforts by financial services firms against tighter EU money laundering laws. Houston runs the European Parliamentary Financial Services Forum, a hybrid organisation of MEPs and banking sector lobbyists.[29] Houston and EPACA, meanwhile, remain opposed to disclosure obligations, arguing that 'the general absence of substantive concerns or scandals about unethical lobbying is striking'. Also business lobby groups like UNICE are not amused with the proposal for improved transparency. 'All proposals that aim for more regulation are nonsense', UNICE's Christian Feustel commented on Kallas's proposal.[30]

Within weeks of Kallas's speech, the opponents of lobbying disclosure played out their main arguments – for instance, that legislation would be unnecessarily bureaucratic and costly. In fact an electronic reporting system would not cost much and certainly would not constitute any burden for those engaging in lobbying the EU institutions. A related claim is that registration and reporting requirements 'will make it harder for smaller interests to make themselves heard', as Rogier Chorus, the chairman of SEAP argued in a letter in the *European Voice*.[31] This is a flawed argument, because these obligations should only be required for large organisations and firms (those with a lobbying budget over a defined minimum, as is the case in the United States and Canada). Coming from professional lobbying consultants whose services are unaffordable for 'smaller interests', such arguments ring particularly hollow. A second argument used by opponents of lobbying disclosure is that, as David Earnshaw of Burson-Marsteller puts it, the European Commission might face 'big problems' defining who is a lobbyist: 'If you are a Socialist, business is the lobbyist; but if you are a Christian Democrat, NGOs like Greenpeace are the lobbyists.'[32] Given Earnshaw's own CV, which spans in-house lobbying at pharmaceuticals giant SmithKlineBeecham, Oxfam, and now corporate consultancy Burson-Marsteller, such confusion over who is and who isn't a lobbyist is rather surprising. In all these roles Earnshaw has been happy to call himself a lobbyist. Such statements are probably intended to cause confusion; in practice it is clear that both business and civil society should be covered by reporting obligations, as is the situation in the United States and Canada.

Commissioner Kallas's speech on the European Transparency Initiative also referred to insufficient transparency by NGOs receiving European Commission funding and suggested improving the current registry of NGOs, including financial information. Improved financial transparency for NGOs should certainly be welcomed, particularly if it also ended the secrecy of corporate-funded think tanks like the Centre for a New Europe. With increasing corporate donations flowing into EU think tanks, from both Europe and the United States, it is of crucial importance that the recipients are forced to provide full transparency. Defenders of the status quo, however, are using Commissioner Kallas's comments to diffuse the debate and undermine the momentum for meaningful lobbying disclosure rules.

Attacks on the legitimacy of civil-society groups are an intensifying trend in which two academics seen as experts on EU lobbying issues play dubious roles. Rinus van Schendelen (Erasmus University, Rotterdam) and Justin Greenwood (Robert Gordon University, Aberdeen) describe lobbying towards the EU institutions as a level playing field where different stakeholders balance out their attempts to gain influence. Van Schendelen even claims that NGOs have an (unfair) advantage over business due to their superior credibility, which helps them gain access to EU officials.[33] Van Schendelen regularly attacks European Commission and government funding for NGOs, while ignoring the imbalance in financial resources between industry and civil society. Greenwood eagerly challenges the representativeness of Brussels-based NGO coalitions,[34] but is uncritical about the role of business lobbying. While presenting themselves as academic observers, both van Schendelen and Greenwood are deeply entangled in industry lobbying networks in Brussels.[35]

ENTER ALTER-EU

While opposed by vested interests, including many 'hired gun' lobbying consultants, the call for improved transparency and ethics around lobbying has broad support among civil society groups in Brussels and around Europe. In July 2005, the Alliance for Lobbying Transparency and Ethics Regulation (ALTER-EU) was launched.

ALTER-EU, a coalition of over 140 civil society groups, trade unions, academics and public affairs firms, was established in order to prevent the European Transparency Initiative from being watered down.[36] Beyond mandatory lobbying transparency, the ALTER-EU statement also calls for an improved code of conduct for EC officials (including limits on officials going through the 'revolving door' to industry) and the termination of privileged access and undue influence granted to corporate lobbyists.[37]

The ALTER-EU launch event on 19 July in Brussels was attended by Commissioner Kallas, who insisted that he wanted an online register of EU lobbyists, but was not yet convinced of the need to make registration and reporting obligatory.[38] The final outcome of the decision-making process on the European Transparency Initiative is therefore far from certain. A worrying scenario is that the ETI might be watered down to a degree that it would not enable any serious and effective democratic scrutiny of corporate influence over EU policy making. If the new rules are weak and meaningless, they will be used to legitimise current lobbying practices around EU decision making. Unless the rules emerging from the ETI ensure meaningful transparency around lobbying, they might do more harm than good. This is why the struggle for a far-reaching improvement of the reporting obligations for lobbyists working to influence the EU institutions must be an urgent priority for progressive movements in Europe. EU lobbying-disclosure legislation would certainly not mean the end of excessive corporate power over decision making, but it is a necessary step in that direction. Whatever the outcome, the heated debate and struggle around this issue might do more to alert the European public about the democratic, social and environmental impacts of the emerging EU lobbycracy than anything we've witnessed in recent decades.

NOTES

1. Corporate Europe Observatory, '"Lobby Planet" Guide to Brussels', December 2004, <http://www.corporateeurope.org/docs/lobbycracy/lobbyplanet.pdf>.
2. 'A spoonful of sugar makes the message go down', *European Voice* 11(33), 22 September 2005.
3. Graham Bowley, 'Brussels' rise draws lobbyists in numbers', *International Herald Tribune*, 18 November 2004.
4. Belén Balanyá, Ann Doherty, Olivier Hoedeman, Adam Ma'anit and Erik Wesselius, 'Europe Inc.: Regional and Global Restructuring and the Rise

of Corporate Power' (London: Pluto Press, in association with Corporate Europe Observatory, July 2000). A second edition was published in 2003, ISBN: 0-7453-2163-1, <http://www.tni.org/books/inc.htm>.

5. See also the presentation by Jorgo Riss of the Greenpeace EU Unit: <http://www.alter-eu.org/launchreport.html>.

6. 'Oxford Council on Good Governance', at <http://www.oxfordgovern-ance.org/index.php/245/0/>.

7. 'EU-US free trade talks ahead?', Corporate Europe Observatory (CEO), June 2004, <http://www.corporateeurope.org/tpntabd.html>; <http://www.netcaucus.org/biography/erika-mann.shtml>.

8. Corporate Europe Observatory, 'House of Mirrors: Burson-Marsteller Brussels lobbying for the bromine industry', January 2005, <http://www.corporateeurope.org/lobbycracy/houseofmirrors.html>.

9. See for instance 'EU and US approaches to lobbying', Euractiv.com, <http://www.euractiv.com/Article?tcmuri=tcm:29-135509-16&type=LinksDossier>.

10. 'PA veteran calls for professional body to scrutinise Brussels lobbyists', 3 May 2005, <http://www.euractiv.com/Article?tcmuri=tcm:29-139066-16&type=News>.

11. Corporate Europe Observatory, 'Bulldozing REACH: the industry offensive to crush EU chemicals regulation', March 2005, <http://www.corpora-teeurope.org/lobbycracy/BulldozingREACH.html>.

12. 'By embracing a pro-business agenda from the start of his term as European Commission president, José Manuel Barroso has already won friends in corporate Europe. "The early signals are very positive", says Baron Daniel Janssen, chairman of Belgium's Solvay chemicals group who also heads the competitiveness working group of the European Round Table of Industrialists, a big-business lobby.'

13. 'The European Commission president tells George Parker and Andrew Gowers that he detects a "new sense of urgency" about the need to deliver economic reforms', *Financial Times*, 2 February 2005.

14. Graham Bowley, 'EU starts war on red tape', *International Herald Tribune*, 24 September 2005.

15. For instance, after the ESF's visit to Geneva in March 2004 (including meetings with the WTO ambassadors of many developing countries), Commission officials asked the ESF for a meeting at which they could be briefed on the outcomes. This meeting took place soon afterwards. Email correspondence (25 March 2004) between ESF managing director Pascal Kerneis and Anders Jessen, DG Trade's deputy head of unit, trade in services, <http://www.corporateeurope.org/docs/email20040325.pdf>.

16. Email (31 October 2003) from ESF managing director Pascal Kerneis to Joao Aguiar Machado, DG Trade's head of unit, trade in services, and his deputy, Anders Jessen, <http://www.corporateeurope.org/docs/email20031031.pdf>.

17. 'EU service shake-up supporters attack "stupid" protesters', Eupolitix.com, 18 March 2005.

18. The country-of-origin principle would mean that services companies can follow the rules and laws not of the country in which the service is to be provided, but the one in which it is registered. See Thomas Fritz (Attac

Germany), 'Transforming Europe into a Special Economic Zone: The EU's Services Directive', June 2004, <http://www.attac.de/gats/hintergrund/Fritz-vs-Bolkestein-EN.pdf>.

19. <http://www.corporateeurope.org/barroso.html>.

20. The official response came from the European Commission's department for 'relations with civil society'. The letter, dated 17 November 2004, did not explicitly respond to any of the demands in the open letter, but simply described the status quo concerning lobbying in Brussels, referred to SEAP's voluntary code of conduct and stated that the European Commission 'in its dialogue and consultation with civil society seeks to ensure that relevant parties are heard', <http://www.corporateeurope.org/docs/lobbycracy/SGtoCEO.pdf>.

21. See link to the speech at <http://www.corporateeurope.org/lobbydebate.html>.

22. There is no mandatory regulation on reporting or registering lobby activities. Registers provided by lobbyists' organisations in the EU are voluntary and incomprehensive and do not provide much information on the specific interests represented or how it is financed. Self imposed codes of conduct have few signatories and have so far lacked serious sanctions.' Siim Kallas, vice-president of the European Commission and commissioner for administrative affairs, audit and anti-fraud, 'The need for a European transparency initiative', speech at the European Foundation for Management, Nottingham Business School, Nottingham, 3 March 2005.

23. 'Brussels lobbyists to come under tighter scrutiny', EurActiv.com, 7 March 2005.

24. The day after the open letter to Barroso was sent, SEAP reacted with a letter in which it argued that its own voluntary code of conduct for lobbyists was sufficient and that there was no need for EU legislation on lobbying transparency and ethics. 'SEAP rejects NGOs request for registration and reporting requirements', 26 October 2004, <http://www.corporateeurope.org/SEAPreaction.html>.

25. Christian de Fouloy sent an email to all signatories to the open letter, advertising the fee-based voluntary registration system on his website. He invited the groups to 'become a Member of EULobby and to voluntarily disclose information about your activities as you have suggested in your collective letter'. CEO responded, 'Such calls for voluntary systems of registration, providing a semblance of transparency, are a common strategy of the PR and lobbying profession, to avoid the introduction of compulsory registration and reporting requirements for lobbyists.' <http://www.corporateeurope.org/EUlobbymail.html>; <http://www.corporateeurope.org/CEO-EUlobby20041112.html>.

26. <http://www.corporateeurope.org/lobbydebate.html>. The letter came in response to a survey which CEO carried out in February 2005 among 35 Brussels-based public affairs firms that are offering services to the chemical industry. We asked them for 'an overview of the clients for which your firm in the last 12 months has provided PA/PR services on the proposed EU system for Registration, Evaluation, Authorisation of Chemicals (REACH), the relevant budget and towards which EU institutions the efforts were

directed.' A month later, after a reminder by fax, only three out of the 35 firms had replied, none of them disclosing any information. This led us to conclude that 'the willingness of Brussels-based public affairs firms to provide transparency about who they are lobbying for is non-existing', <http://www.corporateeurope.org/lobbycracy/BulldozingREACH.html>. EPACA defends the lack of transparency in the proposed 'professional self-regulatory structure' as follows: 'Our code requires professionals to identify themselves and their company clearly, to declare the interests represented, and not to misrepresent their status, during inquires to or lobbying of EU officials and representatives. There is no requirement on them to supply details of such exchanges to other interest groups, or to publish lists of clients and/or lobbying budgets.'

27. As a follow-up to the previous 'Code of Conduct Group' (sometimes referred to as 'Public Affairs Practitioners'), <http://www.corporateeurope.org/docs/EPACA per cent20members.doc>.

28. 'Lobbyists under Brussels scrutiny', *Financial Times*, 19 May 2005.

29. Glenn R. Simpson, 'In Europe, Finance Lobby Sways Terror-Funding Law: Legislators with Close Ties to Industry Water Down Money-Laundering Rules', *Wall Street Journal*, 24 May 2005, available at <http://www.corporateeurope.org/wsj240505.html>.

30. 'Die Lobbyisten werden untersucht', *Die Welt*, 11 March 2005.

31. Chorus wrote, 'Bureaucratic controls and reporting requirements will not improve transparency; they will make it harder for smaller interests to make themselves heard'. 'Fighting funding fraud', *European Voice*, 10 March 2005.

32. 'Analysis: Reining in EU lobbyists', *Washington Times* (United Press International), 8 March 2005.

33. 'NGOs appear to have relatively easy access to EU officials, as the latter consider them less "dangerous" than national government officials and less "selfish" than corporate people, and "closer to the citizens" than others ... That easy access gives NGOs an advantage in PA and lobbying, which makes the playing field less level', says van Schendelen. EurActiv.com public affairs policy section, 'Accountability of NGOs', 27 October 2003, <http://www.euractiv.com/en/pa/accountability-ngos/article-117442>.

34. See, for instance, Justin Greenwood, 'The World of EU NGOs and Interest Representation', <http://www.rgu.ac.uk/files/ACF456B.pdf>.

35. The two act as consultants and co-hosts of corporate lobby strategy events. Greenwood has for many years had a close working relationship with commercial lobbying consultancies such as Ernst & Young and Kellen Europe, which involves hosting conferences in Brussels on how to improve the effectiveness of lobbying by EU trade associations. ('This event is brought to you by Kellen Europe together with Professor Justin Greenwood'.) <http://www.kelleneurope.com/euroconference/2005_agenda.html>; <http://www.kelleneurope.com/euroconference/2006_presentations.html>.

On his website, Greenwood acknowledges receiving funding from 'Ernst & Young and other companies, and EU and domestic trade associations inc. AMCHAM-EU', the main lobby group representing US multinational corporations in Brussels, <http://www.rgu.ac.uk/abs/staff/page.cfm?pge=5373>

Van Schendelen is proud of his commercial lobbying consultancy work for large corporations wanting to influence EU policy making. On his website it says: 'Professional activities are mainly in the field of training, consultancy and research regarding Public Affairs Management and Lobbying at the European Union level for companies, trade associations, NGOs, regional and national governments both domestic and foreign, such as Glaxo, 3M, Philips, Shell and Siemens and ministries in China, Finland, Hungary, Oman and the Netherlands.' Homepage of M.P.C.M. van Schendelen, Erasmus University, <http://www.eur.nl/fsw/staff/homepages/vanschendelen>.

Van Schendelen is moreover a central figure in the European Centre for Public Affairs (ECPA), a commercial seminar and lobbying training organisation with a large corporate membership and a strong affinity with the Brussels corporate lobbying world, <http://www.publicaffairs.ac/inindex.php?in=/community/farfdirectory.php?id=30>.

36. See also <http://www.alter-eu.org/>.
37. <http://www.alter-eu.org/statement.html>.
38. <http://www.alter-eu.org/launchreport.html>.

16

Killer Coke

Andy Higginbottom

At a special presentation on 11 November 2004, Coca-Cola Corporation's chief executive officer, Neville Isdell, unveiled to Wall Street analysts *The Coca-Cola Manifesto for Change*, a master plan to improve the corporation's flagging profits. Flanked by Chuck Fruit, the company's chief marketing officer, and other executives, Isdell presented a new marketing strategy to target sales expansion into India, Brazil, China and Russia. During 2005 Coca-Cola added $400 million to its $1 billion marketing spend outside the United States, and its executives commissioned scores of agencies in the search for new ideas. They call it 'iconic marketing', to promote the core qualities of 'uplifting refreshment, stubborn optimism and universal connections' that they believe consumers associate with company products. Isdell claimed the essence of the Coca-Cola brand is that it is 'a decent thing, honestly made'.[1]

Decency and honesty are not the words that first spring to mind with regard to the Coca-Cola Corporation, but fact and fiction are easily confused by a multinational that spends $7 million a day on advertising. Coca-Cola's problems run much deeper than reviving a tired icon: the corporation's celebrated publicity machine is struggling to recover from a series of PR blunders, such as the fateful British launch of its Dasani bottled water (it turned out to come from the mains supply and was withdrawn as potentially carcinogenic), and medical confirmation that the marketing of fizzy drinks to children has become a major public health concern.[2]

Coca-Cola has an underlying credibility issue that will not go away. Its claims to universalism and decency have been rocked by sustained allegations of human rights abuses and environmental destruction in underdeveloped countries. These are not just 'PR disasters' – surely a devaluation of the term 'disaster' – but real disasters for the often ignored 'unpeople' living in the South of our planet.[3] Moreover, the victims of Coca-Cola's abuses are finding a sympathetic hearing among those in the global North already fed up with being taken for a ride by the corporation.

ASSASSINATIONS OF WORKERS IN COLOMBIA

A can or bottle of Coke is more than the incarnation of expert marketing. The product's ubiquity is the result of a huge collective effort by the usually forgotten yet essential special ingredient – *the worker who produces Coca-Cola.*

Isidro Segundo Gil was one such worker. Isidro worked at the Coca-Cola bottling plant in Carepa in the far north Urabá region of Antioquia department in Colombia. Isidro was assassinated inside the plant on 5 December 1996. He was a leader of the local branch of the food and drink workers union SINALTRAINAL[4] and had one week earlier tabled the union's demands in the annual negotiation round with the bottling company. The plant manager declared he wanted to 'sweep away the trade union'. Shortly afterwards right-wing paramilitaries burnt out the local union office and shot Gil inside the plant, the fourth union member they had assassinated. Two days later the paramilitaries re-entered the plant, called the workers together and made them sign prepared letters resigning from the union. The letters had been printed on company machines and were collected by management. The union branch was decimated. Subsequently, after a four year battle to get justice for her murdered partner, Isidro's wife Alcira del Carmen Herera Perez was murdered in front of their daughters. The Carepa plant was run by Bebidas y Alimentos, a US company owned by the Kirby family based in Key Biscayne, Florida.[5]

Gil's assassination is the most egregious crime in an extraordinary catalogue of violations. In all, nine workers have been assassinated, while three local leaders of SINALTRAINAL at the Bucaramanga bottling plant were imprisoned for six months under false charges of terrorism. Union activists at the plant in Cúcuta have suffered a series of shootings, beatings, kidnappings and intimidations, and local leaders in Barrancabermeja have been the target of threats and assassination attempts by the main paramilitary group, the AUC.[6] Increasingly family members have been victims, with the attempted kidnapping of the four-year-old daughter of one union leader, the actual kidnapping of the 15-year-old son of another, and, on 20 April 2004, the assassination of the brother-in-law, sister-in-law and nephew of yet another.[7]

Many incidents show managers in Coca-Cola's Colombian bottling plants working in collusion with the paramilitaries. SINALTRAINAL reported 179 human rights violations against its members between

1990 and 2003. The data reveal that the threats, beatings and assassinations mostly occurred in the periods immediately prior to and during annual negotiations on collective agreements. Violence against unionised Coca-Cola workers increased dramatically in 1994/5, and again in 1997/8. In 1993 the union had 1,440 members in Coca-Cola plants; by 2004 this had fallen to just 389.[8]

This drastic fall in unionisation, from around 15 per cent to under 5 per cent, represents in microcosm the experience of Colombian workers employed by multinational corporations. The Coca-Cola Corporation is focused on improving the 'efficiency' of its investment.[9] Since the early 1990s three elements have combined to encourage an aggressive implementation of the strategy: state policies, the corporation's employment policies, and the socialisation of class-based violence. The Colombian state fully adopted the neoliberal economic model in 1990, the year it passed Labour Law 50, which was aimed at 'flexibilisation' of the workforce. Law 50 dispensed with nearly every legal protection for permanent employment contracts and encouraged subcontracting and temporary working. Union membership has since fallen to less than a million; and that is concentrated in the public sector, as there are very few private industry trade unions left.[10]

Coca-Cola has taken advantage of this legal environment. In 1990 the 'Coca-Cola system' in Colombia had 12,000 workers, of whom 9,000 had permanent employment contracts. By 2001 there were only 2,500 direct employees, and by the beginning of 2005 fewer than 1,000 workers had stable employment contracts. The current workforce is nearly 9,000, of which over 90 per cent are now 'flexible' workers, engaged indirectly through various layers of subcontracting. Until 2003 there were 20 bottling plants, but as part of a worldwide implementation of new techniques, production is now concentrated in just five mega-plants, with the remainder being reduced to distribution centres. This is but the latest round in a continuing worldwide Coca-Cola strategy to reduce its labour force.[11]

The subcontracting of violence goes hand in hand with subcontracting the workforce, and is just as calculated. Paramilitarism is not unique to Colombia; it was present in the 1980s in Guatemala during the civil war counter-insurgency that claimed 150,000 lives, many trade unionists amongst them. But the phenomenon has been particularly prevalent in Colombia, where human rights NGOs attribute to the paramilitaries at least 80 per cent of the annual toll of 3,000 socio-political assassinations outside of armed combat; and they link the paramilitary groups to the official military apparatus, evidencing a state policy of 'dirty war' against the social movements and political opponents.[12]

INDIA: 'GET RID OF COCA-COLA, SAVE WATER'

A second test of Coca-Cola's honesty and decency is how it treats communities around its bottling plants in India, where the corporation's appropriation of water as a natural resource is a fundamental issue for another forgotten actor: *the communities in which Coca-Cola plants are located.*

The stories of communities fighting Coca-Cola are well reported by the India Resource Centre, which identifies four broad categories of harm: Coca-Cola plants are taking ground water from surrounding farming communities; the plants' output pollutes the diminished remaining water supplies; Coca-Cola bottling plants in Kerala and Uttar Pradesh have been spreading toxic waste (cadmium and lead) onto surrounding land; and the bottled products themselves carry a dangerously high pesticide content (DDT, lindane and malathion) up to 30 times higher than American and European health standards. Farmers in Andhra Pradesh and Chattisgarh are even spraying Coca-Cola on their crops as it is 'more cost-effective than using other branded pesticides'.[13]

Coca-Cola's processes in India use up to 3.7 litres of water to manufacture just 1 litre of soft drink.[14] The effect of Coca-Cola's plants is to monopolise water supplies, dispossessing tens of thousands of already poor peasants from water access and so destroying their means of subsistence. It is not only livelihoods, but the very right to life that is under threat. The resistance has been driven from deep within the communities, with women coming to the fore. The fifteenth of January 2005 marked the 1,000th day of a permanent *dharna* (vigil) by local community groups in front of the Coca-Cola plant in Plachimada in the southern state of Kerala. This plant has been shut since March 2004. Coca-Cola say they closed it voluntarily, but this is untrue: they were obliged to suspend production due to the decision of the Kerala state government to ease drought conditions in the area, and also by the ruling of the *panchayat* (village council) not to renew Coca-Cola's license to operate, a decision that the corporation has appealed.[15]

Plachimada and the other communities in resistance have put Coca-Cola under international scrutiny.[16] The outside world has learnt of vigils and hunger strikes; the sit-in by over 2,000 people in Kaladera, Rajasthan shouting the slogan 'Get rid of Coca-Cola, Save Water'; the march from the Coca-Cola plant in Balia to Mehdiganj in Uttar Pradesh that was attacked by armed police, who arrested 350 people; the defiant rally of community residents outside the Mehdiganj plant.[17] Amit Srivastava draws a parallel with Colombia, highlighting that 'Coca-Cola acts with impunity, and violence is an inherent part of how Coca-Cola does business around the world'.[18]

The issue here is corporate domination of natural resources. The battles for water in India are an example of what Vandana Shiva calls 'the globalization of inhuman rights', the form of economic globalisation that 'places the rights of corporations above the rights of states and citizens'. She argues that this leads to 'food fascism', whereby multinationals' monopolistic control over food production and distribution is killing off the sustainability and cultural diversity of indigenous production. There is a striking convergence with the thinking of SINALTRAINAL, which supports a policy of national food sovereignty and natural fruit alternatives to commercial fizzy drinks.[19]

MULTI-TRACK INTERNATIONAL CAMPAIGN TO STOP COCA-COLA'S ABUSES

SINALTRAINAL developed a two-track international effort to stop the assassination of its members. The first track is a civil action on behalf of the SINALTRAINAL victims, lodged under the 1789 Alien Tort Claims Act with the Florida southern district court, on 20 July 2001, by lawyers of the United Steelworkers of America and the International Labor Rights Fund. The claim is for relief and damages due to a campaign of violence committed by paramilitaries employed by Coca-Cola's bottlers in Colombia, and is against the Coca-Cola Company, its main bottler Panamco, and Bebidas and its named directors.[20] In a ruling on 31 March 2003, the US District Court Judge found that the allegations were sufficient 'to allow the case to proceed on a theory that the paramilitaries were acting in a symbiotic relationship with the Colombian government'. The cases brought by SINALTRAINAL could go forward against Panamco and Bebidas, but the claims against Coca-Cola and its Colombia subsidiary were dismissed 'on the ground that the company's bottling agreement did not explicitly give Coca-Cola control over labor relations issues of its Colombian bottlers'.[21] This ruling is strange, as Coca-Cola did not provide a copy of the actual agreement it has with the Colombian bottlers. SINALTRAINAL appealed Coca-Cola's removal from the case. Indeed, circumstances have since changed and the parent corporation is more involved than ever in what happens in the bottling plants. In June 2003 Coca-Cola FEMSA bought out Panamco for $3.6 billion. The Coca-Cola Corporation increasing its shareholding from 25 per cent of Panamco to 40 per cent of the Coca-Cola Femsa–Panamco corporation, a controlling interest. In September 2006, US District Judge Jose E. Martinez dismissed the case against Panamco and Bebidas.[22]

Meanwhile, SINALTRAINAL opened a second track through a campaign of publicity and mobilisation. Working with support groups, the union organised three 'popular public hearings', in Atlanta, Brussels and Bogotá, to which Coca-Cola was invited, but did not attend. The idea of boycotting Coca-Cola products arose during this process. The union issued a call for an international consumer boycott at the World Social Forum in January 2003. The boycott would not start for several months, allowing Coca-Cola time to respond constructively. SINALTRAINAL makes clear that the boycott of Coca-Cola products is a tactic, not a long-term strategy. The idea is to get Coca-Cola seriously to engage with the union in saving its members' lives.[23] After the corporation had failed to respond, SINALTRAINAL and Colombia's main union federation, the CUT, launched the boycott on 22 July 2003 in Bogotá, matched by public events in several countries.[24]

North America is a key arena. The Campaign to Stop Killer Coke has animated student and union activism, with education and protests leading to the withdrawal of contracts at universities and vending machines from many union branches, and a high-profile intervention by campaign director Ray Rogers at Coca-Cola's 2004 annual meeting. Students have thrown out Coca-Cola products at 13 colleges and universities.[25] Another dimension to the US campaign is the drive to get soda drinks out of schools on health grounds. This represents a head-on challenge to the drinks corporations, for whom 'the school system is where you build brand loyalty', as acknowledged by John Alm, president of Coca-Cola Enterprises.[26]

In Europe the boycott was first taken up most enthusiastically in Ireland and Italy. The John Hewitt bar and restaurant in Belfast became the first public house in Ireland to remove Coca-Cola from sale, as did the Irish language cultural centre Cultúrlann McAdaimh Ó Fiaich. Students of University College Dublin (UCD), the largest campus in Ireland, voted in a referendum on 13 and 14 October 2003 not to serve Coca-Cola in any student union outlet. Despite the efforts of a strange alliance of right-wing students [27] and officials from the Services, Industrial, Professional and Technical Union (SIPTU), who circulated slick publicity proclaiming 'Enjoy choice ... Enjoy Coca Cola' and 'Choice is your right. Coca-Cola is your right', UCD students voted in favour of the boycott not once, but twice. Coca-Cola sent its Director of Communications for Latin America to dissuade UCD students from their decision. The corporation even invited students to a slap-up meal, but these tactics only galvanised support in favour of the boycott. It was endorsed a month later with an increased majority in a second referendum.[28]

The issue continues to be sharply debated in the Irish media, trade unions and political movements. Proceedings at the April 2004 national conference of primary school teachers' union INTO were interrupted when a delegate objected to Coca-Cola's sponsorship of the conference, including a stall from which free products were being distributed. A year later INTO voted to break all links with Coca-Cola. Students at Maynooth college voted not to ban Coca-Cola. It was subsequently revealed that the main anti-boycott campaigner is the son of former Taoiseach (Irish prime minister) John Bruton, who had received fees from Coca-Cola for speaking engagements.[29] Students at Trinity College Dublin voted for the boycott in February 2004; this was followed by a decision of the SIPTU branch representing over 550 staff at Trinity to disinvest any union funds invested in Coca-Cola. And the 2005 congress of the Union of Students in Ireland (representing over 250,000 students) backed the boycott of both Coca-Cola and Nestlé.[30]

In Italy, Rome's mayor organised an event on 13 December 2003 at which Coca-Cola was asked to respond to SINALTRAINAL. The director of external relations for Coca-Cola Italia tried to evade responsibility, but admitted that Coca-Cola has a code of conduct that should be implemented by bottlers using its brand name. Rome's District 11 and the town of Empoli in Tuscany have joined the boycott, as have eleven other municipalities. In March 2005 the Academic Senate of Roma 3 University voted to remove all soda drinks from campus vending machines.[31]

There have been similar initiatives in Germany, Turkey, Brazil, Canada, Mexico, Switzerland and Australia. In the United Kingdom, the Colombia Solidarity Campaign had by mid 2004 gained pockets of support, notably from the Scottish Socialist Party, which hosted a SINALTRAINAL member in the Scottish parliament, from public sector union UNISON, which voted to support the boycott in June 2004, and from activist students in several colleges. Journalist and comedian Mark Thomas took up the case in the *New Statesman*. He and artist Tracey Sanders-Wood added a fresh take when they launched the 'Coke's Nazi Adverts' exhibition, on the premise that since Coca-Cola was not revealing what adverts it used when it collaborated with Hitler's regime,[32] the general public would be invited to submit their reconstructions of what the adverts might have looked like.[33] Mark Thomas visited India and Colombia and integrated the story of Coca-Cola into his stage show. In one of the show's features, 'Coke Facts', Thomas and his researcher swap nuggets of information they have dug up on the corporation. Tens of thousands laughed out loud at these performances – imaginative dissent had been turned on Coca-Cola, and it was beginning to feel the pressure.

THE CONTRA-BOYCOTT CAMPAIGN

There has not only been a campaign against Coca-Cola's abuses, there has been a contra-boycott campaign designed to stigmatise and undermine the corporation's critics. The contra campaign employs two arguments. The first is to suggest that there are other more responsible trade unionists than SINALTRAINAL, which in any case is but one of many trade unions represented in Coca-Cola plants. Coca-Cola often quotes another union, SINALTRAINBEC, saying 'we have not a single indication' that the bottling companies are linked to illegal armed groups.[34] This responsible-versus-irresponsible argument has been taken up by the Trades Union Congress (TUC) and leading British trade unionists, who argue that 'two of the three unions representing Coca-Cola workers in Colombia are opposed to the call for a boycott of Coca-Cola. We led from the front during the boycott of *apartheid* South Africa but cannot support a boycott that most of the workers affected do not themselves support.'[35] The TUC's claim is incorrect on two counts: there are 14 unions representing workers in the Coca-Cola system, not three; more importantly, although only a minority of the workers are in unions, SINALTRAINAL *represents the absolute majority of unionised workers* (417 out of 810 in late 2002; 389 of 550 in late 2004). By contrast SINALTRAINBEC has fewer than 40 members.[36]

The TUC followed the advice of the International Union of Foodworkers (IUF) to reject the call for a boycott.[37] The IUF promotes its own affiliate, called SICO, which is only present in the Carepa plant. To appreciate the origins of SICO, we can consider the report of a Canadian trade union delegation that visited the Urabá region in October 1997, long before the Coca-Cola boycott became an international issue, but just after a bloody military/paramilitary offensive against the left in the region.[38] The Canadians made a point of reporting their concern about another union called SINTRAINAGRO, representing banana workers, whose leaders were exceptional in *not* raising the issue of their members' security, as had all other trade unionists met on the visit. Instead SINTRAINAGRO gave an account that 'coincided exactly' with the briefing on the situation in Urabá by army commanding officer General Rito Alejo de Rio, notorious for his links with the paramilitaries.[39] The general in turn praised SINTRAINAGRO as a 'model' union. Able to work with such endorsement, in 1999 SINTRAINAGRO helped form a new union in the very same plant where SINALTRAINAL had been eliminated three years previously. The new union was SICO.[40]

There are issues with drawing too close an analogy, but taking the example of South Africa, a favourite tactic of the apartheid regime was to put up hired stooges to poison the boycott call. And so it is here, by privileging an organisation with less than a tenth of SINALTRAINAL's representation, the IUF's approach has been deeply unfair to the majority of trade unionists in Coca-Cola plants in Colombia. Worse, it has played into the hands of the corporation's divide-and-rule strategy. After this experience it is unsurprising that SINALTRAINAL does not accept the IUF as an interlocutor on its members' behalf. One of the few surviving Colombian private sector unions, SINAL-TRAINAL's treatment by the official structures of international trade unionism is sectarian and shameful, and should be corrected by the movement as a whole.[41]

Even more sinister has been the Coca-Cola Corporation's suggestion that SINALTRAINAL members are connected with economic sabotage and terrorism. The manager of the Bucaramanga plant publicly accused union organisers of being 'auxiliaries of the insurgency', a claim that was effectively buried when the court case against three local leaders was lost, but resurfaced again spectacularly at a Leeds University student debate in November 2004, where Coca-Cola's presentation tried to link SINALTRAINAL with the FARC and the ELN, Colombia's two biggest guerrilla groups. When challenged by the Colombia Solidarity Campaign, which pointed out that this labelling is normally a prelude to assassination, the Coca-Cola representative denied any such intent. But stigmatisation clearly *is* the corporation's intention: the same presentation quotes from SINALTRAINAL's website that the union is against US military intervention, and that the union president had called for an international campaign against corporate violence, as though both demonstrate subversion.[42] Mark Thomas highlights similar scare tactics in India, where Coca-Cola puts out 'that the protests in Plachimada have been the work of Marxist agitators'.[43] A throwback to 1950s cold war mentality, this is the Bush doctrine put into dangerous practice.

The corporation has set up its own dedicated website – also called 'Coke Facts' – in response to allegations.[44] It claims that Coca-Cola provides security for its employees, and cites a number of specific measures. The results tell a different story; sacking 15 per cent of the workforce in two years whilst stigmatising their main trade union is not conducive to security. Coca-Cola's notion of 'security' is outside normal use. As for specific safety measures, the president of Barranacbermeja branch, William Mendoza, points out that 65 SINALTRAINAL members are threatened with death, and that any protection has come about through the union's insistent campaigning, with the support of the CUT Human Rights Department.[45] Despite these measures, death threats, bomb scares, beatings, assassination attempts and actual assassinations of close relatives have all continued. The more fundamental problem is the impunity that protects the perpetrators of the violence.

Coca-Cola executives make several related points concerning violence: the state is too weak, the violence is prevalent, trade unionists are not the only victims, many other trade unionists as well as Coca-Cola workers are assassinated, managers as well as workers have been killed. The overall picture is one of confusion; the corporation has done all in its power amidst senseless and overwhelming violence in which all sides suffer. This is evasion of the corporation's own responsibility: Coca-Cola must address the specific purpose and connections between its managers and the paramilitary hit squads.

Coca-Cola claims that court rulings in the United States and Colombia have absolved it, but there is a duality in the corporation's stance on the US civil action. In an interview with this author, Coca-Cola's representative took a defensive posture: he said the corporation would not answer any specific allegations while the Florida court case is in progress.[46] Is Coca-Cola involved in the US court case, or not? With its 40 per cent ownership of FEMSA stock, it is certainly very much involved. This reflects a deeper contradiction in Coca-Cola's positioning; are operations in the bottling plants its responsibility, or not? Well, 'yes' when it comes to the claim that employment is being provided, but 'no' when it comes to taking responsibility for the lives of those same employees. As far as justice in Colombia's courts is concerned, the workers' right to life was treated with the utmost cynicism in the judgement, Coca-Cola denying protection for the surviving targeted Carepa trade unionists – as Coca-Cola made clear on its own website.[47]

Coca-Cola and its bottlers continue using Colombian state institutions to persecute SINALTRAINAL. In 2003 Panamco raised charges of 'injury and calumny' against seven named SINALTRAINAL leaders in retaliation for their participation in a press conference launching the US civil action. In Colombia these are treated as criminal offences. Panamco's lawyer, Dr Jaime Bernal Cuellar, was himself the state's national prosecutor in the mid 1990s, in which position he signally failed to pursue any of those responsible for the assassinations. The corporation has also raised injunctions seeking to remove the seven union leaders from their posts. The next move was an attempt to criminalise the union as an organisation. Coca-Cola presented a petition to the Ministry of Social Protection to revoke SINALTRAINAL's statutes, attacking articles that make it possible for shopkeepers, informal workers and other people in the agro-industry to join the union. The outcome of this case is crucial for SINALTRAINAL to be able legally to recruit the 92 per cent of Coca-Cola's manual workers who are outside the collective agreement and employment law – because they are subcontracted, independent or temporary workers.[48] Such battles for the most oppressed 'informal' sectors to organise against the super-exploitation of the multinationals are fundamental for the future.

Coca-Cola's responses to the charges against it were based on literal denial, yet stubbornly the facts kept coming out. The corporation has belatedly moved to a more sophisticated strategy, based on presenting a different interpretation of events and on the deployment of processes seeking constructive engagement with potential critics and probing which of them may be co-opted. The corporation recruited Ed Potter, formerly of the International Labour Organisation, as director of global labor relations to implement this PR-led response. In the case of Colombia, Coca-Cola appointed Cal Safety Compliance Corporation (CSCC) to conduct a survey of its operations. Cal Safety duly found that union officials were able to operate 'free from obstruction and discrimination'.[49] Coca-Cola claims that CSCC is 'a respected, independent third party', but CSCC auditors never examined any past events or even interviewed a SINALTRAINAL member.[50] In short, their report is a corporate makeover. In a related move, Coca-Cola set up a $10 million Social Investment Fund. The trustees are mostly elite businessmen. SINALTRAINAL immediately criticised the foundation, pointing out that none of its riches are going to the victims or their families.[51]

A MANIFESTO FOR CHANGE – THE REAL THING

In conclusion we need to consider what it means to be up against a global profit-making machine.

The significance of overseas markets for Coca-Cola is immense. An industry analyst estimates that 'Coca Cola obtains 75 per cent of its profits outside the United States', and that 'a considerable proportion of this comes from Latin America'.[52] The corporation divides the world into four, according to how deeply it has penetrated the consumer market. The 'leading edge' markets are those countries (Mexico, Spain, the United States and Australia) where the *average* per capita consumption of Coca-Cola products is over 250 'servings' a year, which in 2002 accounted for 47 per cent of the company's sales by volume. Then there are the 'developed markets' (which include the United Kingdom), with an annual per capita consumption of 150–249 servings, the 'developing markets' (50–149 servings), and finally the 'emerging markets' (fewer than 50 servings per person per year), which account for only 11 per cent of company unit sales, but 69 per cent of the world's population.[53]

More and more people in the so-called developed markets want to end saturation exposure, especially parents concerned for the health of their children, who object to the ready availability of Coke and other junk food products. Since September 2005 vending machines have not been allowed in French schools, and the New Labour government has announced similar intentions.[54] Coca-Cola's near-global presence also means that anyone who wants to can join in the campaign, wherever they are. The cases highlighted in this chapter are not the only struggles against Coca-Cola by any means, rather they are the tip of the iceberg. Coca-Cola FEMSA Venezuela's top managers decided to dismiss 50 workers because they could not show evidence of having signed the petition against President Hugo Chávez; workers at Coca-Cola factories in Peru went on strike on 31 May and 1 June 2004 because managers threatened to sack 233 of them, including union leaders; that same month Human Rights Watch issued a report that the sugar used in Coca-Cola products in El Salvador is 'in part the product of child labor'; the civilian resistance to the US/UK occupation of Iraq boycotts Coca-Cola; the residents of the Malvern Hills are trying to protect their flora and fauna from being bled dry by Coca-Cola over extracted mineral water; and so on.[55] As Andy Rowell comments, 'Coca-Cola could become the first global company to face a sustained global boycott.'[56]

There is diversity as well as potential unity in these struggles. There should be acceptance of this diversity, with space created for a democratic hearing of the experiences of groups such as SINALTRAINAL, for in the fight for justice the victims' needs have to be paramount. At the same time, and whilst recognising that the sharp end is usually in the global South, there are many workers, communities and consumers in the North in dispute with the corporation on legitimate grounds in their own right. They can make common cause on issues that connect peoples around the world.

Finally, the problems such as Coca-Cola's operations in Colombia and India cannot be resolved by PR: for the sake of human life they have to be addressed in substance. But, as Mark Thomas concluded from his visit to Kerala, 'it is fairly safe to say that Coke have an image problem that the advertisers might not be able to solve'.[57] Coca-Cola is an unreconstructed profiteer still in corporate denial. It has yet to come to terms with the fact that you cannot sell human rights, nor can you buy them, quite simply you have to respect them. It might well be that we have to get rid of Coca-Cola to save water, and to save life. Returning to that Wall Street speech by Neville Isdell, Coca-Cola's CEO promised that his manifesto 'is a call to action', although 'not a radical change in strategy but in execution'[58] – quite a conservative call then.

We call for an international peoples' coalition of workers, communities and consumers to hold Coca-Cola accountable for its crimes, and to achieve justice for all its victims worldwide. Now that would be a manifesto worth fighting for.

I would like to dedicate this chapter to fellow internationalist delegates on the International Caravan for Life that visited Colombia in June 2004, but most especially to Emilio Rodriguez (whose warm heart has returned the gold a thousandfold) and to the ever militant and fraternal Dave Younger, both of whom carried the load when it mattered. Thanks also to them, and to Amit Srivastava, Gearoid O'Loingsigh, Dan Kovalik, Ray Rogers and SINALTRAINAL leaders for answering my questions and for their comments on an earlier draft. We all draw inspiration from the members of SINALTRAINAL, whose daily courage and calmness under fire is immensely impressive. They, like so many in Colombia, are truly living on the frontline.

NOTES

1. *Adweek*, 'Coke to Increase Marketing in India, Brazil, China, Russia', 11 November 2004, <http://www.indiaresource.org/news/2004/1052. html>.
2. *Guardian*, 28 June 2004; and British Medical Association, 'Preventing Childhood Obesity: A Report from the BMA Board of Science', 2005, <http://www.bma.org.uk/ap.nsf/content/childhoodobesity>.
3. See Mark Curtis, *Unpeople: Britain's Secret Human Rights Abuses* (London: Vintage, 2004).
4. Sindicato Nacional de Trabajadores de la Industria de Alimentos.
5. See ICCHRLA, 'Trade Unionism under Attack in Colombia: Report of the Canadian Trade Union Delegation to Colombia', Inter-Church Committee on Human Rights in Latin America, 1998, <http://www. colombiasupport.net/199802/canadaunion.html>; Daniel M. Kovalik, Terry Collingsworth and Natacha Thys, 'Complaint in the United States District Court: Southern District of Florida', United Steelworkers of America/International Labor Rights Fund, 2001, <http://www. mindfully.org/Industry/Coca-Cola-Human-Rights20jul01.htm>; and Hiram Monserrate, 'NYC fact-finding delegation's report on human rights violations by Coke: Final Report', New York, NYC Council Member, 2004, <http://www.killercoke.org/pdf/monsfinal.pdf>.
6. Kovalik et al., 'Complaint in the United States District Court', pp. 23–34.
7. SINALTRAINAL, 'Urgent Actions', received 19 June 2002, 11 September 2003, 20 April 2004.
8. SINALTRAINAL, report received 17 November 2004.
9. An example of 'efficiency seeking' foreign investment, as described by the Economic Commission for Latin America and the Caribbean, 'Foreign Investment in Latin America and the Caribbean, 2002 Report', LC/G.2198-P (Santiago, Chile: United Nations, 2003).
10. Julio Puig, Carlos Ballesteros, Beatrice Hartz and Hector Vasquez, *Tendencias y Contenidos de la Negociación Colectiva en Colombia, 1990–1997* (Bogotá: OIT, 1999).
11. Comité Internacionalista de Lucha contra las Transnacionales, *Una Delirante Ambición Imperial* (Bogotá: CILCT, 2003).
12. Human Rights Watch, *Colombia's Killer Networks: The Military–Paramilitary Partnership and the United States* (New York: Human Rights Watch, 1996); Human Rights Watch, *The Sixth Division: Military–Paramilitary Ties and U.S. Policy in Colombia* (New York: Human Rights Watch, 2001).
13. Amit Srivastava, 'Coca-Cola Spins Out of Control in India', <http://www. indiaresource.org/campaigns/coke/2004/cokespins.html>.

14. See Nityanand Jayaraman, 'No Water? Drink Coke!', <http://www.
    indiaresource.org/campaigns/coke/2003/nowaterdrinkcoke.html >; and
    'CorpWatch India Responds to Coca-Cola', <http://www.indiaresource.
    org/campaigns/coke/2003/corpwatchindiaresponds.htm>.
15. Srivastava, 'Coca-Cola Spins Out of Control'.
16. Christian Aid (2004), 'Behind the Mask: the real face of corporate
    responsibility', pp. 44–9, <http://www.christian-aid.org.uk/indepth/
    0401csr/csr_behindthemask.pdf>; Venkitesh Ramakrishnan, BBC,
    'Indian court blow for Coca-Cola', 16 December 2003, <http://news.
    bbc.co.uk/1/hi/world/south_asia/3325557.stm>; BBC Radio 4, 'Face the
    Facts', broadcast 25 July 2003; Mark Thomas, 'Wells went dry and crops
    failed', Action Aid, 2 February 2004, <http://www.actionaid.org.uk/433/
    article.html>.
17. Reports at <www.indiaresource.org>.
18. Press release, 25 November 2004, <http://www.indiaresource.org/
    press/2004/mehdiganjattack.html>.
19. Vandana Shiva, 'Food Rights, Free Trade and Fascism', in Matthew J.
    Gibney (ed.) *Globalizing Rights* (Oxford: Oxford University Press, 2003);
    Sistema Nacional Agroalimentario (SNAL), at <http://www.sinaltrainal.
    org/>.
20. Kovalik et al., 'Complaint in the United States District Court'.
21. Terry Collingsworth and Dan Kovalik, 'Court Rules That Human Rights
    Case Can Go Forward Against Coca-Cola Bottlers', statement, 1 April
    2003, <http://www.killercoke.org/cokedec.htm>.
22. Julie Kay, '11th Circuit Asked to Clarify Corporate Liability', *Daily Business
    Review*, 30 October 2006, available at <http://www.law.com/jsp/ihc/
    PubArticleIHC.jsp?id=1161939931304>.
23. The union's demands are summarised in SINALTRAINAL, 'World Wide
    Campaign Against Coca Cola: Statement 13th November 2003' (Paris:
    European Social Forum, 2003).
24. The Colombia Solidarity Campaign held a Coke-free samba party in
    London's Piccadilly Circus. See <http://www.sinaltrainal.org/boikot/
    noconsumo.html>.
25. See the reports at <http://www.killercoke.org/news.htm>; these include
    Jeremy Blasi, 'Coca-Cola and Human Rights in Colombia', UC Berkeley,
    Center for Labor Research and Education, November 2003.
26. Quoted by Ross Getman; see <http://www.schoolpouringrights.com>.
27. Linked to the Freedom Institute and Irish free-market think tank, a
    member of the global Stockholm network of free-market think tanks and
    an Atlas Foundation affiliate – see <http://www.spinprofiles.org/index.
    php/Freedom_Institute>.
28. See 'UCD Students Vote Again on Coca Cola', 19 November 2003 at
    <http://www.indymedia.ie/article/62178> and Indymedia Ireland website
    for more reports and discussion.
29. *Independent on Sunday*, 23 May 2004.
30. Correspondence from Gearoid O'Loingsigh and Cian O'Callaghan.
31. REBOC (Rete Boicottaggio Coca-Cola), at <http://www.nococacola.info>;
    La Republica, 10 March 2005.

32. Coca-Cola was prominently on sale at the 1936 Berlin Olympics, the company's lorries accompanied Hitler Youth rallies and its chief executive in Germany, Max Keith, applauded the annexation of Austria and the Sudetenland. See Mark Pendergrast, *For God, Country and Coca-Cola: The Definitive History of the World's Most Popular Drink* (London: Orion Business Books, 2000), ch. 13, 'Coca-Cola ber Alles'.

33. The show was truly democratic, the display ranging from entries by schoolchildren to those of known graphic designers, and was a great success, with hundreds of entries being shown in two London galleries, and later in a Bogotá social centre – see 'Killer Cola in Colombia', *Colombia Solidarity Bulletin*, 14 October 2004.

34. Interview, 23 April 2004, <http://www.cokefacts.org/labor_union_relations.shtml>; correspondence from Martin Norris, director of communications, Coca-Cola Great Britain, 10 October 2003.

35. Letter from Brendan Barber, TUC, et al. to the *New Statesman*, 12 April 2004. The claim is even more distorted by the Justice for Colombia/TUC report, 'Trade Union Delegation to Colombia, November 2004', pp. 21–2, <http://www.tuc.org.uk/international/tuc-9082-f0.pdf>.

36. Figures supplied by SINALTRAINAL (a) to the Popular Public Hearing, Brussels, 10 October 2003; (b) correspondence, 17 November 2004; (c) correspondence, 23 July 2005.

37. IUF, 'Coca-Cola Affiliates Reject Call for a Global Coca-Cola Boycott', <http://www.iuf.org/cgi-bin/dbman/db.cgi?db=default&ww=1&uid=default&ID=1119&view_records=1&en=1>.

38. See ICCHRLA, 'Trade Unionism under Attack in Colombia'.

39. Ibid., p. 20. See also Amnesty International, 'Report 2002', at <http://web.amnesty.org/web/ar2002.nsf/amr/colombia!Open>; Amnesty International, 'Colombia: NGO under attack', 28 May 2004, at <http://news.amnesty.org/index/ENGAMR23280522004>; Human Rights Watch, 'Colombia: Prosecution Problems Persist', 11 March 2004, at <http://hrw.org/english/docs/2004/03/11/colomb8106.htm>; and 'El General Rito Alejo Del Río: baluarte del paramilitarismo bajo el blindaje de la impunidad', in *Noche y Niebla, Colombia, deuda con la humanidad: paramilitarismo de estado, 1988–2003* (Bogotá: Centro de Investigación y Educación Popular (Cinep), 2004).

40. SICO's president is a member of the IUF's Latin America Committee, and thanks the IUF and SINTRAINAGRO for their continuing support. SICO, 'El SICO y Coca-Cola firman convenio colectivo en Carepa, Uraba', statement, 22 March 2002, <http://www.rel-uita.org/companias/coca-cola/sico.htm>.

41. FENSUAGRO is another important agricultural union facing harsh persecution.

42. Coca-Cola Corporation, 'Why?', presentation at Leeds University, 16 November 2004.

43. Mark Thomas, *New Statesman*, 29 March 2004.

44. 'Coke Facts', at <http://www.cokefacts.org/index.shtml>. The title appears to be in direct response to Mark Thomas.

45. Campaign to Stop Killer Coke, 'Coca-Cola Lies About Providing Security', statement, 14 May 2003, <http://www.killercoke.org/pdf/seclie.pdf>.

46. Interview, 23 April 2004.
47. Decision by Criminal Court 10, Bogotá, 22 April 1997, <http://www. cokefacts.org/facts/facts_co_court_cc10.pdf>.
48. SINALTRAINAL communiques, 6 August 2003, 17 November 2004, 9 March 2005; and briefing report 'Constreñimiento Ilicito' (Illicit Constraint), 17 November 2004.
49. Cal Safety Compliance Corporation, 'Workplace Assessments in Colombia', <www.cokefacts.org/citizenship/ cit_co_assessmentReport.pdf>.
50. At first Coca-Cola agreed to an independent investigation, but then withdrew the offer – see 'Coke's Colombian Conundrum', *Independent On Sunday*, 15 January 2006.

    The omissions are corroborated by careful reading of the CAL report itself, confirmed in correspondence from SINALTRAINAL, and addressed in the document United Students Against Sweatshops (USAS), 'Cal-Safety Compliance Corporation is not a Credible Monitor for Coca-Cola's Labor Practices', USAS statement, Washington, D.C., 2005, at <http://www. studentsagainstsweatshops.org//index.php?option=com_weblinks&cat id=27&Itemid=22>.

    A *Business Week* investigation found that, following the same methodology used to audit a Chinese supplier of handbags to Wal-Mart Stores, CAL had previously 'failed to uncover many of the egregious conditions in the factory despite interviews with dozens of workers'. See Dexter Roberts and Aaron Bernstein, 'Inside a Chinese Sweatshop: "A Life of Fines and Beating"', *Business Week*, 2 October 2000, at <http://www. businessweek.com/2000/00_40/b3701119.htm>.

    For a critical study of CSCC's methodology, see Jill Esbenshade, *Monitoring Sweatshops: Workers, Consumers, and the Global Apparel Industry* (Philadelphia: Temple University Press, 2004).
51. See Colombia Solidarity Campaign, '"Standard Response": Killer-Cola vs the Truth', 19 August 2005, <http://www.colombiasolidarity.org.uk/ UAJun per centD0Sep/standardresponse.html>.
52. See <http://www.finanzas.com/id.4977386/noticias/noticia.htm>.
53. Coca-Cola Corporation, '2002 Annual Report', Atlanta, 2003, p. 45. In 2004 Coca-Cola had a net income of US$4,847 million out of net operating revenues of US$21,962 million.
54. Ross Getman, 'Living Well off the Fat of the Land', 15 January 2005, <http://spinwatch.server101.com/>, and *Guardian*, 29 September 2005.
55. <http://www.handsoffvenezuela.org>; <http://www.rel-uita.org/ sindicatos/sinatrel_28-5-04.htm> ; Human Rights Watch, 'Turning a Blind Eye: Hazardous Child Labor in El Salvador's Sugarcane Cultivation', New York, 2004; Haifa Zangana, speech to War on Want conference, 'Making a Killing: Corporations, Conflict and Poverty', London, 12 March 2005; Nick Britten, 'Coca-Cola plans "will bleed hills dry"', *Daily Telegraph*, 23 November 2004.
56. Andy Rowell, 'Did you have a Coke-free Christmas?', 3 January 2005, <http://www.spinwatch.org>.
57. Mark Thomas, 'Wells went dry and crops failed', <http://www.actionaid. org.uk/433/article.html>.
58. *Adweek*, 'Coke to Increase Marketing'.

Conclusion:
Countering Corporate Spin

David Miller and William Dinan

This book has suggested that corporate power in advanced societies is exercised directly via lobbying as well as indirectly via PR, media and public opinion. We have also claimed that public relations and lobbying are at the cutting edge of corporate power – they represent an important means by which corporate power is defended and extended. The preceding chapters chronicle much of what is wrong with the PR industry, but we have also produced this book as a conscious intervention in the debate about globalisation and corporate power. More than that, we see the exposure of deception and spin as a core part – but only a part – of the struggle for democratic renewal. We also recognise the need to put in place a positive agenda of what we think can be done.

This book has contributed to that agenda by giving some account of what social movements and others have done to counter corporate spin. The chapters on SourceWatch, Coca-Cola, EU lobbying and others, show that different parts of the social justice movement are engaged in positive campaigns to redress the wrongs fostered by corporate power. But to conclude this book we want to give a fuller account of what we can do concretely to rescue democracy from spin and revive our public institutions.

In some respects this volume can be seen as a call to arms to resist spin and to challenge corporate power. We cannot rely on these particular physicians to heal themselves. Instead we need a wider collective cure. An important first step requires those interested in the health of democracy and the conduct of public affairs to recognise self-interested spin when they see it, and, crucially, to expose it. This isn't always easy, but hopefully the preceding chapters have helped to illustrate some of the mechanics and consequences of this spin-led neoliberal assault on democracy.

TRANSPARENCY AND OPENNESS

The most obvious thing to do in relation to deceptive PR and lobbying is to expose them to the light. This means, as a first step, binding regulation, which would require that lobbyists and PR organisations disclose all their clients or principals (those on whose behalf they act), all the issues they are working on and how much money they are being paid for such work. In the European debate on lobbying registration inaugurated by Commissioner Siim Kallas in 2005 as part of the European Transparency Initiative, the lobbying industry naturally mobilised to ward off regulation by launching a new lobby group for lobbying. They argued that their own voluntary code would be effective and therefore there was no need for independent scrutiny or regulation. Amongst other things, the industry wants to pretend that some of its lobbying efforts are not actually about lobbying. For example, Houston Consulting Europe is a lobbying firm that specialises in what it calls 'Client Roundtables': these are 'regular invitation-only discussions with MEPs as well as key EU officials in the Commission, Council and Parliament, to discuss topical issues of interest to industry'. John Houston, the founding chairman of the company, is also the chairman of the lobbyist lobby group EPACA. Houston likes to think that his roundtables are nothing to do with lobbying and are simply an 'event management' function of his firm. This is, of course, plainly nonsense. One such group is the European Parliamentary Financial Services Forum, run by Houston on behalf of the banking industry. It brings together MEPs, including John Purvis, the Scottish Tory, and Chris Huhne (a Lib Dem MEP until 2005 and then an MP) and the banking industry.

According to the *Wall Street Journal*:

The group's chairwoman and several other members are EU legislators. Some of them introduced amendments to the bill that were almost identical to drafts circulated by a banking trade group whose members include several clients of Mr. Houston, Parliament records show. The process led to an unusual protest by legislators on one committee, half of whom abstained on the amended measure. Too many Parliament members introduced 'amendments which had been dictated to them by the bankers,' said Socialist legislator Vincent Peillon of France.[1]

It is clear that any attempt to increase transparency and openness will have to include all such activities and there will need to be significant penalties for lack of compliance. There is already lobbying disclosure legislation in Canada and in the United States (at both the federal level and in most state assemblies). In 2005/6 lobbying regulation was introduced in Poland and Hungary and announced in Western Australia.[2] In the United States, statutory disclosure operates without any of the dire consequences conjured up by lobbyists whenever even minimal transparency rules are mooted. It is plain too that there is a public scepticism about the activities of lobbyists and politicians which feeds through into a desire for openness. In the 2006 US mid-term elections which swept the Republicans out of control, exit polls showed that the most popular of the 'extremely important issues affecting your vote' was 'corruption' (42 per cent of voters).[3]

But the lobbyists do not want any light shone in their dark corners. One tactic is to claim that lobbying regulation is too cumbersome and that compliance will be an issue. All this tells us is that their intention is to defy the law. This suggests more rather than less of a need for binding regulation with teeth. The problem with current US legislation is that it is not strict enough. The lobbyists' attempts to subvert the system have led to attempts to tighten up at the federal level. In early 2006 the then House minority leader, Nancy Pelosi, was only able to have her draft 'Honest Leadership and Open government Act of 2006' referred to various House committees. The Democratic takeover will now give the opportunity (if not the certainty) of further progress on this issue.[4] Meanwhile the corporations are circling the Democrats to try to ensure that they pose absolutely no risk to the interests of big business. Big pharma was early off the blocks, hiring former Democrat senator John Breaux. Others have followed suit, in a reversal of Tom DeLay's K-Street project that ensured that many lobbyists hired only Republicans. According to Ken Johnson, vice-president at the lobby group PhRMA, 'After the election we woke up to a new world ... There will be a renewed emphasis on making friends and reaching out to Democrats, especially pro-business Democrats.'[5]

But there is a model of regulatory penalties at the global level, accepted by most nations in the world, which is already very effective. The World Trade Organisation has an extremely effective and punitive system of ensuring compliance with its judgements, including fines and trade sanctions. Of course this is all put in place in order to enforce corporate power rather than to keep it in check. But it does indicate what can be done when required by the theorists of light touch regulation such as those represented by the lobbying industry.

The scale of the task of regulating corporate activity to ensure social and environmental justice is immense, and transnational corporations will seek to use all their political power to resist binding rules that constrain how they operate or oblige them to behave in a more sustainable fashion. The recent lobbying campaign to undermine the United Nation's Norms on Business and Human Rights illustrates this very clearly. The UN's proposal was that corporations should, 'within their [respective] spheres of activity and influence', refrain from activities that directly or indirectly violate human rights as well as actively promoting and protecting these rights.[6] Those failing to meet this duty of care were to be made to pay compensation to their victims.

This was seen as a threat by many corporations, and Shell was one of those most active in derailing these proposals, acting in concert with many key business lobby groups like the International Chamber of Commerce (ICC). The ICC's 'efforts to sideline the UN Norms [were] led by Robin Aram, Shell's Vice-President of External Relations and Policy Development', reports Corporate Europe Observatory. 'Shell, meanwhile, keeps silent on the issue.'[7] The ICC complained:

We don't have a problem at all with efforts that seek to encourage companies to do what they can to protect human rights. We have a problem with the premise and the principle that the norms are based on. These norms clearly seek to move away from the realm of voluntary initiatives ... and we see them as conflicting with the approach taken by other parts of the UN that seek to promote voluntary initiatives.[8]

Companies like Shell, who are amongst the first to trumpet their corporate social responsibility (CSR) credentials, and organisations like the ICC favour voluntary approaches to regulation precisely because these allow them the freedom to make up their own rules and behave more or less as they please. The relentless promotion of voluntary measures is one of the critical lobbying successes in the past couple of decades. Those interested in reviving democracy and accountability must make campaigns for mandatory controls of corporate activity a priority. One area in which this is achievable, and which will have knock-on consequences for openness, transparency and governance, is that of lobbying itself. Lobbying regulation needs to be introduced at the UN, WTO and EU levels, but also in the United Kingdom and in other nations and in devolved parliaments or assemblies, wherever the lobbyists congregate. That would be a first step.

But transparency and openness depend on more than the existence of regulations and the resources to police them. They also require that activist groups and campaigners devote considerable time and effort to exposing spin, deception and corporate influence. This is the task set by organisations such as PR Watch, Spinwatch, Corporate Watch (UK), Corporate Europe Observatory, LobbyControl, Lobbywatch, GM Watch, the Campaign for Press and Broadcasting Freedom, the Colombia Solidarity Campaign and others, all of which have collaborated in producing this book. Several of these organisations have also collaborated in projects using wiki software. These include Sourcewatch.org, run by the Centre for Media and Democracy (the parent of PR Watch), and Spinprofiles.org, run by Spinwatch.org (in collaboration with Lobbywatch and Corporate Watch UK). There are of course a range of other campaigns and struggles in this area, and we should mention in particular Greenpeace's Exxonsecrets.org, which exposes how ExxonMobil funds climate-change sceptics as part of their deceptive PR strategy. This website allows the dynamic creation of illustrations such as network diagrams, showing how organisations and individuals funded by Exxon link to each other.

These ventures are intended as means of popularising the truth about corporate spin and corporate power, which is part of a wider strategy to roll back corporate influence in our politics and culture. It is clear that exposure and transparency are about more than just disclosure. They are also about using information to hold corporations and governments to account.

REGULATING DECEPTIVE PR

Exposure of corporate misdeeds is of course one aim of transparency legislation or lobbying registration schemes. Lobbying disclosure legislation and the requirement for corporations to disclose which think tanks, front groups and institutes they fund would help improve the ability of citizens to understand and act to hold corporations to account. But another concrete result of opening such activities to public view is that those organisations which depend on secrecy, such as front groups and fake institutes, would be compromised and would have to be either abandoned or changed. This is in itself an important and essential outcome. However, ending deceptive PR requires much more than openness and disclosure regulations. The next step is outlawing deceptive PR tactics and imposing penalties on those who undertake them. The 'third-party' technique is an obvious place to start. This should be outlawed altogether. The pharmaceutical industry, for example, already has specific regulations about advertising medicines. Following a parliamentary inquiry, the pharma lobby group, the Association of British Parmaceutical

Industry (ABPI), adopted a new code requiring drug companies 'to declare on their websites or in their annual report a list of all patient organisations to which they provide financial support'.[9] Clearly this is an attempt by ABPI to ward off statutory regulation, and it is no doubt the case that the industry will do all it can to promote self-regulation. It should be noted that the requirement is simply to list groups which are funded rather than disclosing the details needed for full scrutiny, which would include the sums of money involved and the reasons why the groups are funded.

ROLLING BACK CORPORATE POWER

The use of spin and deception by corporations has reached epidemic proportions, but the problem of spin is a symptom of a wider problem, which is the rise and dominance of corporate power. We don't campaign for transparency or to expose and outlaw deception just for their own sake. At the root of this is the campaign to roll back corporate power. This can be done only by addressing corporate power directly. This is why an important part of the ALTER-EU campaign for lobbying disclosure in Brussels is the demand to end privileged corporate access to the European Commission.[10] The same demand applies to national parliaments and government as also to the UN, the WTO and other international bodies. Parliamentary schemes which allow corporations privileged access, such as the Industry and Parliament Trust, the Scottish Parliament Business Exchange, or the corporate funding of all-party groups and cross-party groups at sub-state, national and supranational parliaments, all need to be abolished and replaced with mechanisms for directly involving citizens in political life.[11] The privileged access of corporations to government also needs to cease. Secondments to and from business, the direct involvement of corporate figures on the management boards of government departments, and government and public advisory boards filled with corporate appointees are all symptoms of the corporate infiltration of politics and decision making. Similarly, privileged access for business to civil servants and ministers needs both disclosure and tight regulation.

The logic of this part of our argument might be seen as suggesting a happy stasis if corporations and their opponents were to get some kind of equal access to civil servants. An equality of access for organised interests would certainly be a lot better than the current state of corporate domination. But the presumption should not be that business and NGOs (including trade unions) get equal access. There are two reasons for this. The first is that many corporate lobby groups are actually recognised as NGOs in international decision making and that many 'genuine' NGOs are actually corporate front groups or take corporate funding, which influences their activities. The second reason is the most fundamental. There can be no substitute for direct citizen participation in government. This can be accomplished by direct representation of popular interests and in part by democratically run and organised unions and campaigning groups. We should not make the mistake of thinking that NGOs which are not run on a democratically accountable basis can substitute for those which are. This applies even to those NGOs of which we might approve. To replace the sclerotic democratic system we now have with one that is responsive at the political level would also be a step forward. But in the end it is only by the serious introduction of political democracy to replace the current dilute arrangement, and by the addition of economic democracy, that the possibility of real and lasting change will be glimpsed. The obvious model for this – suggested by both autonomist and socialist currents in the anti-capitalist movement – is the creation of popular works councils and their equivalents in communities.[12]

In order to do all this – which is, let's be clear, a massive programme of democratic renewal – we would need to roll back corporate power and specifically remove corporate influence from decision making in governmental bodies and in the public services. This will not be accomplished quickly or easily, but it can be done.

WINNING THE BATTLE OF IDEAS

Central to the process will be the battle of ideas. Ideas are not the motor of history, but they are crucial in deciding how resources should be distributed. But the battle of ideas is not something divorced from the battle over outcomes and power. It is an integral part of the same struggle. There is no abstract 'class struggle in language' as imagined by some academic theorists (which, incidentally, played their own part in the disastrous rise of New Labour).[13] Ideas have no independent existence from the material conditions and struggles of life. To understand the real role of the PR industry we should 'not explain practice from the idea but explain ... the formation of ideas from material practice'.[14]

This means seeing the importance of ideas as part of progressive struggles for change and for rolling back corporate power. The PR industry has been at the cutting edge of corporate power and it has enabled the neoliberal revolution. It has done this by virtue of thought and the production of ideas, but also, crucially, by putting ideas into practice. Thinkers, fakers, spinners and spies, the PR industry knows very well that ideas are powerful – but not in the abstract, only in the context of social struggles for power and resources.

The conclusion we draw from this is that it is necessary to take the battle of ideas to those defending the privileged position of corporations, in order to redress corporate power and open the way for thorough democratic reform.

HOW TO GET INVOLVED

The research and campaigning work featured in this book have been the product of collaborative work by the various organisations represented in it. All of these organisations are resource poor and rely on donations and funding from trade unions and public interest charities and foundations. But they also rely on practical help from ordinary readers and citizens. To get involved with any of the projects discussed in this book, simply get in touch with the campaigns, at the websites below.

Lastly, two of the initiatives mentioned in the book are collaborative research ventures. Both Sourcewatch.org and Spinprofiles.org welcome volunteers who can contribute their time (as much or as little as you can spare) to researching and exposing corporate spin and government propaganda. If you have any time to spare and even if you feel you have no special skills, please do get in touch. It is only together that we can turn back the tide of corporate power.

Websites of organisations monitoring corporate spin and corporate power involved in this book:

Alliance for Lobbying Transparency and Ethics Regulation (ALTER-EU) <http://www.alter-eu.org>
Spinwatch <http://www.spinwatch.org>
Spinprofiles <http://www.spinprofiles.org>
Nuclear Spin <http://www.nuclearspin.org>
PR Watch <http://www.prwatch.org>
Sourcewatch <http://www.sourcewatch.org>
Corporate Europe Observatory <http://www.corporateeurope.org>

Corporate Watch UK <http://www.corporatewatch.org>
Colombia Solidarity Campaign <http://www.colombiasolidarity.org.
uk/>
Campaign for Press and Broadcasting Freedom <http://www.cpbf.
org.uk>
Lobbycontrol <http://www.lobbycontrol.de>
Lobbywatch <http://www.lobbywatch.org>
GM Watch <http://www.gmwatch.org>

NOTES

1. Glenn R. Simpson, 'In Europe, Finance Lobby Sways Terror-Funding Law', *Wall Street Journal*, 24 May 2005, <http://www.spinwatch.org/>.
2. Judit Zegnál and Patricia Fischer, 'Room for improvement in Lobby Law', *Budapest Business Journal*, 16 October 2006, <http://www.bbj.hu/main/news_17835_room%2Bfor%2Bimprovement%2Bin%2Blobby%2Blaw.html>; Łukasz Ołdakowski, 'Poland: New Lobbying Law Opens Legislative and Administrative Processes to Lobby', Mondaq com, 23 June 2006, <http://www.spinwatch.org/content/view/3019/9/> ; 'WA to set up lobbyist register', *Daily Telegraph* (Australia), 13 November 2006, <http://www.spinwatch.org/content/view/3673/9/>.
3. The next most important issues were terrorism (40 per cent), the economy (39 per cent) and the Iraq war (37 per cent). Source: CNN News United States General Exit Poll, 8 November 2006, conducted by Edison/Mitofsky.
4. Summary of HR 4682, Honest Leadership and Open Government Act 2006, House minority leader, Nancy Pelosi (D-Calif.), Washington, Public Citizen.
5. Stephanie Kirchgaessner, 'Big Pharma on a mission to woo incoming Democrats', *Financial Times*, 20 November 2006, p. 3.
6. Corporate Europe Observatory, 'Shell Leads International Business Campaign Against UN Human Rights Norms', CEO info brief, March 2004, <http://www.corporateeurope.org/norms.html>.
7. Ibid.
8. Ibid. Stefano Bertasi quoted in 'CSR Europe background note: United Nations Norms on the Responsibilities of Transnational Companies', <http://www.csreurope.org/UNnormsbriefingsheet_pdf_media_public.aspx>.
9. ABPI, 'Code of Practice for the Pharmaceutical Industry 2006', together with 'ABPI Prescriptions Medicines: Code of Practice Authority', <http://www.abpi.org.uk/links/assoc/PMCPA/code06use.pdf>; Sarah Boseley, 'The selling of a wonder drug', *Guardian*, 29 March 2006, <http://society.guardian.co.uk/health/story/0,,1741858,00.html>.
10. See <http://www.alter-eu.org/about>.
11. For more information on all of these organisations, see the relevant entries at <http://www.spinprofiles.org>.

12. See, for example, Michael Albert, 'Anti Capitalist Strategy: Opening Presentation by Michael Albert for a Debate on Anti Capitalist Strategy (with John Holloway)', *Z Net*, 26 January 2006, <http://www.zmag.org/content/showarticle.cfm?ItemID=9602>; Alex Callinicos, 'State of Discontent', *Socialist Review*, March 2003, <http://www.socialistreview.org.uk/article.php?articlenumber=8349>; Alex Callinicos, 'Socialism: Political Vision', *Z Magazine/ZNet* and *Porto Alegre 3, Life After Capitalism Essays*, 2003, <http://www.zmag.org/callinicospol.htm>.

13. 'Almost every fundamental of New Labour can be found in the pages of Marxism Today's back issues', says Decca Aitkenhead, 'These aged teenagers at Marxism Today, guiltily shuffling their feet'. *Guardian*, 23 October 1998, <http://www.guardian.co.uk/Columnists/Column/0,,324997,00.html>; see also Bernard McKenna and Phil Graham, 'Marxism Today Nov/Dec 1998', *Culture Machine*, <http://culturemachine.tees.ac.uk/Reviews/rev1.htm>; Greg Philo and David Miller, *Market Killing: What Capitalism Does and What Social Scientists Can Do About It* (London: Longman, 2001).

14. Karl Marx and Friedrich Engels, *The German Ideology*, 1846, online at <http://www.marxists.org/archive/marx/works/1845/german-ideology/>.

Contributors

Bob Burton is a freelance journalist based in Canberra, Australia and is editor of SourceWatch (www.sourcewatch.org), a project of the US-based Center for Media and Democracy, which documents the PR industry. With Nicky Hager, he co-authored *Secrets and Lies: The Anatomy of an Anti-Environmental PR Campaign* (Nelson, New Zealand: Craig Potton Publishing, 1999; Monroe, Maine: Common Courage Press, 2000). In the 1980s and early 1990s he worked with environmental groups in Australia and New Zealand.

William Clark is the former editor of *Variant* magazine and a public interest fellow at Strathclyde University's Department of Geography and Sociology.

His work is an analysis of a group of organisations and factions which advise and influence government and which engage in deception. Together, these groups covertly function as business lobbyists and propagandists, acting as a conduit for spurious intellectual/political concepts (mostly fed in from the United States), and engage in the quasi-embezzlement of public funds and the corruption of the democratic process. This is a hive of New Labour 'placement', spooks, disgraced lobbyists, right-wing ideologues, pseudo-intellectuals, fake grassroots organisations, and MI6 and CIA agents directing an interlocking network of small unaccountable organisations in control of hundreds of millions of pounds. William is interested in the history of their influence and connections (a continuation of para-political projects aimed at subverting the left in the 1960s).

Aeron Davis has studied or worked in departments of politics, history, media and communications, and sociology. His work tends to combine elements of both political sociology, and media and communications. Between degrees, he spent several years travelling and working abroad, mostly in the United States, Mexico and Central America, Australia and New Zealand, and South East Asia. His research interests span public relations, politics and political communications, promotional culture, media sociology and news production, economic sociology and financial markets. He has conducted research on communications at Westminster, the major political parties, the

City and across the trade union movement. Aeron has published on each of these topics in journals and edited collections and is the author of *Public Relations Democracy: Public Relations, Politics and the Mass Media in Britain* (Manchester: Manchester University Press, 2002).

William Dinan is a lecturer in sociology at Strathclyde University. Prior to joining the Department of Geography and Sociology at Strathclyde, he held several research posts, including research fellowships at the Centre for Risk and Governance, Glasgow Caledonian University, and the Stirling Media Research Institute, University of Stirling.

He has been involved with a number of funded research projects, including Political Communication and Democracy (ESRC Media Culture and Media Economics Programme, 1996–98), Political Communication and the Scottish Parliament (ESRC Devolution Initiative, 1999–2000) and Corporate Public Relations in British and Multinational Companies (ESRC, 2000–03). In the past few years he has undertaken consultancy work for various public bodies, including BBC Scotland, the Scottish Parliament, and the Water Customer Consultation Panels, Scotland (WCCPS).

Will is co-author of *Open Scotland? Journalists, Spin Doctors and Lobbyists* (Edinburgh: Polygon, 2001) and co-founder and co-editor of Spinwatch.org.

Chris Grimshaw has a degree in philosophy and psychology from Oxford University. He has been an active campaigner for a number of years, supporting the Mutilateral Agreement on Investment and subsequent anti-globalisation campaigns. He is a founder member of Corporate Watch and worked for just over three years editing the magazine. Chris now works part time for Corporate Watch, researching PR companies and lobby groups, and writes articles for the *Corporate Watch* magazine.

Andy Higginbottom received a Ph.D. from Middlesex University in 2005 for his study 'Globalisation and Human Rights in Colombia: Crimes of the Powerful, Corporate Complicity and the Paramilitary State'. He is secretary of the Colombia Solidarity Campaign, working with social movements for a just outcome to the conflict. He is on the editorial board of *Frontline Latin America*. Andy was a co-ordinator for the natural resources sector of the Permanent Peoples' Tribunal on 'Neo-liberal Policies and European Transnational Corporations in Latin America and the Caribbean' in Vienna in May 2006, and continues research in this area. He teaches Latin American politics and human rights at Kingston University in London.

Olivier Hoedeman works with Corporate Europe Observatory (CEO), an Amsterdam-based research and campaign group targeting the threats to democracy, equity, social justice and the environment, posed by the economic and political power of corporations and their lobby groups. He is centrally involved in the ALTER-EU coalition for lobbying transparency and ethics reform in the European Union.

Eveline Lubbers is an investigative reporter and specialist activist living in Amsterdam. After finishing university (political science) twenty years ago she co-founded Buro Jansen & Janssen, a spin-off from the powerful squatters' movement of the 1980s. With the bureau she monitored police and secret services, and supported social activist groups against the oppressive surveillance tactics of the authorities. She has published in both activist and mainstream media, and on the internet, and has produced books, mainly in Dutch, on related subjects. Her work is collected on Evel Writes (www.evel.nl). In the past few years she has specialised in corporate intelligence and PR strategies of multinationals against their critics, including net-activists. This resulted in *Battling Big Business: Countering Greenwash, Front Groups and Other Forms of Corporate Bullying* (Foxhole, Dartington: Green Books, 2002; Monroe, Maine: Common Courage Press, 2002). The book has been published in the United Kingdom, the United States and Australia. The Dutch translation (*Schone Schijn , Smerige Streken in Strijd tussen Burgers en Bedrijven*) appeared in November 2002. Eveline is co-founder and co-editor of Spinwatch.org.

Jonathan Matthews is founder of GM Watch and Lobbywatch.

David Miller is professor of sociology in the Department of Geography and Sociology at Strathclyde University. He is widely known for his writings on propaganda, spin and lobbying. Recent books include *Arguments Against G8* (co-edited with Gill Hubbard, London: Pluto Press, 2005); *Tell Me Lies: Propaganda and Media Distortion in the Attack on Iraq* (editor, London: Pluto Press, 2004); *Open Scotland? Journalists, Spin Doctors and Lobbyists* (co-authored with Philip Schlesinger and William Dinan, Edinburgh: Polygon, 2001); and *Market Killing: What the Free Market Does and What Social Scientists Can Do About*

It (co-authored with Greg Philo, London: Longman 2001). David is co-founder and co-editor of Spinwatch.org.

Laura Miller has covered deceptive corporate public relations and government propaganda since 2000 for the Center for Media and Democracy, serving most recently as editor of the quarterly *PR Watch*.

Laura's writing has been published in *PR Watch* and *LiP Magazine*. She has contributed chapters to several books, including David Miller's *Tell Me Lies* and Peter Phillips and Project Censored's *Censored 2006: The Top 25 Censored Stories* (New York: Seven Stories Press, 2006). She has frequently appeared in national and international media, discussing topics ranging from US war propaganda to high-priced campaign consulting to corporate astroturf. She is now happy to be writing on the arts and Midwestern living for her website Miller's Crossing (www.lamiller.net).

Ulrich Mueller is the founder of LobbyControl, a new German civil society initiative that provides information on lobbying, PR campaigns and think tanks and promotes transparency and democracy. LobbyControl is a registered non-profit organisation. It was founded in late 2005 by a small group of people coming from academia and civil society. From 2001 to early 2005 Uli worked for the human rights organisation FIAN, before that at the Max Planck-Institut for the Study of Societies. He is based in Cologne.

Andy Rowell is a freelance writer and investigative journalist. He has over a dozen years experience writing on political, environmental and health issues. His work has appeared in front-page and other stories in the *Guardian*, the *Independent on Sunday*, *Big Issue*, *New York Village Voice* and the *Ecologist*. His articles have also been published in the *Age* in Melbourne, *BBC Wildlife Magazine*, *Earth Matters*, *Delta*, *Mao Magazine*, *New Solutions*, *New Zealand Listener*, *PR Watch*, *Radical News*, *Red Pepper*, *Resurgence* and the *Sydney Morning Herald*.

Andy's books include *Green Backlash: Global Subversion of the Environment Movement* (London: Routledge 1996); *Don't Worry: It's Safe To Eat* (London: Earthscan, 2003); and *The Next Gulf: London, Washington and Oil Conflict in Nigeria* (co-authored with James Marriot and Lorne Stockman, London: Constable Robinson, 2005). Andy is co-founder and co-editor of Spinwatch.org.

Leslie Sklair is professor of sociology at the London School of Economics and Political Science. He is author of *The Transnational Capitalist Class* (2001; Chinese edition, 2002; German edition, forthcoming). His *Sociology of the Global System* (second edition, 1991; revised and updated, 1995) has been translated into Japanese, Portuguese, Persian, Korean and Spanish. A new version of this book was published by Oxford University Press in 2002 under the title *Globalization: Capitalism and Its Alternatives* (Chinese and Portuguese editions, forthcoming). He was the Hans Speier distinguished visiting professor at the Graduate Faculty, New School for Social Research, New York, in spring 2002 and visiting professor at the University of Southern California in spring 2004 and is currently a visiting professor at the Department of Geography and Sociology, University of Strathclyde. He is vice-president (sociology) of the Global Studies Association, and on the editorial boards of the *Review of International Political Economy*, *Global Networks* and *Social Forces*. He is currently researching iconic architecture and capitalist globalisation.

Gerald Sussman is professor of urban studies and communications at Portland State University. He holds a Ph.D. in political science. His most recent book is *Global Electioneering: Campaign Consulting, Communications, and Corporate Financing* (Lanham, Md.: Rowman & Littlefield, 2005).

Granville Williams teaches media policy and journalism at the University of Huddersfield. He is a member of the National Council of the Campaign for Press and Broadcasting Freedom. He is also a member of the Broadcasting Experts' Group of the European Federation of Journalists. He is currently researching the role and impact of corporate lobbying in the revision of the European Commission directive, 'Television Without Frontiers'.

Index